Islanders

REAL LIFE ON THE
MAINE ISLANDS

VIRGINIA L. THORNDIKE

DOWN EAST BOOKS

OTHER BOOKS BY VIRGINIA L. THORNDIKE

Windjammer Watching on the Coast of Maine

The Arctic Schooner Bowdoin: *A Biography*

Maine Lobsterboats: Builders and Lobstermen Speak of Their Craft

How We Got There from Here: Remembering the Days of Steamers, Trolleys, and Model Ts in Maine

On Tugboats: Stories of Work and Life Aboard

ISBN (10-digit): 0-89272-624-5
ISBN (13-digit): 978-0-89272-624-0

Library of Congress Cataloging-in-Publication Data

Thorndike, Virginia L.
   Islanders : real life on the Maine islands / Virginia L. Thorndike.
        p. cm.
   Includes index.
   ISBN 0-89272-624-5 (trade pbk. : alk. paper)
  1. Islands--Maine. 2. Maine--Social life and customs. 3. Atlantic Coast
(Me.)--Social life and customs. 4. Maine--Biography. 5. Atlantic Coast
(Me.)--Biography. 6. Maine--Description and travel. 7. Atlantic Coast
(Me.)--Description and travel. I. Title.
   F27.A19T48 2005
   917.41--dc22

                                                        2005014734

Design by Harrah Lord, Yellow House Studio
Printed at Versa Press, E. Peoria, Ill.

5   4   3   2   1

Down East Books
A division of Down East Enterprise, Inc.
Publisher of *Down East*, the Magazine of Maine

Book orders: 1-800-685-7962
www.downeastbooks.com

Contents

Author's Note

a s always, I have to thank people and explain what I'm up to. The two tangle together more in this book than in many cases, because I have been so dependent on people talking with me—I can't possibly thank them enough, yet I can't identify some of them, either. Many individuals implored me not to quote them directly—island residents don't want to take the chance of being seen as speaking for anyone else, or of thinking themselves more authoritative than anyone else.

In general, I spoke to particular people because someone else told me I should, but sometimes it was pure happenstance. I know I missed speaking with a tremendous number of wonderful people. I wish that were not the case, but I hope and trust that the people I stumbled across are representative of their world.

Specific thanks have to go to every one of the many people quoted by name, whom I cannot possibly list individually, as well as to those who preferred not to be named. All have my tremendous respect and my appreciation for talking with me. The islands are wonderful physical places, to be sure, but without their people, they'd be just rocks surrounded by water.

For the purposes of this book, I have invented an island—which became "Smith Island" for no reason whatever (perhaps only because I know of no Maine island by that name). In retelling various stories I heard, I placed them on Smith Island, so as not to embarrass my confidants or other residents of the island on which they actually took place. Sari Bunker of Matinicus says that when people from any of the islands read one of those stories, they'll believe it took place on their own island. I hope this is the case, as I included the stories of Smith Island because I think they show some aspect of "islandism" in general.

That I have spoken of a particular program or system from one island in no way should be construed to mean it is better in any way than one with a similar goal on another island. I am merely trying to give representative examples of what happens on the islands in general.

THE CONCEPT OF "AWAY"

An important concept in Maine—one that is only more important on islands—is "Away." People come to places from Away. The message is that it doesn't matter where they come from—if it isn't Here, it's at least suspect, and probably bad. On the mainland, so many people come from elsewhere that the meaning of Away has changed—or, more to the point, Here has changed, and it no longer means just one town; it can include most of Maine north of Portland. But on Matinicus, Here means Matinicus, and Vinalhaven is Away, although certainly Vinalhaven is more nearly comprehensible than is New Jersey, say. (Poor New Jersey—in much of Maine, New Jersey is often used as the epitome of all things bad. I'm sorry, I do it myself. There are, in fact, some perfectly good people from New Jersey, and I suspect that a couple may even be on Maine islands.)

Over the years, there has been a lot of cross-pollination between neighboring islands, and of late, connections to the mainland have increased. The overall feeling about Away has softened to the point that on many islands newcomers are welcomed and even courted. That's part of my story.

Islands

When I was a youngster summering on the island of Islesboro, our telephone was on a party line, which we shared with Went Durkee, a lobsterman. His ring was one-four—one long ring and four short ones. That's a hard ring to crank yourself, at least with no more practice than we had; if we wanted to call the Durkees or anyone else on our line, we rang once, for the operator, and asked her to do it for us. Often, shortly after we heard a one-four ring, we'd see Edna Durkee rowing out across the cove to the lobster car [crate], her dog Smoky in the bow of the skiff. Someone was having lobster for dinner.

One pleasant May day about fifteen years ago, as my husband, Phil, and I made our first trip across the bay in our first powerboat (before we learned that the fuel pickup was a couple of inches above the bottom of the tank), we ran out of gas. The wind was blowing such that, with just a little help from an oar, we could drift toward the one dock on Islesboro on which I felt comfortable about landing: Went Durkee was its caretaker. From there, I walked the half-mile up to Went's house, but no one was home. I hitchhiked back to the boat—a nice elderly couple picked me up—and then Phil and I caught another ride to the ferry. By the time we came back to the island the next morning with some gas, Went knew whose boat was at the float and had heard all about our predicament.

People know a lot of things about each other in such a small community. I realize it could be confining, but I suppose I've not felt I was likely to be doing things I'd object to people knowing. Sometimes, in fact, it was useful. The operator was great. I'd ask for the Leonard house—you didn't need the number—and she'd say if you want Sammy, he's gone to so-and-so's, and then she'd ask if she should ring him there.

That awareness is still present, even if the telephone operator is long gone. When I was collecting leads on people to speak with for this book, more than one person suggested someone and then explained why I mightn't be able to reach him or her just now.

"She's ashore today, her mother's in the hospital." Or, "They'll be back from Florida in another couple of weeks."

The islands are still islands; and on some of them, people still talk about going to America when they go ashore. Some of the characteristics of remote places don't change. There aren't many islands that still have year-round populations, but even with satellite TV and the Internet connecting them to the rest of the planet, they remain unique simply because of their physical separation from the rest of the country. "Anything that everyone deals with, on the island it's magnified," says Stephanie Howard-O'Reilly, who grew up on Cliff Island in Casco Bay. "It's not the water—it's the community that is built because of the water." When you're on an island, almost by definition you have a sense of being somewhere in particular. If you're on, you're not anywhere else—nor, without some significant effort, can you get anywhere else. (Islanders speak of "on" or "off" without completing the phrase. "The island" is understood.)

Some of the trust that was part of island life in decades past still remains. A few years ago, my husband and a friend sailed to the island of Grand Manan, New Brunswick, where neither had ever been before. As they tied up to a government pier, they got talking with a fisherman who was headed out to sea. "Take my truck and check out the island," he told them. He wouldn't be using the vehicle during the next couple of days.

Closer to home, when we arranged to meet with someone at Pendleton's Yacht Yard on Islesboro, they left a vehicle for us at the ferry dock. The key was in the ignition.

Traditionally, there has been a big divide between island natives and people from Away, but it has lessened in recent years. "People make much less distinction," says Helene Quinn of Penobscot Bay's Eagle Island. "It's talked about in a certain way, but it doesn't carry over into personal relationships."

On most of the islands, there's a tolerance for "being who you are," as Islesboro's Sue Hatch puts it. (In winter, that is. Summer's a different deal, and opinions about summer people vary from island to island—and person to person.) "Whether your face is purple or whatever, if you're here when the ferry leaves, you're here." That's not to say that everyone is best friends with everyone else, or even that they spend much time together. In fact, says Sue, "There's a quality of giving each other a fair amount of space. You'd think everyone was close, but we're not really close; we need that space." A recurring theme in my interviews was the independence of island people, who tend to be—perhaps need to be—more self-reliant than are most people ashore. "But," says Sue, articulating another common theme, "in a crisis, you won't ever be overlooked if you need something."

"People are fascinated by islands," says Nate Michaud, who spent time on Frenchboro (Long Island) and also with the nonprofit Island Institute, based in Rockland. "It's a metaphor for human existence. There are uncharted waters between each of us and everyone else."

Defining an Island

Let's start with the matter of what is or isn't an island. People on Frenchboro speak of Mount Desert Island (MDI) as "mainland." No MDI resident would do that—to them it's an island. A number of islands along the Maine coast are attached to the mainland by bridges or causeways, including Cousins, Bailey, Southport, Rackliff, Verona, Little Deer Isle, Deer Isle, Mount Desert, and, since 1958, Beals. Although they are still islands, and each is referred to by its residents as "the island," they are different.

(There are also many islands that have people on them only in the summer. Although these are wonderful places—and in most cases they had year-round communities in the past—they are beyond the scope of this book.)

Bridging to Beals—and Degrees of "Island-ness"

A third of the way east in Washington County, Moosabec Reach is a skinny body of water that separates Beals Island from Jonesport. Even though it's not very wide, it wasn't always easy to cross. Some of the region's strongest tidal currents develop here, more than six knots at the extreme. For many years, a passenger ferry connected the two towns, but, says Beals Islander Diana Kelley, "Lots of times you'd have to wait for hours and hours for it to be there." For the last couple of years before the bridge was built in the late 1950s, a car ferry operated for a certain number of hours each day—unless it was rough, and then it didn't run at all. Diana's husband, the late Avery Kelley, said that Beals had been petitioning the state for years for a bridge, but it wasn't until the boys' basketball team won the state tournament a few times that anyone paid attention. The tiny school fielded a state championship team in 1951, 1952, and again in 1956. In any case, work started on the bridge in 1957, and it opened the following year.

"A lot didn't like the change, and a lot did," says Dougie Dodge, who was in his early teens when the bridge was built. "The young who wanted to raise hell liked it, and so did the old, who were scared they couldn't get to the doctor. A lot of others didn't like it"—including him. "I like the rough and tough life," he chuckles.

It was not apparent at first, but the life of every Beals Islander changed entirely after the bridge was built. For years before it opened, there were five stores on the island, and only four vehicles. Some trucks delivered groceries, and there was an oil truck. "You used to be able to get anything you wanted," says Dougie, "and never have to leave the island. Everything you needed to build boats [building boats was the winter occupation of most Beals Island men], clothes, everything to run your house." But none of the island stores could match the prices in Machias, the nearest "big town." Suddenly able to go ashore whenever they pleased and drive back again to their own dooryards, people bought cars and left Beals to do their shopping. One by one, the stores closed; only one lasted into the 1990s before shutting its doors.

Churches was really big when I was small," says Diana, who with nine other students graduated from Beals High School in 1964. "We used to go to the Advent [church], and we'd go to Beals first, and then in the afternoon we'd go down to Alley's Bay on Great Wass." (Great Wass is south of Beals, and connected to it.) Even after the bridge was built, parents forbade their children to go to Jonesport. They thought the kids would be getting into cars, which would lead to accidents and other trouble. Besides, some saw Jonesport as a sinful place. "Our parents kept a tighter strain on us, they wanted to know what was going on. Today you don't have any idea." She does believe that things were so strict on Beals because religion was so strong. She remembers crossing the bridge when she was eleven or twelve—her father always walked across with her. "Even as a high school student, I was never allowed to go to Jonesport."

All five churches are still open, even though there are not as many members as there used to be, according to Diana. "There's too many activities goin' on, soccer and basketball and baseball and all that, and with the bridge and vehicles now you can get to 'em."

In 1969, the high schools of Beals and Jonesport were consolidated, although each town maintains its own independent elementary school. (The Beals elementary school may be in jeopardy now, too.) The fire department is in Jonesport, as is the ambulance; islanders volunteer for both. Jonesporters have always shown interest in the Beals Historical Society, and now that Jonesport has started up its own historical society, people from Beals are going to their meetings. The Masons, Eastern Star, and American Legion all meet in Jonesport and attract members from Beals.

"Beals is still somewhat distinct from Jonesport," Diana says, "but the kids are getting along better than what they used to. Still, there are people who like to say we'd been better off if we'd kept the kids here. Now we have to have the cops over here, kids racing around, all that. Kids today have cars as soon as they're sixteen—in the old days, you wouldn't think of having a car unless you got married, and then your husband would drive it. Drugs are heavy in town—we're getting this bad stuff around. I lock my door now I'm alone. When Avery was here we never did."

Asked about the impact of the bridge, Isaac Beal made a quick and less obvious reply. "Well, I can tell you one thing, we didn't have any skunks before the bridge, nor coons. They came across the bridge.

"And after they took the [bridge] toll off, people started coming. Now they're buying up all the shore frontage, and young people can't buy any access anymore." (He means access to the shore. Like the residents of the offshore islands, Beals Islanders almost all make their living by fishing.) In 2002, he said, 51 or 52 percent of the acreage of Beals was owned by people from somewhere else. "Of course there are some nice people among them," he concedes. He maintains moorings using a scow with a boom on it. "I've run into some difficulties. Not with local fishermen, it's the people from Away." To be fair—though it'll come up any time you ask a Beals Islander about the bridge—this increase in numbers of people from Away can't be entirely blamed on that bridge. But the skunks probably can.

Just as on some of the other islands—and elsewhere on the coast—more and more young people are leaving the area. It's too hard to get into fishing nowadays, Dougie Dodge says. The population of Beals peaked at 695 in 1980, a century after that of most of the coast, but in the decades that followed, it has slowly dropped. The 2000 census counted 618 year-round residents.

"You can go across that bridge fifteen times a day and not think a thing about it," says Diana Kelley. "But the traffic—I don't think I've ever gone across without one or two cars behind me or coming the other direction. It's always busy."

Functionally, Beals is no longer an island, nor are Deer Isle and any of the other bridged islands.

In some ways, the smaller towns of Maine's far northern Aroostook County are physically much more isolated than are the coastal islands. Like all of the islands in the past and some still, "the County" has a net out-migration, which only intensifies the smallness of their communities and thus, in some ways, their insularity. And an argument can be made that being at the end of a long mainland peninsula is more remote than living on Casco Bay's Peaks Island, served by sixteen ferries a day. Still, an inhabitant of a bridged island or a village a hundred miles north of anywhere can leave home at any hour he might choose and drive until he gets somewhere.

Of course, to the residents of the outer islands, the ones closer to the mainland barely qualify as islands. "We don't consider Peaks an island," says a former Cliff Islander. "Fifteen-minute ride to the land, sixteen boats a day, that's no island." Yet to some Vinalhaveners, to whom Islesboro certainly doesn't count (they say you can throw a stone ashore from Islesboro), Cliff might not qualify either, despite its ninety-minute ferry ride, because right through the dead of winter its ferries run early and late enough in the day so people can commute to Portland. (Of course, Cliff is part of the city of Portland anyway, which is nearly as bad as being part of Massachusetts.)

Matinicus is a long way offshore, and there's certainly more weather out there than in the more protected bays where several of the islands lie. The residents of Matinicus think Vinalhaven has it easy, with six ferries a day. The Matinicus ferry runs once a month in winter and only in the middle of summer does it get up to four trips a month—and even then, they're not scheduled so a person can make a round trip in one day. Matinicus enjoys its reputation as a distant and therefore lawless place, one whose rough-and-ready fishermen take care of things themselves. (Reputations often have some basis in fact.) On the other hand, weather permitting, the planes make seemingly infinite numbers of flights between the mainland and Matinicus every day, and perhaps Matinicus is the best-connected of any of the islands, albeit most expensively.

Monhegan is as far out as Matinicus, but even in winter, after they've survived the summer onslaught of tourists, they have mailboat service three times every week. And besides, some feel, it's kind of an arty place, and who can take that seriously?

Downeast, the Cranberry Isles are well connected to the mainland, even though there's no state ferry; the private boats from Mount Desert provide good service, and the waters between the islands and Northeast Harbor are relatively protected. Islands? Marginal, in the minds of some farther out. Frenchboro, with three car ferries a week and a passenger boat on Fridays, sees itself as the most remote island other than Matinicus.

It's all a matter of perspective.

The Islands Enumerated

From some three hundred inhabited islands in the nineteenth century—when of course water was an easier medium to travel through than were the Maine woods—only a very few remain occupied today. There are only fourteen islands with year-round communities including a school, although on more than one occasion, an island has had no children in its school. They do their best not to close a school altogether; it's too hard to reopen one. The islands that have closed their schools—most recently Criehaven, in the 1940s—have soon become home only to people who show up in the summer, either to vacation or to work. Portland's Great Diamond Island has had an increase in population since the development of an old fort site for residential use, but there is no school on the island. A very few other islands are home year-round to small numbers of people.

The islands are arranged physically into three general groups: Casco Bay, Penobscot Bay, and West of Stonington, with Isle au Haut forming the boundary between the latter two. Most of the Casco Bay islands were until recently part of the city of Portland; Long Island managed to sneak out before Portland fully realized what was happening, leaving the communities on Cliff, Peaks, and Great Diamond, as well as some summer islands, to provide the city with ever-more-highly-valued taxable real estate. Chebeague Island plays the same role in its town of Cumberland.

Greater Penobscot Bay's five islands with significant winter populations—

Monhegan, Matinicus, North Haven, Vinalhaven, and Islesboro—vary about as much as any five islands could, with vastly different sizes, populations, and economies. The islands don't share land access; their ferry connections are from Port Clyde, Rockland, and Lincolnville. North Haven, Vinalhaven, and Islesboro are the only Maine island communities with full schools, kindergarten through twelfth grade. As of the 2000 census, Matinicus was the least populous of the Maine islands and Vinalhaven the most.

Like North Haven and Vinalhaven, Isle au Haut is part of Knox County, but Stonington in Hancock County is its service center.

Frenchboro, the Cranberries (Islesford and Great Cranberry), and Swans Island make up the last group; they all are part of Hancock County. Those islands, too, are very different from one another. Access is from Mount Desert, through either Bass Harbor or Northeast Harbor.

Then there are Eagle Island, north of North Haven, where only Bob and Helene Quinn now live, and perhaps a couple of other islands that are inhabited year-round, and you've got it. (In summer, many islands, thriving communities in the past, once again sprout people.)

One tends to think of Maine's islands as rock-encircled, fog-encased, and spruce-covered—and these were in fact typical in the last century or so—but the coniferous vegetation is simply the second growth after every kind of tree was stripped from all Maine land near salt water, and up to ten miles inland, during the nineteenth century. Any wood not used for building local structures or vessels or burned locally was shipped off as lumber, pulp, barrel staves, or firewood. There are still people today who remember coastal houses naked to the wind, with nothing but bare rock and scraggly grass between them, and no shade anywhere. After the arrival of the brush and thorny berry bushes that grow in any abandoned Maine field, the first trees to return are the spruce and the quick-growing woods like alders and poplars.

The rocks are still there, their surfaces broken down over the millennia by fog-loving lichen into a thin layer of topsoil. But larger deciduous trees are making a comeback, some of the many tree species that grew on the islands in their natural state. The names of islands often seem backward, with islands called Bald now growing tall spruce, the many Burnt Islands and Oak Island also sporting a rich growth of spruce and other conifers. On the other hand, Spruce Island off Islesboro, fifty years ago a bright tangle of scrub, not only again has spruce tall enough to attract nesting ospreys but a good number of birch, oak, and other hardwoods. Pulpwood operations, once again economical, are being carried out on Maine islands. Not many of the islands have much open land, and a good deal of that belongs to summer people who keep idled pastures mowed and whose manicured lawns sweep down to the water. Gardens are not terribly productive without serious work. The beautiful flower gardens around some of the is-

The scenery from Isle au Haut is hard to beat—but notice the deer fence around the garden.

lands' statelier summer residences tend to be the product of one of the local industries, gardening.

One of the most fervently held beliefs of the residents of each of the islands is that their own particular island is unique, and it's certainly true, using any standard. Different rock formations, different vegetation, different human use over the years, different economies, different social characteristics. But they do have commonalities, too, and when it's convenient, their people proudly state that as well. When Islesboro was unhappy with Waldo County's taxes in 2003 and 2004, they overwhelmingly voted to join Knox County instead. The reason stated publicly as often as any other was that they could thus be in the same county with North Haven and Vinalhaven. (At this writing, it seems unlikely that the Maine legislature will permit that change. The economic impact on the rest of Waldo County, and particularly its many small towns, would be too great.)

All the islands share the obvious (although varying in degree) physical disconnection from the rest of the country, which leads to at least some feeling of remoteness, and on nearly all, there are but two primary sources of income: lobsters, and summer people of one sort and another. Only the Casco Bay islands are sufficiently connected with the mainland that off-island employment is truly convenient. A few inventive souls on some of the islands are making a living via the Internet or with some small-scale industry (including crafts). But for the most part, lobsters and summer visitors are it. And summer people bring with them not only monetary rewards but also tremendous economic stresses on property values, creating a third issue shared on most of the islands: a lack of affordable housing, which in turn relates to the ability of young people to establish themselves and their families. And all agree that keeping schools alive is essential. Once a school closes, it's a matter of time—and not long—before the community dies.

The numbers of people of the various islands are subject to discussion. The simplest counting method is to use the 2000 census—however they decided to count people, perhaps they were consistent enough that the numbers, while not totally accurate, are indicative of something. The problem, of course, is that if you miss counting five people, that could be 10 percent of the population on several of the islands.

But there is no definitive way to count. The issue isn't as simple as where a person calls home, or where he is registered to vote, or even where she happens to be on April 1. Numbers and categories of people on any of the islands are hard to calculate. Who counts as a year-round resident? On Matinicus, Frenchboro, and some of the other islands, lobstermen who take their traps ashore for the winter often go to the mainland—or even Florida—for a few of the coldest months. Are they still year-rounders? Certainly in their own minds they're still islanders. (You can't take that away from them—even those who have had to move ashore permanently for medical reasons.) Retired summer people have winterized their island houses and sometimes are staying six months or more. They vote on the islands, telling the states they came from that they are now residents of Maine (much to—for example—New York's consternation when they have the gall to die in Maine, leaving New York's hands out of their sometimes significant estates). Their children, too, are taking up residence on the islands, and making their livings there (those who need to). But are they islanders? They're certainly not natives—nor, on some islands, will their children be. As the old saw goes, the cat may have her kittens in the oven, but it don't make 'em biscuits. Despite that, they may well be accepted as part of island life.

Three main categories of people have houses on the islands: Natives, People from Away, and Summer People. On North Haven, some subcategories have been recognized: Transplants (individuals or families from Away, including summer people, who have moved onto the island), Implants (people from Away who have married natives), and Replants (natives who've left and come back). Are people from Away—of whatever subcategory—accepted? "Sure, after they've been here thirty or forty years," semi-joked one native woman from North Haven, but she went on to say that some will always be remembered to be transplants. It's the same deal as that some summer people truly become part of the community, while others who legally and perhaps in fact make their homes on an island will always be summer people.

Acceptance is in large part a matter of having a legitimate reason for being there—a spouse, or a job as teacher or nurse, for instance, and nothing to do with vacationing. Often, what it comes down to is the newcomers' commitment to the island, their willingness to pull their own weight, though that's a tricky line to walk. Too much involvement is not acceptable, particularly if there is too much attempt made to change things. Perhaps it's about showing respect for all the people sharing the rock—not that such respect is a prerequisite for claiming nativehood, as in many cases the natives are the least open-minded of all. You can't be a native without the pedigree—that's that, though having a single native parent qualifies in most cases, and for some, the pedigree is what counts.

Some of the islands—notably Frenchboro—are in a time of flux, and the categories are particularly difficult to master. Because of the successful homesteading program on Frenchboro, there are now thirteen households of people who otherwise would not be living there—thirteen from not more than twenty-five year-around establishments altogether. Many of those in the affordable housing project, having no local roots, are most definitely from Away. But in many ways they're also the most active in town, serving on boards and committees and working to better their community for themselves and their children. And, because often they have young children in school, or fewer financial resources, they are likely to be actually on the island a greater share of the time than many of the natives. They are certainly residents, while someone else, born and bred on Frenchboro, may be gone half the year or nearly. She's native—but is she still a year-rounder?

North Haven village, from the Fox Islands Thorofare

Eagle Island
THE QUINNS

t o us, it's ordinary," says Helene Quinn of the life she and her husband, Bob, share on 280-acre Eagle Island in Penobscot Bay, part of the archipelago between Deer Isle and North Haven. But their life—not only not ordinary to most of us—is quintessential "island-ness." Although rusticators join them in summer, they are the only people on that little island for most of the year.

Even though at one time most of the smaller islands of Penobscot Bay were home to a family or two, if not a whole community, Eagle is the only one that has never been without year-round residents. Bob and Helene are both the fifth generation on the island, and they even share a great-grandfather. Their ancestors settled on Eagle in the early 1800s.

The Quinn family: Helene, Bob, grandson Samuel Quinn Russo, and Treena Quinn-Russo, fifth, sixth and seventh generations of Eagle Islanders. (COURTESY OF BOB AND HELENE QUINN)

Eagle's population peaked at about sixty in the late 1800s, but by the time Bob was born in 1938, only five families remained—twenty or twenty-five residents—and it wasn't many years before most of them moved ashore for the war effort. Bob's father took his family to Camden and went to work in the shipyard. (His father, Cappy, like Bob today, was never afraid of labor. "The Lord ain't made a day so cold that I couldn't work hard enough to stay warm," he used to say.) Only a few older folks stayed on the island, including Helene's aunt and Bob's grandmother and great-uncle.

In 1942, Eagle Island's school closed, creating the benchmark—the official end of the Eagle Island community. On several islands today, there's a justifiable worry about losing the school—and therefore the winter community.

Both Bob's and Helene's mothers came to the island as children, daughters of lighthouse keepers. "That's how the men got their brides," says Helene. "Not exclusively, but that's how those two did."

Bob's mother grew up in one lighthouse after another. Her father worked six years on Boone Island, a rock off Portland, and then a few years on Avery Rock off Machiasport, where the light tower was on one rock and the house on another, with a gangway in between. "The only place they could get outdoors was on that walkway. That's where my mother and her sister used to push their doll carriages. Mother claimed that when they came to Eagle, it was the first time she walked in grass." They stayed twelve years, happy to finally be living in a community, and one with a school. (Their next post was at Marshall Point in Port Clyde, where the lighthouse actually stood on the mainland!)

Even though he was living ashore while he was growing up, Bob spent a lot of time on Eagle with his grandmother. It was always his dream to move to the island full-time. As soon as he finished high school—even though his grandmother had died by then—Bob returned to Eagle. He lived with his great-uncle and Helene's aunt, who was caring for the old man. In summer, he fished offshore with his father, going out for a week at a time; in winter, he did "this and that," as he still does today.

In January 2004, he had just bought a trap to go after the mink that were getting into his chickens. He suspects there's still a closed season on mink—it used to be that trapping was legal only in November—but he also suspects that he has the right to protect his flock. "Those mink come under the varmint category." He hasn't commercially trapped mink for some forty years—back then, you'd skin the mink, stretch the hide, dry it, and send it off to Sears and Roebuck. A check would come in the mail. As a boy, with the help and advice of his father, he'd go trapping over Thanksgiving weekend. He bought a bicycle with the proceeds from his first mink.

Bob was drafted in 1961, and after he came home from the service, he lived in Stonington and fished from there. He looked after the elderly members of his family still on the island—bringing them groceries and fixing their generators and cutting wood for them. Every night, he talked with them on the CB radio, to find out what they needed. Summers, he was back on the island full-time, tending to the rental houses and to the summer cottages that had been built on parcels of land sold to summer visitors who had stayed with his grandparents through the years. In times of bad fishing, he has sold a couple of lots himself, again to longtime renters, and then has built the houses for them. The fall and spring maintenance work on those places has fallen to him since he was a young man.

Helene too spent summers on Eagle and always felt a connection to the place. She and Bob married in 1966, and although they lived in Stonington during the school year, they were on the island whenever possible—weekends, school vacations, summers. Helene worked in the school on Deer Isle, and Bob fished from Stonington until summer. Always he took care of things on the island. Helene's aunt was the last full-time resident of the last generation—after she died, they found caretakers to stay on the island. The last couple stayed ten years and raised and home-schooled two children there. After that family left in 1991, the Quinns moved out to the island full-time, as Bob had always intended to do. Their daughter was away at school, so they no longer needed to stay in town.

Bob and Helene now live in Bob's grandmother's house, built by Samuel Quinn, the first settler, in 1810. "At least he built the beginnings of this house. It's been built on and over a number of times since," says Bob. Samuel's family was the primary family on the island until 1839, when the lighthouse was built. "They got new blood from the lighthouse."

"For me, moving out was a brand-new startup," says Helene. "Different challenges." Not only were they alone on the island most of the year, but for the first several years they had no telephone, just the radio and the Camden Marine Operator. Working in the school on the mainland, she had become accustomed to being in the center of activity, and she admits that she was anxious at first, feeling isolated. "I felt I'd left all my support ashore, and early on, before we had the phone, there was much more time without contact except when we went ashore.

"But once I got myself in hand and had a chance to live with it, it was very worthwhile. It was a life-changing experience—I found my strength and I found my resilience, and just became very peaceful. I came out much stronger. I reflect on that a lot," she says.

"It was a real gift. People are paying money nowadays to do that, going on retreats that cut them off from the stimulation of modern life and allow them to experience quiet and introspection." Did she expect that when she moved out onto the island? "No. I had no idea what to expect. I don't have that kind of time now—it only lasted the first two winters—but I always have that to look back on."

Summers are as busy on Eagle as on any of the other islands. The Quinns have several irons in the fire—not only does Bob fish and caretake, but they still have a few rental cottages, and Helene operates a little bakery business. They have been running the mailboat for the last several years, too. "You attach all kinds of things together, more than you can do, all condensed into three months. You pack it all in," she says. "I kind of relish it after the busy season. We go into a different routine. That's the time when we do the bookkeeping and catch up on correspondence. We're away a fair amount, off and on, during the holiday season, and then in January and February we tuck in to do projects and get ready for the next summer."

Helene says people can't imagine her life. "I've been asked a million times, 'What do you find to do?' I answer different ways each time, for my own amusement, but really my life is just like theirs." She concedes, of course, that it really isn't, but she says she always thinks of life in terms of similarities rather than differences. "There are common denominators wherever you go. We are in contact with so many people, that's the fallacy. It's not like you're going to go to the Post Office and chitchat every day, but we're in daily contact with people on the phone. I think we have more contact than most —people calling about rental reservations or just checking in—and we check with our family pretty regularly." And when she starts to remark that people don't just drop in for tea, she has to correct herself. Just this winter, she says, "three people came over from Vinalhaven. I guess they just wanted to go for a boat ride."

There are always projects set aside for the winter, but it's well into December before Helene wraps up the bookkeeping and has caught up on correspondence, and before Bob gets the boats and moorings taken care of and the summer cottages readied for winter—cleaned up, screens taken off, shutters put on, water drained. Although they have a propane floor heater they can use if they're going off island overnight, the Quinns heat with wood. That alone gives them one good project every year—cutting, sawing, splitting, and stacking nine or ten cords of wood. "There's not much hardwood out here. It's mostly spruce. There's not a lot of heat in that." Bob's been working on his barn for five years now, and says it'll take another five to finish what he's planned. There are plenty of maintenance jobs and improvements to be made on the cottages—always something.

For thirty years, communication from the island was by CB radio. "It was a primary link for all the islands," Bob explains, "and most everyone had it on, monitoring. But there were too many people on it—the government even gave up and stopped making people get licenses. There were rude people using it, and it got all foul language." The Quinns switched to VHF radio and used the Camden Marine Operator when they needed to make calls shoreside. In 1997, when Bob and Helene started running the mailboat for his cousins, they needed a regular phone of some sort. They tried a cell phone, which worked all right but was horrendously expensive. People couldn't keep their conversations short, and although they would offer to call back, they didn't understand that the cell account would be charged anyway. The phone cost the Quinns $4,500 the first year. Bob heard that the then-new 900-megahertz portable phones purported to carry a long distance, so he tested one. Running an extension out in the boat, he discovered that, at least under the right conditions, the handset could be as much as three miles from the base—the distance from a friend's garage on Deer Isle to the Quinns' house on Eagle Island. And among the summer people on the island were engineers and scientists who schemed up an antenna system of a broomstick and coat hangers—since upgraded to PVC pipe and proper wire—that directed the signal toward the island. "It works reasonably well," says Bob. "Wind, rain, foliage on the trees all affect it—and we have only a couple of places in the house where it'll work, so that's where you have to stay. It's cordless but not mobile."

"There's an element of magic to it," says Helene, "but it works almost all the time."

The summer people all have cell phones now, and some have Internet connections via satellite. The Quinns have so far chosen not to take that step. "I can see how as time goes on, you get pulled into that stuff," says Bob. "It's hard to stay current. But we're happy not to be." Bob noticed a distinct change not so many years ago when a summer person a quarter-mile down the island wanted something and called him. "For generations before, if you wanted someone, you put on your hat and coat and went to see them." Now it's not at all unusual for people to call. "There's something about being here, you think you're getting away from it all—a lot of people say they feel they're stepping back in time—but it's pretty thinly veiled."

The Quinns have a diesel electric generator, which they use to run the washing machine and Bob's table saw and other power tools, but for lights and their electronics they use a solar array. (They do have a television, which receives channels broadcast from Bangor, as well as their radios.) "We could stand a few more solar panels, or better yet, a windmill, but if it's cloudy a long time, we always have the auxiliary power if we need it." In summer, refrigeration is provided by propane. "In the winter, you just set things on the floor in the corner," says Bob. He says that ice cream is a luxury they seldom have, as the propane refrigerators just don't keep it cold enough. "The other day," he said in January, "we bought a pint and didn't eat it all, and it's sitting on a shelf in the entryway and it's just fine."

Some of the summer people have generators too, but most of them use candles and kerosene or are installing solar-power equipment. "We don't have the same amenities as in some of the summer places like Camden or even North Haven," Helene says. "It's a much more modest setup here."

"In some ways, I think we're not as inconvenienced by storms and the like as on the mainland," Bob says. "We don't lose our power, and we don't have to go to the hardware store and buy a snow shovel. Everyone else seems to have to—we see them on TV, and stores have all run out. I've got a shovel I bought from my great-uncle when I was in high school, and I'm still using it. What do they do with all their shovels?"

It's a three-mile trip, a twenty-minute run in Bob's lobsterboat, to Sylvester's Cove on Deer Isle, where the Quinns keep a vehicle. Since 1999, Bob and Helene themselves have had the Postal Service contract for the mailboat service. Her grandfather had the first contract, starting not long after 1900 and running up until Bob's cousins, Jimmy Quinn and his wife, Edith, took it over. They had met when Edith, a nurse, came to the island to care for an elderly person, but they moved ashore for their children when the island school closed, and they ran the business from Deer Isle. After Jimmy died, Edith and her son kept on. For fifty years, they always made the same bid, their only increase coming from the fuel adjustment given them by the government. They quit when the Coast Guard regulations started getting too burdensome and the reservations and bookwork were more than Edith wanted to do anymore. Even at ninety-four, Edith still helps, though. All the UPS packages for the island go first to her.

In winter, the mailboat—Bob's lobsterboat—runs to the mainland twice a week. They are scheduled to make the trip on Tuesdays and Fridays, but if the weather's truly nasty, they'll do it the next day or the one after. In the forty-six years that Bob has made the run—for himself or filling in for his cousins—only twice has he missed a trip altogether.

In summer, they run a Coast Guard–inspected passenger boat and serve five islands that have summer residents. Most of the summer people on Eagle and the other islands don't have commuter boats themselves, nor is there any good place for them to land ashore, so they ride the mailboat. Tourists like to make the two-hour trip, too, seeing the islands and wildlife and getting a bit of a feel for life on the bay.

The Quinns' contract expired in 2004. Their son-in-law had been operating the boat for them in the past summers, but 2003 was his last year. "I feel like I'm at the bottom of Tuckerman's Ravine with an avalanche just started," said Bob before the contract ran out, referring to the famously dangerous section on Mount Washington where many people have lost their lives. "There's no way out, and it's headed at me." He goes on. "I like to get a few traps set, and I can't do that and run the mailboat. We need the income from renting and people have to get here. But there's not a big enough volume of people." Bob says they carry about 1,800 passengers a season, and it would be hard to increase that number much, even with day-trippers, because of the physical difficulties on the mainland—parking, and access to the boat itself, which is at a tidal dock that doesn't always have water enough.

They weren't sure they'd put in a bid again. Even just to carry the mail, the Postal Service—probably not aware of what its stipulation actually means—requires that the boat be inspected by the Coast Guard, which considers the boat to be a ferry like any other ferry (to Staten Island, for instance). There are inspections and compulsory drug testing (which with just one operator means tying up the boat when that person has to run to Bangor at some randomly chosen time to pee in a cup). And there are frequent government demands for new equipment. Now under consideration, for example, is a beacon that would broadcast a signal at all times so the Coast Guard—part of the Department of Homeland Security—can keep track of the boat. That alone, Bob said, would cost $9,400 per vessel—obviously cost-prohibitive for such a small operation. There are always niggling details to take care of—for example, the passenger boat has been carrying a life raft for thirty years; the regulation required that it have a 10-fathom floating line attached, yellow or white. In 2003, they had to change that line to a black one. Why? "You don't ask that," he says. "It's just like in a lobster boat. You gotta have a life ring. Well, 50 percent of lobstermen go out alone, so what good's it gonna do you? I guess when you fall overboard, you gotta throw your life ring first.

"You like to think we're out of the mainstream out here, but you can see we're not," says Bob.

For the last hundred years, there has been a mailboat contract. The Quinns worried that if they didn't take the contract, it might be the end of the tradition. Another bid was unlikely, as it would be very difficult just to break even on mail and passengers. Perhaps the Quinns don't really need a mailboat during the months when they're the only people on the island—although never does a trip fail to bring mail—but in the summer, it's a different situation. Bob didn't know what would happen if there was no bidder.

So, when it came down to it, the Quinns renewed their contract for another two years, with the option to renew a year at a time. "Four years is a long haul," Helene says. They were encouraged to learn that a good friend was willing to run the boat at least for a couple of years. The only impact that the government's concern with homeland security had on them was that the Coast Guard inspection, usually in June or July, didn't take place until September. "They're so busy they can't get to do routine things," says Helene. Asked shortly after Labor Day if the fellow running the boat was happy with his job, she replied, "We're all so tired we can't see straight. We'll have to see when the pressure's off how he feels about it." She knows that they'll have to find a relief captain of some sort, so he can have time off. "It's a grueling schedule, seven days a week till the season's over. You get kind of thin."

Helene is sixty, Bob is sixty-six. "I don't worry about medical emergencies," Helene says, "but I do think about them, and we have a contingency plan. If I get hurt, he's strong enough to haul me around to the boat," she says. She'd have a harder time with his bigger body. "We use common sense and don't take risks—knowing that things do happen. We accept that."

They're still the only people living on Eagle full-time. "We talk about it some," says Helene. "Who else is going to come along? You never know. We're here now, and kinda in control of things, so there's no need for anyone, and there's a limit to what people can do out here. But as we get older, it may change. It may generate somebody else getting the idea."

Bob sounds a little less hopeful. "It'll change with the new generation. Part of life is change. There are some younger people coming out here, but not many couples—some of the young couples we have, one will be more interested than the other." That appears to be the case with Bob and Helene's daughter. Her husband ran the mailboat for several years, but, says Bob, "it doesn't quite work for him." He concedes that it takes an odd breed to stay on the island. "Evolution takes care of it—we're all playing out. I realized a long time ago that I was a link in the chain of this family—I worry that I'm the last link. Every chain has an end link.

"My daughter is very interested—hopefully, maybe our grandson will be." He's four now. "I just hope I can hang on till they get rooted. He'll be the seventh generation, if he makes it."

Bob remembers the care he took of his great-uncle and Helene's aunt, chopping wood and dragging heavy cases of canned goods on sleds through knee-deep snow. "I couldn't do it today," he says. "If I could find someone to do that for me, I could live out my life here too. I keep hoping."

North Haven
CHELLIE PINGREE

1 t took a while, but Chellie Pingree, who arrived in Maine in 1971 at the age of sixteen to be with her boyfriend, learned how islands worked—and people, and politics, too—all on the island of North Haven. Thirty-one years later, after a close but unsuccessful race for the U.S. Senate, Chellie went to Washington anyway, becoming president and CEO of Common Cause, a nonpartisan nonprofit concerned with citizens' voices and elected leaders' accountability. She still lives on North Haven Island whenever possible, and she's still very conscious of the lessons she learned there.

Chellie came from Minnesota, and was growing up during the difficult era at the end of the Vietnam War. Her parents were from immigrant families, and she was the afterthought in a family of four children; she describes herself and her siblings as coming from completely different generations: "My sister was a prom queen, and I was a war protester." She met Charlie Pingree in an alternative high school program. What possessed her to strike out for Maine at such a young age? Times were different then—kids were leaving traditional paths, traveling the country, emancipating themselves legally or simply in fact. Some were "going back to the land." And that's what Charlie and Chellie did, Scott and Helen Nearing's books in hand, living on North Haven in an abandoned family cabin with no amenities. Although Charlie had always summered on the island, as had his parents and grandparents, it was then unprecedented that a summer kid would try to stay year-round, and it

Chellie Pingree (COURTESY OF CHELLIE PINGREE)

didn't go over well. No one paid much outward attention to them, but, even though they didn't realize it, of course they were noticed. Who were these kids, and (perhaps more important) who did they think they were? No way would they consider letting "the girl who drives that red pickup truck" even volunteer in the school. Chellie was bewildered. "I was surprised anyone even knew who I was, much less hated me."

They moved away for three years, visiting the island only in the summers while Chellie received her college degree and Charlie trained as a boatbuilder. But they wanted to go back to North Haven. This time, they were determined to fit in. In 1977, married and with their first daughter, they returned with plans to farm and build boats. Farming was a clearly useful occupation, one that was disappearing from the island. It required hard work and knowledge and produced things people wanted. It provided Chellie with credibility. Her egg route and milk sales at the farm occasionally led to the little conversations that become knowledge about people and community—she learned who was related to whom, whose mother was ailing, what other young mothers were going through with their own children. In becoming a real person to her neighbors, she was learning what community meant. "If you've told them enough about yourself," she says, "then you can be accepted. Whether you're gay or alcoholic or difficult or mean, that's OK—but a mystery can't be trusted."

The Pingrees began going to town meetings, and eventually Chellie even dared to voice controversial opinions about taxes or schools or the ferry. But she learned that even when people were angry with her at the time, the next morning they'd still ask the little questions like "How's your wood holding up?" that neighbors ask of one another. She had become an active part of the community. For the first time, she felt the discomfort when someone said they were leaving the island. "What's wrong with us? Why would they go?" she'd ask herself. Many rural communities these days are worried about growth pressures, but when someone leaves an island, the residents are concerned about losing Scrabble or card-playing partners for Saturday night, or losing children from the school. "Survival seems tenuous," she says now. "In few other places do you understand interdependence the way you do here."

Along the way, Chellie experienced the island's summer season the way its winter residents did. Summer people bought vegetables from her during her regular hours on Monday, Wednesday, and Friday—and sometimes expected her to be available on Saturday. Or they would call, asking for special favors, long after she was in bed. "I began to understand the price my island neighbors paid to earn their living. Summer exhausted everyone; winter was when the community reconnected."

When the Pingrees built their own house and finally moved in, Chellie gradually made the change from farming to running a knitting design company. She ended up with ten full-time employees.

It wasn't long before she was also involved in town committees and projects. "There are ninety elected and appointed offices in town, and only 350 of us, and a hundred of those are kids. We have to do everything Rockland does, so everyone knows they have to take their turn. Very few people stay uninvolved," she says. She enjoys the irony that twenty years after she was barred from volunteering at the school, she was chair of the school board. She stepped down in 1992 to run for the State Senate. When she asked neighbors how they felt about her making that run, the reactions were not all positive. "Are you out of your mind?" she was asked, and "Who do you think you are?"

"No one wants to be abandoned," she says. "And you don't want people to think that you think you're better than anybody else."

Among the lessons learned on North Haven was how to work through personal conflicts—"You can't walk away from something." Chellie and Charlie are divorced now, but they still live five miles from one another. She cherishes the fact that her closest friends on the island include people she never would have met elsewhere—for instance, people who can tear apart a diesel engine and put it back together again. It amuses her that she has more skills than the people she meets off the island—she can grow tomatoes, milk a cow, split wood, cook on a woodstove. "It colors your perspective," she says.

A Democrat in a Republican district in 1992, Chellie managed to win her election to the State Senate, where one of the most difficult situations she faced was the adoption of the Monhegan Island Lobster Conservation Area. Friendship, the mainland home of the fishermen who were challenging Monhegan's exclusive fishing zone, was located in her district, but Monhegan was not—yet she voted in favor of Monhegan. "I was an islander first," she says. She was also a major supporter of the attempts by various islands to secede from the city of Portland. Ann Rand, her best friend in the State Senate, represented the city of Portland, which was vehemently opposed to losing tax base, but Chellie felt strongly about the matter. "How could you think of denying the right to self-rule? If any community chooses to govern itself, it's such hard work that, absolutely, they should. The most important thing in democracy is not just to have it, but that people participate," she says.

Chellie ended up as majority leader of the State Senate. After she was term-limited out of office, she made a serious run for the U.S. Senate, garnering far more support than had been initially expected. But she attributes her successes to lessons learned on North Haven. She learned not only about community, but also about being inside or outside of a group. She realized how protective people are of things they truly care about, and how different the ways people perceive you may be from the way you perceive yourself. "This is important in politics," she says. "You have to convince people that they can trust you, that you'd be a good negotiator on their behalf. If you want them to give you something—their trust—you have to meet them on their terms."

As a young woman, she had spent hours discussing utopias, but she came to realize that she didn't want to be part of a theoretical utopia. Rather, she wanted to be part of North Haven's very real community—people who for a variety of reasons had a commitment to each other. By delivering eggs, or by hiring knitters, she was providing something that mattered to them, thereby creating the perfect model for becoming part of a community.

"The political battles in a community that really cares are like nothing I'd experienced," she says. "You learn to be tough when you care about the outcome, and how to survive when you lose, and how to rebuild relationships when you're viciously on the opposite sides."

For more than thirty years, Chellie has lived mostly on North Haven, even though lately she has been active in the Washington, D.C., battlefields of Big Issues. "Everything I need to know about politics I learned here on North Haven. Even though it isn't always pretty, it's the essence of community."

Islanders

d on't quote me! I'll have to move away!" warned one island woman I interviewed. It's true that island people tend to be careful about what they say. Ted Hoskins has summered on Isle au Haut forever—first as the son of the summer minister and then as the summer minister himself—and he spent one winter out there, teaching school. "An old buddy of mine on Isle au Haut," Ted says, "you ask him any question, and he'll think a while, and then say, 'I wouldn't want to say for sure.' Particularly on an island, you get caught on anything you say. You learn not to say a great many things, because you're going to be held responsible for them all. Unless you've gone through a couple of winters, you don't know why you're so quiet in the summer. By the end of winter, you've gone over every one of the summer conversations, and some of 'em don't mesh."

Nate Michaud's island experience started on Frenchboro where he went to work as a sternman when he was a young man. "It's odd moving into a community of forty people," he says. "You start in a bubble and bounce against everyone else's bubbles till you find places where your bubble melds with other people's. No one anywhere is ever completely open, but maybe that's even more true on an island. There are always areas you can't get to. You have to learn to take people for what they are, not to try to change things. That's a mistake a lot of people make. You have to see good in things as they happen. You find your position. People check you out, you check them out, find common ground where you can; it evolves."

"It didn't take long to feel part of this place," says Islesboro's Bill Boardman, whose roots were on the island but whose own upbringing was not. "A few years." (Is time different on islands?) He's been on Islesboro since the 1970s and at Pendleton Yacht Yard more than twenty years now. He's also the code enforcement officer for the island, getting paid for fifteen hours a week. "I work about eight in the office and eight outside, but you're always on the clock. Just like the boatyard—they'll call you at home, see you at coffee. You help on Sunday if a fisherman wants to launch." Same thing goes for the contractors, if they need him to check a septic system. "Island life is like that in general."

"Everyone has been great to us," says Brenda Hopkins, a transplant to Isle au Haut. "They're wary, like anyone would be, if you come in and try to push or change something. You're from Away."

When Brenda and Bill Clark moved onto the island in the mid-1990s, they found the transition easy. They know to respect other people's space and wishes, and to sit back and see how

Bill Boardman

things are done. "You have to take everyone as they are," says Brenda. "They're wonderful people—every one has their special way. You can learn from everybody. You try to be helpful.

"You have to decide what to get wound up about," she says. "If you're a person who's gonna get upset—such as when people know what's going on in your life, or when you can't get a certain thing at the store—you don't need to be here. Go with the flow, don't try to change things. Get along, and agree to disagree. Sometimes you have just too much information—but don't believe everything you hear, and only half of what you see, as they say.

"And always," says Brenda and nearly any other islander, "if anybody needs anything, then everything's forgotten."

"There are certainly people you can't stand, and everyone knows that and acknowledges it," another person told me. "You only begrudgingly say hello, and you bitch about them with your friends, but if their boat's sinking or their house is afire, you go without hesitation."

When a couple from Away moved onto Matinicus, a local fellow took it upon himself to harass them continually and with some seriousness. Nails were dropped in their driveway, and their car was turned over onto its roof.

The woman actually saw the nails being dropped, so she gathered them up with a magnet and took them back to the perpetrator. "I think these are yours," she said. But when her husband died, that fellow was the first on her doorstep offering help. "The guy you sent to jail is the guy who pulls your boat off the rocks," she added.

Only once did I hear the reason articulated—but it's always there: "Next time it might be me." (And no, the Matinicus harasser didn't entirely change his character. After a bit, the pranks continued. The woman had become active in island government and was taking actions disliked by some islanders, including her tormentor.)

Donna Wiegle and her husband moved onto Swans Island full-time a couple of years ago. She does admit that everyone knows your business in such a small community. "If they don't, they'll make it up, so you might as well tell them."

Different sorts of people are on different islands for differing reasons. "Some people think they're going to find themselves," I was told. "Sometimes they do, but when they don't like who they find, they move off!"

A couple from my fictitious Smith Island suggests, "Everyone here who's not from here is hiding from something." Asked what he is hiding from, he answers, "My mother."

Asked what she is hiding from, she immediately answers, "His mother."

(There are those who object to this argument. "There is such a stereotype of us escaping the real world," says Eva Murray of Matinicus. "That's easily misunderstood to mean we're chickening out." No one would accuse Eva of chickening out. We'll be coming back to her.)

Successful island transplants share a disinterest in Wal-Mart and are willing and able to fend for themselves. "Life has to be self-sufficient so you don't need or want to go anywhere," says one retiree on Islesboro. "If the buzz over there on the mainland is going to be important to you, it won't work. I tell people there's nothing to do here—no restaurants, no movies or shopping. We're so busy—but you don't tell them that part, because they don't get it." She was surprised at how welcoming people were and how involved she became on the island, having always hung back from joining things in her earlier, more urban life.

There's one quality essential for island life, even in those places with regular ferry service and connections to the mainland. "You've got to like yourself pretty well," says Ted Hoskins. "If you're not content with who and where you are, you don't fare well. People end up driving around as if they're going to go somewhere they haven't been before. Some enjoy seeing things, but others have an urgency as if they're going to get away."

"Many people think it's quaint to live on an island," says Michelle Wiley, pastor of Vinalhaven's Union Church, "but after three months, they get edgy."

Matinicus perhaps is the extreme, with only fifty residents officially—and probably fewer on any given winter day. It's a place too full of reality to have many romantics wrapped up in the "simple life," and there aren't many immensely rich people like the ones who light on some of the other islands. It's unlikely that anyone would notice any rich folk there might be. "They don't need to be recognized," I was told. "The island attracts interesting people who don't fit into the mold of society—not the John Travoltas, but lawyers who won't practice law, some wealthy people who refuse to put shoes on. They're rebels. They're people who don't really need community. Some of the most interesting and intelligent people I have ever met have come here, and some of the scummiest lowlifes as well. Refugees from either Princeton or the county lockup. No kidding."

Another person is specific about what can happen to people on islands. "If they're not psychologically self-sufficient, they retire into TV and the bottle. The happy ones have enough in their internal life that they don't need external stimulation."

"If you live down here with fifty or seventy-five people," says Bob Howard of Cliff Island, "you're sort of a loner anyway. You're not used to being outgoing and being close friends with everybody. It's not intentional—we're not particularly social with each other, either! We have suppers once in a while, but we don't do a lot of home entertaining."

Says a transplant on one of the smaller islands, "Community has to be intentional."

Television and the Internet have kept people from gathering even as they did in the old days. The Grange, church activities, community suppers, the stitch-and-bitch gatherings of women knitting things to sell at fairs in the summer—if not gone, they are less frequent on many islands than in decades past. "You could go a year without seeing anyone outside your particular group now," says Barney Hallowell of North Haven, which, with a total of 350 residents, is actually large enough to have groups.

But there have always been and still are organizations where people get together, even if times have changed. When I first talked with Donna Wiegle, she burbled about the new garden club on Swans. "It's five weeks old today," she said. More than twenty people have joined, about half of them summer people and half year-rounders. "There are older ladies who know so much, and people like me who want to learn about gardening in Maine, both flowers and vegetables. We charge dues—ten dollars a year unless you're over seventy, then it's a dollar a year, or over eighty, fifty cents." Just from dues, they had $175 in the treasury already to use the next year for projects like window boxes for the ferry terminal. "The terminal is the first thing anyone sees when they come on the island, and it's kind of drab." The members range in age from twenty-six to eighty-four. "That's the way things are out here, young and old all do things together." One man has joined.

Donna particularly likes the tradition of visiting. "Where we came from in Pennsylvania, you didn't just drop in on someone. You waited for an invitation, or at least you called first. But here, people visit each other. On my birthday, a young lady came to visit, bringing a little plant for me. Her mother is younger than I am. But she told me that you can't pick your friends based on age here. If you meet someone you like, age doesn't matter. I thought that was pretty wise coming from a twenty-two-year-old."

Says Chellie Pingree of North Haven, "There's an integration of ages on the island that you don't find in most communities. I never realized it until years later, but my kids never called anyone Mr. or Mrs. Older people come to all the school basketball games, and if you have breakfast with all the old guys at the store, they're as likely to be talking about which sixteen- or seventeen-year-olds are dating as the new sewer plant. Most communities are stratified by age or working group. Not here."

Visiting isn't nearly as common as it was before the days of television, but morning coffee still goes strong. On Islesboro, the Island Market is the place for coffee, and it runs for a couple of hours, with each group of guys having its own time slot—though, depending on the weather, some stay right through. Bill Boardman is there from seven-fifteen to seven-forty. "We talk about everything from prostate exams to the war in Iraq. A lot of them try to be neutral," Bill says, but he admits he's outspoken. "There are a couple that feel as strongly on the other end—but we like each other real well. It just makes for banter. That's what it's all about. It's a good place to promote a cause—sell tickets for a raffle or a benefit dinner. Even if they don't expect to come to the event, they're always willing to throw in ten bucks."

Of course the weather is a very common theme at any gathering. "It took me a long time to learn to talk about the weather," says Nate Michaud. "I realized how many things you can say, talking about the weather. Like, weather in relation to work—it's different in a place like Frenchboro, where weather's so central to life. The first thing you think about in the morning is which way the wind's blowing. And the sound of the surf on the back side of the island. What traps you're hauling today, what they were like last time. If you're able to get off the island or not.

"When he's talking about the weather, a person could be talking about a string of bad luck he's had hauling, or success, or a real sense of pleasure about being on the island, or being sick of it."

Several of the islands have become attractive to retired people, a fact that brings its own problems with it. Says one Smith Islander, "They're self-contained, though they do contribute. But they're opposed to what the locals want. Cut the school budget—taxes are too high. They don't realize how important it is to have young people to do things. And there was a move to have twenty-four-hour police protection. It's unnecessary, particularly in winter—a county cop comes over. At town meeting, the vote, to a person, was that the people who grew up here, young or old, and the youngish transplants were against it. The retired and older new people were for it. One stood up and asked, 'What should I do if something happens in the middle of the night?' The locals know: call your cousin, or your neighbor."

There are still sometimes bad feelings between natives and transplants: "They move here because they like it, and then they gotta have it the way it was where they came from. If they don't like it, why'd they bother to come here?" There is an element of legitimacy to the question—there are certainly some who come with the feeling that everything can be bought. They're wrong. "I don't care if somebody offered me five million dollars," says Islesboro's Sue Hatch, "they couldn't have my house."

But the native who questions why people come if they want it different may not understand that the newcomers sometimes can see threats to aspects of their new home that the person who has lived there all his life might not recognize. "It won't happen here" is heard or intimated nearly as often as the remark about making an island like the place the people came from—and of course it quite likely will happen—whatever the threat may be—and perhaps already has. The lack of affordable housing is a ubiquitous problem on the islands. Some of the issues, like solid waste disposal, are more global than island-specific. Because of the small scale of human activity on the islands, though, practices no longer acceptable everywhere else are sometimes still seen as OK on the islands, and it's likely to be someone from Away who objects enough to do something about it.

Recent transplants to many of the islands are serving as selectmen, school committee members, town clerks, treasurers, librarians, and so on. At first blush, this might seem like the stereotypical "people from Away who come here and want to change things." No doubt, sometimes that's the case, though, one has to note, the islanders voted for or at least allowed those people to occupy these positions. There are times that locals have just gotten fed up enough with newcomers' approach to local issues that they throw up their collective hands, saying, "Fine, you do it."

There are certainly changes occurring because of the foreign involvements. "I don't want to blame it on the facile newcomers, but that's a part of it," says Ted Hoskins. "They get involved in churches and local government, and they've had experience and training and they're assertive and they volunteer to do things, and it's easy for them. But if the islanders feel any push, they back away. The newcomers are only trying to be helpful, but it can be disastrous for the church, and town politics too."

Often, however, it's simply that everyone else—natives and others who've been around a while—have all taken their turn at various town jobs, and they're happy when someone comes along who's willing to pull some of the load for a while. On an island such as Frenchboro, where there are thirty-seven registered voters and forty-five town positions to be filled each year at Town Meeting, willing bodies are welcomed. And, most often, the reasons that the newcomers came to the island are similar to the reasons the other residents have stayed there.

There is yet another reason why committees are apt to be filled by people who've moved to an island, rather than natives—and this may be particularly true on the larger islands. In the past, islanders decided things by consensus. An issue would arise, people would talk it over in small groups—at the store or the post office or boat-to-boat or in each other's kitchens—and after a few weeks, consensus would appear. Then whatever action was required would be taken. There was no formal committee to decide whether the pier would be strengthened, or the road paved, or a school building reroofed.

But now, with more formal town structures and perhaps less day-to-day communication among people—particularly where there are several social groups within the locality—committees are appointed to consider particular issues. Recent-comers hold back waiting for the long-time island residents to volunteer to serve, and when they don't, the people from Away—often retirees with skills learned in the outside world and time to spare—step in. The committees do their best to study their charge carefully and open-mindedly and ultimately make suggestions, and although public hearings are held, no one from the community says anything in public until the Town Meeting at which a decision is to be made. That's when the naysayers show up and become very vocal. Sometimes, with one shot, they will knock down the fruits of many months of work. After such a meeting, hard feelings can develop on both sides and add to whatever division may already exist between natives and transplants.

Sometimes the sides on a particular issue are based on place of birth, but often they may be drawn along entirely different lines: those with kids against those without, rich vs. poor, retired vs. working, house-owner vs. not, or young people against old. Permanent rifts are not common, but occasionally an issue will divide a community so thoroughly that it takes years or even a generation to get over it. Often it seems to be something about the school. Everyone knows everyone else on most of the islands, that's a given. For instance, a sign posted on the Islesboro ferry advertises organic maple syrup. "See Jamie," the poster says, adding a phone number almost as an afterthought.

A recent transplant onto Smith Island points out one clear benefit from knowing everyone. "When you're living in New York City, you don't know who the terrorists are. Here, you do."

There are a lot of little rules—things you just know on an island (and if you don't, it's clear you're not really part of the island yet). Bill Boardman, passing a car on the Mill Creek Road, which leads to the ferry road on Islesboro, explained, "You can't pass on the ferry road, that would be rude. But you can pass here—and I've cut people off on the corner." But never on the ferry road.

Gweeka

"It used to be I'd fight and die for the place, but I won't no more," says lobsterman Richard "Gweeka" Williams of Vinalhaven. (Unusual nicknames are an old Vinalhaven tradition.) "It ain't the island no more—they've turned it into what everything else is. They might just's well build a bridge or a tunnel and get it over with. The place is still beautiful and all that, but you go into the post office and there's people jostling you— used to be everyone knew you. There were people who didn't like you and people who did, but you knew everybody.

"At the Fourth of July parade, I never see so damn many people, and I didn't know nobody. Might as well have been in Rockland or Belfast. The only difference is it's a pain in the ass to get here.

"And with all this Homeland Security, it's a real pain in the ass to deal with the ferry." Of course, Gweeka can't remember the last time he was on the ferry. He has a perfectly good boat to take him ashore if he wants to go. But he's concerned about it. "You don't know if they're gonna have the pot dog sniff you all over, or strip-search you, or what.

"If there was no ferry, that would take care of it." He remembers the days before the state took over the ferry service. The town owned the boat then, and it could carry a couple of cars. There wasn't any population pressure then. Of course, that was nearly fifty years ago.

"There's not the balance of what you're willing to give up or endure. It used to be you were living alone, by yourselves, a laid-back, quiet life. But you ain't got the solitude no more. There's a billion people you don't know telling you what to do and jacking up your taxes. Now you got to go like hell just to keep up. People have groceries flown out here on an airplane, rather than pay the prices here—if you're gonna do that, you might's well be there."

Vinalhaven has just completed a new school. Gweeka's opinion of it? "They went berserk spending money. It's almost like the island bit off more than it could chew, doing all this stuff to a little one-horse town like they're doin' in the big cities. The vast expense of it is mind-boggling. We got a school like you wouldn't believe, like you'd see in New York somewhere, and there're only two hundred kids. They could divide all the money up and, Christ almighty, each kid could go to Harvard!" The

Vinalhaven fisherman Gweeka Williams
(BANGOR DAILY NEWS)

island also built a new sewer plant and reassessed all the property in town to boot. When I interviewed Gweeka, the tax bills hadn't been mailed out yet, but since his house is on the shore, he was anticipating a big jump. "If you can even see the water, your taxes will triple," he says. "Everyone's bracing up." (He was wrong—while his valuation did indeed triple, his taxes only doubled. Only?! Meanwhile, the taxes on some of the island's inland properties actually dropped.)

People are retiring to Vinalhaven, and not just former summer people. "The old summer people, you knew them. Now just everybody's got a little cottage or a camp tucked in the woods and the next thing you know, they're running the sewer board. Town Meeting used to be in March, and all ten of us were there. Now it's in June, when six thousand are here. They all come out to the island because they love the island, and then they want to make it like where they come from."

Gweeka admits that lobstering is good. He'll be able to pay his tax bills. He's unhappy, though, because he doesn't get anything from the town for his money. "I ain't got no kids, I'm not hooked up to the fifty-million-dollar sewer plant, and they want a new fire truck—by the time that got down here this place'd be a pile of ashes." But his real complaint is about the changes in the feeling of the island.

"It used to be you could pretty much do what you wanted. A lot of people, they never even began to think of leaving, and there's a lot of talking about it now. Shit, you go to the east'ard, Washington County, they'd love to see you come." Gweeka talks often about selling out and moving somewhere else—he'd love to be on Matinicus, but, being out of his home territory, he couldn't fish out there. Or maybe he'd buy a piece of swamp on Vinalhaven and put a trailer on it and sell his house for half a million bucks. Or, he says, he'd be as well off ashore in a camp in the woods. He doesn't expect to live another ten years. "I'm a fifty-year-old alcoholic drunk," he says. "Reality is reality. I'd like to think I'd semi-retire here in a couple of years, not have to work, but I don't know if that'll come about. To put my cards on the table, I'll probably stay, but the thought of not being here doesn't bother me like it used to. I'm not saying I hate the place—I still love it to death. But it's been too long, now—she's gone."

Growing Up on an Island

A universal theme on many of the islands is that being a little kid there is idyllic, and freedom is the key word. "At worst, I could be two miles away from home," says Erika Kelly, who lived on Matinicus for eighteen months as a six- and seven-year-old. "There was no calling in, or any of that. Mom knew I'd be around."

Stephanie Howard-O'Reilly says the same of Cliff Island. "At age four, your parents could tell you to go down to the playground, and they didn't have to worry. You just walked into people's houses, got your cookies—you knew who to be afraid of, who not. You didn't tell your parents where you were going to be—who knew? You'd go from one place to the next. You knew every inch of the island."

It may be obligatory on an island that there be a haunted house. Matinicus had one when Erika was there; she remembers it as having only a piano, no other furniture. It wasn't locked. She and her one friend—in the winter, there were just the two girls—used to go there and play the piano and fool around.

"Breaking into houses wasn't such a bad thing as long as you left things the way they were," says Stephanie. "We'd just go in and hang out." There was one house that they were sure had a ghost, Aunt Clara's. Looking through the window, they could see a couch with a long form, under covers, that looked like a body. Stephanie and a group of girls thought they'd check it out, but they couldn't open the door. They found an open window and threw the smallest kid in; she was going to go around and open the door for the rest of them. She was startled to find a woman in there! "Well, hello, come on in!" said the woman. "We all had cookies and told her what we were up to—she laughed and let us check it out." There were just pillows under the cover.

"I wouldn't even consider living anywhere else," says Julie Brown, who grew up on North Haven, married a fellow islander, and has raised their son there. "It's safe and secure. You can let your kids go to school and know they're going to come back."

Eva Murray of Matinicus feels that one of the really good things about being on the island is that the kids get to see a lot of their dads. "They get to see how adults make a living—the adult world is not some foreign world they go off to in the daytime. They're not age-segregated—they play with toddlers and teenagers, and they have adult friends too. Even kids without a real intact family have a chance for an extended family." She doesn't feel that the old idea of every kid being raised by everyone on the island is true any longer, at least on Matinicus—"if it ever was. Kids are just turned loose. But at least they know their neighbors, and they know what people do. It's not like you're supposed to be twenty-one before you know what to do for money or what to do in an emergency."

And kids are part of the emergency system. If people need help, kids go to help too. "For example," says Eva, "if something's going on with the adults, the young kids need to be cared for, so some older kid takes that over. They understand that if there's a problem, you're obligated to be involved. But they also know that you can have fun with people who are not your age."

After television coverage about Cliff Island in the last several years, four families from Away arrived. "Two are single moms. It's a refuge for single moms," says Bob Howard. "There's extended family for the kids—a lot of people looking after them, not specifically, just in general."

But it's not all milk and honey. A mother from Smith Island—I'll call her Marion—says that sometimes her son wants to hang out with children from homes where there is lack of supervision, lots of substance abuse, and weapons and violence. "I can't just say, 'You can't play with so-and-so,' but I still don't want him playing in particular houses, especially in the evening. She doesn't want to seem "stuck up," she says, nor does she want to raise her boy "here-but-not-here."

"How do you answer little kids who ask, 'Why don't you want me to go in little Bobby's house?'" she asks. "Not letting him associate with people I hope he doesn't turn out like does not seem an option." And entering adolescence, she feels, "they have to go mess around in the harbor; boys have to hang out with guys watching movies of questionable taste and swear and brag and talk like idiots with the other teenagers." There's even a practical side of the dilemma: if the boy ever wants to set out a few lobster traps around the island—which he might, whether or not he ultimately wants to be a full-time fisherman—he has to have grown up with the other Smith Island guys.

Marion feels less worried now that her son is old enough to just come home if anything seems amiss, and she hopes she has given him a sense of safety and individual responsibility and ethics. That's certainly the good aspect of an island: no one is ever very far from home.

But Julie admits there is another side to the story, even on seemingly idyllic North Haven, which has a high school. "We're so close-knit and caring—we look after one another. But when they graduate and leave the island—oh, my God!" Sometimes kids have left North Haven for college and come home in a week—and it's not because they weren't prepared academically. "It's culture shock." The same phenomenon occurs on Vinalhaven. Says Susan Lessard, former town manager there, "Some who go away to school have real adjustment problems—life off the island is materially different from life on it. Depending on the degree to which they had time to experience both perspectives while growing up, the degree of a successful transition to America is sometimes very hard."

Stephanie was in the first Cliff Island class to be sent ashore in sixth grade rather than ninth. "People were worried about socialization," she says. "Some had been having problems when they got to high school. Bonds are made in middle school." But even leaving for a bigger school at that age wasn't a panacea. "I always questioned how the island affected social abilities. A lot of us have problems making true friends.

"Growing up, your whole world is small, you live in a bubble. I pushed away the truths about the big, bad world as if they were the lies. You leave, and the truth gets in." Looking back on her childhood, she realizes that what seemed idyllic might be considered weird to people from other places. Her kindergarten year, she was the only girl among eighteen students—later on, a couple of girls came along.

Groups of kids gather, particularly in the summer when the summer people are around, and, Stephanie says, they're friends with kids they wouldn't have been, had they been on the mainland. At eleven, she started hanging out with a group of eleven- to-twenty-five-year-olds, mostly boys; that year, she dated a boy of seventeen, although she didn't lose her virginity until she herself was seventeen. "All the guys protected me. No one would dare mess around with me." Still, during the next couple of years, she was drinking a lot. "I was caught then, and quit till I was eighteen, mostly because I was grounded for a whole summer." Even now, with the perspective of an adult, she seems to feel that even the drinking was safe. "I didn't have to worry. I knew the guys would protect me, and I'd beat the crap out of them if need be. They were all older brothers to me." Her grandmother kept asking when she was going to be a lady, but, she says, "I was a boy on the island, playing tackle football and so on."

According to Stephanie, some things are different now on Cliff, perhaps less so on other islands. "At fourteen, I was driving cars—nobody asked. Nowadays they're all tense—you have to have a license even for a golf cart (or be twenty-one). Everybody knew if you hit a rock or smashed up a car, you paid for it, had a little bit of shame for a while, and then went on.

"Now there are so many off-islanders year-round—when I was a kid, there were only six people I wasn't biologically or marriage-connected to. It's like a marriage—you almost know what someone's gonna say or think so you don't even ask them. But you may be missing surprises. You have a bias against a person easily. I trust my mother or my cousin or whoever; they see something in a bad light, I automatically do too, even though there may be more to it."

Eva Murray and her husband Paul, who are home-schooling their son and daughter on Matinicus through the elementary grades, are aware of the potential for culture shock. They are encouraging their children to be independent of them and of each other. "Part of getting them ready to go away to school at age fourteen is keeping the apron strings loose, without letting them feel all adrift," she says. "So I'm trying to give them both a solid sense of belonging and safety and our attitudes, and also give them as much independence as possible. Like everything on Matinicus, it's both extremes at the same time!"

At the elementary-only schools on many of the islands, similar attempts are being made to expose the children to the world they're going to have to join so soon, and all three island high schools (on Islesboro, North Haven, and Vinalhaven) have recently increased their efforts in that direction. (More about the schools in a later chapter.)

Islesboro: From Summer Person to Year-Rounder

For Sandy Alexander, leaving Pennsylvania when it was time to go out on his own was a given. Like his brother before him and his sister a while later, he moved to Maine. They had spent every summer on Islesboro in their family cottage—one of the Maine-coast summer "cottages" that are larger than many hotels. Each of them started out in one field of medicine or another—though Sandy only used his nurse's training for a year—and they all ended up on the coast of Maine, albeit on the mainland. Sandy spent twenty years in Bath, where he bought old houses, fixed them up, and sold them. But when his children were grown, with no particular reason to stay in Bath, he thought he'd give Islesboro a try.

"Now I'm here," he said to himself, "what'll I do?" For no particular reason—he just realized that he could—he got a Coast Guard captain's license. Once he had the ticket, he asked Earl McKenzie if he might like some help on the *Quicksilver*, the island water taxi. Earl was building a schooner that summer, and he welcomed Sandy. "Earl went on the boat with me twice, and I never saw him on her the rest of the summer."

When Earl wanted out of the business, Sandy bought into the *Quicksilver* and for several years ran her with Tom Daley, Earl's former partner. In the summer of 2003, business had slowed down. For whatever reason, there were fewer bicycle tours, fewer huge parties on the island, fewer large weddings—these were the cash cows. "I could have built half my house on some of those weddings," Sandy remarks. Even the routine runs were carrying fewer passengers than they had in previous years. "But the boat has become a fixture—if it doesn't run, people get panicky." Sandy didn't really want to be out on the water at ten o'clock at night, and he was excited about building a house for himself. "Basically, I said to Tom, 'Call me if you need me,' and he was OK with that. Once in a while, he does call me, but not often." Sandy's at work on his house, which suits him. "I can't do anything a little bit. My house has become my obsession, my mistress—it takes all my money and all my time."

Was the island different, year-round, than he expected? "The winters are a little long," he says, "more so than on the mainland." How about socially? "Unless you're involved in the school, it stinks. But I'm sort of antisocial anyway. They say you're supposed to talk to some number of new people every day—and they're all me." Without planning ahead, he does go off-island once in a while. "I get tired of it here, so I decide I'm going to go somewhere," he says. Then he's off to Portland, where his kids are living, or to Florida to visit his mother, or perhaps even to Florence because it would be fun. "I can definitely hack it here. Probably there's more in the world than I can find here, but I've put down my roots here." After having lived in Maine for thirty-five years, he can't even imagine living in Pennsylvania, but even in his own mind, he'll always be "summer people." "I'm a transplant." But he says he gets along well with the locals.

"More so than with the summer people. I like them—they're more interesting. I'm a member of the Tarratine Club," he says, referring to the upscale summer crowd's golf/tennis/yacht club, "but I could care less about it—I do nothing there. I don't know why I pay the dues money, but I don't want to let it go. It's one of those neuroses we have, where am I? I'm not interested in golf or tennis, and I certainly don't go to cocktail parties, but I gather my grandfather built the yacht club. And maybe there's a practical aspect—if I give it up, it might be hard to get back." Not that he can conceive of caring, but still. You never know.

He doesn't feel that anyone has looked at him funny for staying, "but I'm not very sensitive to that. Maybe they do and I don't care." He tells about a time he went into the coffee club at the Island Market at seven-thirty in the morning. "I'm walking back there to get a cup of coffee and everyone's chatting away—but when I got back there they became silent. I don't think it was anything to do with me personally—it was more that something else was introduced to their environment and they had to stop and look." He feels he could become a part of the coffee-club scene, "but I don't choose to."

Matinicus Local Historian

Suzanne Rankin is directly descended from one of the first permanent settlers of Matinicus, Phebe Young, who came to the island with her husband in 1763 to be with her sister, who had first lived on Matinicus in 1760. Suzanne's great-great-grandmother on her mother's side left the island for good in 1877, but even though no one in her own generation had ever visited it, Suzanne had always heard stories of this island so far off the coast, and she was intrigued by it. After 1978, when the mailboat stopped running, it was hard to get to. But in 1981, Suzanne's husband, Tom, saw an ad in *Down East* magazine for a place to rent that included transportation. The owner was a pilot and would fly them out. The Rankin family took the house for two weeks. "When we got to Rockland, it was thick-o'fog, though, and we ended up coming out with Albert Bunker on his boat," Suzanne says. Neither she nor anyone in her family had ever been in a boat on the ocean, but it was perfectly calm, and they saw a whale and seals on the trip. When they rounded the breakwater into Matinicus Harbor, the sun came out. "I had the most incredible feeling of homesickness," she says, "as if I'd been gone a long time and had come home. It was so profound and strange that for the longest time I didn't tell anyone about it—I thought they'd commit me."

When they had settled their luggage into the house, Tom walked one way with a couple of the children while Suzanne walked in another direction with the others. Separately, each of them ran into someone along the way who said, "Oh, you're the people related to the Youngs." Suzanne knew they had to stay.

They bought a house and visited the island during summers, but it was twenty years before they moved to the island full-time. The first year they were supposed to be on the island, happenstance had them running here and there a lot. "Never knowing where your socks are is stressful," says Suzanne.

Now they make their home on Matinicus. Suzanne has been appointed town historian, and she is doing her best to organize the island's historic papers and documents. Others on the island have connections to the earliest settlers, but none care more about the island than Suzanne.

Waving

In a fashion similar to, if not derived from, the friendly hand gestures still exchanged among mariners, island automobile drivers wave to one another. On the water, it's a simple "I'm okay, are you?" kind of greeting, and that's probably what it is on the islands too. "I acknowledge your existence," it says at the least; between closer friends, the signal becomes more significant.

While on a boat the wave by necessity has to be large in order to be seen, on the islands the gesture can be as minimal as the lifting of a forefinger from the steering wheel —which occurs on many of the islands. (Bill Boardman thinks of Islesboro's one-fingered wave as a Robin Quimby wave, referring to a long-gone and well-respected islander, but he adds that Robin's index finger filled half the windshield.) I always thought of the one- or two-fingered wave as the natives' desire to avoid inappropriate effusion— and that's probably right, but it's reserved for folks you don't know. A flat palm flipped upward but still with the hand on the wheel is the next step. Taking the hand off the wheel is reserved for particular friends.

North Haven Community School principal Barney Hallowell
(COURTESY OF ALICE BISSELL)

In the politically turbulent war-and-elections summer of 2004, I heard that many Islesboro people had adopted the V peace sign as a wave. I asked Bill about this. "I learn more stuff about our island from my mainland compatriots," he remarked. But then he continued: "Come to think of it, I passed someone last night who flashed me a peace sign." Bill had thought it was a wonderful greeting and had decided to start using it himself.

Even the smallest wave can express more than an acknowledgment. North

Haven's Barney Hallowell tells how he felt when he was divorced, which of course everyone knew about. "I didn't think I could put my head out," he says, "but you do, and people wave to you." He was relieved to know he was still accepted as a fellow human being. "Everyone has their problems, things they're not completely proud of—that understanding is what gives us stuff in common. It's not because someone's better than someone else."

The real power of the wave is in its absence. Says Islesboro's Sue Hatch, "You get a clue someone's unhappy with you if they stop waving to you." When an island is divided by an issue, if there could possibly be any question about it, identification of who's on which side can be seen in who's waving at whom.

The Rescue of the *Harkness* Crew

Any mariner will say the same thing: if someone's in trouble on the water, you do what you can to help. Islands are populated by mariners. One bitter-cold January night in 1992, seamen from Matinicus had the opportunity to demonstrate that.

It was around zero degrees and blowing up to 40 knots from the northwest. The tug *Harkness* was headed for home on Mount Desert Island; her captain and his crewman were aboard, as was a friend from Bangor who was getting a ride to remember. As they neared Matinicus Island, they realized the tug was taking on water and radioed the Coast Guard.

Sitting at home on Matinicus with his VHF scanner turned on, Vance Bunker heard the tug's crew talking to the Coast Guard. Hearing the Loran position, he realized that he was a lot closer to the tug than the Coast Guard was. He called Rick Kohls and headed for his boat.

Paul and Eva Murray were having dinner at Warren and Harriet Williams's when the phone rang. The call was for Paul. "Most everyone knows where most everyone else is on the island, this time of year," says Paul.

"Vance says to meet him at the shore," Rick Kohls's wife told Paul. With no idea what was going on, Paul put on his coat and headed for the harbor. He hadn't worn heavy clothes because he knew the Williamses kept a warm house, but he grabbed his insulated coveralls from the powerhouse on his way. He'd been out with Vance on nights like this often enough—taking out ship pilots or picking them off ships—so he felt just fine taking off in Vance's boat, the *Jan Ellen*. The boat was about the best in the harbor, and the three men had experience with and confidence in each other. They hoped it would simply be a matter of giving the tug a tow in, or maybe even just giving her a lead. With each radio transmission, she gave her Loran fix and they wrote them down.

"The vapor was so thick we couldn't see anything," Vance says. It was just sea smoke, down low to the water. They could see lights ashore, but the path ahead was invisible. They were heading into the wind and Vance's boat iced up badly. Although they couldn't make very good time, they kept going toward the tug's position.

"Ten or fifteen minutes out, things changed kind of suddenly," says Paul. The last call from the tug came just after seven o'clock—the men were up to their chests in water in the tug's pilothouse. "It became clear they were leaving the boat—or the boat was leaving them." She was going down, and when a tug goes down, she does it quickly. Suddenly, the *Jan Ellen*'s mission changed.

"We never discussed it afterward," Paul says, "but I know that I didn't hold a lot of hope for those guys. The water was very cold, the air was very cold, they wouldn't last long." Vance headed for the last known position and then let his boat drift, hoping she'd follow the men, that her sail area would let her drift faster, and that they'd find them in time. "Time wigged out, then," Paul says. They still couldn't see a thing on the water.

Suddenly Rick saw a pillar of light coming up through the sea smoke. "Head over there," he hollered to Vance. By the time they all got focused on the light, the men were in sight, too. They pulled two of them from the water. "They were pretty much dead weight," Paul says. "They'd lost all their strength, they were so cold." The flashlight one of them held had frozen to his hand. And then the Coast Guard boat showed up. "It's amazing how fast they got there," Vance says. The Coast Guardsmen plucked the third man from the water, and they all headed back to the island.

The cabin in Vance's boat had a diesel heater, which they had fired up on the way out, and the engine had added some heat too. The men from the *Harkness* went down forward into the warm cabin and stripped off their wet clothes, and Vance and Rick and Paul gave them what dry clothes they could spare. (Paul's wife says he came home bare-armed, wearing nothing but the overalls and his boots.) Because the Coast Guard vessel didn't have a heated cabin, the guy they'd picked up needed days to get rid of the chill.

When they got into the harbor, cars were idling on the wharf, their heaters on full, waiting to take the men to houses. There was food for all the men coming ashore. "Everyone had been listening to the radio—word goes around," says Paul. "Everyone was doing what they could. The enemy that night was the cold."

Says Vance, "I've been out many nights worse'n that—the scariest thing was not knowing whether we were gonna pick them up dead or alive or not at all."

All three men from the tug lived to tell the tale. Vance says that for some time afterward, he could see the tug with his bottom machine—his fish-finding sonar—but after a while, it disappeared. Maybe another storm pushed it into a deep hole or it drifted offshore.

"There's a good possibility that if it wasn't for that light, we woulda been too late," he says. He shrugs off his own part in the rescue. "It seems when anything happens out there near Matinicus, it's usually someone there that gets to the scene first. The Coast Guard is not handy. I'm willing to do it because I hope if sometime we're in trouble someone will do the same for us. It's the same for any fisherman."

Vance's mother, Rena, was in Florida at the time, but when she heard about the evening, she was frightened just thinking about it. She summed it up: "'Course I was scared, but there's a man out there yelling for his life and you can't just ignore him."

North Haven's "Troubles"

A few years back—as happens sometimes in any community and even more so on islands—North Haven was split in two, with nearly the entire population taking one side or the other. It became ugly. Dead animals were left in driveways and mailboxes, nails were strewn around, and, perhaps most poignantly, people crossed the street in order to avoid speaking to or even catching the eyes of former friends. At issue was the school—or at least ostensibly it was the school. Maybe it was really about old ways versus new ways—perhaps, one would think, even native versus newcomer, but maybe it wasn't that simple. Even though the island was divided into two factions, people don't always find it easy to summarize who was in which group.

"It has been said that an island is like a big family," says Herb Parsons, who has lived on North Haven full-time for twenty years, "and it is, with both the pluses and the minuses. When things go wrong, they really go wrong."

"Everyone is interdependent," says Chellie Pingree to explain why an island fight can be so serious and so deep. There had been many big battles since Chellie had lived on the island: affordable housing, certain school-budget votes, the degree to which the island doctor should be subsidized.

Among the biggest of the fights she remembers was the matter of whether North Haven should join with Vinalhaven for a combined basketball team. The issues were both spoken and not spoken, and they ranged from the dangers of crossing the Fox Islands Thorofare in the winter to the necessity of trying out for the team—on North Haven, any kid who wants to play, does. An advantage of a combined team was that it could truly be competitive with the rest of the schools in the state's Class D category, and it might actually win on the state level. Always underneath, though, were the uncomfortable feelings between the two islands—which are totally different both geologically and socially, even though in decent weather one can row from one island to the other in seven minutes.

North Haven was traditionally an agrarian community, with a landed gentry of farmers and boatbuilders living in reasonable wealth and comfort. At one time, it had more sheep than people. The island voted Republican. Vinalhaven, while a true fishing community today, has always been far more diverse than North Haven, due in large part to the historic granite industry, which brought many immigrants to the island. Vinalhaven's stoneworkers unionized—even the island's fishermen at one time were in the AFL-CIO. It has also always had three or four times the population of North Haven and always voted Democratic. North Haven people looked at Vinalhaven as a community of rabble-rousers, as Sin City, with bars and prostitutes. Vinalhaven saw North Haven as an island of snobs.

And yet, for some reason, North Haven has always been quick to question its self-worth. The argument has been raised from time to time that some particular improvement wasn't necessary—"This is only North Haven, it's not Camden." One of the issues in the basketball dispute was whether Vinalhaven would somehow get more than its share—of players, of playing time, of who-knows-what. It's always assumed that Vinalhaven gets more than its share of everything. The Fox Islands Medical Service is supposed to cover both islands, but it's based on Vinalhaven, and many on North Haven feel it's only for Vinalhaven people. The ferry service is another example. If both the North Haven boat and one of the Vinalhaven boats broke down simultaneously, who would get the relief boat? Which island would get a new ferry first? North Haven tends to expect to get the short end of the stick. The final question about joining forces for basketball was, would it lead to combining the schools? No way would North Haven permit that—particularly if, as assumed, the school were to be located on Vinalhaven. No one is going to tell North Haveners how to do anything—not their summer people, and certainly not Vinalhaven.

(Since that time, the two islands have combined forces for some secondary athletic events, including golf, tennis, cross-country, and soccer. In soccer, for instance, together they could compete, but separately they didn't have enough players. Also since then has come a strong suggestion from the state that the two schools should merge, for efficiency's sake. Once again, North Haven says No!)

But the war of 1995 and 1996 was the worst, and the saddest part is that the split has not yet fully healed.

Barney Hallowell, principal of the North Haven Community School, was the lightning rod for the big split—"the Troubles." Several generations of Hallowells have summered on North Haven, and Barney has lived and taught there for more than thirty years. For the last fourteen, he has also been the principal. He has been described by many as a "total visionary," but he pooh-poohs that. "I became principal by attrition—no one else wanted it," he says. "We'd been through six or seven principals, maybe more, in the first twenty years—superintendents too—and I said, 'I'm just not going to sit here and have someone else come in and reinvent the wheel.'" There was a bad feeling in the school at the time—it was the whipping boy of the community, Barney says. Some people said the kids were stupid, others said the teachers were not competent, and overall, there wasn't much support for the school. Kids were angry. Teachers came and went, a third of them every year. Why should the students invest themselves with teachers who weren't themselves committed?

Barney believed in both the kids and the faculty, and his belief was obviously well founded. Teacher turnover is now way down. The strength of the teachers is amazing, Barney says, and the accomplishments of the students are high. In the past thirteen years, 82 percent of the seventy-seven graduates have gone off to two- or four-year colleges, considerably more than the state average of 62 percent who continue to post-secondary education. Thirty-four of fifty graduates have earned a degree or are still enrolled, while only slightly more than half of all Maine high-school graduates who enter college actually earn their degrees. The number of those who have left school may well have been influenced by the current monetary rewards of lobstering. Two young men have come back to the island from the University of Maine, at least for a time, and are now fishing.

All the same, North Haven is increasing efforts to prepare its students for success away from home. Programs include frequent trips off-island to cities and to colleges as well as visits from alumni now away at school. In a particularly dramatic opportunity, in 2004–5, the entire high school—sixteen students, along with three faculty members—spent two weeks in Paris, part of an exchange with a French school that brought sixteen students to North Haven the previous year.

Barney describes North Haven's school as "quite different from the typical mainland school, very personal and individualized, with a focus on experiential education and student empowerment." Each school year starts with a week-long field-study expedition for all the high-school students. They usually go to the mountains and rivers of northern Maine, and the curricula for the first months of school are built on that. "Here we're bounded by the sea and limited by the ferry. They see another part of the world, and it's a time when teachers and kids share what their experience of the year's going to be." Surveys about students' attitudes toward teachers and school show far higher satisfaction since they started the trips—and higher than is typically expected in public schools.

North Haven has offered a surprising number of outrageously bold opportunities to students. A few years back, the junior and senior science students all worked on the school's Tour de Sol entry, a national contest for environmentally friendly vehicles. The school has received two national arts awards. John Wulp, retired from his theater life in New York, has led the school in two or three major theatrical productions in each of the last several years, usually including a Shakespeare play.

Right from the start, Wulp asked the youngsters to put on plays that one might think would be over their heads—an early one was *The Importance of Being Earnest*. One parent called Barney to say that the kids hated the play they were working on and that he should put a stop to it. "We don't need to do anything that good in North Haven," she said. Barney talked with all the kids. The complainer's daughter wasn't coming to rehearsals, but none of the rest of the students wanted to quit. One girl, who had had a reputation for not being very bright, said it was the most important thing she'd ever done. "For the first time, people are treating me like I'm not stupid."

They did the play, and it went over very well. Barney says the girl was brilliant.

"Theater has given the young an incredible presence and sense of self-confidence," says Chellie, whose own son, Asa, a graduate of the North Haven School and the Arts Educational School of Acting in London, is working toward an acting career in New York. (He is more fortunate than some would-be actors in that he can return to North Haven and go lobstering when he's short of money—no need to wait tables.)

Perhaps most impressive was the musical *Islands*, created by John Wulp and summer resident Cindy Bullens as part of the healing after the Troubles. Half the school's students and staff, along with other community members, acted in the production, and they took it to New York for a standing-room-only performance on Broadway. (In one hour, the show manages to demonstrate nearly everything I write about in this book.)

There were some summer people, though, who had a negative attitude about all the attention the island was receiving. *Islands* is great for self-esteem, they said, but enough is enough. Put it away now—too many people might want a piece of the island. (One person admitted being annoyed that a summer person might make that remark at the same time that their new island house was featured in *Architectural Digest*.)

And now, occasionally, teachers wonder if they must themselves achieve such acclaim. Is this a "publish or perish" situation? No, says Barney Hallowell. While acclaim is nice, it shouldn't drive everything. "It's hard for elementary teachers to be thinking all the time about the outside when they're trying to teach basics. It's a mixed blessing."

In fact, there's an aspect to island life anywhere that makes it uncomfortable for anyone to excel. "The instinct is to haul back in," says Barney. "Standing out makes others feel less worthy." But the key is demonstrating that it's not that individuals can't do good stuff—or be given recognition for doing good stuff—but realizing that doing something outstanding doesn't make that person better than anyone else. Barney wrestles with the problem all the time, knowing that resentment comes all too easily. He knows that he could fall any day. "I can never get too big for my britches. It's all fragile," he says. He is careful not to take credit for the strengths of the school. "Nothing is so well institutionalized that it couldn't all change in a few months."

Forming the underpinnings of the Troubles was the belief that some people felt that the school did too much extra, at the expense of the basics. It was possible at least one year for a child to have four and five time-blocks of music each week and only three of math. Occasionally parents will say that their children couldn't really read until almost third grade. "You send your kids to school to learn," I was told, "not to do nothing."

The fire of the controversy was sparked not too long after Barney became principal, when he, the school board, and the superintendent agreed not to renew a particular teacher's contract. She had a following, and at the next town election, a candidate for school board campaigned on supporting her and won. Not only did the new board rehire the teacher but it also refused to renew Barney's contract. That's when everything blew up. Two groups appeared: the Watchdogs, who supported Barney, and the Friends of the School, who were against him. The school board, the selectmen, and the whole island took sides.

The Watchdogs, who felt that the board had acted illegally in letting Barney go, took the matter to court, where a judge agreed, and he was reinstated. The next town vote elected people supportive of Barney, but the problem was far from over.

Some insisted that the quality of basic education was clearly not what it should be—after all, their school wasn't accredited. Perhaps no one knew what that actually meant—it's not a state requirement, and many Maine schools do not have accreditation (at the time, no island school did). But Barney and the school board decided to go for accreditation by the prestigious New England Association of Schools and Colleges. "Accreditation was a wonderful, grueling process," he says. And when it was all over, "They held us up as the poster child of unique, extraordinary schools." Barney notes that the accreditation actually increased the resentment some people felt: "Not only were we not rotten, we were really good, and someone good said so!"

That the whole story was covered by the statewide newspapers shocked everyone. "We're not accustomed to settling family disputes in public," says Chellie Pingree, who was in the State Senate at the time. Islanders sit around and talk and gossip about each other, but never with people from outside. But, she says, because the fight was so public, with reporters watching, state mediators coming to the island, and summer people asking what on earth was going on, people became analytic—and more articulate than they otherwise would have been. A lot of hostile, mean, and nasty things happened, she says, but you don't want a family with members not talking with each other. "Most of us don't know as much about the people we deal with in everyday life," Chellie says. "Here we know thirty or fifty years of people's history—like siblings. You can be supportive, or you can go after each other in the meanest way. You can bring up stuff that happened in kindergarten. We have real vulnerability to each other—but we know it's a spectacular gift, too."

For the most part, the island has recovered from the war, but there still are people who feel that the school is overrated, and who say the split has not gone away. "It never will," I was told. "North Haven won't ever be the same again." Some people still don't speak to certain other people—you can occasionally see it in the Post Office, for instance, when people from opposite sides happen to be there at the same time. They don't acknowledge one another. In the course of business, people sometimes have to deal with people from "the other side" (which is still referred to in those words). "We just don't talk about it." There are people who don't attend Town Meeting any more. "You can tell how things are going to go—you know you'd be outvoted, so there's no sense in going."

"I feel I'm still part of the community," says one former member of Friends of the School. "It's just not the same community as it was."

Was the issue between "old" North Haven and "new" North Haven? "I think that says it pretty well," I was told by a Friend. "They move out here and think it'd be better if we did this and this and this. So why'd you move out here?" Others think it was about power and who has it, and they say it wasn't as simple as being anti–summer people and anti-transplant.

Of "the war," Chellie says, "We're past it." But she adds: "In any battle, there's always 10 percent on each side that either never feels it was righteously solved, or they feel betrayed, and they can't get over it. If you can get the majority to come to a point of agreement, it's important to move on. That's as close to utopia as you'll ever get."

It is ironic that before Barney Hallowell came to North Haven, he taught on Vinalhaven, and his contract there was not renewed. He loved the students, though they were certainly different from those he had worked with at Outward Bound and the conservative prep schools where he'd started his career. He hated the school itself at the time—he felt it was repressive and that the students were totally unempowered. But he thought he was doing well personally. He taught a navigation course, and all the students who were in it are now high-line fishermen. "They came to class even though they were already making more money than I was and they were questioning why they were going to school."

He and another popular teacher—a native son and graduate of the Vinalhaven school—were dismissed at the same time. There was a furor about it, including demonstrations. At the time, North Haven and Vinalhaven shared electricity, which alternated between the two islands—one hour on, one hour off. "For the school board meeting that night, the power was off, the bleachers around the edges of the gym were packed, and the school committee was in the middle of the gym floor with flashlights. It felt like the reign of terror." The superintendent, who served both Vinalhaven and North Haven at the time, told Barney that if he'd resign from Vinalhaven, he could have a job on North

Haven. "It was an ethical dilemma for me, but I admit, not as much as maybe it should have been. I said OK." It was not an automatic acceptance on North Haven, either. "I was hired by a three to two vote of the board," he says. "It was an eye-opener for me. My family was one of the first summer families—to vote against me was courageous. It might have had repercussions—though, in fact, my parents wouldn't have done anything. They might have been happier if I hadn't gotten the job." (He suspects they assumed he'd continue teaching at the prep schools he'd started with.)

"But," he says, "it has absolutely felt right to be on North Haven ever since. If there's a connection between a person and a place, that's how I feel. Every day feels fresh—it doesn't feel like thirty years."

Barney was part of a group who bought the bankrupt and abandoned Waterman's Store building downtown, next to the ferry landing, which had been for sale for seven years. They turned it into a community center, "something to revive the town and give people of all ages something to do in competition with TV and the Internet." The center has a coffee shop, a day-care center, a teen center, after-school programs, weekly movies, a boatbuilding workshop, a 140-seat performing-arts center, and office and retail space. It was controversial and still is. "I've never been in there and never will be," one woman told me. But most people see the community center as a renewal of island spirit.

Barney acknowledges the split between old North Haven and new, though, and is glad for the enthusiasm of the newcomers. "That's how communities deal with change. You can't romanticize—new people with energy and ideas do 90 percent of the work, but you can't be exclusive, you have to bring the others in. They don't volunteer, don't offer ideas—they're focused on other things, fishing or raising their families. One aspect of small communities is that people don't jump onto bandwagons. They approach everything with skepticism. Are these guys going to have the energy to stick with it in adversity?" (Perhaps it's the job of the skeptics to answer that question by providing the adversity.)

Chellie articulates the skepticism. "If you care about something enough, you're going to fight and push back anything you think might do it harm."

"There have been some things that just haven't had the resilience or brilliance that I thought at first," says Barney, "and after a bit, I'll say, 'You know, they're right, this doesn't work.'"

North Haven is in a state of change, which the "Troubles" simply pointed out. Like most of the islands, the makeup of the population is changing. There are more people from Away living on the island year-round, and they bring different ideas with them. That they love the island as much as the multigenerational native families is certainly the case, but it's not always obvious when it appears they're trying to change things. It would be wonderful if the war disappeared, but despite much easing, for a few people it hasn't, and it may not for a generation.

Adultery and Other Social Transgressions

The same things happen on islands as anywhere else, but people's responses on islands may be different—sometimes in intensity, but at other times in tolerance. "The island is a magnifying glass," people say. Not only can events be blown up, but there's no escape from the inspection and attention.

To cite an example, a number of years ago a minister's wife on our fictitious Smith Island became involved with another man. She was shown in no uncertain terms that she was in disgrace. The expectations for a minister, or the wife of one, are always different from those for most of us, and adultery is certainly not in the rules. "Mary"—I'll call her that—never ever felt she had done well in the role of minister's wife, even before she fell in love with "George," a newcomer to the island. She doesn't take full blame for the mess—she and her husband had taken separate paths in the years since coming to the island (neither of them was native). "My ex didn't treat me very well, people saw that."

Still, the divorce was messy, Mary admits freely. Everyone knew everything. "You cannot go anywhere without everyone noticing everything: your mood, what you're wearing, where you're going, what you're doing." Certainly it's difficult to hide having an affair when the only road in town passes by all the places you might want to meet. "Nothing's secret, and nobody wants anything secret—they want to talk about it. If it's not interesting enough, they'll make it interesting." In Mary's case, the rumormongers reported that not only was she sleeping with George, but also with his best friend, and finally with his best friend's wife, to boot. "You hear these things—your friends tell you what's being said," Mary says.

"Island life is like that—you find out who are your friends and who are not." She was surprised by some of the people who attacked her—"people I didn't even know." People on the boat would stroke their pointed fingers at her—tut tut!—and they would assault her vocally in the Post Office or at the store. "Islanders feel they can say almost anything to you, and they did." Even George's supposed friend was antagonistic. "It was a terrible time to go through."

Mary was perhaps even more surprised by some of the people who supported her, including her employer. Friends offered to let her stay with them, if she wanted it to appear that she was not shacking up with George. They then found an inexpensive cabin without running water for the couple, giving them access to their shower. Other friends gave them an old beater of a car to use.

But time is a great healer, Mary says. She and George have been married now for nearly as long as she'd been on the island before the uproar. She has felt no hostility from anyone in several years. "Maybe when they found out I wasn't going to leave, they felt better." Perhaps they recognized her commitment to the island. She enjoys her work on the island and intends to keep her job there.

"It's hard to believe how much melodrama, violence, and adultery can be absorbed and more or less forgiven or accepted," says a Smith Islander. "There are people who are friends, who really count on each other, who have the perfect right to punch one another's lights out!"

A woman of about Mary's age says that the people of Smith haven't forgotten the transgression. "Nothing is ever forgotten," she says. "Once you're branded, that's it. But they'll forgive." In another case of adultery within a year or two of Mary's, the lovers didn't marry. That woman was not forgiven: "She never made it right." The woman left the island and now returns only in summer.

"Becky," an adult Smith Islander who lives ashore now, tells her story: her thirty-year-old cousin sexually molested her when she was eleven. She told her mother a few weeks after it happened and the case was taken to the police, but they dropped it, and no one ever said another thing about it. "I suppose they thought I'd forget about it," she says today. Bad things don't happen on Smith Island. In fact, some fifteen years later, her mother was surprised to discover that Becky even remembered the incident.

Just recently, Becky found out that the guy had done the same thing with several other young girls on the island. Because of the silence, there would have been no way of knowing, at the time. The group of former victims alerted the mothers of all the youngsters on Smith about their experience. They warned of the predator's way of building a relationship with a kid—he had hired Becky to clean his house, for instance. "We told everybody, and then when he'd come into the store, everyone would walk out." It wasn't long before the guy moved off the island. I've been told that freezing someone out is possible in any small community. "You start not talking to someone, pretend they're not there, and if enough people do that, they'll leave."

When Becky was still in grade school, another of her cousins, this one younger than she, molested some three- and four-year-old girls. She knew about that—likely everyone else did too—and she wasn't the least bit concerned at the time. "That's the way things were." She supposes that it's likely the boy had himself been abused, but nothing was ever said about that either.

Both Mary and Becky speak of "the island way" of not allowing emotions to show. "Everything's fine," says Becky—that's the pose of all islanders. Mary—older than Becky and a transplant with a different perspective—analyzes it further. "You don't show your feelings unless you want everyone to know how you're feeling," she says.

"Everyone knows your business," she says; you don't want to open your vulnerable insides too.

"You have to have sensitivity on the island," says "Dora," a transplant onto Smith Island. "You have to be quiet and figure things out." She describes a small controversy that she didn't even recognize, in which a woman in a social group she belonged to was being a little unfriendly, specifically to her. Another member of the group gave her a hint as to what the problem was, and Dora understood why the woman was concerned. "Couldn't she just have said something to me?" Dora asked.

Not on Smith Island. People aren't obligated to tell you what's bothering them; you're supposed to figure it out. Approaching anyone directly is not done. "Things have to be fixed without their being acknowledged as problems, or acknowledged that they are being fixed," Dora explains.

On Smith Island, everyone's related to everyone, and it seems that once married, as anywhere else, they don't always stay home. Someone's husband might have beaten up someone else's because he was sleeping with someone's sister—it's all pretty confusing to an outsider. "So many kids by so many fathers," says one transplanted woman—Gina, I'll call her—who lived on Smith for a while but is glad she doesn't any longer. The last straw for her occurred when an island wife and mother slugged Gina's best friend. "A fist fight between women? I'm going home," Gina said.

Certainly the closeness of people makes any typically human but messy behavior particularly uncomfortable as it's happening. One man on Smith Island divorced his wife and a few years later married her sister. Said the women's mother, "I didn't like him when he was married to my first daughter. Don't like him any better now."

The live-and-let-live attitude may be better for people in the long run, though. The relatively recent ex-wife of one Smith Islander now lives with another prominent citizen on the island. "In the city, you wouldn't have to cross paths with them," he said. "But here, you've got to get past it or you're stuck. On the whole, I think this is a healthy thing. You have to deal with things."

Many islanders automatically seek partners off-island. Seeing little future there, many young women move off their islands, leaving the young men searching elsewhere for their brides. Frenchboro's young men pile into someone's boat and go off-island on Saturday afternoons. "They're all so clean—we don't recognize them," says Linda Lunt, mother of one of them.

There has long been intermarriage between Matinicus and Vinalhaven, as the two islands are closer physically and—despite their size differences—in lifestyle than they are to other places. Swans Island, Vinalhaven, and North Haven seem to keep more of their young women at home than do many of the others. Their populations are relatively large, allowing the younger people to have some choice in partners, even at home.

Margie's Story

A woman I spoke with—I'll call her Margie—spent a couple of years on Matinicus and still talks about how beautiful it was out there. She was considerably younger then—didn't have much sense, she'll admit now. A fellow she met in a bar asked her if she'd like to hang out in the sun and eat lobsters. Sure, who wouldn't? There wasn't much lying around in the sun, but they did eat a lot of lobster, particularly short lobster, particularly in the winter. "We couldn't afford groceries," she says. "I never thought you could get sick of lobster."

Though it did have electric power—like most of the houses "down on the shore" at the time—her new boyfriend's house had no running water. Even on such a small place as Matinicus, there was a bad part of town, and she was in it, along with a group of about twenty young people who came and went, men and women both from the island and from ashore. "Other people had money and groceries and water," she says, "and there were nice, older houses where respectable people lived. Everybody spoke to each other, but I never would stop by and visit any of those people, nor would they visit us." The guys all had a working relationship—they were all out on the water together.

But she liked the closeness of her community, particularly in the summer when everyone was working hard. "Nobody had any money, and they'd get together and make a big soup or something and eat together. You wake up when it's still dark, and you'd work all day long, but it's good work, outside. There's people with you all the time."

They didn't just drink soup together, though. Alcohol and drugs were common and were the reason no one from down on the shore had any money. Honest fishermen will admit that there's a very good living to be made fishing for lobster, but this particular group fished only to make money for their mind alterations. The men were on the water all day, worked hard and long, and kicked up their heels when they came home from fishing.

The island was supposed to be dry, but a lot of liquor was sold out there. "One of the lobster buyers sold liquor, and I thought it would be fun," says Margie, "so I sold liquor too. I kept it in the pantry." She had coffee brandy for the women and a lot of different cheap stuff for the men. Everyone ran up a big tab, she says, but they'd all pay up. "The trouble was, when we sold it, everyone would sit at our kitchen table and drink it. And in the winter when their traps were all up, they'd start drinking in the morning one day and stretch it out for a week." A party might start on a Monday and not stop till after the following weekend—rowdiness wasn't uncommon. Her kitchen table was broken more than once, and there were scuffles and worse among the partyers.

It was during one of these protracted sessions that her boyfriend turned on her for the final time. "I'd been wanting to leave," she says, "and he woke up and started drinking in the middle of the morning and said, 'It's time for you to go.'"

While he became drunker and drunker, she packed, but before she could take her pile of possessions anywhere, he set it on fire. Too convincingly, he threatened to kill her. She hid in a neighbor's closet overnight—"I was shaking so badly I could hear my knees knocking." The next morning, she fled the island, and though she loved Matinicus and many of its residents, she hasn't been back since. "It might be all right," she says, "but it might not."

Another resident of Matinicus Island says Margie would be welcomed. "Everyone liked her. I've an idea he'd leave her alone." Listening to him, you get the feeling that people would make sure the guy would leave her alone.

Alcohol and Drugs

"On the islands, the boys start fishing young and become adults young. They start drinking young," says Sue Lessard, Vinalhaven's former town manager. "It's well known that drugs and alcohol are widely used on some of the islands. The present generation of young fishermen have never known bad times—the older men remember having to work on the mainland in the winter to keep their families housed and fed, or feeding their children lobster because that's all they had. Now everyone has a brand-new boat and a nice house and new trucks, and they don't know the extent of their debt, just the payments. The young don't have a lot of life experience to know how to handle so much disposable income."

Although it's hard to find a lobsterman who'll admit to making more than a nickel, there's plenty of money right now. One fisherman told Sue that you could catch lobsters in a puddle—and you don't always need the puddle. But even before there was so much money around, alcohol was a problem. Many people used to stop drinking for one month a year, just to prove they could. "Drinking is just like breathing to them," Sue says. Not that everyone drinks, but it's not uncommon that when the guys come in from a day of fishing, they sell their lobsters, go home and get cleaned up, and then go to somebody's shop, where they work on their gear and drink a while. Then they'll go home and have supper, go to bed, get up at three or four in the morning, and start over. "Between four and six-thirty in the evening, you go around the Sands (the area where all the shops are), you'll see clusters of vehicles. They're not necessarily drunk, but it's an everyday habit."

"It used to be a big drunk-and-drugged-up community out here," I was told by an Islesboro resident who has been sober for fifteen or twenty years. I'll call him "Charlie." There was an active Alcoholics Anonymous chapter on the island for a while, but the woman who initiated it left. "I'm not going to AA out here—people know too much about you anyway," she said.

"Since we quit using, we think nobody uses," Charlie says. "That probably isn't true. But it used to be that everybody went to the same functions, all ages—ten-year-olds at the community hall dancing, drunk, pot-smoking—there was barely any law enforcement then." The school has changed since—there's more pride, he says. People came in from Away, and those parents got more involved, and the former users started having kids themselves. A young graduate of Islesboro's school system almost confirmed Charlie's impression that drug use on the island isn't extreme. He seemed to feel that pot was of no significance. "Marijuana is legal," he said, meaning locally accepted, "because we say it is. But we don't want to mess with heroin or cocaine. I heard of guys showing up pushing heavier stuff, but they get run off the island. 'We don't need this out here. Get lost.'"

This is not the case on all the islands. On Smith Island, drug use is hardly hidden—some say that drugs are used more than alcohol out there. "There's more drugs than you can imagine," said a fisherman a decade or more past his youth. "It's open." A woman who taught there in the late 1980s says she had students who did not know that pot was illegal.

Drug usage is most common among the young men on the islands, as it is anywhere in the country. It does offer an additional economic opportunity for people from the mainland who are willing to work as sternmen: bringing dope out and selling it to the islanders. "They've hauled a few of 'em off to jail," I was told. "A guy can do a lot better as a sternman out there, and dealing, than with anything he can do on the mainland." Except for Great Cranberry Island, Islesboro has the smallest lobstering community, and it's rare that a sternman comes from off-island; maybe that's why they've seen fewer hard drugs there.

Smuggling offers temptation, too, though I've not heard of recent cases. "I've been propositioned," one person told me. "I was gill-netting, anchored one night, thick-o'fog, and a boat came up and offered me any amount of money to go into some harbor before daylight. I could have got them in, but I guessed not. I didn't think I needed money that bad. But it was tempting. You can pick out houses built on that money twenty-five years ago—guys didn't get caught, and who the hell cares?"

"The people who do drugs pretty much stay together," I was told. "There's a split out here between the way people wish to live. Some want to smoke pot and be zoned out twenty-four hours a day. Fine, just leave us the hell out of the way. Not that I didn't raise a little hell myself. No question but what I drank way too much, but I always did my work."

Both drugs and alcohol, however, have had their impact on their users' work. On most of the islands, serious fishermen are off their moorings and heading out by daybreak. On Smith in years gone by, I've been told, if you saw anyone going out to haul as late as seven or eight in the morning, he'd have two or three cases of beer with him. "But now they just have a lunch bag." There's no saying what's in that.

I'm told that in earlier generations on Smith, the fishermen would have a big party once in a while, drink a lot and have a good time, and then forget all about it and go back to work. Still, there are advantages to some kinds of illegal drug use over alcohol. It's not only islanders who say they'd much rather drive, fly, or work with a person who'd smoked a lot of marijuana the night before than someone with a hangover.

An older fisherman who says he drank more than he should have in earlier years admits he became disagreeable sometimes because of it. "One thing you can say about pot smokers is they never get ugly." He goes on, though: "No one twenty or thirty who's been using drugs since he was a teenager is ever going to amount to anything. They make what they need to buy their drugs, and they use them, and then work to make some more money for drugs."

Drug use is often right out in the open on Smith Island. I was told about the time a grocery delivery came in and guys grabbed loaves of bread, ripped open their wrappings, and pulled out bags of cocaine, "laughing like hell." Another time, a few fishermen were leaning on another fellow's truck, with cocaine in lines along the hood. They saw the owner of the truck approaching and blew the powder away. "Now, boys," said the truck owner, "that's quite a waste!" But, people say, lobstering has been so good it doesn't matter. They have money enough. On the mainland, they'd have to rob stores regularly to get enough money to waste their dope so cavalierly.

Certainly drug use does cause trouble from time to time. On Smith in recent years, when one person—not a youngster—died of an overdose, it was hushed up and kept out of the papers. But, I was told, it did happen. "You feel bad to see people ruin their lives and die over the whole thing, but that's life." There aren't too many illusions on Smith. And people have certainly died due to alcohol abuse, too—on Smith as elsewhere.

Still, on any of the islands, even Smith, a lot more people don't use drugs than do. "It's just like alcohol—some use it to excess and a lot just drink once in a while." One of the best fishermen on Smith still uses drugs, I was told, but only on occasion— just as a member of an older generation might have occasionally binged on alcohol.

Smith Island Hippie

There have always been people coming and going from the islands, and the way some were viewed at the time and in retrospect is indicative of some of the changes on the islands. An example is a fellow from Smith Island—"Norman"— who after high school in the 1960s headed west to seek his fortune. While in the San Francisco Bay area, he popped his share of LSD and joined the Revolution. He attributed great life insights to the acid, and, at least at first, he believed that the young, freedom-loving people he had met on the West Coast would soon be taking over.

But within a few years, he was back on Smith. Perhaps he believed in the Revolution still—but he called it a "damn free-for-all" and felt its leaders were nearly as corrupt as the leaders of the current system. Like many of his contemporaries, he went back to the land. He established a garden and, Tom Sawyer–like, schemed about ways to let other people do the work (and perhaps pay for the privilege). He took pride in not knowing what was happening in the world. He did remark once that he supposed that the Revolution was still in progress: "I can't imagine the whole course of humanity swinging a right wing simply because this feather has fallen from the left." What little money he needed he brought in with some writing, though he felt that the work he could sell easily didn't serve much purpose, and he was working on more political subjects. At the time, he said that he'd love to tell his own story, which he called "sensational"—but not while he still had a family to offend.

A number of "hippies" passed through Smith, joining the kindred folk then living on the island. "We all saw each other socially," says one totally respectable fellow on Smith today. (I'll call him Carlo.) "We partied together," says Carlo, who today doesn't even drink. He remembers what he describes as "some vigilantism" but doesn't give it much credence.

A hint about Norman's recent past came when he was joined on Smith by a tall, good-looking, but extremely effeminate African-American man I'll call Pete. Norman's mother remembers, though in typical fashion she speaks in understatement. "Pete wasn't taken to by some of the goody-goodies," she says. "He worked in the garden buck-naked one time, and the neighbors reported him. I guess they didn't like seeing that! But he didn't care about nothin' or anyone. He wasn't well liked by the rednecks, I s'pose you could say. When they're threatened by something, such as hippies, they get kind of uppity," she says.

"Francie," a native of Smith Island who lives there today, speaks of Pete and those times. "Pete was a sweet, sweet, wonderful man," she says, and of Norman's mother, she adds, "Bless her heart, she was always close to Norman. But there was a huge impact on us. People weren't very nice to Norman or Pete or to any number of us who allied ourselves with them." There were remarks about one-way boat tickets and even halfway boat tickets. "Even my own father, who normally kept his prejudices to himself, made an angry comment about going around with 'hippies, niggers, and queers.' It was confusing to him—he didn't understand why I wasn't being the good girl I'd been and had been raised to be." The mother of kids for whom Francie used to babysit warned the children not to take anything from her garden because she laced the vegetables with LSD. "I was heartbroken when I heard that. But I'm on perfectly good terms with that woman now," she says. "People were just afraid." Of course, she says, there were people who couldn't have been nicer through all of it. Some were just intrigued, and she chuckles as she recalls one who wondered if maybe he couldn't get in on some of that free-love stuff himself.

Francie tries to think of a parallel situation today, looking back on it from the perspective of a fifty-year-old. "If someone were out here pushing crack cocaine on our children, I'd get pretty upset, certainly. I suppose they saw it like that."

She left the island at that time. Pete stayed around for a couple of years, and then gradually he and most of the rest of the hippies from Away moved on. When Francie came home again five years later, she found everything different. She was more grown-up herself, less rebellious, she says, and, like the others who had remained, was beginning to contribute. The former members of Smith Island's counterculture have become the pillars of society. "I'd like to think it's more tolerant today," says Francie, "but we're the generation in charge, now, and we should remember how it was. If we're not tolerant, who will be?" She adds the old saw, "But they say if you can remember the sixties, you weren't there."

Norman died in the 1980s, not long after he turned forty. No one confirms it, but rumor has it that AIDS took him.

"There's a lot of tolerance on the island," says Francie. "Even in times when they're not very happy with you, you're part of the community. You're here. A lot of things went down then," she adds, "and all of it went by."

The Elderly

KATHLEEN AMES, MATINICUS

Kathleen Ames of Matinicus has been thinking about moving to the Methodist Home in Rockland. The idea has come up at the end of the winter for a number of years now—one of these years, she may do it. She's seventy-seven, and she has lived in the same house since she was one week old. There's no driveway in to her house, just a wooden bridge across the ditch and a hint of a path up to the door. She's never driven. Her house is very square, painted bright white with green trim, and the inside looks as if the only change during Kathleen's entire life has been the addition of some stones painted with coastal scenes. The house is tidy, clean, and stark. There's a calendar in the kitchen, but no photographs or trinkets on the wall and no carpet in the parlor. The window and door trim is dark, varnished hardwood.

She wears sweatpants and knit tops and sneakers, and someone from the island comes in and cuts and perms her hair. Kathleen speaks in short sentences. When I

Sharon Daley approaches Kathleen Ames's house.

ask if I might talk with her about life on the island, she says she doesn't know that she'd have much to say but she could answer questions. I can ask questions.

"I like it here," she says. "It used to be more pretty than it is now. I thought it was, anyway." Islanders don't make absolute statements for anyone but themselves. Were there pastures then? "Yes, there were," Kathleen says. "That's when it was prettier. You could see cows in the pastures. It was quite a farm place out here once." How many animals were there? "People would have two or three cows, and oxen, pigs, and hens. And big gardens." Kathleen's mother had a big garden and did a lot of canning. Kathleen used to can a lot too, but she doesn't anymore.

She doesn't see many people nowadays. "I'm the last one in the family," she says. Her mother died in 1967; her brother lived in the house with her until he died twenty years ago. He had a heart attack at sixty-seven. And of the people she grew up with, only a couple are left: Albert Bunker and Kenneth Ames—and their wives are both from Away. The island is full of Ameses, but Kenneth is a third cousin and the rest are even more distantly related. She has closer cousins in Cherryfield, in Washington County— she visits them a time or two each year.

"There's a different class of people out here now," she says. "Not the original people. People came from Away and got married here. They don't associate the way they used to," she says. Did television make a difference? "Yes, it did. When people got their televisions, they stayed at home, and that's what they done [for entertainment]. We did use to have nice social times before."

Not many people visit Kathleen. "When Dot Bunker comes back, Albert's wife, she'll be coming down to call on me, and we'll have cookies and tea." In summer, people come by more often. "They make a dooryard call." Dooryard call? "If I'm settin' down on the porch, they come up and chat with me. That's what we used to call it, a dooryard call." Kathleen never got to know many of the summer people, though. "They go by themselves."

Both the nurse and the minister on the Sea Coast Mission boat *Sunbeam* make a point of stopping in to see Kathleen when the boat's in. "I like it when the *Sunbeam* comes. I look forward to seeing Sharon and Rob [the nurse and the boat minister]," she says, "and Rob's wife, Cristy, and Peter." Rob and Cristy spent a week on the island last August. "I was up there for supper one night," Kathleen says. It looks as if they'll be back for a week this year too, with their new baby. Kathleen is happy to hear that.

She'd move off in the fall, if she went. She likes summer on the island. "It would be pretty inshore in summer, though," she says. And there'd be more people there. "I grew up with a lot of people," she says. There were thirty in the school when she finished eighth grade. Not many of them went on to high school—Kathleen didn't, and she never married, either. "I worked for people on here," she says. Not summer people, island people. "I cleaned house, and I babysitted a lot." I said I bet she was a good babysitter. "People said I was," she says unassumingly.

"I don't know if I'll go this year or next," she said in the spring of 2004. "I do like the island. I'd miss my house. But I can take my cat."

(She didn't make the move that year.)

ALFRED STANLEY, MONHEGAN

A fisherman year-round, Alfred Stanley lived on Monhegan as a boy and all his working life once he'd finished his World War II stint in the U.S. Navy. "I traveled the world pretty good and finally landed back," he says. He met his wife, Dorothy, when he was in the navy. "Getting used to Monhegan didn't seem to bother her." She was from a small town herself, outside Saint John, New Brunswick, and all the men in her family were seafarers. She spent a weekend on Monhegan before they were married. "She seemed to want to come back, so that was that," says Alfred.

Alfred Stanley spent six months lobstering each year—in those days, the season ran from the first day of January until June 26—and the rest of the year, he went line-trawling, stop-seining, tuna fishing, and fishing for anything else he could find. When he'd been married fifty-seven years, a friend asked him how he and his wife had gotten along so long. "I wasn't home often," he replied. For the same reason, he says he never minded the tourists on Monhegan.

They never had children. "It'd be nice to have someone now," he says, without complaint but with a note of sorrow.

More than fifty years later, Dorothy had health problems that forced them to move ashore. He sold everything he had on the island: his house, his boat, his fish house, his gear. "Hadn't been for my wife's problems, we'd probably still be there," he says. She's been in a nursing home for two years, suffering from Alzheimer's. He hasn't been on the island in a couple of years—since the time he went out to see a friend who was on his last legs. "I could go anytime," says Alfred, "but I haven't got up the motivation, I guess. Sometime I'll take a ride."

The Maine Accent

The coastal Maine accent—with its particular rhythms, intonations, images, vocabulary, pronunciations, and local variations—can still be heard on the islands. Says Ben Doliber, a transplant living on Swans Island, "All the islands have a different accent. I hear someone on the [VHF] radio and I can tell immediately where they're from."

On my way to Vinalhaven, I overheard an older fisherman talking with one of the ferry attendants; with the diesel droning behind him, I absolutely couldn't understand more than the occasional word. Once on the island, I needed directions, and there he was sitting on a guardrail, apparently waiting for someone to pick him up. I approached him with a little concern and greeted him. His eyes immediately dropped to his feet. "'Lo," he said. I asked how to get where I was going, and without looking at me, he told me clearly enough in his quick, swinging rhythm and readily identifiable tune. I thanked him. "Hope I've been of help to you," he said. I assured him he had.

Even more unusual than the actual sounds of the local language might be the images. Willis Rossiter, gone these past twenty years, said that when he was young, he used to crawl around boat rigging like a cat but that toward the end of his life, he was feeling more like a woodchuck. At ninety-plus, Went Durkee still lives on Islesboro and still drives very slowly down to meet the last ferry every day just to see who's coming onto the island. He has a wonderful way with words, and describing boats is one of his fortes. He thought the world of the old *Owl*. "Some boats when they hit a wave, it stops 'em or slows them up," he said, "but not the *Owl*. She just separates the water and goes on through." And describing a trip he took with her in a real sea, he said, "She buried her bow right up to the windshield three times, but she'd get up and shake herself off."

Gweeka Williams of Vinalhaven is a lot younger than Went, but he has the same way with words. For instance, there was the time they used airplane fuel in a racing lobsterboat. "You talk about makin' an engine happy," he said. "She was smilin' from valve cover to valve cover."

But the local Maine ways of talking are disappearing. I've not heard anyone under the age of thirty with any distinctive speech, and when I ask others if they have, they often pause and think about it, and end up agreeing that the young people all talk like the television now. While various southern accents remain, as do the several variations of eastern urban accents and dialects, perhaps there just aren't enough Maine-speaking people to maintain theirs. For whatever reason, it's disappearing—even on the islands, where it has traditionally been strongest.

The Business of Lobstering

obster fishing remains the major industry on nearly all of the Maine islands, with most of the men and some women out in boats at least six months of the year. While the methods and rituals vary somewhat from island to island, as from community to community on the mainland, the issues are the same everywhere: weather, equipment, trapping, maintaining territory, containing costs, and selling. Of course, there are ancillary businesses too—buying lobster and selling bait and fuel, and the occasional trap-building operation. A fellow on Swans Island builds traps on a quintessentially beautiful point of land. It's said that he has been offered huge sums for his property. "Why sell?" he asks.

Everyone understands the importance of lobstering. "I was late to a wedding recently," says Swans Island's Donna Wiegle, who told the bride and groom: "I'm sorry, I had to haul."

"Oh, that's fine," they said. Everyone knows and accepts the fact that an island wedding that happens to fall on a good day after several foggy ones may not have very many guests.

Weather is certainly an issue for lobstermen—fog, wind, heavy seas. Some fishermen take particular pride in going out no matter what, while others, perhaps older and wiser, are more willing to lie low for a day or two until conditions improve. Matinicus, stuck way out in the Gulf of Maine, has more weather more of the time than do the islands closer to shore, and Vance Bunker admits that in his younger days, he had knots in his stomach in a lot of different situations. "You learn over time that if you stop and think about things, it generally works out," he says. "And if it doesn't work out, there's not much you can do about it."

It used to be that a lobsterman's main wintertime endeavor was taking care of equipment, although some used to go scalloping or shrimping, too, back when those catches were profitable. He'd build traps, knit "heads" for them, carve and paint buoys, and take care of his boat—or perhaps build a new one. (On Beals Island, each winter many fishermen built a boat to sell, in addition to taking care of their own.) But now traps are made of wire mesh, and most people buy them ready-made, complete with nylon netting. Buoys are Styrofoam, and painting them doesn't take much time. Boats are made of fiberglass, and while sometimes a fisherman will finish his own, in this time of high yields, they often just order a boat from a boatshop, rigged set up just as they'd like it. What maintenance it needs each year is minor, though many fishermen do take pride in keeping their boats in tiptop condition. It's always fun to check out the new electronic gizmos and perhaps purchase a new radar or bottom machine, but these aren't time-consuming tasks either.

Trapping is a matter of baiting the trap in a manner that lobsters find attractive, throwing it where they happen to be, and coming back to haul in the catch. Of course, there are some variables involved there . . . and significant ones they are.

Bait is one of those variables. Herring is traditionally the bait of choice, but it's not always available, nor is it always the most economical option. There are probably nearly as many opinions about what's most successful as there are fishermen, and availability varies from place to place. Many fishermen, particularly on the islands, tend to buy their bait from the person who buys their catch—thus, a fisherman often takes whatever bait his buyer offers. *Uncle Henry's,* Maine's weekly classified-ad magazine, advertises various cow and game hide-based baits, though these are the subject of some controversy, as lobsters have been known to appear on plates with undigested hair inside them. Many fishermen, understandably thinking this might affect sales, want to see these baits made illegal. Other people—concerned about overfishing of herring—are pushing for a limit on how much bait can be used at all. (Says one fisherman: "I don't want to think about that.") Various other fish products are used, including frozen fish and fish by-products from Canada, the Great Lakes, and occasionally even as far as Portugal. Bait used to be nearly free for the taking, but nowadays it represents a major expense for fishermen, who might use ten or fifteen bushels a day, at twenty dollars a bushel. But, say some, it's a good investment—not just in trapping lobsters, but also in feeding young stock. It's a common belief that part of the reason for the recent boom in lobster landings is that the baited traps act as feeding stations. The state of Maine passed a law that required vents in the traps to allow undersize lobsters ("shorts") to escape so they wouldn't be injured when they were thrown back in the water. At the time, many fishermen disliked the new requirement, but they've come around. Without the small lobsters, the traps are easier to handle, but there's more to it. Many fishermen say that the little ones learn to come in, chow down, and leave again. Eventually—perhaps sooner than if they'd had to scavenge harder to make a living themselves—the lobsters grow into "legals" and can no longer escape the trap.

"It's the biggest aquaculture industry," says one lobster-catcher. The scientists don't generally accept the concept, but no one really knows.

Then comes the matter of how to set the traps. To some degree, this is regulated by the state, and to some it's a matter of personal preference, though the preferences are regional in nature and in some areas were taken into consideration when the rules were set. Offshore, beyond the three-mile limit, where a federal license is required, trawls (or strings) of fifty traps on a single buoy are common, but the number of in-shore trawl traps is limited by the state, with limits varying from zone to zone. In Casco Bay, up to twelve traps may be set in one trawl. Most of the zones allow three traps, though often only a pair is set, simply for ease of setting and retrieval. In very congested areas, fishermen set singles, as they do in shallow water around ledges. When there are only inches between your boat and the bottom, you want to zip in and out as quickly as you can.

And where to set the traps—that's the biggie. Territories aside, it's that choice that determines who's the high-liner and who's just another fisherman. Lobsters move with the seasons and with their personal development: when they shed their shells, they hide among rocks, closer in; once well protected in their hard shells, they move farther offshore. And what human being understands all the particulars that affect a lobster's choice of habitat? But some people just know where the "bugs" are, and everyone accepts that. Others, says Went Durkee of Islesboro, "couldn't catch a lobster if they was spread two feet deep all across the bottom." Everyone knows who's who, and some less-savvy fishermen simply try to set as close as possible to one of the high-liners, even with no knowledge of why that might be a good place.

Territory is the most dramatic issue, certainly. The license a lobsterman receives from the state says that he can fish anywhere along the coast, but no one is foolish enough to believe that. "The fishermen say, 'Sure you can, but you may not find your traps in the morning,'" says Ted Hoskins, the Maine Sea Coast Mission's minister to coastal communities and fisheries.

Fishing grounds have always been well-defended resources. The concepts of defense remain the same as they always have been, but the specifics have tightened up. The lines between territories aren't visible, but they are very precisely located and well known. It used to be the rule that several warnings would be given when a trap was set on the wrong side of such a line. "First, they'd tie a hitch on the line, so the buoy dragged the wrong way," explains Ted. "Then they'd go up past the second toggle, cut the line, and re-tie it with a big knot on it. No way could anyone miss that." Next, Ted says, they'd empty the trap. They'd never take a lobster, he says (that would be theft); instead, they'd throw any catch back in the water. And the final warning was to cut off the trap. "Four steps over a period of time to warn someone to move back." But now, in some places the process has been abbreviated. The first warning is made over the radio—it's innocuous enough, even though everyone knows everyone else's voice on the VHF. The meaning is clear, even though the words are unobjectionable. "Gee whiz," someone says, "what's this funny-looking buoy over here by this ledge?" And if the funny-looking buoy is still there by the next haul, it gets cut. Sometimes the warning starts a battle, with traps being cut by fishermen on both sides of a dispute.

To be caught by the Marine Patrol for molesting traps brings a three-year loss of license, but the Marine Patrol hasn't the manpower to halt all such activity. For the most part, they don't get involved "unless someone's on a cutting frenzy and there's buoys floating all over the bay." And when they do catch someone cutting traps, everyone is treated alike, regardless of the local status of the cutter—whether he's interloper or enforcer.

Sometimes things get worse, as in a story I heard about our fictitious Smith Island: "One fisherman was an import, thought he'd go fishing out there. He had a fire in his house. They drove him off the island."

Isle au Haut faced the opposite problem in the middle of last century. "Fishing got so poor," says Danny MacDonald, manager of the Isle au Haut Lobstermen's Association, "that people moved off." The year-round population, still nearly three hundred in 1880, had dropped to forty-five by 1970. There were so few people fishing the shores of Isle au Haut then that, for safety's sake, a few men from Stonington were allowed to set their traps in traditional island waters. "If you break down, somebody's around to lend a hand." But then the fishing got better again, and more and more Stonington people came in. "Brothers, cousins, fathers, sons—now we're outnumbered ten or twelve to one." There are still places the Stonington fishermen don't go, but there are also some areas around their own island where Isle au Haut fishermen can no longer fish. They've become part of Stonington territory.

Everywhere, if you pull back, someone else moves in, and you'll never reclaim that area.

This matter of territory is particularly significant on the islands. Without local bottom—literally, sea floor—available, there's little reason for a fisherman to live on the island. It's a matter of economics, since it's far more expensive to live out there. On the other hand, in order to maintain rights to the bottom, there are rules to be followed in every area. And even though the rules are well understood—or, if in question, everyone knows that too—no one wants to talk about them. But, in general terms, the criteria for acceptability relate to blood connections, perhaps connections by marriage, and residency. Whether a new fisherman is liked makes a difference, too. On Smith Island, a prospective fisherman has to own a house, and the current fishermen formally vote on his entry. But even this system is not written in stone. "The stupid bastards change the rules at every meeting," says one of the older members of the group. One of the other islands requires that the fisherman live on the island; having grown up there isn't sufficient. "Cousins cut as much as anyone."

One island with an entirely different way of managing access is Criehaven, where no one lives year-round anymore. The people fishing the grounds around Criehaven have limited themselves to a certain number, and no one else is allowed in until someone leaves. His slot then goes up for sale, and there seem to be no criteria beyond dollar bills to decide who can buy it.

Unlike the rest of the coast, which is open to fishing year-round, Monhegan has a limited season of 180 days, starting in December. But in most places, the season is determined either by tradition or by the lobsters—for example, they usually don't come up Penobscot Bay as far as northern Islesboro until summer is well underway. That the fishery has been so generous of late has allowed for a more comfortable fishing schedule everywhere than was possible in leaner years.

Another kind of enforcement occasionally is required when someone is helping himself to lobsters from other people's traps. Foggy Sunday mornings are a choice time—even after Labor Day, when Sunday fishing is permitted, many boats don't go out. On Smith Island, I was told that people were suspicious of one particular fellow. "Suspicious!? We're not suspicious—we know. He hasn't many traps, but he comes in sometimes with as much as eight hundred pounds to sell." One of the other fishermen said he was planning to watch from the shore, and when he saw something he didn't like, he'd give the guy a call on the radio. "Look over here," he'd say, and he'd wave. "Next time I won't be waving." A shotgun would make quite a hole in the side of a boat.

Licensing is limited now. Youngsters can get a student license, which allows them to set up to 150 traps. When they turn eighteen and can show they've put in a certain amount of time, they can automatically get a full license. Otherwise, a would-be fisherman must go through an apprentice program, keeping a log of time spent fishing and working on gear and getting it signed regularly by a warden or the Marine Patrol. After two years, with enough hours documented, he can apply for a license and get on a waiting list—and it may be several years after that when he finally receives a license. "It's a long process," says Jill Philbrick of Swans Island. She knows someone who has been waiting four years. Even when armed with a full license, a new fisherman is only allowed three hundred tags, which means three hundred traps. Each year after that, the number increases until it reaches the maximum—eight hundred on most parts of the coast.

Swans Island is unique in that in 1984, the fishermen voted to create a conservation zone around the island. The specifics have varied over the years; currently, the rule says that anyone who sets a single trap within the bounds of the zone is limited to

475 traps in all, both within the zone and outside it. A very controversial scheme when it was adopted, it is no less so today, and it is often questioned. It's hard to watch the fisherman next to you fish eight hundred traps and only have 475 yourself—but within the zone, at least, the per-trap catch is higher and the expenses are lower. No one actually knows how the net proceeds compare, since no lobsterman will ever talk about such things. "There are good fishermen everywhere, and better fishermen, and top-gun fishermen," says Swans Island lobsterman Ben Doliber, who has friends fishing all along the coast. "It's a matter of knowing the bottom, when to move your traps, how to read the lobster, and so on, but every place I go, I don't see that anyone's living any better than the guys fishing here," he says. "The younger guys have never seen anything different, and they think, if I had more traps, I'd do better. They don't realize that everyone else would have more traps, too, and there are only so many lobsters on the bottom. If you have eight hundred traps, you just catch 'em up quicker." But Ben says he can understand both sides. There are some who think Swans should keep the conservation zone but also increase the trap limit, to six hundred. "I'm in a quandary, how I feel—I go back and forth."

In the fall, the lobsters move away from the shore, often out beyond the three-mile limit and into federal waters, where an entirely different fishing permit is required.

On Isle au Haut, no one presently has an offshore permit, even though there are many boats out of Stonington fishing federal waters in the winters. Men from Isle au Haut used to have offshore permits, but nobody kept them. "Years ago," says Danny, "all you had to do was sign up if you were going to go beyond three miles." Now that they've limited the number of permits, the only way to get an offshore permit is to buy one from someone who is retiring from that fishery. That will set you back twelve to fifteen thousand dollars. At the same time as the limits on numbers of permits were adopted, new Coast Guard requirements came in for offshore waters: EPIRBs (Emergency Position Indicating Radio Beacons), life rafts, survival suits. "You gotta catch a lot of lobsters to pay for all that. Ain't worth the hassle for a couple of weeks of fishing."

On the other hand, the offshore demarcation is so close to the outermost islands that many of the fishermen on Swans, Vinalhaven, Matinicus, and Frenchboro feel they must have a federal license just to follow their local lobsters when they move away from the shore in the fall. "It's very difficult for Swans Island people not to go outside," says Belinda Doliber. "We're already offshore." The need for a federal license is a problem for young people entering that fishery, too. As young children, they can get student licenses from the state and bypass the apprenticeship program, but they still have to wait for a federal permit-holder to retire before being able to get that piece of paper. Setting up to fish on the outer islands becomes an expensive proposition.

Still, many fishermen think the expense and discomfort are worth it, and they fish offshore for at least part of the winter. Most of them only set one or two days' worth of traps, though, which allows them to haul on the good days and not go out when it's too horrendous.

Lobster Cooperatives

In the early 1980s, lobstermen of Isle au Haut joined together formally in a cooperative association, and today nearly all the island's fishermen are members. The association buys lobsters like any other lobster business, and sells to dealers off-island. They also operate a "pound", where they store lobsters. On Isle au Haut, they pound lobsters caught when they are shedding ("shedders") and prices are low, usually starting around the first of September. They take the lobsters out in March or early April, when it's warm enough to transport them and prices are high. "It's a crapshoot when to start taking out," says Danny. "Like the stock market. You put 'em in and hope the price'll be there in the spring. Some years it is, some years not."

Burnt Coat Harbor, Swans Island. That's the pound on the far side of the cove.

Swans Island also has a cooperative, to which about half the fishermen on the island belong. There have been three other buyers coming out to the island, too, keeping things competitive. "It creates a little price war in the harbor," Ben Doliber says. "But I'm a believer in the co-op; I never sold anywhere else. We've got a good core group of members, loyal—we're in it together."

Kathy Clark is the manager of the Swans Island Fishermen's Cooperative. She and her husband came to the island indirectly from a small town in Vermont, and have no regrets about the move. "We didn't come out trying to change things. I fell into my job—if I'd set out to come out and do it, it would never have worked." Kathy had been doing the co-op books on a part-time basis for several years before she took over as manager. Her husband is a carpenter and roofer who finds plenty of work on the island.

As on Isle au Haut, the Swans Island co-op has a pound, but they pound lobsters at two times in the year. When the shedders come in strong, during the summer around Swans, the co-op pounds them and feeds them. They feed dry fish racks—the leftovers after salt fish have been filleted—which have been shown in tests to be the best feed available for the job. The calcium in the bones helps the lobsters' shells harden, and in six weeks they have shippable lobsters when there aren't any others around. Hard-shell lobsters are always in demand: "They'll survive air freight."

Then they fill the pound again in late September or early October for the winter. "Not too early," says Kathy, "but not too late, so the lobsters can eat before it gets too cold." There's a balance to feeding pounded lobsters. "You have to kinda keep watch. We leave some bait bags on the side that we can keep track of and see how they're doing. You have to feed enough so they don't chew on each other, but you can't overfeed them, particularly if you're feeding herring, or it rots and eats up the oxygen." The lobsters won't eat at all if the water freezes over, which it has done twice in the ten or so years that Kathy has worked for the co-op. "They used to have a saying," says Kathy, "'No ice, no price,' but I don't know if there's anything to that. Last winter the price was OK, but the year before, it was really good. That was just after 9/11." Worried about the economy, no one wanted to put a lot of lobsters in their pounds. "We put in less too, but the price was great. This year, everyone put more in. It's a gamble."

The Swans pound isn't aerated. In theory, it can handle a hundred thousand pounds of lobster, and it could be more with aeration, but they've never put in more than eighty-five thousand pounds, for both the co-op and individual members, who receive the average price after deducting the "shrink." To minimize shrink, the lobsters are checked out before they're pounded, and the "culls"—any with breaks, such as lost claws—are sold. They wouldn't make it through the pounding anyway. Some loss is inevitable.

In the spring—usually in March—they sell the pounded lobsters. Ben used the same term as Danny MacDonald: crapshoot. "Some years are better than others. You wonder if they're all down there dead, or if there's a hole in the wall—it's a lot of money tied up there." Feed, labor to get them in and out, equipment, interest on the money paid to the fishermen to begin with, and maintenance of the pound—it's an expensive proposition. The timing for taking them out is key, of course, and entirely unpredictable—the price is determined by the economy and by what kind of season Nova Scotia had. The fall price might be three and a half or four dollars a pound, and Ben says that usually they bring between five and six dollars when they come out. At the very end of the pound season, they might get as high as eight dollars. "Nobody waits for that high price, though," Ben says, "because when it starts down, it drops by dollars and nobody wants your lobsters when they know tomorrow the price might be a buck less."

Then comes the annual co-op meeting, after all the expenses and income for the year are calculated. At the meeting, the members decide whether a bonus will be paid—and if so, how much. "More people come to that meeting than to any other all year," Kathy says.

Kathy's job entails more than just dealing with lobster and bait, though those are certainly a big part of it. In 2002–3, just to pick a year, the co-op handled 689,862 pounds of lobster, plus crabs; for bait, there were 9,431 bushels of herring and 122 bushels of redfish, pollack heads, and hake heads. It's an unwritten rule on Swans that a fisherman sells his lobsters to whoever sells him bait, and the co-op pays the going price off the boat. The co-op gets its bait by truck, and the lobsters go out by truck, daily during the summer. "We have excellent lobsters," Kathy says. "They're in demand." Because there are only two reserved spaces available for trucks on the state ferry, and those can be booked no more than thirty days in advance, Kathy stops in at the ferry terminal every week during the summer to reserve space for the lobster truck. The bait people, with a less predictable schedule, make their own reservations. The reservation costs $5.75—far less than for standing in line waiting for a place while the ferry goes back and forth without you. As a percentage of the cost of the whole trip, the reservation fee isn't much, either. Trucks going on the state ferry to Swans (or Vinalhaven or Frenchboro, for the same size truck) pay $87.50 for the round-trip, using the lower rates charged for tickets bought on-island. The bait truck going to the co-op on Islesford, however, is barged over at a cost of $150.

Occasionally a truck might get on without a reservation—the middle line on the boat is 115 feet long, and the reservers have specified the length of their vehicle, so the attendant knows how much space should still be available for anyone willing to wait in line for it.

The co-op also carries marine gas and diesel, outboard oil, transmission and hydraulic fluids, regular oil, bleach, Dawn dishwashing detergent (no other will do; the fishermen say it cleans up their boats better than anything else), Bounty paper towels, and a variety of tools and fuses and hose clamps. Windshield-washer fluid is important in freezing weather for some boats' wash-down pumps. Auto (and truck) gas is available, too. In a given year, they sell incalculable amounts of coffee and about four thousand pounds of the rubber bands used to clamp lobsters' claws closed. The co-op is a gathering spot not only for its members but also for other fishermen. It opens at four in the morning, and often someone is there even earlier.

Sternmen

Before he came to Swans, Ben Doliber fished in areas of Massachusetts where everyone set long strings, twenty traps apiece. "Whack, hack, and set 'em back," he describes it. "Everyone tried to set in the same direction, but it didn't work." The strings were always getting entangled. "If you didn't know any different, it was normal." By contrast, 475 traps set in pairs is pretty simple. In fact, although he always had a sternman in Massachusetts—he had to—he's only recently started regularly taking one again. "I'm getting older now. But going alone was wonderful—no worry about whether someone was going to show up in the morning or not."

Most fishermen nowadays take an assistant with them, a sternman, or even two, though a sternman—or the fisherman—may be female. (No one talks of sternwomen or sternpeople, or even fisherpeople. That's foolish.) Increasingly, women are getting into fishing. It's not unusual now for a young woman to "stern" (work as helper) for her fa-

Cranberry Isles Co-op on Islesford

ther or someone else. She may continue in that role for her boyfriend or husband—or she may end up marrying the fellow she's working for, as Barbara Fernald of Islesford did more than twenty years ago, and Frenchboro's Linda Lunt did last year. When the wife goes with her husband, says Jill Philbrick, "all the money stays in the house—you don't pay out 20 percent to the sternman." Sterning is usually paid as a percentage of the take, although some fishermen pay their help by the hour. Jill grew up sterning with her stepfather and now, though she doesn't yet have a license, she owns a boat with one of her sisters. More women these days are getting their own licenses—and not just the high-profile ones such as writer Linda Greenlaw of Isle au Haut and *Survivor*'s Zoe Zanidakis of Monhegan. On Swans Island, there are three or four women with their own boats, and fifteen or twenty who go stern.

Paul Waterman and his sternman, daughter Liza

Liza Waterman is one of four or five women who stern on North Haven. She has sterned for her father, Paul, for years now. "She's an old pro," says her mother, Bonnie. Liza is just finishing up her training as an early childhood teacher. She would like to teach on North Haven someday, but, says Bonnie, "I need to retire before she can do that." Bonnie teaches first and second grade. "I told her, 'I think an awful lot of you, but I'm not going to give up my job for you.'" Bonnie sterned for Paul herself one summer. Says she emphatically, and with respect for her daughter, "It's a job I wouldn't want in the long haul."

Because of the rigors of the job, it's not always easy for islanders to find stern-men. It's hard work, and wet and cold and messy. The rubber gloves they wear become slimy, covered in bait. It's slippery hanging on in a sea anyway, and even more so for the sternman. The captain can grab onto the wheel and the trap hauler, and, most important, he can see what's coming.

Most young fishermen on the islands have their own boats. Danny Lunt of Frenchboro started fishing when he was nine or ten, as did his father and grandfather, and as his sons have too. Danny had his own outboard skiff at ten, fishing about fifty traps, like his father before him. When he graduated from school, he was fishing 150 traps, setting them ten at a time, making three trips a day when he couldn't borrow his father's or grandfather's boat. Eventually he was able to move up to a bigger boat. Why would a fellow who was doing all right on his own settle for sterning?

About half the fishermen of Frenchboro have assistants, and all of those are connections of some sort—friends of theirs, or friends of friends, or someone's relatives. Occasionally someone chooses to stay working stern and not bear the responsibilities of the boat, but usually a sternman would like to fish for himself—or he moves on to another job, somewhere else.

The job of sternman has a number of facets. On the one hand, the job has the potential for good financial reward, and it provides an opportunity to get time in toward the state's apprenticeship program. A good sternman is certainly a plus for a fisherman. But often it's a position held by young men who have few commitments and enjoy their off hours to a degree that interferes with their work. I was told of a sternman who borrowed $300 from his boss and then wanted a ride to the ferry. "We're going to haul tomorrow," the boat owner said.

"Oh, yeah," the guy said. "I'll be back." He never returned.

"Typical sternman stuff," says the fisherman. "But that's normal when you deal with young men." In some cases, the captains should expect little else, since they hired the guys in bars in the first place.

And then there's the other side: "Many lobstermen go through sternmen, whoosh," says one man who has done his share of sterning. "They treat their sternmen like shit. They feel like a god and figure if they're making the guy a thousand or fifteen hundred dollars a week, that's good enough." But, he says, it can be a different deal altogether. "If you get someone you like, or who likes you, it's nice. Every once in a while, you find people who don't treat you like shit, and you bend over backward for 'em."

DONNA WIEGLE, SWANS ISLAND STERNMAN

Each summer for the first fifteen years of their marriage, Donna and Charlie Wiegle spent time with friends on Swans Island. He had come to the island since he was five, and it was always his dream to live there, but when it came time to do it, she was the one who "really, really wanted to stay." They lucked into a house when their friends bought shore access from an old lobsterman and didn't need the house that went with it. They look out over the lobster pound and Burnt Coat Harbor. "We were very fortunate. We have a view, but we don't pay the taxes of shore frontage." When they bought the house, they didn't intend it to be their year-round home. They rented it out the first summer and came out in September, "and we've been here ever since," says Donna. "It's been two winters now, so I guess we're good to go."

Charlie, a good builder, has found that there's plenty of work on the island. He's booked up more than two years ahead, in fact. Donna has a degree in medical technology and kept it current so that if she needed to, she could work in the hospital in Ellsworth, on the mainland. She kept a subcontract for computer work with the company for which she had worked in Pennsylvania, and during the first summer she mowed lawns.

Then she took a job sterning for Rusty Crossman, who she got to know while working on a play. Swans Island has put on a number of plays every year since Rusty moved over from Frenchboro more than a decade ago, and he's been in every one. "I'm kind of a ham anyway," he says, "and I love it." Rusty came to Swans because his then-wife's children were getting to high-school age. They didn't want to move to the mainland, but from Swans, the kids could commute to school on the state ferry. (She has since moved ashore. Go figure.)

Charlie and Donna Wiegle of Swans Island

Donna never thought of herself as an actress, but someone asked her to join the cast. "Basically, if you had a pulse, you got the part," she says. But she enjoyed it, and got a job offer besides.

"The more we talked about it, the more I thought, I'm forty-four now, and not getting any younger—if I don't do it now, I never will." She signed on to go with Rusty starting in April. For 20 percent of the total catch, she is at his beck and call to work on traps, paint buoys, paint the boat, or haul—whatever he asks.

(The norm on Swans for a stern who only hauls and doesn't do any maintenance is 15 percent. Donna kept a log to judge at the end of the season whether it paid to take on the extra work.)

She is perhaps a little proud to say that she has never been late. She knows that if a fisherman says he wants to leave the dock at five, he wants to leave right at five. In fact, sometimes she gets to the co-op before Rusty does. "They get right on him if I'm there before him. Someone's on the radio, 'Rusty, where are you? Donna's been here a half-hour, pacing the floor.' Of course it's only been five minutes, really."

Donna told him that if she ever wasn't there when he was ready to go, he should call her. He said he wouldn't. "You call me," she insisted, "because if I'm not here, something is wrong."

When she and Charlie first decided to stay on the island through the winter, a long-time summer person told her she'd never make it. "You're too friendly," they said. "Island people will be very nervous about you."

But she found that not to be true. "People treat you as you treat them," she says. She feels that she and her husband are respected as hard workers. "People out here keep their eyes open, and they see what you're doing." Rusty said something to her about having a lot of money, because many former summer people who move onto an island are well off. "If we were really rich, would I be getting up at four-fifteen in the morning to go with you?" she asked him.

"We're able to fit in because we're hardworking people. We don't have fancy cars. And mowing grass, building, lobstering—that's all hard work. They appreciate that."

In August of her first season of fishing, when asked if she would go stern again, she said it was too soon to make that decision. "I want to see how rough the fall is. It's not the cold, I can handle that, but we'll be offshore farther, and it'll be rougher. I've only thrown up once, and that was back early in the season. You hear about people who get sick every day. I don't know how they can keep going out there, knowing they're going to be seasick—there's nothing worse. I think you do get used to it out there, but I want to see."

She got a taste of it in early September, the day after the tail end of what had been Hurricane Frances worked its way out into the Gulf of Maine. It may then have been only a tropical depression, but it still brought a good blow with it, and there was plenty of sea remaining the next day. Rusty's was the only boat out from Burnt Coat Harbor. She told him her life was in his hands.

"Well," said Rusty, "today, your safety's only as good as you can hold on."

She figured she only had one of two choices: go, or quit. Rusty said no, actually she had three choices: go, quit, or just not show up for work. She wouldn't lose her job—there aren't many lined up wanting to work, he said. That third option might be typical of some sternmen, but that's not Donna.

A clue to what was in store for her is that four times a week for six years, Rusty ran the mail from Frenchboro to Swans Island, or, if the Swans Island ferry wasn't running, to Bass Harbor, and he only missed two days because of weather. One of those was the famous Perfect Storm. When Donna heard that, she asked, "Does that mean we're not going to miss any days lobstering because of weather?"

Rusty didn't answer.

By Thanksgiving, she had agreed to go again the next year, though she wondered if she had spoken too soon. "It's getting a little choppy out there," she said. "'Course we're fishing offshore, now." And it was getting cold. "You get there in the morning and the hot water barrel's frozen solid—but you suck it up and you dress appropriately. I wear so many clothes in the morning! But the days that have been cold in the morning it's been nice in the afternoon—forty, even." At that point, they were only going out two or three days a week, "and I know there's an end in sight," she said.

"One more year, that's it," she told Rusty.

"Oh, no," said Rusty.

"You mean I gotta go with you forever?"

"Yeah."

"Till you die."

"Yeah."

"Well, don't say that, or I'll be praying for you to die," she told him. She says she's getting too old for this kind of work. He's got a number of years on her, of course, and he's not quitting.

Donna says they probably would be all right financially with just Charlie's work and her Internet job. She doesn't want to commute off-island, that's for sure. "Go on the ferry every day? No way!" Two women do commute ashore from Swans, to work in boatyards, and of course the high-school kids go off. That's not for Donna. She and Charlie had plans to go grocery shopping the Wednesday after we first spoke. She hadn't been ashore for twenty-eight days. "It's such a hassle. In summer, it's a big problem just dealing with the ferry. It only takes fifteen or sixteen cars, and there's a lot of construction and trucks, so it's difficult getting on and off. You lose a whole day, and there's all the traffic going to Ellsworth or Bangor—you adjust to being out here with no traffic or traffic lights. I dread the idea of it. In the winter, it's fine—just drive on the boat and drive off, but in the summer it takes planning."

In any case, she loved her first year sterning. "It's been a great experience," says the ocean-loving Donna, who is a certified scuba diver. "To be on the water is wonderful. I'm so excited about all the things in the traps besides lobsters. Every once in a while, Rusty says, 'Donna, this ain't no nature cruise, throw it back!' I know the job is all about being as fast as possible, so I have a little bucket on deck and I throw stuff in there to look at later, when we have a break." She has checked out starfish and snails and tiny blue lumpfish two or three inches long and living sand dollars, brown and furry. She loved the year, even if she was working hard.

Kyle Spratt, Young Lobsterman with a Backup Plan

In June 2004, as he has been nearly every summer since he was a young teenager, twenty-one-year-old Kyle Spratt was on Frenchboro full-time, fishing for lobster. He had been home from the University of Maine for six or seven weeks. During the fall, he comes back to the island every weekend to fish, and he has recently bought a house on the island. It was shortly after the summer solstice when I spoke with him, and his regular schedule was to get up at three every morning. "You're supposed to be on the water by dawn," he says. That's what the fellows on the island have told him. "I ended up liking it. It's a quiet time, and the sunrise—it's incredible out here." From Frenchboro to the eastward, there's only ocean, no land. "I try to catch it every morning."

In previous years, Kyle had been fishing on a student license and had built up to 150 traps. He was paying his way through college on what he had made. Once he'd become eligible for a Class I license, he had to wait for eighteen people to die before he could actually receive the license—three years. Each zone has its own regulations, and in Zone B, where Frenchboro is, the limited entry rules stipulate that three licenses be retired before a new one is given out. "No one gives up their license anymore, they just die," Kyle explains. If an older fellow gave up his license and then decided he wanted to start up again, he'd have to go work for some young fisherman, and no one would want to do that. In February 2004, Kyle finally got his Class I license. He bought a twenty-six-foot fiberglass boat to replace the old skiff he had been using, and he increased his trap count to three hundred.

Kyle says that the hardest aspect of fishing for him, not having grown up on the island, is that he's always trying to prove himself to his contemporaries. He has known these young men ever since he started spending summers on the island. In their eighth-grade year, Zach Lunt, Kyle's age, had lived with Kyle's family from January through the end of the school year in order to get accustomed to the mainland before he went off to high school. In return, Zach's parents invited Kyle to spend the summer on the island and learn to fish. (After that, Zach's parents split up, and some years after that, his father and Kyle's mother married, making the young men of Frenchboro his stepbrothers or stepcousins. But that's another story.)

"I try to work what they think is the hardest." (I've been told that on Frenchboro in years past, boys were brought up to think that work was all-important. Play wasn't a part of life once a kid was old enough to work, and they all were out fishing by the time they were ten.) "They say this is what you should do—and sometimes they're mean about it, but they don't realize it." It took him a while to understand that even though they're sometimes crude in how they say things, they do want to help him. "Because I'm not from here, they want to teach me. And they're not trying to tell me to leave the island!" Once in a while, without saying much about it, one of them will do something big for him. Last year, Zach set out all of Kyle's traps, for example, and once in a while they'll haul for him when he's at school. "Then they'll come up to my house and borrow stuff when I'm not there, but it's all part of it. The whole island is one family, which is intimidating sometimes."

Kyle has changed his routine this year. "Last year, I stayed up till eleven every night, got up at six or seven, and dragged all day." By the end of the summer, he was exhausted and hadn't worked as hard as he thought he should have. He decided to change the schedule to the three o'clock rising, "so I can focus." He says he's already gotten more work done, and has caught three times as many lobsters as he did last year. He does have more traps now—but only twice as many. And having let it be known that's what his schedule was, he's felt committed to it at least until the days get shorter. "People know I'm up at three, and if I change, they're going to ask why!"

During the fall, he spends the week in Orono going to classes at the university and studying, and Friday night he's back on Frenchboro to work all day Saturday and Sunday. One semester, he tried to carry nineteen credit hours. It was too much. "It felt like everything was in a tornado all the time." More recently, he's cut back to only twelve credits. It'll take him an extra semester to graduate, but he makes enough money just in a few weekends to pay his whole school bill. When he graduates, he'll have a degree in mechanical engineering, which he doesn't actually like very much—it's all inside work, and technical, and you never talk to people. "But people respect you for doing it because it's supposed to be a tough major, and if I ever get hurt, it'll be a good backup." Not to mention he'll have no debt from his education.

Fisherman Ben Doliber Comes to Swans

Ben and Belinda Doliber's mailbox looks like a lobster. Before the 2004 election, they received a phone call about the Kerry/Edwards sign hung on top of it: "Looks like your lobster's got shell-wasting disease." Democratic political signs were unusual on Swans, but the Dolibers are certainly part of the island now.

Each summer toward the end of the 1980s, when the lobsters started shedding off Ben Doliber's hometown of Marblehead, Massachusetts, he and his wife, Belinda, would fire up their Nova Scotia–built lobsterboat and cruise to Maine. Their children were grown and gone, and they could just enjoy themselves. The first year, they only took a week, and they got as far as Casco Bay, which they thought a wonderful place. But the next year they had more time and kept going. One year, they made it all the way to the Canadian island of Grand Manan, where a mistake in the cruising guide sent them into the harbor that had no customs officials. But their lobsterboat fit right in with all the other Novi boats, so they went ashore and wandered around anyway.

It was during the second summer that they found Swans Island. They were out in Toothacher Bay one morning and saw a guy in a blue boat pulling traps—Ken Lemoine, best of friends today. They asked him if they could buy a few lobsters. Sure. He gave them four lobsters and named a price just barely over boat price. They didn't have the right change, so they overpaid him by two dollars, thinking it was still a more-than-fair deal. Then they asked about a picnic spot. Ken sent them to a sandy cove on Marshall's Island. After they'd eaten their lobsters there, Ben looked at the chart and thought Burnt Coat Harbor looked good for the night. Of course, they didn't know the area yet, and Ken's boat hadn't had a hail port painted on the stern, so they didn't ex-pect to see it again, but there was that same blue boat, moored out in front of the co-op in Burnt Coat.

Ben met Llewellyn Joyce at the co-op, where he'd stopped to ask about a moor-ing for the night. Llewellyn was headed across the island with his son. "You need any-thing at the store?" he asked Ben.

"We really didn't," Ben says, "but it was a good opportunity to see the island, so we went along with him. Saw the store and the dump and met Llewellyn's wife, Jeannie. Later, after having supper on the boat, we saw a skiff with a couple and two kids rowing out."

It was Kenny and his wife, and, wearing footed pajamas, their children. "Boy, am I glad you're in the harbor," said Kenny. "That two dollars was bothering me all day."

Swans was even better than Casco Bay, and the Dolibers re-turned on their next few summer cruises. They couldn't get enough of Swans Island. They started think-ing that maybe they should buy a re-tirement place there. To see what the island was like in winter, on Fri-day afternoons when Belinda got out of work, they'd get in the car, drive to Bucksport and spend the

Swans Island's Ben and Belinda Doliber
(COURTESY OF DONNA WIEGLE)

night, and get on the first boat Saturday morning from Bass Harbor to Swans. They'd spend the day on Swans, take the last ferry off the island, and head home again. On Saturday, they'd hang around the co-op—"I'm a gas bag anyway," Ben says—and got to know a lot of the islanders. "It got to the point we were coming so often, people would just say, 'When are you just going to move out here?'"

Before long, they had bought a house. That made the weekend car trips a little easier—at least they could spend Saturday nights on the island.

In Massachusetts, Ben had been lobstering half the year and dragging for groundfish the other half; when he was on Swans, he'd been looking the bottom over. "There's gotta be tons of flounder here," he said. "It's beautiful flounder bottom." One cold February, he steamed up to the island. One of the guys with him, Mike, had just met a new girl the night before they left Massachusetts, and he had no desire at all to be there. They came into Swans in a snowstorm.

"Where in the world am I?" Mike asked.

They made six or seven sets, Ben says, and caught one flounder. He tried for shrimp, then, because the prices were high in Portland, but after a month they went back to Marblehead. He wasn't disillusioned, though. The following year, Ben and Belinda made twenty-seven weekend trips during a six month period, and they realized two things: first, Ben probably was never going to retire, and second, they didn't want to wait. They decided to make the move. "The worst that could happen," said Ben, "is that we'd have to move back to Massachusetts." No big deal.

They have not had a single regret. "Never a minute," says Belinda, and Ben says, "It's the best thing we ever did." Marblehead was building up too fast, and they thought Swans wouldn't change too much during their lifetime.

By the time that Ben first set lobster traps, he knew most of the fishermen. "I've been fishing all my life, and I settled in without too much problem. It all worked out."

Although fishermen were scalloping, gillnetting, and shrimping in winter when the Dolibers first came to Swans, none of that pays now, so Ben just chases lobsters—and he does that during months of better weather. They don't believe winter lobstering is worth it, either. "There are guys who leave gear out all the time," says Belinda. "They might get out to it only once a week, or once every couple of weeks if the weather's bad. If they had something more productive to do, they'd do it."

Belinda says Ben couldn't stretch his winter work to fill the time, and he was lost. "He'd go out to the shop and paint one buoy, then go down to the co-op to buy a piece of sandpaper and have a cup of coffee, and then go back and paint another buoy. Then he'd need a paintbrush and go back to the co-op and have another cup of coffee." Now they go to the Bahamas for two months each winter. One year, they rented a speedboat down there, but it wasn't boat enough, and they kept thinking how nice it would be to have their lobsterboat there. The next year, they took her. They left in December, traveled down the Intracoastal Waterway, and went across to the Abacos from Florida. "It was a neat trip, but it was long." Because the days were so short, it took a month to get there. It didn't take so long to get home. The days were longer, but more important, says Belinda, "He'd grown his lobster mask. He was hustling to get home. He's hell-bent on getting home by April first; sometime in March, he's thinking of buoys that need to be painted, of lobsters crawling in traps, and that lobster mask starts growing."

Since then, they've bought a used trawler to use in the Abacos.

Not long after they moved to Swans, the real estate broker who had sold the Dolibers their house asked Belinda to join her in the business, to relieve her of having the whole responsibility. Belinda got her license, and she enjoys the work—even though, as she says, "the first few years, I didn't make enough to pay the phone bill. We moved here right at the end of the active market." It's still a low-key, part-time thing. The other woman has retired, and Belinda now has been joined by a younger woman. Despite changes in the law that permit an agency to act both as seller's agent and buyer's, they have to act solely as seller's agent—in order to offer both services, the state requires that there be three people in the office. Besides the seller's agent and the buyer's, there has to be someone to watch over them to be sure they don't share information they shouldn't. But Burnt Coat Harbor Real Estate is just a two-person operation. "We're just honest and up-front with everyone, the old-fashioned way." Who would misrepresent anything to their new neighbors? "You can find out whatever you want to know just by asking on the ferry, anyway," she says.

On a visit to Swans, the Dolibers' daughter saw a sweatshirt for sale in the island store with the slogan "Life in the Slow Lane." "This isn't life in the slow lane," she told her mother, "this is the dead lane."

"I don't think island life would be her thing," Belinda says. "The people who have settled here from away seem to be happy. They don't need a lot to be entertained, they're happy to entertain themselves—reading, knitting, gardening, kayaking, or just sitting quietly and listening to the birds. They didn't have unrealistic expectations."

Of course, there have been people who've come to Swans Island and moved off again. In general, though, Belinda feels that the process of buying property would take long enough that people would have a chance to think about it. "There has to be something in island life that they like."

Swans hasn't yet exploded with retirees the way Islesboro has, though some have come, and other people are buying or building summer places with an eye toward eventually spending the year or at least a long season there. Nor has the island had to attract young people from Away. Anticipating a potential problem, in 1991 the island received a grant and a state loan for affordable housing. The town subdivided some property it owned into two-acre lots, installed a well and septic system on each one, and sold them to people within certain income guidelines. It's all sold now—eleven town lots and another three that the town assisted with well and septic systems. The new owners could build or put a trailer on the property, as they saw fit. Three have changed hands since then—there are covenants that limit the resale price, and the new owners must fit the same financial profile. The island has very few year-round rental properties other than eight subsidized units for the elderly in a private apartment building.

"Sometimes young people can build on family-owned land, too," says Belinda.

In 2003–4, there were twenty-some students in the island school, in three class-rooms; as recently as 1990, there were more than forty, but there isn't too much concern yet about dwindling numbers. Most young men come back to go lobstering when they have finished high school, and some of the young women do, too. A number of women run their own boats now, and quite a few are sternmen, taking time off only to raise their children. And while the trend is increasing, it's not a new practice. The late Roberta Joyce fished with her husband until fifteen years ago, quitting when she was in her sixties.

While there are just over three hundred year-round residents today, in the summer the population rises to over a thousand, Belinda says. But, she points out, at the turn of the century there were almost that many. (Census reports show Swans Island's peak at 758 in 1900.) Those were the days of quarrying, boatbuilding shops, and fish-processing plants. "When those jobs went, those houses were sold off as summer homes. A lot of the old original houses, built by standards of year-round life then, are now summer houses." In fact, the Dolibers have one of them. Nowadays, new houses are almost all built with winter use in mind.

Lately there has been an increase in construction. Gravel trucks come onto the island regularly, and lumber trucks arrive two or three days a week. And the building styles are changing. Dexter Lee, longtime selectman and town father, reports that recently there has been an increase in "trophy houses." In one recent year, there were three building permit applications for houses of more than three thousand square feet. Swans may be catching up with some of the other islands.

The Future of Lobstering

Although many of the young lobster fishermen can't imagine hard times, their elders remember years of bad fishing and try to warn them not to spend all they earn. "They're the best group for gloom and doom," says Kathy Clark. "If they were knee-deep in lobsters, they'd predict it might stop tomorrow."

It's easy to be complacent, even in the face of the devastating wasting disease that recently killed a large proportion of Long Island Sound's lobsters. Gweeka Williams of Vinalhaven is not concerned about Long Island's experience. "They know goddam well what they done there. They poisoned 'em. Where we are, out to sea, I don't think that'll happen, unless they dump enough in the river to pooch it."

Youngsters typically can't imagine times being any different than they are at present. An older man told me of talking with a high-school boy who was getting his gear ready to set. Lobstering is the only thing the young man cares to do. The older fellow gave him a word of warning: "You've got to diversify, pick up trades, gain as many experiences as you can." But the kid didn't hear. "Lobsters are just getting better and better," he said. And in his memory, it's been true.

But it takes seven or eight years for a lobster to grow to market size, and some researchers are saying the little fellows aren't out there. Warren Fernald of Islesford doesn't believe it. "They just haven't found 'em, that's all." He sees large numbers of egg-carrying females, particularly in the fall, before they migrate offshore, and he's sure those eggs hatch out somewhere.

A female lobster carries eggs on her abdomen for ten or eleven months until they hatch. Maine fishermen who trap them are required to cut notches in the tails of these "eggers," as they're called, and release them to reproduce. No one may keep a notched female. Warren says a notch lasts three sheddings or so, and if a fisherman catches a female whose notch is disappearing, he'll re-notch her before tossing her overboard.

Lobstermen feel that the resource has been protected by the notching system, along with the measuring device that determines whether a lobster is within legal limits—a lobster that is too small or too big is returned to the ocean. A lot of juveniles and oversize lobsters are caught and thrown back every day.

Scientists have observed that the single dominant male lobster in an area is responsible for breeding all the females, so there's no harm in harvesting a disproportionate number of males. In some magical fashion, females can store sperm from one service over a year's time and through more than one spawning. Males are necessary for reproduction, yes, but only in minimal numbers. Warren has been through hard times fishing before, but it doesn't seem to him that there's any shortage coming now.

Even in good times, when the lobsters are plentiful and bringing high prices, the weather is beneficent, and no one's misbehaving, lobstering is hard work. And lucrative—now, anyway. "A guy's a sluggard if he doesn't make a hundred thousand dollars," I was told, and the number was confirmed more than once.

The axe may be ready to fall, though, and the impact on the islands would be devastating.

Matinicus

atinicus Island is all about lobsters. Until the mid-1980s, there was a store; there's still a post office; there's a bed-and-breakfast whose owner doubles as the office person for the local electric company; and there's one man who takes care of the electric plant and propane sales and 'most everything that needs fixing on the island. But the rest of the working men on Matinicus—more than thirty boats' worth—fish for lobster. "You'd have a hard job to make a better living anywhere else," says Vance Bunker, who for more than forty years has fished from the island where he grew up. "Everyone says get a college education, and that's fine, but there's not too many that makes as much money as a fisherman out there who pays attention and takes good care

Matinicus Harbor

of his stuff." You'll rarely find a lobsterman who admits that—they're all as poor as can be, to listen to them (and of course one never does know what will happen in a living resource-driven occupation). But take a look at their trucks or their boats or where they take their vacations.

Matinicus has seven or eight hundred acres and claims about fifty residents, though in winter many of them are somewhere else, or come and go. There were nineteen on the island one particular day in February the year I happened to ask—everyone always knows who's on the island and who's not, and if they're not, where they've gone. Usually, even in winter, there are more like twice that number, and by March or April, the fishermen are back and at work until Christmas.

Vance and his wife, Sari, came ashore in the end of December this particular year. "When it come time, I got my traps up, got my boat up—I guess I was tired of the snowy weather and the ice." He suggested to Sari that they stay on the mainland a while. But by the end of February, they both were getting anxious to be home. "I'm not tired anymore," said Vance.

A half-dozen lobstermen fish through the winter; they deserve the money they get. "Where you gotta go, you're running outside," says Vinalhaven resident Gweeka Williams, who has fished year-round from Vinalhaven himself and also went stern with a friend on Matinicus for a couple of winters. "The sea acts different in the winter, and it's cold. And if the boat's gonna break down, it's gonna do it then. You got no daylight, and it's always rough." And as for Matinicus, "That's a lonely piece of real estate," he says. "Come spring, the pegs will fall right over in the cribbage board, and you've played poker so much you can't read the dates on your pennies."

No one fishes from Matinicus who didn't grow up there or have family connections, now or historically. A time or two, someone has tried. It doesn't work.

"They're gently motivated to move on," I was told. "You try to do it in a reasonable way," they say, but if need be, things can get rowdier. No hindrance—or help—will come from law-enforcement officials. "The state's not involved," I was told. "They can't do anything on a foggy day, anyway." And if someone from the Marine Patrol were to query the island people about their ways of limiting competition, they're ready to reply that it's simply conservation of the resource—just what the state has been struggling to accomplish for years now.

"I know people everywhere," says Vance, "who come to me and say they're coming to Matinicus. 'No, you're not,' I say, and walk off with a smile on my face."

The local fishermen protect the resource from other interlopers as well. I was told of the time that a group in a large sailing yacht anchored at Matinicus and made a big production of cooking lobsters on deck. Someone asked where they got the lobsters. Their naiveté is hard to imagine, but they answered—perhaps even bragged—that they

Vance Bunker getting ready to set out in the spring

had pulled a few traps outside the harbor and helped themselves. Somehow, a bucket of used motor oil flew up over the rail of the yacht and fell down the companionway, dousing everything in reach—splashing all over the cabin and back up onto the deck and sails. The Coast Guard and the Sheriff's Department investigated, but not a soul could explain what had happened.

Among the men who fish the Matinicus waters in spring, summer, and fall are some who commute to the island from the mainland every day. With today's big-engined boats, it takes only an hour or less to get there. "The new lobsterboats nowadays, they seem to want 'em to go as fast as their cars," says Vance. Also, wives don't seem as enthusiastic about living on the island as they once were. "When I was young, if you married a fisherman, you went where he was. Now they don't bother. They don't want to leave the convenience of the mainland."

For many decades, the young women who grew up on Matinicus have almost always left. There are only a very few women on the island today whose families go way back. Once in a great while, one will stay on and fish with her father. Rarely do they return to the island once they go off, but Vance's daughter is the exception. She had her fishing license when she was in school and let it go to live ashore and work in real estate. But she went through the apprenticeship program and is again licensed and running her own boat. She lives on the island from early summer until it gets cold.

By contrast, almost all the boys follow in their fathers' wakes. Some of them have their own boats; some work for someone else. "There's a lot involved in owning your own boat," Vance says. "There's half a million dollars invested." And because of the island's remoteness, a Matinicus boat has to be a bigger, more rugged vessel than some of the inshore lobsterboats.

The majority of the boys in school when Sari Bunker taught in 1980–82 are now living on the island and fishing; one girl, gone for a number of years, has recently come back. Young men tend to find wives from off-island. It has long been a tradition to check out the women who come to the island temporarily. Vance's mother worked on Matinicus as a nurse, and Sari taught on the island. She is now on the school board. When it was time to hire a new teacher, one young fisherman told her, "Get a young one."

The school had no students in 2001–2. "It didn't close," says Sari. "It just didn't open." No teacher was hired, but the school still existed. Opening a closed school is very difficult—probably impossible, in fact—because of state requirements. There was one student in 2002–3, plus two home-schooled children; the next year, the school population increased to three, at least part of the time. The Matinicus school has never gone beyond eighth grade, anyway. Like many island youngsters of his time (and since), Vance went to boarding school for high school. He'd have been happy not to go, because he knew he wanted to fish for a living. "I was born and brought up to it."

But Vance's mother told him he was going to graduate from high school if it took him the rest of his life. "Mum said I had to go and I was frightened of her, so I went," he says with a twinkle. "It's the best thing that ever happened to me. If I hadn't gone to school, I'd have been a worse idiot." He notes that it's easy to think that because your father did something a certain way, and your grandfather did, then you're going to, too, and it's just too bad if someone doesn't like it. "You have to get away so you can see there's something else." Then if you come back, it's because you've chosen it.

Although ten years earlier there had been thirty students, no more than fifteen were in the Matinicus school during Vance's time there. At boarding school, he liked being exposed to so many different people of different backgrounds, and having the opportunity to decide with whom to hang out. The only disadvantage he sees today to living on such a small island is that you can't choose your associates—but, he says, going away for those four years taught him how to get along with anyone he might not like so well. There will inevitably be those types in any group, no less just because everyone knows everyone—not that it matters in time of trouble in a fishing community. Never mind your good or bad relationship with a person, you help. If you want, you can go back to not speaking with one another when it's over.

Matinicus is a plantation, a Maine designation sort of halfway between a town and an unorganized territory; the island officials are known as assessors. They have authority over the day-to-day running of the island's government, but the state is responsible for land-use ordinances and the like. It was only a couple of decades ago that Frenchboro changed from a plantation to a town. Actually, it was their second foray into independence. For a year in the mid-1800s, they gave township status a try, but then abandoned it. A town has much higher costs than a plantation. When they considered reincorporation in the late 1970s, Rusty Crossman, now of Swans Island, was an assessor on Outer Long Island Plantation, as Frenchboro was then known. "You had to enforce all their rules?" I asked him. "Yup." "Did you?" "Nope." The state wanted to set guidelines for building docks—that may have been the last straw for Frenchboro. As Rusty tells it: "They was tellin' you as a commercial fisherman you couldn't build a dock over here, 'cause there was a clam over there. Finally we decided it was too much bullcrap—that's when we went to Town Meeting and voted to go to a town.")

Vance was an assessor on Matinicus for more than thirty years. He wouldn't have stayed in the role so long if it weren't for the younger fellows who joined him toward the end. "I told them, anything reasonable you do, I'll back you up. I told them they were the future of the island, they couldn't sit back and whine, they had to take care of things. And they have."

There was the incident of the gun, for instance. The villain has since then made the news as part of a white supremacist group protesting against foreign immigrants statewide; he was living on the island at the time, and he confronted some yachtsmen about their dog killing his duck. He shoved the gun in their faces, demanding a hundred dollars from them. They paid up, but the islanders weren't happy about the event. "One of the younger town officials got onto him pretty heavy," Vance says. "Told him he'd take the gun and shove it somewhere if he didn't get off the island. And he told the guy's boss to get rid of him." The fellow left Matinicus soon afterward.

"The island is one place those people he joined up with won't come and protest, either. We might have a bad reputation, but we have a good one, too," says Vance.

The cruising guides tell yachtsmen to stay clear of Matinicus, the natives aren't friendly. When Paul Murray's father was cruising along the coast in the 1960s in a small boat that hailed from Cape Elizabeth, he stopped for gas in Port Clyde, and they asked where he was headed. "Matinicus."

"Do you know people out there? You better!"

Some say that the people of Matinicus cultivate their reputations as pirates. The image of a rough-and-ready group who'll take care of things themselves and let people know what they think is not unearned. Before he died, cat-lover Charlie Pratt ran the power company and took care of the phones. One day, he found all four tires flat on his van, and a dead cat was tied to it. "I musta hit somebody's cat," Charlie said.

Moving into any small community can be tricky, and an island can be more so. Sari says that the island values education, however, so the teachers are always welcomed "as long as they don't make too many waves."

When sixteen-year-old Warren Williams moved onto the island in 1935 to work for the storekeeper, it wasn't so easy. He happened into the job through a friend at home in Mount Vernon, Maine. "I always wanted to see what's on the other side of the mountain," Warren says. At the start, even his trip to the island made him wonder if this choice had been a good one. It was the last day of April when the young high-school graduate caught the mailboat from Rockland. The *Calista D. Morrill* was an old sardine carrier, converted for the Matinicus mail route. It was a miserable, foggy day, blowing southeast and starting to rain. Even at the Rockland pier, the boat was bobbing up and down. It only got worse on the trip across the bay—the old carrier rolled and tossed and fussed throughout the two-and-a-half-hour trip to the island. "I wasn't sick, but I was squeamish."

The Henry Young Company store had opened up before 1900 to serve not just the islanders but the whole area. The company built the wharf that's there today, bought fish, and, after digging an ice pond, sold ice to the Gloucester fishermen working on the Grand Banks. The schooners would come in for ice if they had only a partial load of fish and weren't quite ready to return to Massachusetts. This ice trade was gone by 1935, but the local business continued. The owners had a farm and raised potatoes and other vegetables, and they had a few cows and a pair of horses—one red and one black—used to pull the hearse. It was Warren's job to tend the farm as well as to help with the store. No island boy would take that job; they were fishermen out there!

When Warren put his suitcase on the dock at Matinicus, a man loading produce into a wheelbarrow asked if he was the boy who was going to work for Aunt Marion. He was. "Follow me," he said, and led him up to the store. Aunt Marion Young was post-master as well as storekeeper; when Warren walked in, she told him the boat was going to Criehaven and would be back in an hour, and she had to have the mail ready for it. "Sit right there," she said.

During the time he sat and she sorted mail, a number of people came in the store. "Who's that?" they'd ask, and someone would say, "Oh, that's Aunt Marion's boy, he isn't going to last long." Of all the stoppers-by, only one person approached Warren and introduced himself—Aunt Marion's brother Leon.

"It cost me ninety cents for that boat ride. If I'd had ninety cents, I'd have got back on that boat," says Warren. But he stayed a year and a half. "I got thirty dollars a month in summer," says Warren. He got room and board, too, year around, but the pay went down to twenty dollars a month in winter. "They figured I didn't have to work so hard in winter." He tended the livestock and the farm, and he met the boat every trip—three times a week in summer, twice in winter—and carried boxes up to the store. "If the tide was so low that the boat couldn't come in, I'd take out the skiff and bring in the fresh stuff, ice cream and produce, and row it in." They'd plan the arrival of heavy cargo—flour and molasses and sugar and those other things that came in barrels—for times when the tide was high enough that the boat could get right up to the wharf. Then he'd take both horses and the jigger wagon, manhandle the barrels onto the wagon, and unload them at the store.

After the second summer, "I figured there must be an easier way to make a living," Warren says, and he went back to school. But he returned to Matinicus the next few summers to help Aunt Marion with the haying, and soon World War II came along.

Warren's parents came out to visit him in the summer of 1936. A minister, Warren's father ended up working with the Sea Coast Mission. An elderly islander who had to move into a nursing home ashore asked Warren's parents to stay in her house, and soon they were spending more time on the island. Ultimately, she left the house to them, and for many years, they stayed on Matinicus from April until Labor Day. After Warren's mother died in 1976, Harriet, Warren's wife, stayed there with her father-in-law, and Warren, who then had a job ashore, flew out to visit from time to time. A lot of the older people knew Warren from when he'd worked for Aunt Marion. "We were accepted, no problem," they say. "Someone said, 'He was pretty near born here.'"

Harriet says that anyone coming to the island with a connection to someone who lives there is taken in with no difficulty. "If you have a visitor, within an hour, everyone knows it. Those people are accepted. Renting a cottage is different. You may hear someone say, there goes a 'germ,' or a 'summer complaint.'" She describes the experience of a visiting friend of hers. At five-thirty one morning, she was sitting on a rock by the wharf. At that hour, there's usually no one but fishermen out there. When she heard a fisherman coming, she said good morning to him. "She jumped the wits outta me," he said later. "What you doin' here?" he asked her.

"It's so quiet and peaceful, I'm reading my Bible and taking it all in," she told him.

"OK, fine, to each his own," said the lobsterman.

Says Harriet, "A cottage-renter would have got a different reaction."

It's understandable, though, when you hear some of the stories about visitors picking pansies from people's dooryards and otherwise making themselves disagreeable.

Harriet herself—the sort of person who would be cherished wherever she landed—found it particularly easy. She was sitting in The Breezeway, the little lunchroom that Madeleine Young ran at the time. ("The place became famous," says Warren, "when her halibut sandwich was named in some publication as the best on the East Coast.") "I could see she was having problems," Harriet says, "and I asked, could I help?" Madeleine said that if she could just take orders, it would help a lot. A college girl was supposed to be there, but she hadn't shown up. "A day or two later, she bounced back across the plank, 'I'm back!'

"Madeleine says, 'That's nice, but you aren't back to help me anymore. You go on and enjoy yourself.'" Harriet worked with Madeleine the whole summer, and she met a lot of people while she was in that lunchroom.

"I always tell people, there's no Mr. In-Between. You're going to hate it out there or like it," she says. They've had visiting couples who came out for a weekend, and right from the start, one of the pair would be on edge and nervous, while the other loved it.

Starting in 1983, the Williamses stayed on Matinicus year-round. The next year, he and Harriet were elected tax collector and treasurer—positions they held for sixteen years. Warren, officially retired, went stern from time to time with one fisherman or another, and Harriet still runs the Matinicus Island Chamber of Commerce, fielding queries about places to stay on the island.

"It's much different now than when we first were out there," they say. "They had the boat, then, and for two or three dollars you could go ashore. Today it costs fifty dollars to fly." The store had to charge a premium for what they sold, but in the early days it carried everything you could want. "They had a deal with the Clark Stove Company in Boston," Warren remembers. "If you wanted a stove, you'd look in the catalog, and they'd call Boston. That night, your stove would go on the train to Rockland, and it would come out on the next boat. They knew what they were doing, then."

The store owned the wharf, and though they didn't say you couldn't bring groceries to the island, they frowned on it. In 1960, Warren saw someone bring seven hundred dollars' worth of groceries on the boat. A friend with a dragger had ordered them for him from the same distributor that the store used. Clayton Young, who had bought the store from his aunt Marion, looked at the boxes and wasn't happy. He would have had some leverage with the company if the guy had bought them himself, but since he hadn't, there was nothing he could do.

After changing hands a few times, in the early 1990s, the store closed for good. By then, the mail came out by air. Shaw's Supermarket made a deal that still exists today, packing orders for people and sending them out in the mail plane.

In the fall of 2002, the Williamses felt it had become too expensive to live on the island, and they were concerned about the lack of medical facilities, so they moved ashore. ("Matinicus is a bad place to get sick and have to get to Rockland—that wind blows all winter long," said Vance Bunker's mother, Rena.)

The act of moving ashore takes a different kind of planning. Arrangements for the ferry's limited space can be complicated. The truck has to go in the center of the little ferry, and you may not be able to get a reservation. "You can't go the bottled-gas time—that truck takes three spaces." It took the Williamses three trips to move all their possessions ashore. Each time they were bringing the empty truck back to the island, they put out the word that they'd be happy to transport stuff from the mainland for people. "People usually do that," they say. They brought a stove and refrigerator for one couple and a load of lumber for the owner of the island B&B. Once while they were waiting in line, three different groups of islanders added things.

At one time, there were three private planes on the island; now, Vance Bunker's is the only one. Vance and Sari say they've become spoiled by having the plane—it's so easy for them to go to the mainland. "When I'm working, though," he says, "I don't come in any more than I have to." But in addition to paying his helpers a percentage of what they catch, the deal is that he'll take them back and forth when they want to go, "if I feel like it." (This last is a refrain you hear a lot from Vance. He has set up his life so he doesn't have to do too many things he doesn't feel like doing. Matinicus both allows that approach to life and encourages it.) And, apparently, Vance felt like taking his help in often enough. As a Christmas present one year, they gave him a warming cover to put over the nose of the airplane to protect it from the cold.

As long as he can work, Vance expects to make his home on the island. "If I quit fishing, got lamed up so I couldn't go at all, I couldn't stand it. But retirement? It's fine if we want to go somewhere for a month or two, see places we'd like to see, but I'd only retire if I had to. I love fishing. Why would you quit what you like doing? No use to set around and die two years later, bored, doing nothing."

Lobstering, and perhaps all fishing, is a part of the men who've done it all their lives. If for health reasons a Matinicus fisherman can't set his traps any more, he'll usually move ashore, though he might come back for a while during the summer. It's not unusual that the older men keep working until they die—like Emery Philbrook, who fished into his eighties. Vance Bunker knows a seventy-five-year-old fisherman in Spruce Head who just got a new boat. "Good for him!" says Vance. His brother Albert, seventy-four at this writing, is among the oldest fishermen on Matinicus today.

"Fishermen are a weird bunch. We've worked hard all our lives, and most of us love to. If at seventy-five or eighty I can't go, I couldn't stand to set around and watch it go on around me," Vance says. "If I don't die with the boat, or right here at home, I'll be moving off. Dad was that way too."

Harold and Rena Bunker left the island when Harold was sixty-two; he had struggled all his adult life with a bad back, and finally he couldn't work anymore. He returned for three summers and fished, but his back couldn't take it. "If he coulda gone easier, he would have lasted," says Vance. "But that's the way we all are."

Harold didn't want to stay on the island; he said it had changed. "There's nothing for anybody who's retired out there," he said. "You never see anybody anymore. After television came in, people knocked off going to people's houses, playing cards and all. It isn't the same now." He was disgusted that Vance had to hire someone to help him do some work on his wharf. "In my day, they'd all come and help."

The arrival of television is often mentioned as a turning point in island life. The Matinicus Ladies' Aid used to meet every Tuesday night. After supper and chores were done, and the men were asleep, the ladies had free time to gather and do the handwork they sold at the summer church fairs. According to their minutes, much of the discussion in March and April of 1954 was about the installation of gas lights, but by the mid-1960s, islandwide electricity had come along. Because only five members were present on November 23, 1966, the planned annual meeting had to be postponed until Friday night, "when there is nothing on television that anyone wants to watch."

It's not certain that Rena Bunker ever liked the island, but she certainly didn't want to be there when she was approaching ninety. "That's a scary place to live, out there," she said at the time.

"What's scary about it?" Harold wanted to know. "You could die anywhere, going out in a gale of wind in the winter. It ain't half so scary there as walking down the street on the mainland."

"I don't care if I ever go out there," Rena said. And Vance says that the twenty-seven years his parents spent in Florida after retirement were the happiest of their hard lives.

But Vance knew when he finished school that he liked the quietness of the small community. By February, he's looking forward to returning to the island. "I go down to the shop, and I don't mind not seeing anybody all day. I come home and have a drink if I feel like it, maybe watch a movie, go to bed. It don't take much to entertain me," he says.

When Sari was interviewed for the island teacher's position, the superintendent asked her what her social life was like. Did she like to go out to supper? He explained to her that these might not seem like the right kinds of questions, but if you have to be with a lot of people and doing things all the time, this isn't the job for you.

"I can put up with myself," she says. She hesitates, and looks over to Vance. "Oh, and you," she adds.

"If you don't need a lot of people around, it's a great place to be," says Vance.

"You always complain I'm so slow doing things—I've got plenty of time to be slow, out there," Sari says.

Matinicus is unusual in that no matter what value is assessed on their land, the Bunkers say, the taxes won't drive anyone off. Its summer people go there because they like what it is; it's too inconvenient to change much. And the expenses of running the plantation shouldn't be such that the taxes need rise unreasonably. In fact, that there are as many properties owned by seasonal residents means that even if assessments go up, island expenses and therefore tax rates stay low.

The one problem with summer visitors that Sari and Vance mention is the people who rent a cottage for a few days and bring their cars. "We wanted the ferry for building materials and so on, and when they use it like that, it takes away from locals who want to bring stuff across." The small state ferry only runs four times a month in summer, and it's sometimes hard to get a space. And it's not as if Matinicus is so large that a car is needed to get around.

Matinicus and lobstering are synonymous. The few nonlobstering people know that the island depends on the crustacean. It's not likely to become a community of retirees—if lobstering fails, it's hard to imagine a year-round community remaining there.

Summer People

Since the end of the nineteenth century, summer has brought vacationers to all Maine's islands, in huge numbers or small. Whether they're welcomed or not, which, for the most part, they are, at least begrudgingly, their contributions to island coffers are significant. Maybe best known are the owners of the immense "cottages" of the super-rich in Islesboro's Dark Harbor (and on some other islands), with ten or twenty bedrooms plus servants' quarters. Many other vacationers have far more modest properties, some simple traditional houses on the main roads, and others farther off the beaten track.

The only land-side access for one tiny summer home, for example, is a small path that wanders three hundred yards through the woods to a long private road leading to the town road. At first glance, it's hard to imagine how the house was built in this remote spot, but the property includes the site of an old quarry and has a pier where a century ago schooners were loaded with granite paving stones bound for Philadelphia and New York. The ledges on either side of the approach still have heavy iron staples that the schoonermen used to kedge their vessels into the dock. Although in relatively recent years the owner has brought in electricity, the house is still served by an outhouse. This summer home is in one of the most comfortable and beautiful settings on the face of the earth—looking out across rocky ledges, small islands and bigger ones, and the mainland hills beyond. When the lobsters are crawling in close the passage is nearly filled with buoys of all colors of the neon rainbow, a striking sight but a hazard for any approaching vessel.

The appeal to "rusticators," as the summer residents were titled in the late nineteenth century, is obvious, but there's no doubt that their arrival changed life on each of the islands, one way or another. Construction and caretaking—along with shopkeeping and other services needed in any self-contained community—have provided

A remote summer house . . .

. . . and its view

work opportunities on some islands that had lost their earlier economic viability from farming, quarrying, groundfishing, boatbuilding, and shipping.

As mentioned earlier, there has always been a distinction between people from Here and people from Away, but relations between islanders and summer people have varied over the years from one island to another. Also, there's a clear distinction between summer people—who own island houses and to one degree or another become part of island life—and people who only rent cottages a week or two at a time. Some of the latter, however, come back year after year and almost cross the line into being summer people. Others are essentially day-trippers on an extended visit. With some exceptions (most notably Monhegan), day-tripping tourists are rare on most of the islands, and they're not appreciated by many islanders. While they do bring money, day-trippers find that the islands offer few places for them to spend it. Bicycle tours—or even just individual bicyclists—sometimes are attracted by the relatively quiet island roads, but islanders and summer people alike are annoyed by cyclists who take up much of a narrow-laned roadway. Many islands actively discourage day-trippers, knowing that neither their expectations nor even their needs will be met on-island. Even Monhegan has relatively few amenities for the masses of visitors who arrive there each day. The owners of the only restrooms available to the public request a dollar donation to offset the costs of keeping up the facility.

Matinicus people have always had—and deserved—a reputation for independence, which carries over into their relations with summer people. Harold and Rena Bunker, who left the island themselves in the mid-1960s, were open about their feelings. "We didn't like the summer people. We wouldn't pay any attention to them or answer their questions or anything," said Rena a few years back.

Harold spoke of going squidding in the early evening. "You learn how to haul the squid up outside of you, because they squirt that ink. Used to take summer people and not tell 'em and they'd pull 'em up and get a face full."

Vance, Harold and Rena's younger son, says that there is still a segment of the Matinicus community that couldn't care less if the summer people ever came out there. "There's a small few who don't get along with anybody and don't want them. But we don't have the kind of summer people they have on the other islands, where there are hundreds of them going back and forth. They have people who say, 'You're just dumb fishermen.' That's not the way you do things. Most of ours have had property here in their families as long as I can remember, and they want their property to stay just as it is. Most of us get along fine with them, and we do anything we can for them. Most of them keep their property nice and do what they can for island projects."

Many of the kids on Matinicus mix with the summer kids—even if their parents aren't crazy about the intermingling. The island's teenage boys are more interested in the fresh meat the summer girls represent than in what their parents think. And younger kids are happy just to have more playmates.

On North Haven, there has been a dependence upon summer people for generations. It used to be a feudal caste system, says Chellie Pingree. In the 1920s and 1930s, island parents instructed their children to stay clear of the summer children. "The summer people felt that way too," says Erma Peters, who grew up on the island. "It could only cause problems; it was two different cultures." Erma says that some islanders had married people with money, and it didn't work.

It's certainly different on North Haven now, as on many other islands. Kids hang out with each other all summer. Even though the summer residents of some islands are likely to be immensely wealthy CEOs of enormous corporations who love the beauty and the yachting lifestyle, they typically aren't pretentious. They are hugely generous to the school and other community projects, but they might have holes in their sneakers. "They court their caretakers' wisdom, too," says Chellie. "They want an islander to come to their cocktail party. It's reverse snobbery, but a lot of respect has evolved over the years. Summer people want to be liked by islanders." It's not always quite egalitarian, though. Islanders dress up to go to work for the summer people, even if it's just in khakis.

On many islands, however, the majority of summer people are just regular folks whose houses are no different from those of the islanders around them. It's not unusual to hear of a marriage between a native and a summer person now—sometimes after the summer person works a spell as sternman and ends up married to her captain.

"There's less of a complete contrast with summer people than there used to be," says landscape gardener Sue Hatch of Islesboro, whose childhood on the island was in the 1960s, "but I still struggle with a chip on my shoulder. I grew up in that, and I don't know how it manifests itself till it appears. 'You may go now.' It still happens—not to me, and less than it used to. But it's hard to have a friendship with someone you work for." She says she manages to a certain extent with a couple of her clients—"sort of. But it's harder to be friends with them than for my crew to be with me."

On our fictitious Smith Island, one summer person–dependent business has taken away most of the customers from a similar company on the island. The proprietor of the successful one ponders the phenomenon. "It's a mystery to me what's so tough about being nice," he says. "All of us have mixed emotions about being run over by summer people, but they're how we make a living."

In Casco Bay, the distinction is perhaps smaller than on any of the islands to the eastward. For one thing, transportation is so easy that it's hard to define who lives on the island how much of the time—people have homes in the Greater Portland area as well as on one of the islands, and they run back and forth more than is possible farther east. Commuting to work is easier in Casco Bay, and cross-pollination comes from that contact.

On Cliff Island, Bob Howard is a former summer person who not only has lived his whole adult life on the island and married a native, he has become an important member of the community. One of two building contractors on the island, he has chaired the Cliff Island Association, which acts as the connection between the city of Portland (of which Cliff Island is a part) and the islanders. "He's the quintessential," says his stepdaughter, Stephanie Howard-O'Reilly. "Everyone calls him in an emergency. There's not a person who'd say a bad thing about him, except my mother and my grandfather." (That's just marriage, and not to be taken seriously.)

He shrugs off his role. "Most people seem to like me—I don't cause trouble." But the Cliff Island Association itself shows the island attitude toward summer people today. Anyone may join, and any paid-up member present at a meeting may vote. Certainly there are summer people on Cliff who are looked upon with more favor than others. Families who come and put $250,000 into a big house are appreciated—the construction work being the livelihood for a number of people—but those who also join in and contribute to island projects are accepted, while those who don't are not.

There are always concerns that divide island communities, and inevitably there are times when the division line comes between summer people and year-rounders. Deer have caused such a rift on Cliff Island—there are a lot of deer. "Some want them shot—others don't want anything done. It's a major political battle," explains Stephanie. "You can't have a garden—no way. There are few coniferous trees left, or ferns. And they tested ticks and found 11 percent of them carried Lyme disease. Summer people don't want the population thinned." They enjoy seeing the animals and don't like interfering with the natural ways. "Sure—they don't have to deal with them all year."

Deer have been an issue on a number of islands, often with the same division of opinion about what should be done. An anonymous poster to one online island bulletin board articulated the islanders' usual point of view about deer—first mentioning the health hazard caused by deer ticks and then speaking of the hazard they cause on the road. The writer continued: "Rats with hooves is what they are. I for one would turn a blind eye to anyone shooting a deer anywhere on the island except maybe if it was having communion in the up-island church."

"It can get kinda nasty. Like the deer issue, things got kinda out of hand, things were said that shouldn't have been," Bob says. "But if people say things, I don't worry too much about it. I think in the end, people will get back together. We all have to live on this rock, and we probably won't have to shoot each other.

"And always, if anybody needs anything, then everything's forgotten." This goes for summer people as well as islanders.

That many of the islands depend on their summer people economically is a fact, however well liked. And in many cases, it's liked just fine. "Sure, you grumble about

The Charles Dana Gibson cottage, Seven Hundred Acre Island, off Islesboro

them," says Brenda Craig of Islesboro, where summer residents are said to triple the population on the island, though no one has actually figured it out. "They take up space in the store or crowd you off the ferry, but that's harmless. We need them, and they need us. Frankly, I think we kind of miss each other in the winter."

And, says David Bunker of Great Cranberry Island, "It's a comfort, not having to wonder what to do if we need this or that. Doesn't matter what it is—library, historical society, CIRT [the affordable housing project in the Cranberries], the fire department, whatever—the summer people come forth generously. They employ people, too—caretakers, gardeners, boat captains for those well-enough off to have a boat and want someone to run it. There's a lot of income from all that. It'd be very different without them."

On the other hand, sometimes it can be difficult to take the attitude of the occasional summer person. It might not even be disrespect for a particular islander providing a service so much as a lack of awareness of what would seem to be obvious facts of local life. A celebrity with a summer residence on Smith Island wanted a ride ashore to a gym at two o'clock every morning—the privacy of the middle of the night is understandably attractive to someone trying to avoid constant recognition. For the fellow driving the boat, though, it was impossible to live a normal life and make that nightly run. He kept raising his rates, and the passenger just kept paying, no questions asked. Money isn't an issue for some. Rumor has it he paid five hundred dollars a trip at the end, but finally the owner of the boat said "No more."

The other extreme is Frenchboro, which, perhaps because it has little land available and infrequent ferry service, has a smaller number of summer residents than the other islands. There might be a couple of dozen all told. Only two or three are said to be truly wealthy, and their presence is negligible. They don't spend much time on the island and they're less involved with the island's concerns and projects than are people on some of the other islands. They hire locals to care for their property, and that's about the extent of it. The others who come to Frenchboro in the summer are very likely to have ancestral connections to the island. "We don't feel overwhelmed," says Donna Hasal, herself now a summer person. Though she grew up on the island, she spent many years away. "Our people come and go, and there's not a big influx. Plus they're helpful. They're very generous with their time—they volunteer at the museum and at the library. They're a big asset. Everyone is glad to see them coming." Interestingly, a rather large percentage of the handful of people who have summered on Frenchboro seem to end up living there year-round.

Robert Young of Vinalhaven speaks in the same way as many islanders about summer people and tourists: "Some of them have a lot of money and think they deserve special treatment, but most are nice even if they have money." But then he continues: "When we go to the Caribbean in the winter, we're tourists and we ask stupid questions just like they do."

One Smith Islander was amused when she and her husband were invited to the island B&B for supper. There were guests there too—overnight visitors, not summer people. "When they learned we were fishermen, they asked all kinds of questions. I told my husband, 'I think we're the entertainment!'"

Islesboro's Changing Class System

Islesboro, like each of the other islands, is unique, but the ways that its social structure has changed over the years is probably not entirely unlike that of other islands, particularly those with wealthy summer visitors. On many, population numbers peaked in the middle of the nineteenth century; more recently, a few of the islands, including Islesboro, have seen increases again. Natives, summer people, members of the 1960s counterculture, and retirees—all have influenced many of the Maine islands.

"We were fortunate, out in the world," says a retiree who has fairly recently moved to Islesboro. She and her husband retired while in their mid-forties and accidentally ended up on the island—a place where, if you intend to make a new home, frankly, nowadays it's as well to have been fortunate somewhere else. But the island, in the past a clearly stratified society, has changed tremendously in the last decade or two. Where there used to be two main castes—the natives and the Dark Harbor summer people, with a less-striking subset or two—now there is a third group, people she describes as "middle-class people like me," retired people from somewhere else. That they have a more significant income than many middle-class folk is irrelevant, at least to them.

Islesboro's year-round population peaked at 1,276 immediately before the Civil War and bottomed out 110 years later at 421. The numbers have been rising again since 1970; first a group of back-to-the-landers came to the island, and then the retirees came along. The 2000 census showed 603 permanent residents.

In comparison to the summer people, the natives have been seen as one group, although of course there have always been economic and social differences among them, too. Lydia Rolerson, born in 1919, recalls her childhood living on the northern end of the island. She was one of ten children abandoned by their father before the last was born; they were "on the town," supported at least in part by tax money. At the time, there were four schoolhouses scattered around the fourteen-mile-long island and no cars; Lydia and her siblings walked three miles to the Ryders School rather than go to Pripet, where they were ignored by the children of families who looked down on them for needing financial assistance. Even when they walked down-island to the high school, she says, "Those that had a horse and buggy would never pick you up. Many's the morning in winter that my legs were purple with cold when I got to school."

Two neighbors treated the family awfully well, Lydia says. When her sister had polio and they were quarantined, one neighbor would make a big meal for them and set it out on the road, and they'd go and pick it up. At that time, the island consisted of neighborhoods, whereas now, with the exception of a couple of summer enclaves, it is all one physical community.

For more than a hundred years, the summers have brought a great influx of people. There are two original summer colonies—Dark Harbor with its huge "cottages" on the southern end, and the less splashy, slightly older cluster of houses at Ryders Cove, up-island—but now summer people are found all over the island with immense houses or smaller ones.

During the first decades of the twentieth century, people with unimaginable amounts of money built the original Dark Harbor cottages. These were the summer homes for successive generations of families from Philadelphia, New York, and elsewhere. The names of their mid-century owners would fill any "Who's Who" list: investment banker C. Douglas Dillon, high up in the Eisenhower administration before being appointed secretary of the treasury by Kennedy; Winthrop W. Aldrich of Chase National Bank and ambassador to England; internationally known yacht designer Clinton Crane; department-store magnate Marshall Field, to mention a few.

Their visitors, too, have been men and women of importance. One summer, Adlai Stevenson was visiting Mrs. Field. Willis Rossiter took care of her boats and sailed as crew for her in the semiweekly Twenty-footer races. He knew every rock and ledge in the racing grounds, but somehow, the day that Stevenson was aboard, Mrs. Field's boat hit bottom. No damage was done, but someone asked Willis later in the day how that could possibly have happened. "Got sick and tired of them damn Democrats,"said Willis.

That the summer experience was significant for many of the summer children of the middle of the last century is evident from the number of them who have since made their homes on the Maine coast, if not on the island itself.

But there was always a feeling among many of these summer people that they enjoyed—and felt was their due—the superior position they held compared to their dependents, as most of the islanders had become. (Unlike most of the other islands, Islesboro does not support a true fishery any longer. It's a short season for lobsters up in the bay; most lobstermen fish as a sideline to their other jobs in trades or service.) The big-house rusticators did not look upon the native caretakers, kitchen help, and providers of various services as equals. You might like the fellow who brought you lobster, but you'd never invite him to dinner. Cocktail parties and dinners and tennis games and golf and sailing have always been the rituals of the Dark Harbor summer life.

It must be said, too, that the islanders knew that the summer people, however rich and famous, were not any better than they were. In fact, they felt there was no one any better than—or perhaps even as good as—an islander. Lydia, a quiet-spoken and respectful person who obviously likes people in general, remembers the end of one summer years ago. Her employer, preparing for the trip back to her winter home, wanted Lydia to come early on her last day of the season. But Lydia knew that everything was all packed and the woman had plenty of time for her breakfast before the first ferry, which departed in those days at 8:30. Lydia came at seven as usual. Her employer wasn't happy. "When I want you here at a certain time," she said, "I expect you to be here. Things will be different next year!"

"You don't have money enough to hire me another year," Lydia told her. Today, she says, "They thought they owned you. Well, no one owns me!"

The old summer families did take seriously what they saw as their aristocratic responsibility to the island. They loved the place, and they donated large amounts of money to various island projects of which they approved. (Of course, the tax base they provide has given the island an extraordinarily low mill rate or high spending power, though no Mainer—possibly no human being—is likely to admit that his taxes are fair, let alone too low.) At the same time, legend has it that occasional summer people have said they don't want island education to improve much, for fear of losing their underclass of service people. I would like to believe this to be myth, and I feel fairly certain that if there ever was any such feeling, it's long gone.

An occasional retiree has been heard to say it wouldn't be bad if the school closed altogether and workers came on the island on the first ferry and left on the last. Perhaps they are being shortsighted, for most certainly they want to be able to call for medical help at two in the morning; they may want to enjoy coffee at the store, and not just during the hours when the ferry is running; and they probably don't want the expense of importing everyone to work in or on their houses nor to have to go off-island for car repair.

More recently, big houses have been changing hands, at so-many million dollars a pop, as old family fortunes have dissipated with new generations coming along, or people divorced or died off. The island has become the vacation home for some whose wealth and fame came from more visible endeavors, like Hollywood stars Kirstie Alley and John Travolta. "Celebrities come because they can be here and not be mobbed," says Bill Boardman. It's not likely that any visitor to the island would be shown where their houses are, and on the street, they'd not be treated any differently than anyone else. No one is.

After many decades without new construction of big houses, starting in the 1990s, there was an explosion of huge cottages being built all over the shoreline. It continues today. Not all the owners of these new houses are being accepted into the traditional (one could say "snobby") Dark Harbor clubs and social circles, though some are.

But it's the year-round community that has seen the most changes. There's now a large population of transplants, an increasing proportion of whom are retired and some of whom are also building big houses. A surprising number of them are, like one woman with whom I spoke, geeks retired from the high-tech world of the West Coast. They are educated and well heeled, and whether or not they have past connections to the island, they have respect for it. They can mix with either of the original groups, the natives or the summer people, though they may not feel entirely welcome in either camp. Perhaps they have changed the balance on the island, taking away from the power to which the Dark Harborites have been accustomed.

People who might describe themselves as "former hippies" are now a significant subgroup on the island. Now in their forties and fifties, most of them are transplants, though a few are natives; their marriages and close relationships cross the boundaries. Some may still wear their hair long, but their children are in the school now, and they are active in town affairs. They're mainstream. "They're fat and old and comfortable, now," I was told.

Native islander Don Pendleton, who approaches seventy, says that the class system on the island had already started softening even before the recent influx of retirees. For the change, he credits the historical society, which attracted both summer and local people, and then the library, the Islesboro Islands Trust, a couple of good restaurants, and finally the Island Pub, which was open for several years in the late 1960s and early 1970s. Each brought natives and summer people together. All these things happened right in a row, he said, breaking down the divisions.

"Then came a big transition," he says. "There were no more servants." For the first seventy years of the Dark Harbor summer colony's existence, the big houses were staffed by Irish or other (mostly immigrant) servants who came to Islesboro for the summer with their employers. But then it became much more difficult to find live-in help—especially people who were willing to pack up everything and go to a Maine island for the summer. "They had to hire locals. That did wonders," says Don.

The jobs offered in the big houses now are good jobs. Islanders can work for the summer people and make more than they could elsewhere in the area using the education many of them have. Housecleaning pays twenty or thirty dollars an hour. And few summer people treat islanders like indentured servants, the way some of their predecessors did. "They can't get away with that!" says Don. "There's too much Yankee here."

Relationships do grow between employers and employees, even if they don't attend the same parties. Some islanders are invited to visit their employers in their winter residences, and their young children do play together.

It would not be surprising if before long the island were to become primarily a retirement community—the summer colony having shrunk and younger island people having had an ever-harder time finding housing. It's questionable whether there will remain significant numbers of people who grew up on the island—let alone those with multigenerational native ancestry—even though there are economic opportunities on the island for young people with the right training. "We're short on plumbers, electricians, landscapers," says Don. I was told by one island resident that the state technical colleges are not seen as worthy schools for Islesboro's high-school graduates. "They're afraid that people won't think theirs is the best high school," she said. Don also feels that the young people of the island are not being encouraged to enter these trades. But most of the young people look ashore for their futures. Most graduates of the high school head off to higher education or the military and at least postpone the decision about where to work, but few plan to come back. Little prideful crowing was heard over the one boy in a recent year who chose to stay on the island to work in a trade with his father. Those who do want to return after college, like one of Lydia's grandsons, find it very difficult because of housing costs.

The retirees are very active both politically and financially, says one of them, Marny Heinen. She worries, though. "We have to watch out for the presumptuousness that we know what's good for the people here." Perhaps, in her admirable respect for the natives, she forgets that now she and her sort are also residents of the island—people who love it as much as the lifelong islanders do. She herself is more comfortable on the island than she has been in any other place she's lived. "We've never stayed any-where more than three years," she says of her husband and herself. "That we've been here seven years already says something."

It's Marny's belief that people do well living in groups of five hundred or so. "It's big enough so you don't know everyone—it surprises me still to run into people I don't know—yet small enough that you care about everyone." You do recognize almost every-one, she says; you have day-to-day dealings with half of them, and you like most of those people. Yet you're far enough apart that you're not on each other's nerves.

"In the World, you see people in just one dimension," she says. Insurance Man, Schoolteacher, Auto Mechanic. All you know about the bad driver on the freeway is that he cut you off, but on the island, you know a person even if he makes you angry. He's your neighbor. He might also be running the snack shack, or plowing the roads in win-ter—and whatever else he's doing, you know about it. As an example (though not one she's been angry at), she mentions a fellow who runs a service station, is a good welder, sets moorings, takes his tiny dog lobstering with him, works on boats, and doesn't like any dessert that started out as a vegetable. "You see someone as a whole person," Marny says, "which makes you kinder. You can't be angry at a whole person."

The one social distinction that does still remain divisive on the island—and that only sometimes and from some people—is what might be called Nativism. The major intercultural tension on Islesboro, I'm told, is between natives and transplants, no longer between year-rounders and summer people. Some of the native-born-and-bred islanders, particularly those who have never spent time off the island, look down on any-one without their island connection. And from some of the transplants, there's a reac-tive response: "You don't see natives stepping up to the board of selectmen or the plan-ning board. They just sit there and grumble." (To be fair, at this writing, Islesboro's five-member board of selectmen happens to include three natives and two transplants.)

But all the year-rounders cross paths all the time, and amity grows between trans-plants and natives. "Retirees make good friends," says Don Pendleton. Brenda Craig, the editor of the island newspaper and a transplant, says that her close friends are divided between natives and transplants in about the same proportion as the current year-round population.

While perhaps there aren't many truly intimate friendships between summer people and year-rounders—one well-educated transplant notes that she doesn't have the money they do, and (therefore, she implies) has little in common with them—at least there is now mutual respect, and the symbiotic relationships between islanders and seasonal visitors are recognized and enjoyed.

Beyond Lobstering:
Making a Living

While lobstering is the primary means of support of most families on the majority of Maine's islands, there are, necessarily, other ways to make a living. Certainly the second industry on most islands is that of support to summer residents: building, fixing, cleaning, and caretaking of their houses; landscaping and gardening; and maintaining and sometimes running their boats. Though other islands have a small number of visitors who come for a few hours on the mail or tour boats, and there are a few bed-and-breakfasts here and there, Monhegan alone has a truly significant day-tripper and short-visit business. For the most part, it is not tourists but summer residents who provide the most nonfishing employment on the islands. "It's a service-oriented island," says Bill Boardman of Islesboro. "It's all or nothing. It's not unique to Islesboro, but there's so much focus on the June-to-September work schedule. The thing we do in summer is work"—with scant time for play. They're not all in typical bottom-end jobs, however. "Here we have people doing summer yard work and caretaker jobs and then spending the winter in the Cayman Islands."

It's not uncommon that well-educated women clean summer houses in the spring and continue working as housekeepers and cooks throughout the owners' stay. "They want staff and they demand a lot from them," says Bonnie Mowery-Oldham, who used to work in that capacity. "Things are tight—there's enough demand for cleaning, and you get paid well. And they're desperate for cooking help. They're paying retainers now through winter so people will stay. In the past, that was unheard-of except for caretakers."

There are other businesses, quirky and otherwise. The traditional island way is to do a little of this and a little of that. A woman on Swans Island, for instance, runs a small take-out restaurant in summer, but when school opens, she works for the school as bus driver, secretary, and teacher's aide.

Peter Gasperini
Jack-of-All-Trades, Vinalhaven

"It's very easy to be self-employed," says Peter Gasperini of Vinalhaven. "I can go in a hundred directions every day." He says there's always something to do, and he likes the variety. "I almost need a calendar."

Peter first came to Vinalhaven some twenty-odd years ago on an offshore fishing boat. He came back to stay, and he still looks to the sea for much of his support. Every good day between November and April sees him diving for scallops or urchins. "I'd like to think I have a wonderful lifestyle. Under water, I have a lot of time to think." (Thinking has its pluses and minuses. The Iraq war was fairly new when we talked. "If you actually think about everything going on, how can a normal person not be depressed? You have to balance the good day-to-day life with the other stuff and hopefully it tips a little bit to the positive.") He describes late-winter diving: "It's easy pickings, though it takes a lot of courage to get out some days." He says an old Vinalhaven lobsterman told him diving is like a vegetable garden—"You go in with a little carry-basket, pick up what's ripe, and don't disturb anything else. Go back later for more." Peter loves the fact that diving is a low-impact pursuit—the proof being that he's been doing it in the very same places for more than twenty years. But it's not always entirely pleasurable. "Last Thursday I was doing urchins on the southern end of a hurricane in bumpy seas—underwater it was pretty, but it was hard on the guy running the boat, and I was getting queasy on board in between tanks."

The best reward is finding old objects on the bottom. "I can be having a great day scalloping, but if I find something, it's like, Yahoo!" He has discovered all manner of things, including a big rudder fitting he found while he was urchin diving from Beals Island. Peter showed it to Beals Island boatbuilder Calvin Beal: "He ran his hands all over it like a grandfather with a newborn granddaughter." Calvin reminisced about working with his father and grandfather, repairing coastal schooners. Rudders went all the time. Calvin told Peter the gudgeon was actually small—though not when compared to a similar fitting on a normal sailing yacht today.

Peter used to have a bike repair shop and still does a little of that work, and he caretakes for a dozen summer places, three of which have no access by car. "Floats, boats, water systems, house maintenance. A month before they come, I get my first two or three floats out." From the middle of April through September, Peter stays busy with his diving business: freeing propellers tangled in fishing gear, and building, delivering, repairing, and inspecting moorings. He does about 250 inspections on North Haven (where there are more pleasure boats) and about a hundred on Vinalhaven. "The lobstermen think they can take care of their own better."

He also fills in as sternman for a couple of lobstermen, one of whom is an older fellow. "He has no radar—he has a computer on the boat but never turns it on. Everything's in his mind."

From outboard boats, Peter's two teenage sons have fished for lobster with student licenses for ten years. "They love it," he says. "Well, the older one loves the money. The younger son is into it. He leaves house at 5:30 in the morning and bikes three miles to spend more time on the boat. Some weeks, working three partial days, he makes more money than I do. He sets ninety traps and brings home $450 after he has paid a friend. He's got an IRA and a Roth IRA and a fat bank account. When I was his age, I was helping in Gramp's grocery store for ten dollars a day and all the candy I could eat."

Recently, a Vinalhaven eighth-grader bought a twenty-eight-foot lobsterboat with cash he had earned fishing.

"I live by the tide chart," says Peter. "Fifty percent of Vinalhaven people do." In the spring, everyone is loading gear and setting out. "The boatyards are abuzz now—you gotta know when the big tides are."

On Vinalhaven, everything is hustle now, Peter says. No longer is it the laid-back place it used to be. "Here anyone who wants a job has one—every direction you turn, something is happening. We almost need a stoplight downtown." The local builders are all booked up well in advance, and many construction people are commuting from the mainland. There are a couple of electricians on the island and six or seven plumbers, and they're all busy. The motel is very active in the spring, when workmen are staying there during the week. There's a lobster-freezing plant that works seasonally. Quality houses sell by word of mouth, and everything rentable gets rented. There are five bed-and-breakfasts open in summer. Vinalhaven is hopping.

"It costs 30 percent more to live out here," Peter says, "with transportation, freight, fuel, and so forth. But you make 50 percent more than on the mainland, and you have 50 percent less opportunity to spend it."

Peter has been told that in a heartbeat he could get a quarter of a million dollars for his inland house and seven acres—property in which he says he has perhaps fifty thousand invested. "I'm possessions-rich, land-rich, but where you gonna go? You can't replace it." He loves the island. He has good friends there—"not the kind you check in with every day, but if they don't see you, they'll call or come visit. You know that any time of day you could call any of those people and you got help, and they know the reverse is true. Doesn't matter what it is—could be something illegal. Unsaid, you got help."

Vinalhaven has a great community of organic gardeners, Peter says, "living clean and healthy"—although, like him, they're mostly transplants who came for the simplicity. "It's easy to be simple when you're pulling in two thousand bucks a week." He notes that there's a lot of resentment toward "blatant trust-fund babies who put up a front of making money." Some of those are on the island year-round.

But all in all, for Peter, Vinalhaven is a wonderful place to live. "That's why I'm here. You consider the inconveniences, what other people would consider terrible drawbacks . . . ." He shrugs. "My house is a sanctuary, warm in the woods; I have a beautiful workshop. I have my own niche. That's what it takes. It's fun. You never get tired of doing the same thing. Someone asks, 'What are you doing next Wednesday?' I haven't a clue. That's the beauty of it—there's no structure. Also no guarantee of income, but everything works out."

Sue Hatch
Landscape Gardener, Islesboro

Sue Hatch has been landscaping and gardening on Islesboro for more than twenty-five years. "It's hard work and the responsibility is huge, managing everything. Deadlines, arrivals, garden tours, and all subject to the weather. I wish it weren't all so much at once—May and June are tense, ninety-to-nothing." Sue does all the bookkeeping, management, design, and accounting, but recently she has hired a payroll service. "I don't know why I didn't do it sooner."

Sue Hatch

Sue has plenty to do without worrying about payroll. She caretakes for four families (five houses), as well as doing the gardening work for about thirty people all over the island. The occasional special project finds her building fences and stone stairs and walkways, as well as planting and caring for trees. "We were all women, but lately there have been one or two guys, even three or four. It's hard for them to work with the women—they have to be nonmacho types, willing to work in a team. When I pick employees badly—not often—it's usually people who don't fit in the group, not that they can't do the work."

Sue is lucky that she's found enough help. "I treat them well," she says, "maybe too well. I pay them as well as I can, and I know they have another life. I get a lot of returning people, and I don't have a reputation for being hard to work for." Only once did she have to advertise. She hired a woman from the University of Maine who worked for her for three years—she rented a room at first, then found a boyfriend on-island.

Finding a place to live is a huge problem on Islesboro, as on most of the islands. "Property is so valuable that an ordinary house is more than an ordinary person can afford." Sue knows she was lucky that her parents had land, and she now lives in a house that once was her father's vegetable stand. "It's harder for people with less to begin with—it's a lot tougher for kids who didn't get given much." But things are different from the way they used to be. "People aren't as poor as they were—not us, because we always had food, but for some people, it was minimal. And the generation before was really minimal." Sue has described the days of her childhood as being a time "when short lobsters, deer meat, and the largesse of the store owners were what fed many families through the winter." Now, she says, there's always work if you want it. Maybe things are too good. "People are handed occupations without knowing what's elsewhere. We're paid more here than on the mainland for the same work."

The season is eight months long and starts on April first, although it takes Sue all winter to plan for the next season. She's designing gardens and landscaping and ordering plants and scrounging in catalogs for things she'll need come summer. As spring moves along, members of her crew—six at the start, a dozen or so later on—show up to help as they're available and as they're needed. When school's out, her sons work with her now; other helpers have been with her for many years. The main core of the team is made up of people from the island, but not natives, she says.

Most of the kids on the island today are leaving, according to Sue. Many go to college and don't return; some try college, can't make the transition, and come back. Sue herself did all those things.

Her parents sent Sue and her sisters to boarding school. She had no wish to go, "but it was the best thing our mother did for us," she says. In her 1970 class on Islesboro, there was only one student, a girl who graduated and got married on the same day. No, it didn't last, and she's not on the island anymore. Sue went on to the University of Colorado, and although she loved the mountains, it wasn't a good fit for her. "It was the first time I'd ever been entirely anonymous. I was a little distressed realizing nobody gave a damn." She was surprised and hurt that things were stolen from her in the dorm. "It doesn't happen here on the island, hardly ever. Nothing significant." She returned home broke, looking and acting like a hippie, upsetting her parents. She wanted to go to art school, but her parents wouldn't hear of it. So she enrolled in the first class at the College of the Atlantic in Bar Harbor and became their first dropout. The school was all science then, and she says she's not a scientist.

The next few years, she roamed around—from Connecticut to West Virginia and finally to Alaska for three years. She took classes at the University of Alaska but never got a degree. "I haven't needed one. Sometimes I think I should, but why?" She answers her own question. "If someday I wanted to stop doing this, I haven't any other choices. I promote education because it gives choices." Her husband, Tom Tutor, started teaching when he was forty—he already had the degree and only had to update his certification after twenty years as a furniture maker, boatbuilder, and computer programmer.

Sue's father, too, because he already had his degree, was able to start teaching when he was in his fifties. Like many islanders, Henry Hatch did all kinds of things to support his family. "You have to, and even more so, then." He sold insurance, was a surveyor, did some building, landscaping, gardening, caretaking. He ran the vegetable stand for a few years. Sue always loved flowers, and she helped her father in gardens even when she was in grade school. When she came back to Islesboro in 1978, her father turned over to her a couple of his caretaking jobs. Then she got another job at a new house, where she met Tom. He came and went for a few years, but now they are married and he teaches math at the Islesboro School. Over nine years, they had three children. The oldest is now at Bennington College and loving it. "Having kids is the hardest and best thing I ever did. I wanted the age spread—I had to keep working. With kids close together, there's no way you can work."

And working is only part of what Sue does—she's not one to be idle. She's on the board of the Islesboro Islands Trust, which she describes as being interested in the whole ecology—including humans, not simply preserving land and animals. She's concerned about the effects of development—not just on schools but also on the ferry service, the water table, the fire and medical services. She feels the island is nearly maxed out, but development continues.

Foy Brown's Boatshop
North Haven

Making a living on an island often is more than just bringing home money. Sometimes the livelihood is also part of the structure of the island. That's the case with Foy Brown's boatyard on North Haven.

"You'll know my yard 'cause it looks like it just came out of *Cosmopolitan*," Foy told me on the telephone. We certainly had no trouble finding it, located just east of the ferry landing and marked with a big sign, J. O. Brown. The sign informs passersby on the water side that the boat business was founded in 1888. J. O. was Foy's great-grandfather. Foy himself was named for his grandfather, but he has no idea where the unusual name originated.

We came alongside Foy's boat, *Centerfold*, as he'd suggested on the phone. As we tied up, not particularly gracefully, none of the several people coming and going on the dock showed any interest in us. We walked up the dock and into the shop, where one man was on the phone, an older fellow was sanding a little spar, and a roundish middle-aged guy was sitting in a chair observing; we later learned he was named Dale. No one acknowledged us for a time. Looking around, we saw evidence of current projects (a brand-new North Haven dinghy, ready to launch, for one), older ones (an old wooden sailboat being used partly as storage for miscellany), and representations of older interests and jobs (two models: one of the distinctive Brown lobsterboat hull, with its high-sheer bow, and one, in a glass case, of a six-foot-long four-masted schooner under full sail). Of course, there were the usual tools and signs about their usage and general boat-

Foy Brown

shop clutter. Posted in the dark under a shelf was a required notice about workers' comp. A very old-looking, overweight Labrador retriever lay on the floor—motionless but noticing everything going on.

The fellow sanding the spar stopped, turned as if he had just noticed us, and asked if he could help us. "I'm looking for Foy," I said. The two men gestured at the fellow on the phone, a tall man I'd guess to be in his fifties or maybe sixty. "OK," I said. The older man walked away.

When Foy hung up the phone, we introduced ourselves, and I told him about my project. "I can tell you everything I know in just a few minutes," he said in his slow, careful manner of speaking that is deceptive—taking notes is harder than one would expect, as every word is worth recording. I often throw out a random kind of question just to get someone started, so I asked him if there weren't disadvantages to running a shop on an island.

He didn't have a chance to answer, as a fellow came into the shop. "When I grab onto my wheel, I get a hell of a shock," the fellow told Foy.

"Well, don't grab onto it," said the man sitting down.

"It's kinda hard to steer without it," the guy replied. "I grab on with two hands, I get a hell of a jolt right across me."

"You need that, don't you?" Foy asked. "Defibrillate you?" He asked Dale to check it out and then turned to my question. "Sure, there are disadvantages. You can't run to the parts store—lots of times you've got to improvise. You want to put in a thing, and you've got to do something else to get to the same place. You plan ahead to get your stuff. And lots of times you just have to go and get it. Sometimes you can get someone who's going on the ferry to go into Hamilton's [a marine supply store, in Rockland] for you."

We talked a bit about how the business has changed since he's been in it—every year, a few new boats to take care of, more outboards. "And they can't seem to keep 'em running more than a few minutes," Foy said. More floats and more docks. A lot of building going on all over the island, and taxes going up all the time, mostly because of state and federal mandates, Foy believes. "I tell you, if they're gonna keep mandating stuff, they're gonna mandate us right outa business. Dump, sewer, school. We've got a good school, and the kids like to go to school, but there're almost as many teachers as kids, and most of it 'cause the state says you gotta supply this or that."

The phone rings. Foy answers it. "You're who?" "Is that right." "Well, whaddya think I'm gonna do with that?" "You'd better not talk to me about it, 'cause me and computers and credit cards don't get along—and cell phones either." "Probably before I get to swearin' we ought to end this conversation," he said, and hung up.

Some say that business this summer was down, but Foy didn't notice it. "We were putting boats overboard same's usual. The people who come here were coming here. Now there's boats all over." A lot of big yachts pass through the Fox Islands Thorofare between North Haven and Vinalhaven, "not that they do anything for us—they got all they want already. 'Course this is Route One, you know."

Foy's son, also Foy, is the fifth generation in the shop. (His boat is named *Fifth Generation*, Foy tells us with obvious pleasure.) J. O. started the yard when the summer people, already coming to the island in the 1880s, wanted boats to sail. "And there was a lot of market boats to get over here—it's a lot shorter by water than going around to Vinalhaven Town with a horse and buggy." In the 1920s and 1930s, there were twenty guys working at the yard, building boats. Now there might be a little more than a half-dozen most of the time, nearly all family members. Foy, his brother, his son, two nephews. "Father's here, too, sometimes helping, sometimes hindering." A cousin is there all summer answering the phone, and so on.

Often in the winter there's a big project—building a boat, or fixing one. Last year it was the classic Beals Island boat, the Harold Gower–built lobsterboat *Tidewalker* from the mid-1960s. "It was fun to have something to work with other than fiberglass," Foy said.

A summer-looking man in shorts and a polo shirt came up and stood quietly, waiting to talk to Foy. "You can break in here a minute," Foy told him.

He wanted his engine looked at. "It's not working very well."

It was a Yamaha 150. "That should work perfectly," Foy said.

"It always has, but lately it's been missing."

"Plugs been changed lately?"

"No, not so's I know."

Dale had come back from somewhere, and Foy sent him off to look at the Yamaha. Herb Parsons appeared. He too owns an old Harold Gower boat, the *Brimstone*. She's had episodes of black smoke, the possible causes of which Foy and he discussed. Herb hadn't been using the boat much, and not at all for three weeks. He fueled up back in June, more than two months ago. Foy suggested he check the filters. "That's what I'd do." But it might be something about the turbo. "That wouldn't be good."

How the business has changed since he's been in it is just that there's more of it, Foy said. In the 1960s, one person could tend the place. The crew would go home at four o'clock. There'd still be people coming in—he'd be out buying lobsters—they haven't done that for a while—and someone would want to pay for gas, but he could handle it. In 1973, they got the Travelift, allowing them to move boats easily. "We used to move them around with ropes and a winch and planks, and it would take all day. Now we have two hydraulic trailers, and two storage lots—one where we put forty or fifty small boats, and a yard above here with a hundred boats in it. There's a forty-by-seventy-five-foot metal building we're just getting ready to add onto, and a Quonset hut we put up last winter—Eric Hopkins had it as an airplane hangar, and we got it off him and bought more bows to make it longer. And there's another building here we got to store boats in, but we've been finishing off boats in it."

Dale came into the shop with a piece from the outboard. "The last time I did one of these I almost started drinking again," he told Foy. They talked about the problem for a bit, and Dale left again. A woman came along: "You going to haul tonight?"

"Yuh." As if Foy doesn't have enough to do at the shop, he also hauls two hundred lobster traps, which he says is more than he's ever had before, but he has a sternman, too, which he's also never done before. He goes out at five and comes back at dark.

"You back by 8:45 usually?" the woman asked.

"Yuh."

She asked him to pick up two kids "over across"—meaning on Vinalhaven, across the Thorofare.

"Yuh."

"You going to remember it?"

"Yuh, prob'ly."

Foy built a new boat for himself a few years back, but he'd like to sell her now. Her name is *Pa's Angels*. There's a *Pa's Angels* over on Swans Island, which he spotted on one of the family picnics they enjoy on Sundays. "This is my angel right here," he told the person in the other boat, pointing at his granddaughter.

"These are mine," the man said, gesturing toward two little girls beside him.

Pa's Angels is bigger, faster, and dryer than *Centerfold*, but she's a little too big for what he wants now. "She draws a good bit more water—she swings a thirty-two-inch wheel," Foy said, referring to her large propeller. With her, he has trouble getting into some of the little coves where he has to set moorings and floats.

A woman came in looking for four lobsters. "I don't see anyone else around, I'll grab 'em for you," he said. The dog got up when Foy left but came back with him and lay down again. After giving the woman a handful of lobsters, Foy sat down on a stepladder.

Foy told us that Dale's family was originally from North Haven, but they moved away when he was three years old. He'd been living over in western Maine somewhere. "He asked me for a job and I said OK."

It sounded like that had just happened. "How long ago was that?" I asked.

"Thirteen years," said Foy. He told of a night when he and Dale were out setting a float until midnight. But now that he has the boys in the shop, he doesn't have to do so much. Last winter, he had triple-bypass surgery: "It slowed me down for three weeks. After two and a half weeks, I was here till five, that's a short day for me, but once I got going, it was all right."

Foy's son, in his mid-thirties now, studied mechanics at Southern Maine Vocational Technical Institute after high school. They checked out the boatbuilding school at Eastport, "but I was afraid he'd get bored—most of it he'd already done. But I wish he'd done that—lofting and stuff, I don't know much about.

"Most of the stuff, he's learned right here. Something breaks, you've got to fix it. You call someone up and ask a few questions and a light bulb goes off in your head and you've fixed it. The stuff we do, the stuff we know, we've learned right here. You can't go next door and see how anyone else does it, and of course salesmen never come here showing you the latest—we're usually behind a few years, but we always get the job done."

Foy himself came to the shop from the time he was in diapers. "When I was in grade school, I'd come down and get a nickel, go up to Waterman's Store and buy a Milky Way—that's most prob'ly why I had to have a triple bypass—and then I'd come back and watch these guys. I'd be making something. When I was twelve or thirteen, I made my mother a birthday present, a footstool with a pull-out drawer, and it's still over to the house. And I'd be helping on boats. My son wasn't doing that so much when he was that age. But he's good. He's way fussier than I am."

Foy's daughter has a little boy and a little girl. "They're all right here, so I can visit 'em any time I want." His daughter's young ones went lobstering with him recently. "Payton was all excited, he's just a bundle of energy, jumping right up and down. He's a redhead, and isn't he fun!" Kennedy is seven. "She'll tend the store for me when she's bigger." He thinks Eliza, young Foy's daughter, will help in the shop too. He expects Payton to go carpentering with his father.

We talked about the occupations of islanders—only one full-time fisherman, he said, and he goes to Florida in the winter. Including sternmen, about forty altogether are at it part-time, like himself. They caretake and cut wood and do one thing and another in the winter. There are electricians and plumbers on the island—"they do a good job." Another employer is the Community Center in the old Waterman's Store building. "The Waterman Center, I don't know what they're doing, but it takes a lot of people to get all that lined up and situated and going," he said. This time of year, everyone's busy—mowing lawns, cooking and cleaning, gardening. A lot of carpenters come over from the mainland by private boat—two boats for one company, and another "has a girl from here hauling them around."

A man who looked like a summer person came in with a woman. "This lady needs a ride across to meet a cab to the ferry," he said. She had missed the North Haven ferry and could just make the last Vinalhaven boat if she hurried.

"Dick's out there," said Foy to Dale, who'd appeared again.

"No, he ain't."

"Well, you take her then." There was a discussion about who'd be paying, but Foy said, "Don't let her miss her taxi. We'll straighten that out later," and off they went.

"Is this place the center of everything?" I asked Foy.

"Pretty much," he said. "Sometimes I wonder what anyone wants to come to North Haven for. You get away from the shop, though, and things are a lot quieter. The other day I went out to Crabtree Point to work on a boat and it was all peaceful down there. Here, the phone's ringing off the wall, somebody wants something all the time. That's what I try to teach these kids—don't do just one thing. Work on an outboard, run a boat, cut some glass. It would be nice to build some wooden boats, though. Working on *Tidewalker* was more fun than a dozen fiberglass boats."

Someone came in with a few lobsters in a box. "Gonna feed half the island," he announced.

"Don't look like it would feed half the island," Foy said.

"They're gonna eat light."

We thanked Foy for his time and stood up to leave. He stood too, and shook my hand with the biggest, solidest hand I've shaken in a long time. "It's been fun sitting down and talking for a few minutes. I don't get to do that much."

Brenda Hopkins
Librarian, Isle au Haut

Although Brenda Hopkins has no formal training, she is the librarian on Isle au Haut. It is one of several things she and her partner, Bill Clark, do to keep food on their table and help toward having a house of their own on the island. When they first moved to Isle au Haut, they planned to fish, and during the lobstering season, she goes stern with Bill on their *Double B*. But they need income year-round, and again like many islanders, they do a little of this and a little of that. They have the trash contract with the town—once a week in summer, every two weeks in winter, they pick up garbage and recyclables and take it all to the transfer station in Stonington, on Deer Isle. People are allowed one bag a week. "Sometimes they call and ask if they can have

Isle au Haut's Revere Memorial Hall

another this week. If it's high tide, OK, but if it's low tide, gee, can you wait another week? It's a lot of lugging and tugging."

Bill is second selectman, a position that doesn't add much to their coffers but certainly contributes to the well-being of the island. When the library position came up, it appealed to Brenda. She thinks she was the only applicant, but in any case, she got the job, which pays by the hour.

The library is in a small space in the Revere Memorial Hall, home to the town office and a gym with a stage. During the winter, the library is open only a couple of hours a week (currently Mondays from three to five in the afternoon). In the summer, when the population explodes and things are hopping, the hours quadruple, with a couple of hours on two mornings and a couple of hours on two evenings. But, says Brenda, most everyone who uses the library has a key anyway. Or, if anyone calls and asks her to open it, she'll be happy to do so. And sometimes in the winter, the door is left open. In November, for instance, there aren't a lot of strangers wandering around.

Because Brenda is on the boat during the summer, she only works one of the library days herself; the rest are covered by volunteers from the summer community—

of whom one or two are trained librarians. Brenda is appreciative of the volunteers' work, as well as their suggestions. Recently they've been reorganizing an entire section of the library. "It's a community effort," she says.

The town budgets a few thousand dollars for the library, but this is augmented by donations of money and books, an annual book sale, and grants. The credit-card company MBNA has an educational foundation based in Belfast, which has been working with local communities on particular school and library projects. The previous librarian got grants for videos, audiobooks, and music CDs. Brenda has found grant money herself, one for a collection of Maine books and another for a computer. Not that the library itself is computerized—the card catalog is still just that, and book loans are recorded on cards, too. People sometimes pick up books from the book return, or pass one along to someone else when they're through with it, but Brenda always manages to track them down—someone always knows where they went. Sometimes donated books also appear in the book return—often the latest hot reads. "At a mainland library, you have to wait in line for that new book. Not here!" Brenda wishes she knew who dropped those off so she could thank them.

Taking out a video is officially done by the honor system—borrowers just sign their names on a list.

The library computer is available to anyone for e-mail or other Internet projects. There are computers in the school, but high-school students who go ashore to school and have no computers at home use the one in the library for research and word processing. Adults use it, too. "One person wanted to use the computer to take an exam for a summer course he was taking, and another submitted his photographs to a photo contest over the Internet."

Brenda loves her job at the library. "There's a need, so you fill it," she says. "Enthusiasm goes a long way. You have to listen and be willing to learn. It gives my mind something to do, too. "

Bill Hoadley
Tuckanuck Lodge, Matinicus

Call the telephone number for the one bed-and-breakfast on Matinicus, and if Bill Hoadley's not there, you get a recording that says, "Tuckanuck Lodge, Matinicus Island Electric Office, and Democratic Party." Bill Hoadley, like so many islanders all along the Maine coast, has created a niche for himself—or, more properly, several niches, and finally he's making a go of life on the island.

Bill had no connection to the island when he landed there for the first time at the age of forty-eight, but he says that within five minutes he had decided that Matinicus was where he wanted to be. How did he know that? "The feel of it," he says, but he can't articulate it further. Originally from Nantucket, and then in Boston for a number of years, he moved to Peaks Island, near Portland, in the mid-1970s, in an attempt to combine city and island. "I wanted my front door to open on the Empire State Building and to look out the back window at the Grand Canyon." But Peaks was too crowded. On a trip to Vinalhaven, he picked up a flyer that talked about Matinicus and its two sandy beaches. It was four years before he even found out how to get to Matinicus. After renting a cottage there for two summers, he decided to go into business for himself. He had been in the U.S. Navy, had worked in a state court system and in the business world, and he wanted to go it alone.

Bill looked around on the island for a location off the beaten path yet close to things—not that anyplace on Matinicus is terribly far from what few "things" there are on the island. Unlike Frenchboro or Monhegan, the houses on Matinicus are spread out, and he found one on a dead-end road with just two others, a short walk from the harbor. Of his efforts to rebuild the house, he says, "I knew it was going to be a lot of work, but I didn't know how much." He bought the cottage next door, too, and he spent the first year just cleaning up. The second year, he ripped everything apart. "At the end of that season, my bank account showed zero." For seven years, he had to leave in the winter and get a job ashore—in Rockland, on Peaks, even in Portland. "It felt as if I'd take one step forward and two back," he says. And then, in the eighth year, he was offered a job on the island as the clerk of the electric company. That made the difference. No longer did he have to commute ashore—forty-eight bucks a trip it cost then—and he could finally get his house fixed up the way he wanted it. By then, his Social Security and state pension had kicked in. "I wasn't rich, and everything I made went back into the house. But I was in fairly good shape."

Although there were once three B&Bs, back in the 1980s when there was regular boat service, Tuckanuck Lodge is now the only place to stay on the island, and Bill has built up a steady clientele. He has five rooms, which he now advertises only in *Down East* magazine. "A lot of places I ran ads, I was spending more than I got."

Bill will make supper, too, although he's not technically licensed for that. "People gotta eat somewhere," he says. "I'm afraid that if I go for the license, people are going to start showing up saying, 'We want dinner.' But I'm getting frazzled. Sometimes I need three of me to get everything done."

Some people return every year. One group has stayed with him for the three-day Memorial Day weekend for fifteen years now. He's open year-round; once, people came for New Year. They wanted a quiet place, and they got one. Sometimes he discourages people from coming. "As soon as they ask what there is to do, I know they're not going to be happy here."

Bill says he's getting as much business as he wants. "I don't want to be overwhelmed, for fear I might get the wrong people. I'd prefer to have people who are going to enjoy the island rather than bitch about it." Occasionally someone has come who has been very unhappy—like the New Yorker who made a reservation as a surprise for his wife. "She was certainly surprised!" he laughs. "But it's a great place for kids. Kids love the beach. They can play on the beach all day long."

It can be hard to plan. Sometimes, even in summer, there might be no one visiting, so it looks like a slack time is coming. But then the phone starts ringing. "For the incoming ferry tomorrow, I went from having one to three to four and now I'm full. I hope it's flying weather tomorrow, so I can get some groceries. But I'll do something, even if I have to borrow."

Herb Parsons
Artist/Teacher/Shopkeeper, North Haven

"My roots were sunk deep, very early," says Herb Parsons. He and his parents before him summered beside the Fox Islands Thorofare between North Haven and Vinalhaven. After decades of wondering how he could afford to live permanently on North Haven, in 1984 the opportunity came to artist and teacher Herb Parsons in the form of an offer for a job with the University of Maine at Augusta's center in Rockland/Thomaston.

Although Herb had supported himself on a quiet scale with his teaching, his father had distributed some stock to Herb and his siblings from time to time, allowing him to buy the old Calderwood community building when it came available. With two thousand square feet of retail space on the first floor and another thousand square feet upstairs, it was perfect as an art gallery. (Ironically, twenty years ago, Herb took North Haven's former community center and turned it into a store, and just recently, the defunct Waterman's Store has been transformed into a community center.) Herb sells his own paintings and T-shirts and notecards and hooked rugs of his own design and he takes work on consignment. Having all that room means he can offer things for sale simply because he likes them, not because he expects them to bring in vast amounts of money. Since the beginning of the Calderwood Hall operation, island resident Sue Staples has made lampshades and wooden toys and boxes—and her daughter joined her when she was old enough—but no longer can Herb count upon island people, or even people with island connections, to provide all the merchandise. He still attempts to carry mostly Maine-made products. He has a variable commission schedule, with smaller percentages taken from the proceeds of island-produced items than from those from Away—although he says he charges less even for those than do most shops on the mainland.

He would love to find a manager for the store, so that he'd have more time to paint. "I don't paint at all from mid-April to November," he says. During the summer, Herb is running at a hundred miles an hour; immediately after Labor Day, he's only going forty-five. "It changes so precipitously," he says. Most of the business is with the summer people on North Haven—although at first he thought he might try to attract people from the mainland, he decided against it. The island isn't set up for significant numbers of day-trippers.

A lifelong runner, Herb feels that one reason why he was accepted by the people of North Haven was that even when he was a young man, people on their way to work at six in the morning would see him out running—at least he was up at a decent hour! Of course, he was familiar to everyone, as had been his parents and grandparents—that also helped. And he lived right in town, where everyone saw him all the time. He wasn't hiding away in the backwoods somewhere.

For the first dozen years, Herb continued teaching two days a week in the University of Maine system in Thomaston, and he ran the shop in the summer. When his parents died, his financial situation changed, freeing him to stay on the island and work there. He began coaching the Fox Islands cross-country team, officially open to eighth-through-twelfth-graders from North Haven and Vinalhaven, but the kids start running as early as third grade. For most of one recent season, there was only a single girl running, but she and Herb were at similar fitness levels. "I was stronger and she was faster, but by the end of the season, she was stronger too. We ran every single step together. That's unique—it would never happen anywhere else." That she came in third in the state meet was very satisfying for both of them. In 2004, as a senior, she placed second at that same meet.

In 2004–5, with some help from adults on Vinalhaven, a dozen kids from each island participated, and there are hopes for that level of interest to continue.

Herb has been involved with the island's monthly paper since its beginning— also not a paid position.

Herb says he's fairly well accepted in this community, which is perhaps more dependent upon its summer people than any other Maine island. He feels entirely comfortable on the island, even though he says that his own background may limit his ability to understand some people's points of view. He sees the disparity of rich and poor around him, particularly in this time of construction of huge summer houses, whose impact on the islanders so far has primarily been in jamming up the ferry. The poor self-image of some islanders leads Herb to imagine how difficult it must have been during the first building boom, a century ago, when the super-rich of the East Coast came to build their "cottages" on the island. He feels that this low self-esteem sometimes results in defensiveness—or a prickly pride.

"But that's part of what makes the island neat," he says, "maintaining the specialness of a place. The prickliness is kind of neat, too, even if it's rough on outsiders sometimes, but the reverse is true, too—outsiders are rough on island people." He considers how difficult it must be even today for a local man who's a town leader, perhaps on the board of selectmen, making decisions all winter, and then come summer, the high-powered lawyers and corporate CEOs show up and make condescending demands of him. No wonder there's sometimes a little prickliness.

Doing Business on Swans Island

While the proceeds from fishing and handling lobster feed more families on Swans Island than all the other occupations combined, the island does have a handful of other businesses. None of them are very big, but they are either typical of other islands or at least examples of what can be done on islands to make a living. Many of these pursuits are seasonal or part-time or both.

There are three places to stay: two B&Bs and a four-unit motel that rents bicycles and kayaks, too. There's a general store. There are places to eat or buy food, at least in summer: a bake shop, a seafood establishment, and a takeout that specializes in fried food. A mechanic works on cars and a number of people are in carpentry (some of them also lobster in summer). A gift shop is open in summer and then a couple of days a week until Columbus Day. There's a laundromat with four washing machines. When the weather is particularly cold, as it was in 2003–4, people whose wells freeze up are grateful for the alternative laundry facility.

The island has had three companies manufacturing something: a lobster-trap company; Saturn Press, which prints notecards and stationery on old hand presses; and, until recently, Swans Island Blankets.

John and Carolyn Grace (COURTESY OF THEMSELVES)

SWANS ISLAND BLANKETS

For twenty years, Swans Island summer residents John and Carolyn Grace had thought about living year-round on the island. Finally, with their four children grown or nearly so, they started thinking in earnest about how to create a viable life on Swans. Certainly lawyering was out of the question, even though both had successful practices in Boston. An idea came to them. The old, summer-weight wool blankets that had come down to them from John's family were no longer being made. Would there be a market for this sort of blanket if they were to make them?

In 1991, they visited woolen mills across the country and in Ireland, and they were convinced that creating blankets was a life they would enjoy. After a brief apprenticeship in a small cotton-blanket mill in Maine, John studied weaving techniques and the art of blanket-making at Rhode Island School of Design. In 1993, at their first craft fair, in Blue Hill, Maine, with only a few sample pieces to show, John and Carolyn took orders for eight blankets. That was the beginning of the Atlantic Blanket Company (named for Atlantic, one of Swans Island's settlements). That winter, they wove blankets in their dining room in the Boston area; the following year, they were weaving on Swans Island. They lived in their uninsulated summer house the first winter, burning wood—cords and cords of wood—and they wove.

Their aspirations were modest—simply to support and occupy themselves on the island, not to make a lot of money. They had no difficulty selling all they could make, going to craft shows around the country and telling their appealing story. "Drop your law practice in the city, move to a remote island, and become weavers. Sounds a like a scene from a movie, right?" They had a good catalog, and the Internet provided even more of a market.

The Graces hired islanders to weave for them and finish blankets. At peak production, they were selling five or six hundred blankets a year—blankets that even in the smallest crib size sold for $275 and up. They were doing well. Six people worked for them, at least part-time. They treated their staff well, allowing people to set their own hours and take time off when needed. Most of their employees had small children in school and sometimes a second job, and the schedule flexibility was ideal. "We had a close and intimate relationship with the people working for us," John says. Getting help can be difficult on an island, particularly during a period of lobster-fishing prosperity. Some islanders who in another time might have enjoyed working for the company were simply not available. When fishing is lucrative, some men don't want their wives working, and many women are happy to have the freedom to be home with their families.

As their business flourished, the Graces thought a few sheep would complement their lives and their business. First, a small flock of Shetlands on the mainland needed summer pasture, and the Graces' place seemed ideal. Soon they had fifteen Corriedale sheep of their own, and the Graces had their wool spun to use in the lightweight blankets. For the winter-weight blankets they had added to their line, they bought half the wool from a larger flock that lives unattended on Nash Island, downeast. The last child of the last lighthouse keeper on Nash had kept sheep there for seventy years. She has now died, but her sheep will continue to live on Nash Island. When grass is available, they eat that, and when there is too much ice, they live off seaweed from below the high-tide level.

During 2004, the Graces invited their friend Tom Laurita and his family to join them in the business, so the company could grow and the Graces could back off a bit. The company is weaving and selling the blankets in Northport, Maine. John and Carolyn still live on Swans and remain stockholders in the company, for which they continue to develop blanket designs. They expect always to have sheep and to make things from wool. They have always wanted to make bedroom rugs and to work with felt. Now they will have time to do both.

Looking back on his experience starting a business on Swans Island, John says, "If it's possible, it was even more exciting than we thought it would be." The community was so different from where they had come from, the way of life so different—"The extent of the difference was surprising, but in a positive way," he says. "We enjoyed being completely immersed in our work, and with the people. We were most gratified by being able to supply employment, because there are not a lot of opportunities. And I don't think we expected the business to be so startling a success."

Certainly companies like this could be very helpful to the local economy on many of the islands. What are the secrets to success? John suggests two aspects that are important. First, the project must be an export business. There isn't enough traffic on an island, even in summer, to sustain a company. And second, he says, there needs to be a story. He feels that their tale—two lawyers abandoning their professions to create beautiful things—is a large part of the success of their marketing. There's more to it, of course. Swans Island Blankets has lovely, functional, and very special products, and the people who are part of the company are happy. I'd like to think those two factors matter, too.

John tells of an earlier endeavor on Swans. Between 1920 and 1945, a former Pennsylvania man raised begonias and sold tubers from them. The climate is very good for begonias, and the island tradition of applying seaweed to the soil agreed with them. He prepared the tubers and shipped them around the world, creating a very successful mail-order business in an era when there was no such thing. "For us it was an inspiration, an indicator we could do this," says John. "I hope our business can serve as the same kind of inspiration for other people, sometime."

Whether or not the company will continue to have a significant presence on Swans Island remains to be seen, but it has clearly demonstrated that such a project still can work on a small Maine island.

SWEET CHARIOT MUSIC FESTIVAL

In the mid-1980s, Doug Day was living in a New York City apartment whose owner decided he wanted it back. It crossed Doug's mind that if he owned a house, never again would he have to move his great-grandmother's 1887 Steinway. He liked Mount Desert Island, where he had spent a summer gillnetting and writing a book, but Mount Desert real estate was beyond his means. An ad for a little house on Swans Island attracted his attention, and while that house wasn't what he wanted, the one across the street seemed to be. Before too long, he was a property owner on Swans, a place to which he had no connection aside from midnight trips past it, returning from fishing. "The whimsical need to put my piano somewhere changed my life," he says.

A musician who has supported himself performing and doing artist-in-residence programs in schools, Doug never has truly become part of the Swans Island community. "Early on, I had a naïve notion that I might be accepted," but a season on an island softball team opened his eyes. "I was subbing for an islander who wasn't as good a player as I was." He says he let it go, but he then consciously chose not to ask to be a fully integrated part of the community. In any case, he was traveling a lot.

Fortunately, Doug didn't make some of the faux pas that many island newcomers do, and in fact, his early actions gave him credibility. Soon after he moved to the island, his house needed to be reroofed, and even though that was by no means his field, he went up on the roof with hammer and shingles and did the job. He put in a garden, he paid people on time, and he didn't proclaim himself to be too much of anything. He explains the latter. "Modesty is respected and honored everywhere we turn. Blowing your own horn is absolutely suspect. If you have done or are capable of doing something remarkable, it's best to keep it quiet."

At first, the people of Swans Island assumed he was a drug dealer. He came to the island wearing a suit and carrying a suitcase, with no visible means of support— what else could he be? Guys he hired to work on his mooring would ask for dope in payment, and they didn't believe him when he told them he really wasn't in that business. In fact, since Doug is a Christian Scientist, drug use or sales are less than likely.

What finally allowed Swans Islanders to put Doug in some kind of context was the founding of what's now known as the Sweet Chariot Music Festival. Beginning in 1987, once each summer, he has brought his world of music to the island. The first year, he tore the siding off his barn and set up an informal stage for a gospel group to sing to an audience in the field beside it. After the concert, he simply tacked the boards back on, thinking he might run an event like that again the next year—which he did, with two acts. And so it went, growing every year. By 2004, there were twenty different acts in three sold-out performances in the island's Odd Fellows Hall, as well as a fourth (free) concert in the park. "I won't have the thing become an elitist show that islanders can't attend," he says.

Although Doug has never attracted as many fishermen to the concerts as he would have liked, the retirees and non-native island people look forward to the annual event, as do the guests on the windjammers that crowd into the harbor for the festival. When Doug announced a few years ago that he could no longer run the festival by himself, an instant force of volunteers emerged, mostly from the Swans Island retired community. "I raise the money and do the artistic direction, and the nuts and bolts are taken care of by that hard-core group. It's sold out before we print the tickets." Among other tasks, the volunteers find housing for all the performers and their families—no simple job in August, the height of the season.

Doug admits that the festival started out as a unique offering by yet another eccentric newcomer—a category of person he says is common on the islands. "It's an outgrowth of my needing to share with the islanders what I do, and it's romantic fun for the performers—it's an island retreat."

For twenty years, even if Doug wasn't a fully committed member of the Swans Island community, his only home was there. When he decided to have a family, though, he chose to move off the island in the winter. He researched carefully those places he thought might be best suited for raising his children—and Swans would have met many of the criteria. Kids can get around on their own bicycles and not be chauffeured from activity to activity, as happens in suburbia. There are none of the dangers of the big city—kids have safety and autonomy. But in order to make a living as a musician and teacher, Doug had to be away from the island for significant chunks of time every year. Being on the road isn't OK anymore. He chose Ojai, California—still a rural community, but one where there are a thousand schools within daily commuting distance. There, the kind of artist-in-residence work he has done from Swans would be much more easily joined with a committed family life.

He still has the Swans Island house, and the piano is still there, along with another given to him by an old Swans Islander, whose parents used to play it for dances. He has mixed feelings about the Steinway—in one breath he says it's destined to live out its days on Swans Island, and in the next he talks about rebuilding it and taking it to Ojai. "It's quite playable still," he says. Perhaps Steinway can rebuild it to a like-new state, and perhaps he can trade the work for time in his Maine island home. Or perhaps it'll just live on as is, where is.

There are twenty apple trees of old island varieties on his Swans property. The year his son entered first grade was the first apple-picking season Doug had not spent on Swans since he bought the house. "No matter what I'm doing the rest of the year, I always try to be here for the blossoming of the apple trees, and again for the shortening of the days and picking apples."

Pendleton Yacht Yard, Islesboro

Stanley Pendleton's great-great-grandfather built all the houses in Dark Harbor village for his children, and his grandfather ran a livery stable there until the day in 1933 that automobiles were allowed on the island. The first automobile to show up on the island, in 1912, annoyed some people so much that it and all its kin were banned from the town roads—first by the town and then by the state legislature. The next twenty years witnessed a significant war between the natives and the summer people. Islanders wanted cars to get around their fourteen-mile-long island, while most of the summer people didn't want the noisy, smelly machines destroying their rustic heaven. In fact, they threatened to leave if cars were to be permitted to keep them awake at night and frighten their horses. With increasing frequency, the issue came up before regular and special town meetings during the next two decades. Finally, in 1933, the town, more concerned about fire engines and convenience than the possible loss of its wealthy rusticators, voted unanimously to allow automobiles, and the state legislature rubber-stamped the town's vote. Since that time, there has never been a shortage of summer people.

Stan Pendleton's grandfather and father took all their buckboards down to the shore and burned them. Then they turned to the care and maintenance of automobiles, tearing down all the barns. And now Stanley has built them all back, and more, to house his Pendleton Yacht Yard.

Stanley himself left the island after he finished high school. "The name of the game in winter was to see how far away you could get," he says. One year at the University of Maine at Orono, another in Bangor, then to the University of Georgia, then Europe, the West Coast, South America, the Caribbean. All during that time, he came back to Islesboro every summer "to make a buck." He and his cousin David Pendleton ("DP") opened the Island Pub and ran it a couple of summers before selling it. But, he says, "I never did get

Stanley Pendleton

far enough away or long enough," he says. Over the years, he learned about sailing, navigation, the ocean, boats, and island life in general. One summer, after he had run and cared for a fleet of boats on the island, the owner asked him to haul them, paint them, and put them in the water the following spring. He guessed he could do that—his father had retired from the garage business by this time, so the property was available for storing boats, and DP helped him with the actual work.

One thing led to another, and more and more people asked Stanley to take on their boats. He got married along the way, had two kids, and was no longer packing up on the spur of the moment. "Before I knew it, I had thirty boats. That's when I realized I was having a boatyard." Gradually, more and more of the Islesboro yachts came to Stanley's yard; nowadays, he has all but three of the beautiful old wooden Dark Harbor Twenty class boats, as well as many other classic wooden boats. In 2004, there were some three hundred boats in the care of the Pendleton Yacht Yard. Depending on the season, the yard has between seventeen and twenty-six employees. About 40 percent commute onto the island every day; of the islanders who work for the yard, the greater share are people who came from Away. The yard hires three local fishermen every winter when there is a special project.

It was one of these special projects that changed Stanley's yard and gave it an entirely new reputation—one that extends far beyond Penobscot Bay. When Parker Stevenson and Kirstie Alley were still married and living in one of the cottages on Gilkey's Harbor, Stevenson bought a Bunker and Ellis picnic boat. Although Raymond Bunker and Ralph Ellis built a score of working lobsterboats, the Southwest Harbor pair are better known for the forty or so pleasure boats they built on the same model. The boats are not only comfortable, well built, and seaworthy, they are elegant of line and pass through the water with ease. Traditionally, the pleasure versions were finished with gracefully curved windshield sides and a canvas top, and the houses were bright-finished mahogany.

Bellatrix

The largest of these well-known boats were 44 feet long, and one of these was the *Water Rat* that Stevenson bought. She was built in 1956, and despite her impeccable heritage, at the age of forty-three she was in need of serious restoration. Pendleton Yacht Yard had already restored a Bunker and Ellis, so at the time it felt like just another routine job, and Stanley didn't document the process. Stevenson's project had a higher profile, though, and the coastal boatshop world noticed. The end result is the epitome of classic yacht beauty, now called *Bellatrix*, finished in the highest quality and with all original fittings or copies of the originals.

Since then, the yard has restored another Bunker and Ellis, the former *Nannal*, now *Elysium*. Suddenly, PYY is the yard for Bunker and Ellises. When the 1964 classic *Kittiwake* was to be offered for sale, the venerable and well-honored marine surveyor Giffy Full sent the owners to Stanley. It was never Stanley's intention to become an important person in the world—particularly the classic yacht world—but now he is accepted as the Bunker and Ellis specialist. When Giffy Full says you're It, you're It.

In the meantime, Stanley has offered to build what he's calling a Pendleton 43. Although there are plans for a particular hull shape for the 43, he says he will build it however a client would like it. The one thing he promises to deliver is the defining "look" of the Bunker and Ellis boats. Beyond that, it depends on how a client would like to use the boat. Want to go fast? Perhaps a hard chine would suit. Or for puttering around the islands on picnics, perhaps a traditional round bilge. Anything is possible under the water. Twin engines? Or a single screw? Perhaps a little shorter, or wider? "The only thing set in cement is the look."

There are builders who are turning out boats with curved-top side windows and soft tops, with glossy bright mahogany houses and high-quality finishes—some of them even claim to be modern equivalents of the Bunker and Ellis boats—but, Stanley says, they don't quite look the part. Worse yet, you go below and they smell like fiberglass. The Pendleton 43 would have no fiberglass—it would be cold-molded. "That's my one concession to high tech," he says. He says that a boat built to the existing design would cost a million bucks—plus or minus a couple of hundred thousand. That's competitive with high-end fiberglass boats. And there would be something special about having it built at PYY.

Getting
To and From

O f course, a particularly significant (not to say defining) aspect of living on an island is that it's surrounded by water, and crossing that water, or carting stuff across it, is not always easy or even possible. Says Eva Murray, who's on Matinicus, "No matter what you're trying to do on Matinicus, it all boils down to freight handling."

People who don't have or choose to use their own boats (or planes) have to travel by ferry or mailboat or commercial airplane. Options vary from island to island. "Stuff," on the other hand, may come or go by one of those means, or it may go by barge, or another dedicated freight-carrying vessel may carry it.

Ferries

Through the Casco Bay Island Transit District (CBITD)—a nonprofit corporation owned and operated by the residents of the six islands it serves—Casco Bay Lines provides car and passenger ferry service year-round between Portland and these half-dozen islands. Even in winter, the boats to the islands closer to the city run from before six in the morning until ten at night—or, on weekends, until nearly midnight. Even the farthest flung, Cliff Island, has early morning service and a last boat to the island at quarter to six. It is possible to commute to Portland to work from any of the Casco Bay islands.

This is only marginally true on some of the islands farther east. On others, it's impossible to depend on public transportation in order to work ashore—and even running errands can be difficult at best. Matinicus, nearly twenty miles off the coast as the crow flies, is on the one hand the most isolated of all—it has only a single monthly ferry run in the winter and three or four a month in summer. On the other hand, it is more closely connected to the mainland than any of the others, because of the fifteen-minute air service to and from the island. In summer, it's not uncommon for twenty or more flights to land on Matinicus every day; even in winter, the mail comes out on one flight

Peaks Island ferry Machigonne II (COURTESY OF A.D. STANKOWICZ)

and is picked up again later in the day on another. Passengers fly at a slight discount with the mail, and planes come and go with passengers paying full fare all day long.

Maine State Ferry Service

"The ferry" is the subject of much griping on most of the islands. When Brenda Craig took over the *Islesboro Island News* from its founder, Agatha Cabaniss, her predecessor advised her that she'd have to be careful in what local issues she became involved, but the state-owned ferry was always fair game. (So was the state government in general.)

On several of the islands in summer, it is difficult to get a car on the ferry. Some people don't like to go ashore at all unless they plan to stay overnight—the pressure of getting back to get their car in line for the boat is too great. Even on Matinicus, where the state ferry doesn't even run once a week during the summer, there is pressure from too many people wanting to move automobiles on or off the island. Frenchboro residents don't have the option of going off-island on a ferry and back again the same day.

MATINICUS FERRY

Ferry day at Matinicus is a big deal, particularly in winter. A crowd—a Matinicus-size crowd, anyway—shows up at the harbor to see the boat come in, to see who's coming and what they've brought, and to visit with one another. One of the islanders—often, but not always, Paul Murray—will catch the lines thrown from the ferry, and the same person will run the ramp. Even though the state operates the ferry, it has no presence on Matinicus (or, for that matter, on Frenchboro).

There's a schedule now—at least specifying what day the boat will come—which wasn't the case not so many years ago. It has to be planned around the tides, so there is enough water at the pier for docking, unloading, and reloading. There's one trip each month from November through April, and that increases to three trips in May and October. June, July, and August get four round-trips a month. The schedule has been adjusted so that trips are spaced a couple of days apart in summer, allowing people to go ashore, stay on the mainland a couple of nights, and then get home again. More important, their vehicles may need a couple of days for repair or to load up for the trip back. The next pair of trips comes a couple of weeks later.

The old eight-car ferry *North Haven* usually makes the trip to Matinicus, although sometimes it's the twelve-car *Everett Libby*. And recently, it has most often been Captain Walter Wotton in charge of the run. If Walter isn't captain, it's likely to be Doug Blasius, whose regular job is running Hartley Marine's tug and cement barge out of Rockland. Doug is unusual in that he holds all three Coast Guard licenses—Able-Bodied Seaman, Engineer, and Captain. If he doesn't run the boat, he might be acting as engineer. "I like going in the hole," he says, referring to the engine-room job. "I can read the whole way across." Each of the five regular state ferries has two complete crews, who work one week on, one week off. Relief people fill in when need arises.

Since the Matinicus schedule is so infrequent, the whole Matinicus ferry crew of four is made up of relief people, or occasionally men on their off-week who want extra work time.

Most of the full-time ferry captains won't take the Matinicus run, "or they complain loudly until they get off," says Walter, who was manager of the Maine State Ferry Service for five years and knows firsthand about the griping. He first worked on the ferries in the mid-1960s, soon after the state took them over. He was in the merchant marine for twenty years and came back to the ferry service in 1987, filling in during his time off overseas runs. Finally, he went to

Matinicus ferry North Haven

work full-time on the Swans Island route for a year and a half, starting in 1989. Then came his five years in the office; in 1995, he took the North Haven Island run until 2001, when he retired to his current position as relief captain. As relief, he has run each of the five routes at one time or another, and Matinicus has most often fallen to him. He knows about islands—as a kid, he spent his vacations and summers with his father on one small island after another, lobstering and tending fish weirs.

"Often the Matinicus trip is an adventure," says Walter. It is a long trip, for one thing—two hours or more across open ocean. There's no protection from the wind, and little from the sea. An east wind makes landing on the island—or getting out again—very difficult. "By today's standards, the *North Haven* is a barebones boat," Walter says. She's kept only for the Matinicus run, although at very rare intervals she might be called in to fill in somewhere else. The pilothouse is stark. She has radar, but no plotters or autopilots or other electronic toys that the other boats have. Then there are the issues at the island itself. There's only water enough for the ferry from half-tide coming to half-tide going, leaving six hours in which to make the turnaround. Both landing and unloading have been interesting, too—particularly before a new ramp was built quite recently.

Only a few times has Walter ever left Rockland and had to turn around without completing the trip. "And I've done a lot of trips," he says. One aborted trip was in the winter of 2003, when a truckload of coal was to be delivered, along with a car and a pickup truck. A reporter from the *Bangor Daily News* was along for the ride. The situation was nowhere near as dramatic as it appeared to be from the write-up in the paper, though. There was a nasty northeasterly wind, so they planned to take the *Libby*, which, being bigger, rides a little better in rough weather than the *North Haven*. First they couldn't get her port engine started, and then they had trouble starting the *North Haven*, too—so they ended up leaving Rockland two hours late. That was the real problem—they didn't get underway till one in the afternoon. Though the wind was howling, the first part of the trip wasn't too bad because Vinalhaven and the other islands were blocking the seas. But when they cleared the islands, the going got heavy. Water was coming over the bow, but you expect that, Walter says. Supposedly the coal truck slid on deck and nearly went overboard aft, but that wasn't true; the truck was chained down, as is standard for that time of year. When a bigger wave than usual would come along, Walter would pull back on the throttle, and they were only making about half speed to begin with. By three o'clock, they were only a little more than halfway out, and that meant they'd be returning to Rockland in the dark. "It wasn't worth continuing," Walter says. He wouldn't have been able to see the big seas coming in the dark. "I would have continued on if we'd had daylight, if we'd got off on time."

Another couple of trips were planned and canceled before finally, on the fourth attempt, the coal got to Matinicus—but not the reporter, who was seasick on the first go and had no interest in trying again. But despite the newspaper's implication that everyone on the island would freeze to death without that delivery, it was hardly a critical situation. The islanders know not to count on a particular ferry trip to bring out supplies, particularly in winter. The coal was an annual delivery to only a couple of people, who had plenty left before it came. The statement in the paper that everyone burns coal because there are no trees on Matinicus is just nonsense.

On another aborted trip, it was thick-o'fog. He'd just turned the corner into Matinicus Harbor and the radar showed a big, long blip in front of him. "I didn't know what it was, so I eased on in up to it. Turned out to be a big, two-masted yacht anchored right there. I couldn't get around it—I tried a couple of times, and almost got on the ledge. I didn't touch it, but the guys on my bow were screaming at me, 'Back off! Back off!'" They couldn't raise anyone on the boat, and no one on shore seemed to know the boat was there (certainly Matinicus Islanders would have been able to deal with that problem, had they seen it, but the fog was so thick no one could see a thing in the harbor.) He turned around and went back to Rockland. The next day was fair and good sailing, and he made the trip successfully.

When Walter first started going out to Matinicus, there was no ramp on the island; they built one out of planks when the boat arrived. Then for a time there was a pair of aluminum ramps on hinges with an electric hoist, but the only adjustment was the tide. It was hard to keep the boat lined up on those ramps, and unloading was difficult, too. "A big heavy truck goes off and the boat goes up—that caused some big adventures," Walter remembers. A dump truck full of sand or gravel or salt puts all its weight in a small area, and as it moves forward toward the ramp, the bow of the boat drops a foot and a half or two feet. Then, as the truck gets its wheels on the ramp, the boat whips up, and the ramp comes up and snaps the truck in the rear end. Too often, the truck driver would panic, says Walter.

One of the problems is that often a company sending out a load of something— lumber, say—will send out the truck with no driver, not wanting to tie up a driver all day. "That's fine," says Walter, "but somebody has to get down to get the truck off, and most of those guys out there aren't truck drivers. They'll start up and try to drive right off without warming up the truck. They'll go halfway over the ramp and, with that heavy load, the truck will stall. You have to line up and kinda go for it," Walter says. He shows with his hand how the ramp goes up and down if the driver puts on his brakes. "There've been a lot of loads dumped on deck."

The islanders say that the problem is more apt to be the ferry deck crew's insistence on unloading before the tide can come in and lessen the angle of the ramp.

Doug Crute sometimes works the deck on the Matinicus run. He is neither a young man nor a very slim one. He describes a time when islander Eva Murray saved the day for them. "We can't lift twenty pounds between us," he said of the men who happened to be working on the ferry the day someone hit the brakes partway along the ramp and a truckload of cement on pallets fell onto the bow of the boat. "She [Eva] jumped down and she's throwing cement bags around like they were soccer balls. Hadn't a been for her, we'd still be there."

There've been a number of predicaments unloading, but according to Walter, "so far we've been able to get out of them. Island ingenuity." And luck helps. The time that one rear wheel of a truck went off the side of the ramp, there happened to be a backhoe working on the island. "He came down, and by hook and by crook, he got it back on the ramp and over to the dock."

Posted on a bulkhead on the *North Haven* is a photograph entitled "Going to Matinicus." It shows a compact car squatting under about twenty sheets of plywood tied on, slanting from the roof to the rear bumper. "That about sums it up," says Walter.

Eva Murray concurs. "Islanders consider it nothing less than unethical to deliver any empty space. All possible freight capability must be filled!"

VINALHAVEN FERRIES

Three times a day, one ferry leaves Rockland toward Vinalhaven and, midway across Penobscot Bay, passes her counterpart, which started the reverse trip from the island to the mainland at the same time. Through the crooked narrows by Lawry's Island the ferry travels, across Hurricane Sound and out The Reach, whose channel in 3,000 yards twists and turns eight times, from buoy to spindle to buoy, with little extra room. Finally she makes the ferry pen at Carver's Harbor. There she discharges her load, takes on a new one and makes the return trip, again passing her compatriot in mid-bay.

One of the ferry captains is Danny Martin, who came up through the hawsepipe on a world-traveling research vessel. When he married and started a family, he looked to the ferry service for a job. There's not much turnover in the wheelhouse, which means a lot of turnover on deck, because opportunities for advancement are so limited. Danny happened to come home just as there was an opening for a captain of the ferry running to and from his native Vinalhaven.

Only three of the sixteen regular crew on the two Vinalhaven boats live on the island. "There used to be a lot more," Danny says, "but they retired. The money's much better in fishing. No one wants to be an able-bodied [seaman] on the ferry—the pay isn't quite as good as being a manager at McDonald's." The ferry service has housing on the island for the mainlanders who work on the island-based *Captain Charles Philbrook*.

The weather's certainly one of the biggest issues he faces. "It's either so good it's almost boring, or it's nasty—you can't see the water—or it's rougher than hell." Traffic is another problem. He's had many near-collisions, having to back down to avoid sail-boats, cabin cruisers, lobsterboats. "The only time the lobstermen are a problem is when they're busy and they have their radar on low scale—by the time they see you, you're already slowing down." But for the most part, the lobstermen know his schedule as well as he does. Sailboats can be a problem, though, because they think—they know—they have the right-of-way. "But if you can't see them, they don't," says Danny. (And who in his right mind would insist on right-of-way from a large commercial vessel going about his business, anyway?)

The radar and the VHF radio are important in keeping track of other traffic. In fog, Danny and any other commercial vessels on the bay monitor channels 16 and 13 and broadcast security calls, so every professional mariner has a pretty good idea where all the others are. Lobstermen usually monitor their own local channels, which Danny often puts into his scan, too. But pleasure boats often aren't listening to the radio.

"I've had more near-misses than I can actually count," he says. "Seems like there are days when it happens four or five times, and then months when you don't have to slow down at all." Those months are most apt to be between October and May.

The radio is helpful in other instances, too, such as making calls to help fisher-men in distress. Once, a fellow was stranded on a tiny rock near the approach to Carver's Harbor. The guy had gone ashore after some trap buoys, the tide was coming, and his outboard drifted away. Danny called another fisherman who was still out work-ing and could go capture the boat. "It was a cousin of mine, actually." Does he have a lot of cousins? "Too many of them. My wife says we don't have family trees, we have family hedges." She's from North Haven. "I brought a small-town girl to the big city," he says with a smile.

The route from Rockland to Vinalhaven is tricky. A few years back, one of the captains ran a ferry hard aground coming through Lawry's Narrows. "He just didn't make the turn," Danny explains. "He just sorta went straight. A few days later, the peo-ple on Lawry's Island put up a sign: 'Keep Left.'" The fellow went aground a little while later in The Reach, but even though he told one of the deck crew that this was the eas-iest run he had ever had, he left the service after another two or three months. "He wasn't from Vinalhaven." Danny does say that anyone could touch through that stretch. "I bumped once, on a low-dreen tide, thick-o'fog. There's a shoal spot right in the mid-dle that wasn't on the chart and I didn't know was there. I do now!" Even after a little touch, the Coast Guard had to check over the whole boat, and a diver was sent down to be sure no damage was done.

NOAA has since charted the spot.

The sea can be a problem, too, of course. "I've read the weather wrong and got-ten out there on a few rough days when I wished I hadn't. And I've read it wrong a couple of times and stayed home and shouldn't have." It's up to the captains whether or not to make the run, and Danny is glad to work with the fellow starting on the other side to make that choice. A southerly wind is the worst on the Vinalhaven side, and an easterly is most difficult in Rockland, but "I can't read an easterly from the island because of the shape of the harbor, and they can't read the southerly." The state tried to say that the crew wouldn't get paid if they didn't make a trip, but the captains got together and announced that they'd be going every time. "We might not go very far, but I wasn't going to be responsible for taking food off anyone's table," says Danny.

Probably the boat could make it in any weather, he says, but cars move and start bumping into each other, and an older person might slide off the bench seats in the cabin and land on the floor. "It wouldn't be good." In bad weather, they chain trucks to the deck, and sometimes they refuse to take any heavy ones. "Thirty knots is about maximum in a southerly—a southerly blows right into Carver's Harbor, and if we got in trouble, we'd go on down through all the lobsterboats. But with a north or northwest wind, it wouldn't be a problem up to sixty miles an hour. There's no room to build up a sea."

Even working as ferry captain, Danny does some lobstering on the side. He saves up comp time and uses some vacation so he can go out one or two days a week during the summer. Usually he sets three hundred traps, but the summer I talked to him, he only put out two hundred. The catch was down.

For the most part, he likes his job. He's been working for the ferry service for more than fifteen years, and he expects to stay with it at least until his kids are out of school. "My income needs will be totally different then," he says.

There were six people in the *Everett Libby*'s passenger cabin with us, walk-ons, headed to Vinalhaven in the middle of a late March day. The *Libby* is the small ferry that fills in for the regular, ferry, at that time in the yard for spring maintenance.

The passenger cabin on the *Libby* is on the main deck level. A row of plastic double seats runs down the outside, and there are a few more on the inner side. Each passenger commandeered a whole double seat; trying to sit side by side, we saw why. There was less room than in a subway seat. The ferry squatted when a big dump truck boarded. Too late, a passenger shut the door to the main deck. The diesel fumes stayed with us all the way across.

The sea looked flat, with just patches of light breeze ruffling it, but the ferry felt a gentle swell. She whistled a shrill, high pitch that was audible over the roar of her engines.

A young man was reading *Sports Illustrated;* a guy a decade or two older slept for a while and then stood leaning on the bulkhead, gazing across the gray water, spitting regularly into a plastic bottle. A middle-aged man wearing an *F/V Starlite* cap slept through the whole ninety-minute trip. Behind him, a woman read a romance novel. And across from us were two girls, perhaps eleven and twelve, or maybe one was just small. Her body was just starting to make the changes to distinguish her from a similarly aged boy. Each girl had a book.

Like her friend or sister, the smaller girl was dressed in jeans, running shoes, and fleece jacket. Before we were halfway across, she finished her book and went on to a *Seventeen* magazine. Her friend started a library book before the ferry left the dock in Rockland; mouthing the sentences as she read and tracking the line with a bookmark, she had time to finish it before landing in Carver's Harbor. The few words between the two numbered more than those of any of the rest of our companions, who simply acknowledged one another as they sat down.

It was routine to them all. There were no other boats out along the way, and no one paid any more attention to the markers, islands, and rocks than the gulls en route paid to the boat.

JACK LEACH AND THE ISLESBORO FERRY

Ever since 1951, twice a day—at least three times a week and often five—Jack Leach has ridden the Islesboro ferry. He's been a regular on each of the three ferries that have made regular runs to the island: the *Governor Brann*, the *Governor Muskie*, and the *Margaret Chase Smith*.

Jack carries freight onto the island, always in an International truck. There's a new one every so often, but they're always the same particular green color—the color of money, he says—and the white box is equally distinctive. I see one in Rockland or Camden nowadays and immediately recognize the truck as Jack's.

He's on the first boat off the island every day, and he has a standing reservation to go back again on the one o'clock ferry. His regular route goes to Rockland Food Service, the marine-supply place in Rockland, the bread place, the dairy place, and so on, because he supplies businesses on the island. He also will stop anywhere else if he's asked to do so. Perhaps one of the summer people wants some shrubs picked up, or someone needs a sofa taken to be repaired; Jack's the man to call.

He also meets the FedEx truck in Lincolnville every day.

In the winter, on the days when he's not scheduled for the regular route, you might find Jack waiting for the ferry just the same. One Monday, he was in line with a dump truck full of cow manure. Part of Jack's job is knowing where to find everything. Cow manure is valuable stuff these days, and most farmers spread what they have on their own fields. Not everyone would know where to buy a load. Jack does.

He makes some long-haul deliveries, too, bringing furniture to a summer cottage from New York, for instance. "I might go a month or two or three without making a trip, and then all of a sudden I get five or six. That's in spring, summer, or early fall, usually."

Jack likes his business. "I was born here and never ever wanted to leave," he says. "I coulda gone to college, I guess, but I knew what I wanted to do, and I've been doin' it ever since. I like trucks, and I like what I do."

When Jack started trucking, straight out of high school, the *Governor Brann* was the ferry making the trip to and from the island.

I can remember the *Governor Brann*. If the vehicles were arranged carefully, she could carry ten passenger cars. The crew knew just how to give directions, their fingers beckoning a driver to come forward an inch, or to turn the wheels a whisker or perhaps hard over. They chocked the wheels of the vehicles on the ends, which often would get totally covered in spray. Sometimes, when it was really rough and the little ferry bucked and rocked, I'd wonder if our car would fall off.

In those days, they'd run an extra trip if cars were left behind. There was a break long enough at lunchtime to put in another run then, and they'd add one at the end of the day if need be. Coast Guard oversight, OSHA, and unions had not yet been heard from, and the ferry belonged to the island.

On the very low tides, the ramp would get so steep they sometimes had to winch vehicles up onto hard ground. Jack remembers many a time being winched off the *Brann*. "They had a big cable and a double chain, and after they hooked on, it was pretty easy. You came right along." But loading his truck onto the *Brann* wasn't always so easy. "If you were top-heavy, they'd try to get you crosswise up front."

I used to like to read the fares on the ferry ticket: car and driver, $1.25; passenger on foot, 25 cents. I never saw a horse or cow led onto the ferry, but the fare was printed on the ticket. I don't remember the cost now. The rates for trucks of various axle configurations didn't interest me so much, but I'm sure Jack knew them cold.

In 1959, the Maine State Ferry Service took over the run with the *Governor Muskie*, building new pen and ramp systems. "Looks like a clamshell with a house on top," said Went Durkee of the *Muskie* at the time. She carried twenty-eight cars, but people still had to be left behind occasionally. Like the *Brann*, she was a push-me-pull-you boat—she went back and forth across the bay without turning around. Trucks all had to load on one side; the lifeboats hung out over the cars on the other.

Thirty years later, the *Muskie* was sold—she went to Costa Rica, I heard—and the *Margaret Chase Smith* came into service. She carries upwards of thirty cars. Vehicles still drive on one end and off the other, but she makes two turns on her way to the mainland so she can cross the bay bow-first.

There was something of a kerfuffle about the pens when the new boat arrived—seems no one had considered the fact that the *Smith* had an entirely different shape from that of her predecessor, but it all worked out eventually.

Jack thinks very highly of the *Margaret Chase Smith*. "She'll take a truck across the bay when it's darn rough and be pretty comfortable," he says. She's easier for trucks to board—he can drive straight onto her. "And on the *Smith,* if something did happen, you aren't goin' to tip your truck over."

"I've been on the ferry a long time, and I couldn't tell you one ill thing about it," Jack says. He admits that occasionally it's aggravating when something doesn't go just right, but each boat has been an improvement over the previous one, and he says that both the current crews are terrific.

"I know that if I called them and asked them to wait a minute or two, they would do it," he says. Of course, he's never done that in nearly fifty years. "I never would, unless it was an emergency."

At eighty-six, Went Durkee remembered the earliest days of ferries to Islesboro. "There wa'n't no cars on the island till 1933. They fought it a long time, the summer people did—and theirs were the first to come on, once they allowed it. The first ferry was Lee McCorrison's old scow, the *Redwing.*

"He'd come in on the mud at low water, stick two or three planks down, and you'd drive down on the beach—everybody pushed to beat hell to get you on. He used to land you right on the beach in front of the garage in Lincolnville, and I can tell you, it took some pushin' to get up the beach. There might be someone there with a horse to pull you up. That old scow had two Dodge car engines in her. Took two or four cars, I don't remember for sure.

"I'll never forget when they brought the first scheduled ferry here, the *Governor Brann,*" said Went. "It was the clumsiest thing you ever seen. Built like a chopping tray. They could bring her into the pen and she'd turn around right there. She was just about round. The sea'd come right in on deck two feet deep, and it'd all just run right off again. Can you imagine the purser walking around with hip boots, collecting fares?

"Mel Trim, first selectman, said, 'We'll never see the day she won't carry all the traffic here.' In three months, they took her to Rockland, chopped the middle out of her, and stretched her out to take more cars.

"And they've been fighting ever since to keep ahead of it."

Ferry Service Advisory Board

The Maine State Ferry Service Advisory Board is made up of representatives from each of the communities served by the state ferries. This also includes the mainland towns from which the ferries run, but certainly, the representative from Lincolnville, for one, has always believed that it's an island show. It's the islanders whose lives are affected—though parking becomes an issue on the mainland. The board meets bimonthly to consider the issues facing the ferry users, schedules, and proposed plans for construction or other changes. Unfortunately, from the islanders' point of view, the state has the last say on everything, and all too often, it comes down to a matter of dollars. Some time back, for instance, Islesboro was given a generator to power its ferry ramp should there be a power outage. But no such provision was made in Lincolnville, where the ferry lands. "In theory," noted the *Islesboro Island News*, "passengers might be able to leave Islesboro in an outage but would be left floating in the bay if Lincolnville were also without power." It turned out that the generator on Islesboro was inoperative, at least for a time, anyway.

Ten-thirty in the morning is the designated time for Rockland meetings that hope to attract island residents. It's still a very long way from Frenchboro. David Lunt was at the Advisory Board meeting in May 2004. (He has a house ashore, but he couldn't have gotten to Rockland or home again to the island on that day if he had needed or wanted to.) Kathy Clark from Swans Island was also there, and Sari Bunker from Matinicus (for whom the trip was perhaps the least trouble, since her husband flew her ashore). People also came from Islesboro, North Haven, and Vinalhaven. The state had nearly as many representatives as did the islands—including the manager of the Maine State Ferry Service, the Rockland port captain, someone from the Maine Department of Transportation (DOT) Finance & Administration, and a couple of others. Two mainlanders represented the city of Rockland and the town of Lincolnville, where the ferries land. No one was there from Bass Harbor, the base for the Swans Island and Frenchboro ferries.

The meeting began almost on time and followed its agenda faithfully. Along with the routine minutes and reports on the condition of the particular ferries (the most interesting aspect of which was the remark that the *Smith* had had "quite a lot of painting, as much as we could afford"), there were some significant matters of concern to all—and plenty of time for board members to bring up their own issues.

One issue Jim McLeod, the manager of the ferry service, spoke about was the Maritime Transportation Security Act of 2002, which required that by July 1, 2004, the worldwide rules for security had to be in effect. "There's been no slippage in the deadline date," he said. This was despite the fact that some of the plans had not been approved and the security equipment had not been purchased. Everyone around the table was hopeful that the Coast Guard would continue to be supportive of the commonsense approach they hoped to take to the program. "This is no LNG facility, and it's not a high-value, high-visibility target," someone remarked. Certainly, inspecting every vehicle would wreak havoc with any schedule, and the schedules were tight enough to begin with. Sari asked how the ferry service was going to deal with the issue of driverless vehicles, which are common on all the routes, in both directions. Cars that miss a boat are often loaded onto the next one by friends of their owners, who meet them on the other side. And junk cars come off Matinicus and are hauled away on the Rockland side. "Without proper notice, we're going to have some cranky people," Sari said.

Jim McLeod was the spokesman for the ferry service. "At Security Level One, they'll all be screened," Jim replied. "If it goes up a notch, there will be no driverless vehicles." Yet another reason to hope for quiet on the international scene. Who'd think that everyday life on a tiny hunk of land off the Maine coast would be affected by Osama bin Laden and his ilk?

Unattended freight was a potential problem, too. It would be easier for the ferry service to just say no to the auto parts and other cargo carried unaccompanied on the ferries, but they were trying to accommodate the islands. "We're hoping the Coast Guard doesn't come along and say, 'Don't do that,'" Jim said.

Although the ferry service's huge parking lot in Rockland is only a few years old, it has been filling up and creating problems. People are willing to pay for a permit to park there, but they're unhappy to have no guarantee of a space. Jim wondered whether yet another committee ought to look into it. And space on the ferries continued to be a perennial concern, even off-season. Trucks were part of the problem. One company, reported Bump Hadley, town administrator of North Haven, was running just as many trucks as possible on every trip. A new house was going up—one of some size, apparently—and for a couple of months, there had been a minimum of six daily loads of loam, stone, and other landscaping materials going to the island—five and sometimes six days a week. Rumor had it the situation would continue for several months.

Periodically, the idea floats around that any island could designate trips just for trucks or just for passenger cars, but no action has ever been taken. The islands need the trucks, too, so there's no easy answer. Besides, what's a truck and what isn't?

Sari Bunker raised a question about Lermond Cove, beyond the ferry pier in Rockland, where some of the schooner owners have made a proposal to dredge and build a pier for their vessels. Quarters are tight, and it seems likely that the project would affect the part of the dock where the Marine Patrol boat ties up. Sari asked whether it would also have an impact on the Matinicus ramp. She was concerned about the Sea Coast Mission boat, *Sunbeam,* docking there; that's the largest boat likely to use it.

"No," said Jim. But on further questioning, it appeared that while the Matinicus ramp itself wouldn't be affected, the maneuvering space around it would be. So the ramp itself would be fine—but using it might not be? The ferry service was not challenging the plan, but it had not yet been finalized, and they intended to keep track of it. "We'll let you know," Jim promised Sari.

"Yeah, so we know if we have to picket or not," she replied.

When the meeting adjourned, several people grabbed their lunches and ran, leaving in the room only the DOT people, those from the mainland, and David Lunt, who wasn't getting home that day anyway.

Mailboats

THE *LAURA B.* AND THE MONHEGAN RUN

It doesn't require a gunboat to make the run to Monhegan, but for the past fifty years or so, a former gunboat has been doing the job, taking freight and passengers to the island year-round.

The *Laura B.* was built in Solomons, Maryland, as T-57, a gunboat for World War II; it appears that she served in the South Seas. After the war, she came to Maine with little palm trees growing through her decks. For a few years, she ran lobsters from Vinalhaven to New York and Boston, and after one particularly unpleasant northeaster in the early 1950s, her owners decided trucks were a better way to transport lobsters. That's when she started working the Monhegan run.

Jim Barstow, owner-operator of the Monhegan Boat Line, spent half of each year on Monhegan as a child. Although his mother hated the city, she refused to carry water, and when the island water system was turned off each November, she took Jim back to New York, where his father was an editor with the *New York Herald-Tribune*.

Mailboat Laura B. *has served Monhegan for more than fifty years*

"In New York, I was a Mainiac, and in Maine, I was a New Yorker," Jim says, "but the education I got living as a young boy on Monhegan was well worth it.

"In those days," he says, "a twelve-year-old boy could row a dory to the end of the island and get three or four hundred pounds of cod, pollock, cusk, sometimes haddock, hake, and once in a while a halibut. The sky was the limit for a kid out there. You had as much as your imagination allowed." He says he learned his work ethic on the island. "The people work very, very hard out there. In those days, there was no fooling around—I was busy, growing up out there, but it was a great time."

One of the great adventures for Jim was to go with Earl Field on the boat to the mainland. Earl founded the company in 1914 and operated a series of vessels before he bought the *Laura B.* in the early 1950s. In the winter of 1975–76, Jim bought the business from Earl, including the *Laura B.*

"Earl used to go out, regardless of the weather," Jim says, "but people don't like it." The *Laura B.* now stays home if it's blowing around forty-five knots from the northeast or northwest, and thirty or thirty-five knots will keep her on the mainland if it's coming from the southwest.

"You can't land at the dock out there in a sou'west, there's such a surge," Jim says. There's a cooler on the dock in Port Clyde to hold the perishables until they can be taken to the island. It's rare they miss a trip, though.

Jim's had the old girl in some pretty good weather, and he speaks well of her. "She'll scare you to death before she'll kill you," he says. "If you let go of the wheel and fall off a wave, she'll swing herself into the wind like a sailboat. And you can slow her down so she becomes one with nature."

These days, Dave Hall usually runs the *Laura B.*, unless he's on the other boat, the *Elizabeth Ann*, which joined the company a few years ago. Dave describes the kind of weather Monhegan can dish out: "It was a flat calm and we were unloading the *Laura B.* There was sea smoke hanging on the water, and suddenly the sea smoke started getting sucked out. The temperature dropped fifteen or twenty degrees and the wind was howling northwest. It went from zero to fifty-five miles an hour in fifteen or twenty seconds." When they headed for the mainland, Dave decided to get a better angle on the wind by going around the back side of the island, where the eider ducks hang out. "They jumped up to fly away from us and started going backward!" But with a northwest like that, the sea doesn't have much chance to build up inside Monhegan.

The *Elizabeth Ann* is licensed for 149 passengers and can make them more comfortable in bad weather, compared to the *Laura B.*, with her 92-passenger limit and sparse cabin space. But the *Laura B.* can carry a pickup truck (for the heavier ones, they lift one end at a time with the hoist), or three dumpsters of trash, or great piles of palletized freight. She can move moorings up to seven or eight thousand pounds. In summer, she makes a daily run at seven in the morning, delivering to the island all the groceries and goods for the stores and inns, along with other freight, and taking back trash and recyclables. The two later trips each day are usually made by the *Elizabeth Ann*, but she gets laid up for winter, leaving the *Laura B.* to take care of Monhegan, as she has done for so many years.

"Everything's a lot different in winter," Dave says. "It's three times a week, instead of three times a day, and we're the only boat out there. There's a different tone on the island, too. People mellow out. Everyone's a little on edge by the end of the season."

THE ISLE AU HAUT MAILBOAT

Isle au Haut's connection to the mainland—actually to Deer Isle, a bridged island—is the mailboat. For years, the *Mink* and the *Miss Lizzie* have been carrying both passengers and freight between Stonington and Isle au Haut. A single boat works in the winter, and both run back and forth from mid-June until mid-October. The boat was privately operated at first. In the 1970s, a group formed the Isle au Haut Company; more recently, a new group of summer people and year-rounders took over and are running it as a nonprofit. It's tricky to meet the needs of both the year-round community and the summer people, and even more so to make the enterprise pay its way. Two round-trips each day during the season take fifty to seventy day-trippers to Duck Harbor, on the southern end of the island, where a chunk of land is preserved as part of Acadia National Park, and bring them home again. These trips help pay for the cost of operating the boat.

Particularly in winter, they don't like to run in the dark—it's too hard to see ice. This forces a short schedule, leaving Stonington at seven in the morning and three in the afternoon from the end of October until mid-February. By the end of March, the afternoon trip goes at four. But a passenger from the island doesn't get ashore until eight forty-five in the morning, which means that high-school students commuting to Deer Isle–Stonington miss the first class every day, and they can't participate in any sports or after-school activities unless they stay overnight. And islanders going ashore for other reasons know they'd better be back in time to catch the boat.

"Out of courtesy, we tell the boat crew our plans," says Dianne Barter. "I usually threaten them—'Don't you dare leave without me!'—but most people are more tactful. If we're not coming back the same day, we tell them so they'll know and not worry. You miss the boat, you're in trouble till seven in the morning." They don't cancel the boat often—not if they can help it—and they warn passengers that they might miss a trip when they've heard that the weather is going to act up.

The adult fare is sixteen dollars one way, although books of twenty tickets are available at a discount. It's still expensive to get ashore. Dianne says shopping is easy, though: "You just go online." By April, she has done all her Christmas shopping for the next year. "The only thing I have to lug back is wrapping paper." And the Postal Service is certainly the way to have things delivered; carrying them doesn't make sense, as passengers on the mailboat are limited to two bags and must pay a surcharge for each additional parcel; the boat charges a couple of bucks to handle even a small UPS package.

The boat trips all originate in Stonington—unlike the Maine State Ferry Service, which wants its boats on the islands in case of emergency (except, of course, for Matinicus). Dianne, an EMT, has called for the boat at midnight or two in the morning, and they come right away. There has been talk for years about having a boat on the island overnight, but it would be difficult to have licensed crew live on the island. "Most newcomers don't stay," says Dianne. "I feel better when the boat is in Stonington."

Air Service to Matinicus

There has been some sort of airfield on Matinicus for fifty years or more; Vance Bunker doesn't remember when there was none. Since 1980, the mail has come to the island by air; five days a week, a plane comes out in the morning with the mail, and another plane arrives in the afternoon to pick up the outgoing mail. For a number of years, Telford Aviation had the contract; for a short time, Maine Atlantic Aviation took it over. Like their predecessors, they served Vinalhaven and North Haven as well.

It is Matinicus that most depends on the air service. The state ferry is very infrequent, and it's a long trip by boat. In fifteen minutes, for around fifty dollars a person for a shared flight (or less on the mail run), people can fly to or from the island, and that's the way many people reach Matinicus. In 2003, around two thousand passenger trips were made by air between Matinicus and the mainland.

Kevin Waters was the manager of Telford Aviation's Owls Head operation (at Knox County Regional Airport) and continued on with Maine Atlantic, both of which ran the island service and charter work of all kinds. They had a diverse crew of staff: "Mostly, our pilots are prior heavy iron," said Kevin at the time. "Commercial pilots, corporate, commuter, or military—they now like to live in midcoast Maine instead of in hotels all the time." Some of the pilots had only recently gotten their commercial licenses. "It's an opportunity for pilots getting their start. It's a challenge—you have to be thinking on your feet—the runways are short, up and down hill, there are trees, water on the ends. It's a unique situation for the lower forty-eight." They might be flying islands one day, then the next day be headed off to Dulles, where totally different skills are required. "A lot of corporate pilots come in and watch the show," said Kevin, "and they say they're making good money where they are, but there's an appeal to what we do." He described the group as a team. "It's an advantage for new-hire pilots being

Building at the Matinicus airstrip

nurtured under the wings of guys with real-world experience—it's their way of paying back for when they were taken under some older guy's wing when they were starting out."

Phil and I made a trip in May 2003, when Telford still ran the service. Gary Price, our pilot and tour guide, said he'd flown this kind of stuff for forty or forty-five years. He obviously loved it. The goals of this trip were to pick up the outgoing mail and deliver two boxes of groceries. Island residents could fax an order into Shaw's supermarket in Rockland by ten o'clock in the morning; Shaw's faxed Telford to tell them how many banana boxes of groceries they had and for how many customers, and Telford picked them up in the early afternoon. At the airport, they had commercial refrigeration to hold perishables until the flight departed. If they couldn't fly, they made arrangements with the boats—ferries, in the case of North Haven and Vinalhaven. Matinicus was more difficult. "We're trying to have a boat as part of our services," Kevin said. "A few of us have 'six-pack' licenses." A Coast Guard six-pack license allows a captain to take up to six paying passengers in an uninspected boat. "Otherwise, we work with water-taxi operations."

The little Cessna 206 Stationair—a six-seater, single-prop plane—took off in a small fraction of the Owls Head runway and headed directly out to sea. We flew very close to Large Green Island, where there's a grass airstrip; it's such a short hop to Matinicus, Gary said, and if they make just a little detour to the south toward Large Green, the plane is always within gliding distance of somewhere. "It takes a certain kind of a cat to fly over the water," Kevin said. "Even though we have a good safety record, with a lot of missions, odds are odds."

The owners of Large Green hired the air service to take them back and forth, and Telford could use the island in cases of emergency. But it was pretty unlikely that should be necessary. "Engine failures are almost all fuel issues," Gary said, and they're so careful about fuel now—bad fuel just doesn't happen. But if a problem should arise, said Kevin, "we have keys to a couple of houses on Large Green, with heat and grubbed up, so we could hang out there if we needed to."

Gary circled around Matinicus for our benefit and then made his approach to the dirt strip. "It's a little rough," he said, "but this is what we like. The uphills and down, that's what makes it more interesting."

The Matinicus airstrip

Kevin described more of the possible hazards. "Pilots have to deal with cross-winds, dirt and grass, deer, snow and ice, maybe a broken-down car or an ATV on the runway. Stuff you don't expect. We preach to the flight people all the time, don't get complacent. You may make thirty trips and be fine and then the thirty-first time could be a whole different experience.

"You fly these things enough," Kevin went on, "you get to feel the vibrations, know if something's a little off. You get used to looking at smoke to see which way the wind is blowing, or which way the boats are going—and is that wind-generated, or tide? You get a real shearing in the last 150 feet. Like water in a river going over rocks. It can be really smooth till you're right there." And on Matinicus, in a northwesterly—which is usually a strong breeze—there's a crosswind. "You get real shearing, then, things moving around. You gotta be anticipating. Some guys say, 'This isn't for me!'"

There's a barn at the inland, uphill end of the runway; sometimes pilots fly thirty feet over the barn and land downhill with nothing but ocean beyond. "It unnerves some people," said Gary. There are jokes about grooves in the barn's ridgepole to fit the planes' landing gear.

But our landing was uphill—comfortable and uneventful. We stepped out of the airplane onto the grass; the only building around is a small storage shed with a sign: Matinicus International Airstrip. There were a few pickup trucks parked nearby, and no people. Gary said that he loves landing at Matinicus. "It's so quiet. You land here and there's not a soul around—you just go do your job and no one knows." The air service kept a ratty old blue van next to the shed. It was registered, but not inspected.

"Sometimes it doesn't work," said Kevin, "but people make sure we get the mail, or get groceries to people."

Gary stowed the groceries in the back of the van and we all climbed in; Phil and I shared the single passenger seat. Gary remarked that the roads were rough and that was just fine. "We're lucky the state hasn't come in and paved everything. It just makes people drive faster." No one's going to drive fast on these roads—they have holes ground out of the gravel and rocky bones sticking up. Some roads are barely wide enough to pass another car, widening out only in front of the school and the town building where more than one person might want to park at a time.

The first stop was to drop off a sweater that someone left aboard the plane in the morning. Gary didn't know if the owner would be home, but he would leave the sweater anyway. He went around behind a white clapboard house and returned without the sweater.

Then he pointed out to us what he considered the ideal little white house with its little white picket fence and the view to end all views: the bluffs, an undisturbed cove, and, twelve miles out, Matinicus Light.

A little farther along the road, on the harbor, were a few houses close together and David Ames's three-story building, where sternmen from the mainland stay. It's pretty rough. A sticker on a pickup truck said, "Don't hassle me—I'm local."

"It's an interesting transition out here," Gary said. Summer people stay longer than they used to, though there still are folks who come only for a few days or weeks each year.

He took us to one house that had only a path leading to it; farther along the path is a house whose seasonal residents would be coming soon and would stay into November. The two houses look out on the island's main harbor; the second one also has a view to the open ocean eastward.

Gary couldn't remember whose groceries he was carrying—Ken someone. He passed one Ken's house; Ken's wife was in the yard. "We owe you some groceries?" he asked. Nope.

But Ken himself came around front. "Hey, how familiar are you with the office in there?" he asked Gary. He had a question about fares, but Gary didn't know the answer. "You guys are totally confused in there," said Ken. "Thank God you can fly good."

Gary looked at the grocery boxes and saw they were for another Ken. He knew where that house was, so he started to turn his van around. "Don't do anything I wouldn't do," said Ken.

"That gives me an open book," said Gary.

Mrs. Ken agreed. "That's an open book," she said. At the other Ken's house, a well-used-looking man met the van. He and Gary carried the two boxes of groceries into the house, and Gary came back to drive us to the end of the road to show us another place he particularly liked. As we returned, Ken was waiting in the road. "There's s'posed to be milk," he said.

"Gosh," said Gary. "I didn't know anything about milk. There isn't any in the cooler. What did you order, a couple of gallons?"

"Yup, couple gallons," said Ken.

"I don't know if we have it, but we'll find it for you," said Gary. There would be another flight to the island later in the afternoon.

"You have to learn to get in and out," Gary told us as we drove up the road again, speaking of the mechanics of landing on a small island, "but you also have to keep your mind on stuff like that with Ken and the milk. The job doesn't pay much—it's stuff like that that pays you."

He continued with our tour of the island. On the east side is a long, concave beach with a freshwater stream leading down across it. There's not a building to be seen along it, nor from it, nor anywhere on the horizon. Isle au Haut stands tall and closest, but it's still several miles off; the mountains of Mount Desert Island are in the distance farther to the left, and there's just open ocean to the right. "An unhurt vision," Gary called it. He could live on the island, he said. "'Specially if I had an aircraft like this. But I couldn't afford to pay the airline what these people do to get off and on." The lobster economy pays well.

We heard a plane taking off on the other side of the island. "There goes Rich." He had come across the bay, delivered whoever or whatever he was hired to deliver, and left again during our time on the island. We hadn't heard him land. The planes are unobtrusive.

Back to the center of activity at the harbor—the Post Office. The ferry had just left after its monthly visit. Monday at the Post Office is busy anyway, said postmaster Wanda Philbrook. (The term *postmaster* is, at least in Wanda's eyes, like the terms *fisherman* and *sternman*—there's no need for fluffy political correctness with any of them.) The ferry just made things that much more hectic. "People like to come down on Monday and get things moving," she said. "It could be start-and-finish too, if the fog comes in." There must have been all of three people coming and going; two pickups passed us.

Gary had told us about fog. It was the air service's responsibility to get the mail to Matinicus, North Haven, and Vinalhaven, regardless of the weather. "When it's foggy, it's labor-intensive," he said. "Coordination—and the ferry service is no help."

A woman walked down toward the Post Office and saw the Telford van. She asked if she was too late for the mail. "No, we'll take it," Gary told her. He took her letter and walked partway back up the road with her. When he came back, he asked Wanda how the other woman was doing—she'd lost her husband not too long before.

"She's doing OK," Wanda said. "She went off a weekend or two ago, four or five days." Not only does everyone know if someone's on the island or off it, but they know whether it's a good thing or a bad thing, to boot.

Summer is busier; the air service typically made fifty or sixty flights a day, fifteen or twenty just to Matinicus. "It's a magic show in summer," said Kevin. "Dispatchers have five balls in the air at any time. Planning fuel, loads, schedules—a flight might not end up going where expected—you might start going to Matinicus and home, and then end up going to Vinalhaven too."

"You have to keep your wits about you," said Gary. "Everything is going on at once. There are so many variables, and they never repeat themselves." People usually picked up their groceries at the airport, and sometimes sternmen, who didn't have accounts with the air service the way most of the islanders did, would take theirs without paying for it. It's hard to keep track.

Often they're strictly a taxi service, he said, "but we end up being so much more. And that cuts both ways. If our van's broken, or the airplane's stuck, the guys rally around and bring their skidder or a truck. Whatever goes around, comes around. We barter with people a lot—it's the fair and right thing to do." Sometimes people would be out fishing when their groceries came in; then the pilot would take the boxes to their houses and put the perishables in the refrigerator or freezer for them. They delivered FedEx and UPS, too, and they ran errands for people—picked up a gallon of milk or a prescription. Or delivered a brown paper bag. One time such a bag had $80,000 cash in it, from a lobster buyer to a fisherman.

Things used to be paid for in "Matinicus Ones," Kevin said—hundred-dollar bills. That's what lobster buyers paid with and what the island economy ran on. The pilots had to have change. Kevin worried what would happen if the lobster industry ever failed.

The mail picked up, the groceries delivered, and the island covered from one end to the other, Gary took us back to the plane and home to the mainland.

Telford's operation was considerably more than just island mail, of course. Their chartering took them to Bar Harbor and Portland and Dulles and the north woods and wherever else, and also out and around the islands more, too. Said Kevin, "We're getting a dynamic like Martha's Vineyard or Nantucket—folks are discovering they can do business from the islands as well as from New York City, with fax and Internet. If they need to blast off to a board meeting in New York, they call up and off they go."

Sometimes the human aspect needs to be considered. "You gotta think about who's flying with whom," said Kevin. "Sometimes you get push-me-shove-you deals, and you're the referee."

They did get called on in medical emergencies, too. "We used to get set up a lot on medical deals," Kevin said. "Now we don't go unless there's medical control involved—an EMT or a doctor or someone. We used to get calls from individuals and it wasn't as advertised—they just wanted to get off the island. Now, we might be getting ready to go, but we'll check it out, best we can, for confirmation from someone. It may not be possible—they might not want the law involved, if there's been a stabbing or gunshots or substance use.

"If someone's intoxicated or too weird, we sometimes do choose not to take them. It's a small flight deck." Kevin lost a friend in another part of the country when a suicidal passenger overwhelmed the pilot and ditched the plane.

Kevin tells of getting a call one night from Florida. The woman who called was there with family, and the guy she was calling about was on Matinicus. "He and his brother have issues—there was some kind of a go-round, a vehicle accident, shots fired. She calls, he's been shot, he's in a tree, can we come get him? The sheriff says, 'Let them kill each other.' We went out in the morning—it was a little tense."

People have threatened to sue the flying service when they haven't responded in a medical emergency. A woman under the influence of various substances had driven her car into a tree. With the wind blowing twenty-five knots across the runway, a 150-foot ceiling, and half-mile visibility, they didn't go. She was unhappy. "Another time, a girl got stabbed and then stabbed her boyfriend, and because of the weather, we didn't go. The Marine Patrol went out later on, and then the people refused to go off with him. Then, three weeks later, we were threatened with a suit for not having gone.

"But we're appreciated 95 percent of the time," said Kevin. "All in all, the people are great. It's a privilege doing the service."

Turns out Kevin himself is very much appreciated on Matinicus.

On Monday morning, December 13, 2004, with no warning, Maine Atlantic's owner, Roland Lussier, announced that he was finished with losing money on flights to the islands, and they were stopping right then. Kevin and several of the pilots were told their services were no longer required. The postal contract didn't expire until December 31, but there would be no more flights to Matinicus or anywhere else. North Haven and Vinalhaven of course had ferry service, although Vinalhaveners are reported to have been upset because they didn't get their mail until nine in the morning instead of seven. But Matinicus had nothing. "He closed the thing down and didn't give a shit if we had air service or not," says Vance Bunker, who, along with his wife, Sari, received new titles in the course of the next couple of weeks: point people. Sari says she hadn't run across the term before, but she was told it was just a fancy name for someone to call. That's a position she's held plenty of times before.

It's perhaps not surprising that Maine Atlantic wasn't making money with the island runs. The weather can be tough for the financial side. In 2004, Maine Atlantic lost twenty-two flying days in June to fog and twenty-one in July. The bank wants to be paid even if the plane isn't in the air. But being entirely abandoned, the islanders didn't feel much sympathy for the air company.

Kevin Waters and three fellow former employees of Telford and Maine Atlantic announced that they wanted to create a new company to serve the islands, and Matinicus supported him. "We didn't waste a lot of time wondering who was going to fix things for us," says Eva Murray. With Vance and Sari in the lead, they started raising money to help Kevin get going.

When the newspapers reported that the Rockland-based Island Institute had arranged for Lussier's airline to fly for another ninety days until something could be worked out, some people on Matinicus were upset. The catchphrase on the island—which has long been suspicious of the nonprofit Island Institute—became: "Before they speak FOR us, they should speak TO us." With the full support of the island, Victoria Ross, the summer person who owns the airstrip, told Lussier that his planes were not to land on Matinicus anymore. "We told the only pilot he still had—and he's a friend of ours—that if he landed here, he might not leave," says Vance.

Sari explains, "It's an easy matter—once the plane's down, park a truck here, park a truck there, take the keys, and walk off. We're resourceful out here." Their resourcefulness also carried through to getting the mail to and from the island after Maine Atlantic shut down. Vance flew it out several times in his own plane and brought it once by boat; others brought it on their boats a few times. The Rockland postmaster, Larry Hoodack, rode out with the mail on the single December ferry, impressing the islanders. Wanda assured her stamps-by-mail customers that they would still be able to get their stamps. (Stamps-by-mail is a program in which customers order stamps from an island post office, thereby increasing the business done on the island and, it is hoped, encouraging the authorities to keep post offices open. Island post offices now receive stamp requests from all over the country—and even from expats in other parts of the world.)

Eva Murray reported at the time that the lack of air service was "not unlike a long stretch of summer fog, only without so many boats in the harbor. Vance has his own plane, and that brings us some comfort when we worry about emergencies. He has promised the new teacher he will get her off the island for Christmas." Many people helped the islanders. The propane-truck driver on the December ferry filled his cab with groceries ordered from Shaw's that a Matinicus Islander had delivered to the ferry terminal from the supermarket. And an islander telephoned Viking Lumber in Belfast about his inoperative chainsaw. "Just send it in," said the Viking guy, but when he understood the impossibility of that, he talked the customer through a successful repair.

Despite the slant of press reports, it was never the intention of the Island Institute to promote Lussier's business. Their interest was simply to get the mail moving again, somehow, even on a temporary basis. On December 22, the Institute convened meetings of the various players: representatives of the Postal Service, the Chamber of Commerce, Senator Olympia Snowe's office, the affected islands, the Knox County airport manager, and the county commissioners, along with State Representative Hannah Pingree of North Haven and some others. Sari and Vance attended on behalf of Matinicus. At separate sessions, Lussier and Kevin presented their plans for the islands. Sari says she's not much of a student of body language, "but there was quite a conversation going on that was not being spoken at that meeting." It was clear that just about all the affected people were backing Kevin.

It's a major project—and costly—to start up a company like what Kevin was proposing. Before they would get a penny for themselves, Vance figured it would cost them close to $10,000 a month, not counting any breakdowns that might occur. "If they can make it from now until spring, they'll be OK," Vance predicted.

"The guys are all psyched, even if they don't get paid," says Sari. "They want to do this." In fact, they offered to fly the mail for free during the time there was no service, but the Postal Service wouldn't permit that.

Sari reports that following a letter sent to all the taxpayers on Matinicus—plus anyone else that anyone could think of—they had raised at least seventeen or eighteen thousand dollars, and she'd heard of more that had been sent directly to Kevin. "My respect for Matinicus is immense," says Kevin. "They're real stand-up people when the chips are down."

On January 19, 2005, Kevin announced that his new company, Penobscot Island Air, had received six-month contracts from both the Postal Service and FedEx to serve Matinicus, North Haven, and Vinalhaven. He had leased one plane from Telford and had plans for another before long. Many of the per-diem guys who had been working for Maine Atlantic were ready to help when they were needed. Kevin and his partners were on their way.

Other Independent Cargo Carriers

ISLAND TRANSPORTER LLC

Since she was launched in the spring of 2000, the *Island Transporter* has made herself an essential part of Maine island life. More recently, the parent company, Island Transporter LLC, purchased the smaller landing craft *Reliance* and the pushboat *Pioneer* and her barge. These vessels all have the capability of landing vehicles and products on the shore, and they've carried everything from concrete trucks to salmon fry to destinations from Eastport to Portsmouth, New Hampshire. More normally, the *Transporter* ranges from Mount Desert to Pemaquid, while *Reliance* and *Pioneer* serve Muscongus and Casco Bays. It has worked out well having the other boats available, because even though the *Transporter* could reach the western areas, it was time-consuming and expensive for the clients.

The *Island Transporter* is, above all, versatile. She was designed to be able to land in the state ferry pens stern-first, and she has used them a good bit when possible. On Vinalhaven, when the Maine Department of Transportation built a new ferry pen, they left the old pen in place for the *Transporter* to use during the construction of the town's new school and septic system. With those projects now complete, they're now threatening to take away the old pen, which will hurt the *Transporter*. There is no immediately obvious alternative for her on Vinalhaven, but people are trying to puzzle out the situation.

"They've been very good to us so far," says General Manager Dave Whitney about the Maine State Ferry Service. "We do ease a lot of their burden." Truck traffic is one of the big issues on more than one island served by the state ferries. The *Transporter* does indeed take pressure off the ferries by carrying heavy trucks and taking products such as trash that the ferry doesn't want to carry. But some people question the appropriateness of a private company using the state-owned pens. Fortunately, the *Transporter* also can come into a shoreline and drop her long hydraulic ramps from her bow, allowing vehicles to roll right off at an improved boat launch ramp or even on the beach. She only draws three feet at the bow, and she has skegs outboard of the twin propellers that not only protect the wheels in beaching situations but also limit the number of snags underway. Lobster potwarp slides right under the boat.

Causing more difficulty than the beach itself in many instances is the vehicular access onto the island from the beach. At North Haven, for instance, there's good beach access at Pulpit Harbor—but the bridge at Pulpit isn't adequate for the heavy trucks

The Island Transporter

that tend to take advantage of the service. The islands and Island Transporter are look-ing into more formal options, perhaps leases or construction of facilities where the *Transporter* can land. More than half of their landings now are on beaches, Dave says, not at ferry terminals or boat launch ramps.

Routinely, the ninety-five-foot vessel carries trucks of loam, gravel, paving ma-terial, building supplies, and concrete. Other cargo that travels on the *Transporter* includes well-drillers, excavators, blasting rigs, mobile and modular homes, septic sys-tems, precast concrete products, explosives, petroleum products, and propane trucks (which require extra space around them on the state ferries). She has carried pulp-wood, deckloads of dead cars, and other solid waste off the islands. Although most trash goes off Vinalhaven by ferry, sometimes the ferry people refuse to handle it. "*Transporter* gets juicy garbage or trash with goodies coming out of it," says Dave. "We just wash it off afterward and go on to the next." *Transporter* has provided good serv-ice for Monhegan with demolition debris, old appliances, and the like.

The *Transporter* opened the way to poured-concrete foundations on Matinicus, where previously the single, quick in-and-out trips with the small ferry made delivery of cement all but impossible. The *Transporter* can handle three trucks simultaneously, al-lowing a couple of projects at the same time. The superstructure of the ferries limits the width of their load, but *Transporter* has no trouble with extra-wide machinery, and she has a hundred-ton capacity. She has spent a month each spring stocking salmon pens way downeast, in Lubec and Eastport, and she goes to Isle au Haut once or twice a month most of the year, Dave says. "It takes two and a half hours to get there—if we can, we make it efficient." There's a ramp in Oceanville (Deer Isle) they can use, and they might move gravel trucks back and forth all day, or people might want building sup-plies at the same time. "The road commissioner on Isle au Haut, Bill Stevens, acts as our agent out there. He's done it with us so much, he knows how to take advantage of the tide and just how much to get on the boat."

Surprisingly, Dave says that the tide isn't too much of an issue in the *Transporter*'s area. "It's in the back of my mind when I'm scheduling, but it's not that big a factor up here." It's important in Portland, though, where the company's two smaller vessels op-erate. They take a lot of trash ashore from Long Island and Chebeague in Casco Bay. "Throughout the bay down there, most of the islands have some semblance of a ramp—they've had a need for one."

Dave keeps his ears open for opportunities for the vessels all along the coast. *Transporter* has yet to go to Frenchboro, and she doesn't go much to Swans Island. The Cranberry Isles are well served by the Beal and Bunker ferries, and it's only when a paving project comes up that the *Transporter* is called to help out.

The vessel is licensed for forty-nine passengers and has gone through the same

Coast Guard testing required for any other vessel that takes passengers for hire, including stability and all the other safety issues. A man-overboard drill is different on her than on many vessels. While the skipper maneuvers the boat, the engineer/deckhand, equipped with life jacket and safety lines, goes out on one of the ramps and picks up the victim. The captain's elevated station and his clear visibility—combined with the rescuer's position close to the water—make the exercise relatively easy. Still, everyone hopes the maneuver will never have to be more than a drill. There's no posh accommodation for passengers, but they'll get where they're going. So far, she has only been called on twice to carry passengers. "They milled about smartly and waited for the boat ride to be over," says Dave.

COASTAL TANKERS

Fuel can be purchased on each of the offshore islands, and houses are often heated by oil or kerosene, just as in other parts of Maine. All that petroleum has to get there, though. The Cranberry Isles are served by Beal and Bunker, and Swans Island gets its liquid fuel products by truck and ferry, but Coastal Tankers and Petroleum Corporation's little seventy-two-foot tanker *William McLoon* delivers them to mom-and-pop operations and fishermen's co-ops on the rest of the midcoast islands from Frenchboro to Monhegan. "Sixty-five percent of our business is lobster fishermen," says Captain Rob Jongerden.

"Mom had such high hopes for me," sighs Rob. "I just thought I'd like to work on boats for awhile." But for some twenty-five years, he has been running fuel all along the Maine coast. Until recently, if the *McLoon* was down, his backup was one of the last remaining wooden tankers, the fifty-five-foot *Rockland Gulf*. The *Rockland Gulf* has been a familiar sight around the islands for many decades. She was built in 1933 in Brooklyn, New York, for Gulf Oil, specifically to transport fuel in Penobscot Bay. But wooden boats are always in need of something, even if they're not seventy-plus years old, and the Coast Guard needs to be convinced that the *Rockland Gulf* is still seaworthy.

By 2015, all petroleum-carrying vessels must be double-hulled. It is company owner Ed Polk's position that the *Rockland Gulf* is already double-hulled—or has a double containment system as effective as a double hull—because she has a wooden hull and steel tanks. At this writing, engineering plans had been submitted to the Coast Guard, but they were still reviewing them, and the fate of the old wooden vessel was in the air. Meanwhile, the company is working up plans to double-hull the steel *McLoon*, a relative youngster. She was built in 1954, also for Penobscot Bay. If the plans are not acceptable to the Coast Guard, it will be the end of Coastal Tankers. Although some islands are now trucking petroleum, others, not served by regular ferry or barge service,

The William McLoon

have no good way to do that. "We don't want to stop serving," says Ed. "But I'd just as soon sell out, myself," he adds. Let someone else worry about the Coast Guard.

A crew of three runs the *McLoon*; Rob is captain. The Coast Guard requires him to carry a 100-ton master's license, and a member of the crew has to have a tankerman's endorsement, showing that he or she knows how to transfer flammable liquids.

"The third guy can be rail meat," Rob says, although often all three of the crew members have both master's tickets (licenses) and tankerman's endorsements. "Mostly, you just have to find someone who likes the whole thing." Apparently he has been able to do that. His first mate has been with the *McLoon* more than fifteen years.

In the summer, keeping the islands supplied is a five-day-a-week job for the *McLoon*. In winter, three days usually suffice.

The *McLoon* can carry fifty-two thousand gallons in ten separate tanks—five times what the old *Rockland Gulf* can manage. By comparison, a small Irving Oil tanker—such as might come up Penobscot Bay to Searsport—carries a couple of million gallons, and ships with twenty million gallons dock in Portland.

Rob used to take the *McLoon* to Portland to fill up, but Irving now trucks ten thousand gallons at a time right to the dock in Rockland. "That changed the complexion of the job a whole lot. Portland was a two-day trip in itself. In the winter, those passages could be fun," he smiles, obviously glad at the change.

"It costs an extra three cents a gallon having it trucked, but it's worth it—to me, anyway."

The vessels can take whatever weather comes along, but depending on the route, some winds are more difficult than others. "If it's a northeast gale," he notes, "it's a drag to get over to North Haven, but once you're there, it's beautiful. Southeast is fine going across to Vinalhaven, but then you can't get away from the dock once you're in."

Some of the harbors to which Rob makes deliveries have other challenges. The most difficult is the Pendleton Yacht Yard on Islesboro—their dock dries out on every tide. "You have to get in there a couple of hours before high water and get out just as soon as you can," he says.

The *William McLoon* isn't always seen in a favorable light. "There are two different worlds out there," Rob said. "No one waves at us—dirty tanker, you know. I always ask people, 'Do you know my name?' And when they don't, I say, 'Well, that's good.'" If the *McLoon* ever were grounded, everyone would hear about it.

But those same people who don't wave at him from their boats are very glad to be able to fuel up on the islands.

SEA TRUK

Roaring down the bay, the Sea Truks are outrageous—their immense tires just appearing over the water and looking for all the world like a mistake. Captain David Barrett owns two of the Lighter Amphibious Resupply Cargo LXs (LARC-LXs), which were designed for the U.S. Army in the late 1950s and saw service in Vietnam, moving sixty-ton tanks and other large machinery. Since 2000, Dave has been using the vessels to carry equipment and materials to and from islands all along the Maine coast.

To a nearby listener on the bay, the vessel's noise is astounding. Dave says that he and his crew wear ear protection, but the exhaust system, pointed straight out, sends most of the sound overboard. "If it went straight up, you couldn't stand on the deck," he admits. The LARCs have four 165-hp engines, which, traveling from one place to another, he normally runs at 1500 rpm. In close quarters, he runs more slowly than that—"I don't like ruffling feathers." LARCs require the most power when they're climbing out of the water, and they rev up to 2100 rpm. "That's where the engines are tested." In water, the vessels top out at six knots; on land, they can do fifteen miles an hour. The army tried getting a major increase in power on a couple and got them up to thirty mph on land. But with no suspension, they were unsafe at that speed, and they still made only about six knots in the water. They're hardly an ideal hydrodynamic shape.

What they can do—and what no other vessel in the area can do—is crawl right up the beach to deliver their cargo. Just as they did for the army, they can take heavy equipment—bulldozers or well-drilling rigs or cranes or cement mixers or loaded dump trucks—and deposit it all on dry land. The largest machine Dave has carted around is a seventy-ton rock crusher that he took out to Vinalhaven and brought back again after it had processed the rock required for the new school. "That's one machine I wouldn't

A Sea Truk

care to see again," he says. All its weight was on one end; its jaws, engine, and wheels left the Sea Truk seriously bow-heavy. When they landed on Vinalhaven, in spite of the tremendous flotation from the Sea Truk's nine-and-a-half-foot tall, three-foot-wide tires, they broke through what looked like a hard gravel beach into soft mud underneath. They got the machine off the Sea Truk the following morning, using crane mats and pushing and dragging with a tractor.

But loading or unloading generally is easier with an amphibious vessel than with a barge or landing craft, says Dave, as it's on solid ground when the vehicle disembarks. "We're sitting on all fours. And if the ramp angle needs lessening, we can just let air out of the tires and lower the front of the boat. It would be a high-wire act to get a seventy-ton machine onto a floating boat, other than a huge barge." Big barges with a tug to move them cost more than three times as much as Dave charges for his Sea Truks.

The vessels run on compressed air, rather than the more common electrical systems. There's an electric alarm system and lights, but everything else is air-controlled. Throttles, brakes for land operation, engine cutouts—all are air-activated. "They're self-reliant for air-start," Dave explains. "You can tap into reserve air in the tires if you need to, backfeed into the system to start the engine, and, once you start it, the compressor can regenerate."

Usually, if you're going to get stuck, it will be in the muck at low water, and since the Maine tide is usually at least ten feet and the boats draw eight, at high tide the Sea Truks can float off. Bulldozers sunk into the beach don't have that ability.

Where the vessels excel, however, is carrying bulk raw materials. In many cases, this works out better than taking loaded trucks. With a forty-one-foot-long, thirteen-and-a-half-foot-wide cargo hold, the LARC-LX can carry eighty tons of loam, sand, gravel, crushed rock, or what-have-you. That's sixty cubic yards—the capacity of three large dump trucks—which can then be offloaded on-site by an excavator or bucket loader. Some of the islands that the Sea Truk can access have no roads, so dump trucks would be useless if they could land at all. Dave can deliver the equipment and materials needed to build those roads. The cost of the delivery is lessened also because there is no need for truck operators and no need to tie up trucks.

The Sea Truks carry island-harvested timber to the mainland—tree-length, thirty cords at a time. A log truck meets the boat on the mainland and picks off the logs. He has delivered precut timber-frame houses out to islands, all ready to be put together. He has taken down a big, never-finished house on Jordan's Delight off Milbridge, burning what could be burned on-site and carting off the rest in a Sea Truk. He has worked with septic-system contractors, either taking the subcontract to transport materials or, if he had the contract, subcontracting the actual system construction. Either way works—"It depends who gets the call," he says.

Dave usually keeps the Sea Truks at Mack Point in Searsport; it's central along the coast, not too far from Islesboro, where Dave and his wife, Marianne, have been living for several years, and convenient to services. Hamilton Marine, the largest marine hardware store around, is just up the road, and there's fuel at hand. The facility is big and has a good landing site and asphalt pads for parking. "They're fairly enormous," Dave says of his vessels, which are more than sixty-two feet long, nearly twenty-seven feet wide, and almost twenty feet tall, out of the water.

Unlike the amphibious trucks, DUKWs, or Ducks—which have hit the news for sinking and taking lives of tourists in recent years—the LARC rig is designed so that it is not susceptible to water intrusion. The wheels are suspended from above the water-line on vertical columns that turn at the wheel end. There is no exchange with sea water; cooling is by keel coolers and radiator. Even so, LARC-LXs are best stored on the hard; the seals on the wheel ends eventually would start to seep if they were in the water constantly. But these are boats, not land vehicles retrofitted for amphibious work; they are fully documented with the Coast Guard. Dave's vessels—originally named *LARC 52* and *LARC 53*—were built in 1965 and 1966 and have been kept in good shape. He bought them from a U.S. Army Reserve unit in Florida, where they had undergone a complete refit a couple of years earlier; he has renamed them *Sea Truk 52* and *Sea Truk*

53. There were only sixty built, and, like all military vessels and vehicles, they have enthusiastic followers. From his website, he gets e-mail from people who have served on such vessels, though he hasn't heard from anyone who was on either of his.

When he moved to Islesboro, Dave had been thinking he'd like to work for himself. He had seen landing craft running between the Caribbean islands, and he knew there were some in Casco Bay but none east of there. In 2000, he brought in the two LARCs. Though he didn't know it, he arrived at the very same time that the *Island Transporter* was launched. Apparently it was an idea whose time had come.

The trip from Florida took seven weeks, running the two vessels in convoy. He hired three guys; that crew lasted two weeks. He hired three more, and they also lasted two weeks. From Annapolis to Penobscot Bay, there was just one person on each boat. "Not the smartest thing to do," he admits. "There's a lot to handle." Normally, he operates with a captain and one other man, who keeps an eye on fluid levels, greasing, and all the systems, as well as providing an extra set of eyes in close quarters. "Backing into a mooring field in the fog isn't a one-man job."

On the trip to Maine, they made sixty or sixty-five miles a day and pulled in overnight, sleeping in a Winnebago Dave had bought in a used-car lot and parked in one of the LARCs. It was a long trip.

But once he got Sea Truk going, Dave's marine interests were satisfied. "It's a work in progress," he says of the business. "I knew there were possibilities and thought that it was viable, and it's expanded along the way. On every job, I see neat little islands that, even when sailing, I didn't see; sailing, you're going from A to B and you have to watch out for the hazards and stay clear. Now I'm going right into the hazards." He enjoys getting a call to go to some island that he's never heard of—one where he has to look it up and also figure out how to get into it.

"I feel proud to have initiated and executed an idea with a little bit of frontierism in it. These days, it's hard to find opportunities to do something different, of your own making." The boats aren't stereotypically beautiful, to be sure, but to Dave, "the most beautiful boat is one that makes money. This gives me the opportunity to be on the water and make a living." Not that it's making him rich, he quickly adds. "It's been an experience for me being in business. A character-builder."

the Cranberry Isles

t he town of Cranberry Isles is made up of five islands; of those, Sutton, Baker, and Bear have only summer residences. Each of the two year-round islands is usually called by a name different from the ones on maps. Little Cranberry is called Islesford, and Great Cranberry is known simply as Cranberry, or sometimes Big Cranberry. ("Great" is a bit much.) The two year-round islands are connected to each other and to Northeast Harbor by a regular privately operated mailboat service; in summer, a boat runs from Southwest Harbor, too. Both of these boats will stop at Sutton on request. Since the turn of the twentieth century, Big and Little Cranberry have had significant numbers of summer people who, as on other Maine islands, provide work for islanders. But there is a variety of other employment as well—though as on many other islands, there are more job opportunities than people to fill them.

Although it is smaller in area, Islesford, with sixty or seventy year-round residents, is more populated than Big Cranberry, with only thirty-five or forty. For several years now, the school on Great Cranberry has had no students, although it has not been officially closed. As noted before, a closed school has traditionally been the last straw for an island community. (In 1914, Town Meeting on Sutton Island voted to keep the school open for one more year for two students. That was it for Sutton; since that time, it has been a summer place only.) Nowadays, reopening a school is impossible, practically speaking, if only because the building would have to be brought up to modern code standards. At this writing, on Big Cranberry there is only one young child, a baby. The two children approaching school age moved off-island before the 2004 school year.

The Islesford School is thriving, although no one ever knows for certain how many students there will be. In 2003–4, there were thirteen pupils; the following year started with seven.

There is a store on each island (though the Cranberry store has more to offer), and a library and a historical society, and gasoline is available. Diesel fuel is sold at the Cranberry Isles Fishermen's Co-op on Islesford. Construction is going on all the time, with as many as thirty or forty workmen aboard the mailboat every day. On Islesford, women have found ways to support themselves, as have men who don't choose to fish. "If anybody really wants to, they can live on this island," says Ann Fernald, who has lived there since 1950. "It's a matter of the will." Computers, of course, have opened new avenues, and some women go fishing, but Little Cranberry is home to several artists and artisans. Perhaps the best known is Ashley Bryan, the African-American author and illustrator of children's books, who has owned a home on Islesford since the mid-1940s. He has been recognized with several national prizes, but nowhere is he more cherished than on the island. "We're very honored to have Ashley make his home here," says Ann. "He's such a gentle soul."

There have been and still are jewelers and potters and sculptors as well as painters and other artisans on Islesford; some have their own shops in summer. Cranberry has always had its share of artists, too, though their sales are made elsewhere. Cranberry is also home to two boatyards and a seasonal gift shop.

There are quite a few automobiles on the two big islands; a few years back, the people on Big Cranberry built—mostly with donations—a four-thousand-gallon gasoline storage tank. It has a key-entry system that allows islanders to drive up at any time of day or night, put in the key, punch in the code, and get gasoline. A young couple who moved to Big Cranberry from North Carolina takes care of the gas business, doing the bookkeeping and billing and keeping track of the supply.

On Islesford, the Fishermen's Co-op takes care of fuel. Coastal Energy has tanks there, and the co-op has a little truck for making deliveries.

Among the people who grew up on one of the two larger islands, it would be an unusual individual who would want to live on the other. Relations haven't exactly been rancorous between the islands, and with Town Meeting alternating from one island to the other each year, everyone has been respectful of the wishes of the other island for the most part—but there's something. That's just how it is. Little complaints are mentioned by people on both sides: Islesford doesn't provide much in the way of a lunch when Town Meeting's there—just a potluck meal—while Cranberry perhaps goes overboard, with Cornish game hens and wild rice. Perhaps the solid-waste dumpster area is tidier on Cranberry than on Islesford—but it must be pointed out that the fellow who takes care of solid waste lives on Cranberry. There are people on Cranberry who'll say that the greater number of objects left inappropriately at the transfer site on Islesford—one time, an entire skiff was thrown into the dumpster—is evidence of a different, even disgusting, attitude of the Islesford residents. But others are pleased that rejects that previously would have ended up in the woods are now being removed from the island. Soon there will be a compactor in place, at least on Cranberry, and a person to tend it during the hours for bringing trash. Someone didn't think much of this idea—it's very expensive, if nothing else—and expressed his unhappiness in big red letters on the new building constructed to hold the compactor. "I gather it wasn't anyone from our island," I was told. "Doing something like that just shows the stupid mindset."

"People are insular, of course, living on islands," I was told (it's true by definition), "and tend to think theirs is the best. It's the same ocean surrounding us, and we breathe the same air—I think the difference is fictional, but some believe theirs is better. It's like competing high schools."

Beal and Bunker Serve the Cranberries

A lot of freight has to be carried to the Cranberry Isles, in addition to all the people who want to come out or go ashore. Less than half an hour is scheduled for the boat trips between the Cranberries and Northeast Harbor, and fifteen minutes between Islesford and Big Cranberry; the islands are well connected through relatively protected water.

Beal and Bunker, Inc., has been running the Cranberry Isles mailboat for nearly fifty years now, as well as providing charter service and barging. David Bunker is now the president of the company. Chances are, if something's on one of the Cranberries, one of David's boats got it there, via either the mailboat or his barge.

In the winter, three round-trips are scheduled between Northeast Harbor, Great Cranberry, and Islesford each day, leaving Northeast at seven-thirty and eleven in the morning and three-thirty in the afternoon. This schedule allows people to come across to the islands to work each day—and, even in the dead of winter, there are always twenty and often forty who do. Later in the spring, they add a trip; in the summer, Beal and Bunker has seven scheduled trips.

Beal & Bunker's Cap'n B *and barge headed out*

One or two barge trips a week usually take care of the needs of the islands during the winter—fuel, construction lumber, bait for the co-op in Islesford, and trash on the return. In summer, "it's just as fast as we can do things," says David Bunker. There are three trips a week just carrying trucks of lobster bait. The fiberglass lobsterboat-style *Cap'n B* noses into the deck barge and is tied in place with a wire. She pushes the barge onto the boat-launch ramp in Northeast Harbor, where it drops its own ramps so trucks can drive on, and then they head out across the two miles of the Eastern Way. Pretty soon, back she comes, with the empty truck(s) on the barge. David has a new barge that can carry considerably more payload than the older one, perhaps even ninety or a hundred thousand pounds.

When the gasoline supply on Cranberry gets down to five hundred gallons, the caretakers call David and he gets three thousand gallons in a truck from Coastal Energy. "I used to have a dock, and delivered fuel and had gas, and it was a pain in the butt, particularly in winter. It took a long time to get your money back," he says. "This is better." But still, David's barge carries the fuel.

David's father, Wilfred, founded Beal and Bunker with the late Clarence Beal in 1950. David has been involved with the company since he was in high school, and he started running boats full-time as soon as he finished high school. His father, born in 1920, still is involved with the business: "He's outgoing, and if anything's going on, he's always wanted to be in the middle of it." Retired now, Wilfred lives in Florida in the winter. When he's in Maine, he makes his home on the mainland, in Trenton. "He's still right back and forth to the islands and in the middle of the company," says David. Wilfred always tells his son he doesn't know how much he can do, and then he volunteers for a lot. "He ran little charters last year, and he made the mailboat trip once in a while when the regular crew was fitting out the other boats. As long as he has his captain's license, I'm going to let him do as much as he wants to do. He doesn't want to stop," David says.

Great Cranberry's Boatyards

David and Barbara Stainton are among the outright transplants to the Cranberry Isles. They'd been living in Vermont until about twenty years ago, when they saw an advertisement for a boatyard on Cranberry and bought it. They have lived there ever since. "We got some sidelong glances from people," she says, but they're well ensconced in the community now, involved in many community efforts. "I can't say we've had terribly many regrets."

The first two winters, they rented a house; in the summer, they lived some of the time in an old shack and part of the time on a boat. The third summer, they moved five or six times, until they lucked into a little piece of land. Eventually, they had a home of their own. But because they had firsthand experience with the housing shortage, it's not surprising that Barbara became involved in the effort to create affordable housing in the town. Housing has been an issue for their boatyard employees, too; two commute from East Blue Hill and one from Mount Desert. In winter, with a short lunch, they have seven hours in between the first boat on and the last boat off. "They've been coming five or six years and they do a fine job," she says.

Their Cranberry Island Boatyard stores and maintains fifty boats, and David designed a 19-footer, for which there's a market for all they can build, Barbara says. "The question is, how long do we want to keep doing this? I'm seventy, he's coming up on it. Are we gonna die with our boots on? I don't know. We tell people we can make them one of these in a year and a half if we all live that long."

The other boatyard, Newman and Gray, stores a few boats but specializes in boat reconstruction and new boat construction. Ed Gray manages the yard, and he has two year-round employees—one who commutes from Ellsworth and one who lives on the island. When they're not doing something else, Ed's children work in the yard or for his partner, Jarvis Newman, in Manset (part of Southwest Harbor). Martha, Ed's daughter, has started a successful landscaping business on Cranberry Island that keeps her busy working for the summer people. "They want services," says Jarvis, "and getting help is very difficult."

Islesford's Fernald Family

It's an old joke, but I don't know how many times I've walked into it. Asked if he'd fished from Islesford all his life, Warren Fernald answered, "Not quite all my life yet." Like many islanders, as a youngster he set a few traps from a skiff, and he has made his living from the big crustaceans ever since, except for the five years he was in the U.S. Navy. The day I met him and his wife, Ann, he'd just been given permission to haul for the first time since surgery six weeks earlier. He was anxious to get going. He was seventy-eight, and I suppose she must be about that age too, but I would not have guessed that of either of them.

Warren's is one of twenty boats selling his catch to the Cranberry Isles Fishermen's Co-op—most are from Islesford, and a very few are from Cranberry and Northeast Harbor. Three of Warren's sons are among those fishermen who grew up on the island, and there are also a few who either came from Away or were summer people who stayed on the island full-time and went lobstering. Of the young people who leave the island, many—including the Fernalds' children who live off—come back for their summers. "I'd say nine out of ten do," says Ann.

Ann and Warren's youngest son, Paul, is a contractor who repairs, maintains, and sometimes does some construction on twenty or twenty-five summer houses. "It's constant upkeep—decks, roofing, painting, plumbing. I'm a jack-of-all-trades," Paul says. "I started doing it and learned as I went along."

He says that he got seasick, so he's not fishing like his brothers. "The last day I went, I was sick all day. It was November, and freezing. 'OK,' I said, 'I'm not going to do that again.'" His mother says he just didn't have fishing in him the way his brothers did. Paul admits that he can be on a boat all day long and be fine unless he's filling bait bags. (Rusty Crossman, a lifelong fisherman from Frenchboro and now Swans Island, says he was seasick every single day that he sterned for his stepfather, from when he was nine until he was thirteen. "Never been sick since." Makes a difference whose boat it is, perhaps.)

Paul and his wife, Brenda, live ashore because their two sons "got itchy" as they grew older. They're both playing football, which of course they wouldn't have had the option to do if they had stayed in the Islesford School. Brenda works at Mount Desert Island High School, but Paul commutes every day to the island, and they're all on the island in summer.

Except in the dead of winter, Paul comes across in his own boat. "The mailboat is a drag," he says. It's a long trip, stopping at each island—sometimes Sutton even in the off-season if there's a construction project there—and you're stuck with their schedule.

Islesford seems to have an unusually easy relationship between its summer and winter populations. (Warren remembers when it wasn't that way.) Lobstermen who do well sometimes also live ashore during the winter, but that doesn't make them summer people. They still work island waters. Some choose that their children not go to school on the island, and they sometimes come back full-time once the children have finished school. Warren's son Bruce did.

One of the Fernalds' daughters has married a former summer person, as has their son—she worked stern for him—and a summer person works for Paul. The interests of summer people and natives aren't totally separate anymore, either. One of Warren and Ann's sons, Danny, is an artist and runs a gallery on the island as well as fishing, and at least one summer person has moved onto the island to fish full-time.

A Year on Islesford

When they enrolled their children in the Islesford School for a year, Chris Wriggins had spent every summer of his life on Little Cranberry Island, and his wife, Marian Baker, had been running her pottery shop on the Islesford dock a dozen years. "We already knew the year-round population pretty well," Marian says, "and it was totally easy to turn up and bring two boys to school." The school, which then had about eleven students and was happy for more of either sex, happened to be heavy on girls, so the boys were particularly welcomed. They were seven and ten years old. "It was a fantastic experience," Marian says, and Chris agrees. If they had any discomforts at all, neither of them mentions them. Everyone recognizes the importance of the school to the well-being of an island. Chris is on the board of the Cranberry Isles Realty Trust (CIRT), the affordable housing group.

The family moved into a winterized home in the village for the school year, which was good not only for its central location—"Being in the middle of town, in the middle of the pathway," says Chris, "we got visited a lot more often" than in their own house on the shore—but it allowed Marian to continue with her pottery. Their own house is not winterized, and she would not have been able to work there in the cold weather. Chris, an architect, could maintain his business from the island in winter just as he does in summer, commuting back and forth to Yarmouth in southern Maine when need arose. After the one planned year on the island, the boys really wanted to stay on, and so did Chris and Marian. But she couldn't ask for an extension of her leave of absence from the Maine College of Art (MECA) in Portland. So, as a part-time instructor at MECA, she managed to commute each week, leaving the island on the last boat on Mondays and taking an early boat back on Fridays. That second fall, they stayed in their own house on the shore, perhaps three-quarters of a mile from the village. "It felt isolated," Chris says. Marian says it was a little harder for the kids to get together with the other kids, particularly as the days got shorter, but they still did play flashlight tag. Someone would call and say they were meeting at such-and-such place, and kids and any grown-ups who wanted to join in would all get together and play flashlight tag.

The school at that time was divided into two sections, K–4 and 5–8, with about equal numbers in each. One Wriggins boy was in each group. The two teachers divided classes and activities as they chose, and every student had both teachers both years. (In 2004–5, with just seven students, there was only one teacher, with an aide to help.)

When Marian and Chris first planned the year, they weren't certain the boys would want to spend a whole year on the island. "I was going to make them do it anyway," Marian says. "They'd get over it. But they were excited." Even though they were leaving friends in Yarmouth, they had friends on the island, too. The boys had no trouble adjusting—not to the new school nor to Yarmouth when they returned after a year and a half. Academically, too, they did fine, even though they changed schools in the middle of the second year. They didn't have much homework in Islesford, "but they didn't need to—there was so much one-on-one and no waiting in lines and so on."

The school had a lot of off-island field trips, and either Chris or Marian always went along. Much of the material was related to life on the islands—a long science project was devoted to the study of lobsters, for instance. (Danny, who his mother describes as a wiseacre anyway, said they didn't need to spend quite as much time on lobsters as they did.) And a major assignment—one that took a couple of months, off and on—was their book project. Each child chose an island person, usually an older resident, and created a book about him or her. That required writing a letter requesting the person to be the book subject, and interviewing, and photography, and finally compiling the research into some kind of book. A visiting artist came to the island to show them various ways of making books—some of them nonconventional and not only creative and interesting but also particularly appropriate for younger children whose work wasn't primarily in words.

At the end of their first year back in Yarmouth, even though the boys were glad to be back in some ways, they still were saying they'd like to return to school on Islesford. Marian probed that a bit, finding that part of what they so liked was the autonomy. "They could bike to school—Danny could even walk to school on his stilts," Marian says. Danny did that for a time—until he decided it was easier to ride his bike. In particular, they had after-school freedom they'd never had before—"taking off on bikes, not having to be schlepped around." No doubt their parents enjoyed that, too. "You don't have to call people to arrange for friends to come over and play—the whole gang runs off to play in the woods," says Chris.

"We'd ask where they were going," Marian adds, "and ask them to call if they were going somewhere else." But on an island only a mile long, they were free to go anywhere they wanted. Marian liked the physical safety on the island. "They're not going to get abducted—though of course they could fall off a rock and need stitches." But everyone knows them, and if a kid should get hurt, he or one of his friends can go to anyone nearby and get help.

"Everyone helps each other," Marian says. "It's taken for granted that you'll be helped and you'll help. If you're out of eggs, you borrow a couple, and if someone's going off the island, they'll say, 'I'm going to Bangor, need anything?' 'Sure, vanilla,' you can say, and not feel bad about asking. Or if your kid does need stitches, they'll drop what they're doing and help." Of course, she would do the same. And you learn to improvise, make do, and stock up so you don't get caught short the same way again. "I'm OK with not having conveniences," she says. "You share a lot."

In more public matters too, people pitch in. Marian tells about new playground equipment that had to be assembled. Someone put up signs at the store: "Anyone interested come and bring tools." "The men who understand tools have to show up—there is no professional to do it. If you can't use tools, you bring lemonade and carry things around." The only people exempt are old people who've done their share and young mothers with babies.

Marian admits, "It's nice to have the anonymity you have off-island—in Yarmouth, I volunteer when I can and don't feel guilty when I don't. On the island, I did feel guilty. But I like both ways."

Both Chris and Marian remark on the connectedness of the people. "In time, we became very close to some people," Chris says. "You almost needed a pressure valve to get a release sometimes. Everything on an island is personal, and you can't just walk away after some negotiation and never see that person again."

"I found out an interesting thing," Marian says. "There's a lot of diversity even in such a small community, at least on this island. You learn a lot about getting along with people who are really different. With some, you just don't bring up politics, for instance." (That's true 'most everywhere, no?) And you're careful what you say. "I'm not a person with much to hide, no skeletons in the closet, but you do learn to be very careful if you're talking about someone. I'd be very positive, or at least think twice before saying anything that could be interpreted negatively, and be aware who's in the room."

On Islesford, everyone's aware of every single person in the community, like family, says Marian. You know where people are by where their car is, or by their routines, but there's respect for a certain kind of privacy, too. "Sure, everyone knows everyone's business to a point, but they leave it alone. It's a nonjudgmental attitude."

During their year on the island, Marian enjoyed having more time than she has in summer to get to know people. She loved hanging out with people "our age"—by which she meant people between twenty and sixty, not just ones within three years of her own age. When she'd visit with Warren and Ann Fernald, even though their children are her own age, she felt they were all peers. She had time to cultivate relationships with other older people on the island, too, including two or three who don't get out much. When there is a function with food at the Neighborhood House—like graduation or the harvest supper on Columbus Day—before the food runs out, someone will make up three or four plates and take them to people who aren't able to be there. Marian made the deliveries a few times.

She loves knowing everyone, talking to the captain on the boat, and even griping when conditions aren't good. "People mutter and moan and bitch in bad weather, but they almost embrace the bitching—it's a reward, thinking you're all right with the hardship. We fuss about the wind but love the commute across the water—who wouldn't?" She understands now the dichotomy that year-rounders have about summer people, knows that they love to see the summer people come and also love to see them go. "I work when I'm there; I'm not vacationing the way most of them are. I kill myself out there, but I love every second." She feels fortunate—blessed, even—that her family had the opportunity to spend a year and a half on the island as year-rounders, that they had the chance to know many people on a different level. "That won't change now, for us."

Island
Schools

t he one universal among all the island schools is that by mainland standards they are small. The teacher/student ratios are beneficial—if not extreme— and it is harder to lose an individual kid through the cracks than it is ashore. But there's a big difference between Vinalhaven's two hundred students (kindergarten through grade 12) and the single-teacher schools where in any given year there might be six students in grades K–8, or there might be two, or none at all. The residents of several islands—understanding that a school is essential to a viable island community—have attempted to attract newcomers, particularly newcomers with children, or to help their own young people to remain on the island. They have had varying degrees of success.

Island schooling is a paradox, always coming under pressure from some quarter or other to close a school or to combine it somehow or at least to limit the number of grades taught. Almost always, these concerns are brought up for financial reasons, and they are rarely raised by island-educated people or by the parents of children in school at the time.

Monhegan Schoolhouse

Each of the K–12 schools (Vinalhaven, North Haven, and Islesboro) has a definite flavor, distinct from the others, mirroring its community and its leadership. The islands downeast send their children ashore to high school after eighth grade; on the Casco Bay islands, where there are frequent ferries, kids travel to the mainland after fifth grade. Even the youngest of Great Diamond Island's few students go off-island every day. For those on the farthest-out islands—Matinicus and Frenchboro, as well as Monhegan—commuting to school is impossible. In years past, students were sent to boarding school or to live with relatives, but more and more often nowadays, whole families move ashore when the first child reaches high-school age. Ironically, the very factor that made island communities invite new families to move in—children—more than once has become the reason those same families moved off again as their children were ready for high school.

On all these islands, as in any school, the school experience for one child can be entirely different from that of the next. Islesboro's Dan Tutor went to Gould Academy for high school—it was his choice, and the school provided enough scholarship money to make it possible. "He was lobbying for it from seventh grade," says his mother, Sue Hatch. "He wanted more—more people, more sports, more art, a bigger world. It's the luck of the draw what people you have around you on the island. He only had one friend here, and he was the most academic of the kids around his age. School here was no challenge for him." On the other hand, other students have commuted from the mainland to Islesboro and have been pleased by the experience.

Monhegan School

Retired after twenty-three years as superintendent of School Administrative District 28 (Camden/Rockport), Tom Marx has recently taken up island work. For five years he made monthly trips to Monhegan Island to work with the teacher and the school board out there, and then he began a stint playing the same role on North Haven. He is clearly very taken with both of those island schools—one tiny, the other merely small. While obviously very different, the two schools have much in common.

Monhegan, for many years averaging four students, jumped to seven in 2004–05. The pre-K–8 program occupies a single room in a classic old school building, well supported by board, town, and parents. It takes an unusual teacher to handle the spectrum—there may be one child struggling to learn his numbers at the same time that another is working on algebra. "The island teachers," Tom says, "are usually young, adventurous, intelligent, creative, imaginative, romantic, idealistic, hard-working and caring." He adds that the key to success on the island is "how quietly confident you are within yourself, how balanced"—traits that are important for any island resident. "You have to have the ability to be introspective, self-analytical, and to introduce questions and see and hear what someone might say."

Monhegan, like many of the islands, long had a policy of keeping a teacher a maximum of two years. Tenure kicks in after that, and understandably there has been concern about the impact on children who conceivably could have only one teacher in nine years of schooling. "Every teacher has strengths, weaknesses, interests, and cold spots," says Tom. The problem with a two-year limit is that it takes even the best of teachers a time to adjust, perhaps the whole first year to become familiar with an island and how it works. When winter closes in and the boat's not running, the teacher has to be able to stay holed up and comfortable. The first year, says Tom, they're bound to have doubts—"What's going on in the classroom? Am I really teaching these kids what they need?"

It's difficult to teach such a wide grade span, but, says Tom of the island schools with which he's worked, the students are nearly ideal. "The types of people who end up living on islands," he says, "almost all have the same qualities as do the teachers. They're independent, self-motivated, and hardworking, and they see opportunities. Genetically and socially, their kids are the same way. They're unusually bright, creative, and gifted—all are capable and achieving students."

Monhegan has put together an ancillary support team that makes the teacher's admittedly challenging job somewhat easier. A special education consultant on the mainland comes out a few times each year but is always on call should the teacher want to speak with her. There's a similar arrangement with a gifted-and-talented specialist, and usually a guidance counselor, also. This year they've increased the ed tech (teacher's assistant) help the single teacher gets, and they always make an effort to find ed techs with artistic backgrounds.

Not everyone can do the job. It helps, Tom says, if the teacher has a spouse or partner, which was the case with the last two of the three Monhegan teachers with whom he worked. They came on-island with the teacher and found jobs carpentering— they were skilled, hard-working, nice guys. Tom throws out some more adjectives about the right teacher—eclectic, diverse, multitalented, and disciplined. And Monhegan now has a teacher so well matched to the island that the board waived its two-year policy. Sarah Conefry is working under a continuing contract. Unless she truly screws up, she can stay as long as she likes. Tom thinks very highly of her: "I would hire her anywhere."

The multiage classroom provides opportunities for the students unlike anything they'd find ashore. "The older ones assume responsibility for the younger." It's not just tolerance—which would suggest they might not choose that role. "They are lovingly accommodating to one another."

The islands are by nature like families, Tom says. "Doors are left unlocked, any-body can come in, and people are responsible for each other. Neighbors take note of things—where's that kid going? It's only eleven fifteen and school's not out yet." Children are assimilated into adult activities and even as youngsters become a valued part of the community.

Of course, on Monhegan the trauma comes after eighth grade. All the children leave the island for high school, either a public school somewhere or a private boarding school. The transition is hard, no matter how it is made—whether the child boards with a relative or friend or at school, or one or both parents move ashore. (Monhegan is unusual among the islands in that the lobstering season is in winter, so it's less likely that fathers will leave the island during much of the school year.) For each high-school student, the island pays the state's average tuition—$7,700, last Tom knew—plus about the same amount for board and books. Still, the cost of a private boarding school, commonly the choice of Monhegan students, now exceeds $30,000 a year. Bright island students (not just those from Monhegan) tend to be of interest to prep schools—they're not quite foreign students, but they certainly come from an unusual background, and they're well prepared academically. They are encouraged to enroll with offers of signif-icant scholarships. Inevitably, though, there will still be out-of-pocket costs for parents.

Wherever they end up, the Monhegan kids do well.

North Haven School

North Haven is one of the three islands with K–12 schools. "It is a quality school sys-tem that truly captures the concepts of responsibility to self and one another," says Tom, who obviously enjoys his superintendentship there. "It has a project-based curriculum that allows students to be studying several different disciplines at the same time within the project." Of Principal Barney Hallowell, he says, "You'll walk a long set of miles be-fore you find another like him." But he adds that they have a heck of a fine staff, too, caring and thoughtful and mature. No longer is there the turnover there once was. "Now we're so stable we're getting old and expensive!" he says with a smile. He likes the ex-peditionary learning that the school emphasizes, with kids adventuring on and off the island, the whole school at a time going off to Mount Katahdin or Washington County (Maine) or Washington, D.C.—not to mention Paris. Asked about the few remaining peo-ple who think Barney and his way of education are evil, he's not terribly polite. He goes on: "We're doing a quality piece of work here, and Barney is largely responsible for that, along with the staff and the parents."

In 2004, the island started a $3.8 million capital campaign to build a new school—no help can be expected from the state for such a small school in this age of consolidation.

Islesboro's Magnet School

Jon Kerr was principal for only three years at Islesboro's K–12 school. He had taught in Washington County, Ellsworth, and Deer Isle/Stonington before coming to Islesboro, where he first taught science. Like the other islands, Islesboro is facing declining enrollment, dropping from a hundred students to eighty in recent years, and, as on the other islands, the major issue is the lack of affordable housing. "It'll be the demise of the culture of the island," Jon says. Islesboro has made an effort to make its school a magnet school, thus attracting a number of kids from off-island. "If they come in middle school, they like it. Coming as high school kids, it's hard," says Jon.

"The magnet kids are great," says Sue Hatch, whose three sons have all attended Islesboro's school for several years. She likes the diversity, noting that "Any problems are strictly because of the individual."

Ben Roberts of Lincolnville came to Islesboro in seventh grade and stayed through graduation from high school. His parents were concerned about whether he'd stick it out, since he'd never been a bookish kid, but he worked hard to keep up his grades and thrived on the island. "It just seems like Ben was the missing piece of a puzzle out here," adult island friends told his parents.

Ben would have gone to Camden Hills Regional High School if he had stayed in Lincolnville. "There, you might know ten or twelve of the kids in your class," he says, "and not the other thirty or forty. On the island, I can tell you the names of all the kids down to kindergarten. It's nice. At a big school like Camden, rarely will you see a senior hanging out with a freshman or eighth-grader—here no one bats an eyelash at an eighth-grader and a senior at a party. Nobody really worries about age differences, and everyone gets along."

There's a downside to that closeness, too, from a kid's perspective. "You can't skip classes or anything," Ben says. "News travels fast. You get in an accident down-island, and up-island will know about it ten minutes later. If it's something you kinda want to keep quiet, it won't happen."

Had Ben gone to Camden Hills, he might not have had a chance to play basketball, but on the island, he was on the starting team. He admits that many people can't make it on the island, and they last only six months before they move away. "There's not a lot to do out here," he says, "and you end up doing a lot of hanging out with friends." But for him, the only bad part of going to school on Islesboro was the ferry. He commuted on the ferry through his junior year, though because of sports and plays and other events, fairly often he ended up staying on the island overnight. Always someone offered him a bed. After his junior year, he moved onto the island, staying with a good friend's family. During the summer, he worked for a landscaping business, making ten dollars an hour—in previous summers on the mainland, he'd made $7.50.

The fall after graduation, he joined the U.S. Marines. He doesn't anticipate moving back to the island after his hitch is up, though, "unless I'm rich."

Jon Kerr speaks of the message from rap music, MTV—"It's so full of hatred, no hope. Maybe for the older kids on the island, that's compounded by isolation." Interestingly, he's not talking exclusively about islands at all, he's talking about youngsters in general—and islanders are no different. "With technology, they don't go outside and build forts anymore. They don't enjoy playing—they're encapsulated by Nintendo. There's more electronic community—instant messaging all over the country—it'll be interesting to see the effect over time. But the media have a real negative effect.

"Still," he says, "there's an advantage to the island: making relationships with significant adults. The kids have a better understanding of how to act with adults. It comes out loud and clear on field trips—people always say how articulate our kids are, how well they get along with adults. The flip side is that with the summer partying, there's no boundary between ages, and they grow up fast. They're exposed to stuff."

Vinalhaven School

By island standards, Vinalhaven's school is very big, but with ten to twenty-six students in each of its thirteen grade levels, it's still tiny compared with most mainland schools. It has just moved into a brand-new building that—although controversial mostly because of the expense—has tremendously improved morale among students and teachers alike, as have some recent changes in how the school is run.

The old school, described as having been like a prison, was an ugly, small, crowded cinderblock building. In the dozen years prior to 2004, there were eight principals, all of whom had strengths but faced what may have been an impossible situation. They might have come in with all sorts of innovative thinking, but for the staff, it was very hard to invest in the "flavor of the year," knowing the likelihood that the new ideas would be replaced by the following September. Skepticism was natural. Even aside from job issues, such a position is hard for a family person from Away, too. Even if it were perfect for the principal and vice versa, a spouse would most likely have to sacrifice his or her own career objectives for a time, and the family might not like island life. "It's a weird place to live," says Yvonne Thomas, the guidance counselor, a transplant who now wouldn't want to live anywhere else, "and it's not for everybody."

Now the school has far more physical space and can offer more extracurricular activities. Eighty-five percent of the students in the sixth through twelfth grades are involved with at least one sport, and not just basketball, as it used to be. Cross-country, soccer, spring and fall rowing, baseball. There's a full-time music teacher, and art, dance, and drama are available. In the afternoons and most evenings, the new school is

Vinalhaven School (COURTESY OF ALICIA WATTS)

buzzing with school and community activities. There are adult-education classes and University of Maine courses via television. Adults are playing basketball, and both adult and children's plays are produced. The annual auction to benefit the island eldercare center is held there.

"The new school is the nexus of the community," says School Leader Mike Felton. That's his official title. The twenty-seven-year-old Felton, who doesn't yet have full credentials to be a principal, came aboard in the fall of 2004. Mike had lived on Vinalhaven for two years as an Island Institute Fellow, teaching aspirations and social studies in the middle school, after which he spent another two years working for the Island Institute in education outreach. He knew the island, and the island knew him.

A new, team-based leadership system has been created, with leaders from the elementary, middle, and high schools, plus Yvonne and Mike. They meet regularly to make policy decisions about how the school will run. "Nothing is all the principal's fault, nor are there any willy-nilly principal ideas," says Yvonne.

"It's bringing out the best in a lot of teachers," Mike says. "It's like living your belief about what education can be. We're doing what other people are just talking about. It makes you glad to go to work. There's lots of energy there." Mike says that he doesn't anticipate changing the team approach when he obtains his principal's credentials. Why change what's working?

Everyone's pushing schools to raise students' aspirations these days, from the federal government on down. But the issue of aspirations on Vinalhaven is unique, even among the islands. The lobster fishery is the primary industry on the island, and as long as the lobsters last, it's a good one. About two hundred and eighty boats work from the island, most of them providing a good living for their people. With a K–12 school, kids stay on the island until they're of legal age, and they start fishing long before that. For many, it's hard to see any advantage to leaving for any reason after high school, let alone spending money to go to college. "Why should I, if I can stay here and make a bundle?" they can ask entirely legitimately. Says Yvonne, "There are boys in the high school who make more in the summer than I do all year." She knows it's hard for parents to encourage their children to go off to college, too, knowing that they're probably pushing them to leave the island and, likely, not come back. Still, she says, "I want them to go. I always say to kids, 'Wherever you live, have some other experiences, see what's there. Then, by all means come back if you choose to.'" There are fifty-to-sixty-year-old alcoholic lobstermen on the island who are just going through their lives, talents never developed. "They're just here—they're never going to leave," she says. No one wants his or her child to end up like that.

Vinalhaven has a strong vocational education program. In some recent years, they've offered both building trades and marine project development courses. The voc-ed students have been involved with the design and construction of the timber-framed shop at the new school, and they built two cold-molded. six-oared Cornish rowing gigs. The gigs have since been used by a variety of island groups, including both high-school and middle-school rowing teams as well as adults, competing in races around New England.

The latest project is the refurbishment of a donated thirty-foot steel sloop, scheduled to be relaunched in the spring of 2005. Voc-ed teacher Mark Jackson hopes to use her in a seamanship program that would include a yearlong trip to Florida with three students coming aboard at a time. He sees the vessel as a metaphor for a little spaceship, as self-sustaining as possible. They would anchor out and prepare their own food. Trips ashore would be only to visit museums or other local sights, or to take a run for exercise. "A major goal is to take the romantic notions out of cruising—but show that while it's not always fun, it's always rewarding."

There are presently fifteen students in his shop class—as many as he's ever had, because of the interest in this program. "I'll be trying to talk them out of it," Mark says. "This won't be a good way to get out of school—they'll be using math in navigation, science in weather observation, and English in journaling." He plans to have the boat equipped with communication systems so they can be in constant contact with Vinalhaven—and report to and involve the elementary school with their progress in real time. "We're a long way from setting sail yet," he said in the fall of 2004, "but the discussion has begun among the faculty, administration, students, and parents."

While there are already academic sail-training programs for self-motivated and self-assured students, Mark sees this program as offering something to kids who might not have such strong academic and personal confidence. It would give students the opportunity to push themselves beyond what they've done before and to realize that they are capable of more than they had expected.

Vinalhaven used to have a higher dropout rate than many towns—again, why go to school when you obviously can do well fishing already? And women often started families at a young age. The school is making greater efforts to reach at-risk kids and to work with their families as well. Many more young people of both sexes are finishing school now, unencumbered by families of their own. "It's still a small school," says Yvonne, "and the teachers know the kids. If a kid doesn't show up at school, we can usually find out why. Someone comes in to school and says he saw so-and-so get on the boat this morning, he won't be coming to school, and I say to myself, 'I'd better see what that's about.' Falling through the cracks doesn't happen—we know each other so well. Poor kids, they can't get away from us!"

A Schoolteacher's Life on Matinicus

At a small school, like that on Matinicus, the mail is interesting, says Sari Bunker, who is also known as "S. T." She came to teach on Matinicus in 1980 and returned a decade later to marry Vance. Some island people never bother with schoolteachers' names, since they stay such a short time anyway, and many on Matinicus found Sari's Hungarian first name difficult to pronounce. (It is not the same as the Indian dress—it's more like "Shah-ree.") So she was called "the schoolteacher," or simply "School Teacher." She suggested the initials S. T. instead, and that has stuck, even though she hasn't taught school on the island for well over twenty years.

She was hired to teach nine students, but when September rolled around, there were thirteen, in grades three through eight. By the middle of January, she was down to just three students. "It was kinda fun, because sometimes two of those were gone."

It's hard on any island to know how many students will show up, but Matinicus is particularly difficult, as people move ashore and back unpredictably. "We never know till school starts," she says.

Even in a tiny school, the mail brings the usual catalogs and official notices from the state and information about various programs. "Lunch programs—yeah, right," says Sari. "You know where we are?" (On some of the islands, including Matinicus, students go home for lunch. Not only is it easy for them, being in such small geographical places, but that's the only time in the school day that a lone teacher has to herself.) But the senders of all this promotional stuff don't sort through where it's going. "You'll get copies of the same catalog addressed to Grade One Teacher, Grade Two Teacher, and all the way up. Plus Gifted and Talented Teacher, Business Manager, Physical Education Teacher, and Principal."

Although there have been and continue to be exceptions to the rule, on Matinicus, as on most of the smaller islands, teachers typically stay only two years. As noted, tenure becomes an issue after two years. "Even if everything goes wonderfully, with nothing but highly motivated families and kids with breakfast and enough sleep and all that, you don't want them to have just one adult in that role for their whole school career," says Eva Murray, who came to teach on Matinicus in 1987. (Like Sari Bunker, Eva met her future husband there. They now make the island their home.)

And sometimes things don't go wonderfully. It's sometimes said that Matinicus chews up and spits out teachers. Since lobstering is about the only way to make a living there, the students who are not members of long-time Matinicus fishing families tend to be transient, being offspring of sternmen or, even more tenuously, of sternmen's girlfriends. At one time, few parents on Matinicus were supportive of the education process. Teachers found themselves acting as social workers and in need of services that weren't available to them, such as a reading specialist, a guidance counselor, or Alateen. "For a teacher, it's certainly nice to have less oversight from your administration, less paperwork and hassle," says Eva. "But you have no peer or moral support, no specialists to help, no substitutes, and nobody to back you up when there's a fight. When the kids' families aren't going to support you, that's asking more than you can ask of a teacher." Two years can be plenty long enough for a teacher.

Isle au Haut School

Dianne Barter is one of five school board members on Isle au Haut, where there were nine students for most of the 2003–04 school year, in grades two through eight. Her own eleven-year-old son, Nicholas, was in sixth grade. Prior to the fall of 2003, all his school memories were with Judy Jipson as teacher. Judy left Isle au Haut when her family needed her on the mainland. "Judy's a dear friend and we miss her out here," says Dianne, "but after five years with a single teacher, the kids know what buttons to push, what they can get away with." The change was difficult at first. "Judy was all structure," says Dianne. "Joy [Seaver] isn't. Nicholas didn't like it at first—he's a scheduled child, and if the schedule got disrupted, he'd go wild. But he's adjusting. He's done well. It's good for him to learn different ways.

"This was my first year choosing a teacher. Scared! This is my kid! But it was so easy," she says. There were twenty-four applications, but all five board members selected the same group of five or six as the strongest candidates. "They've got to have a lot of experience, and in a multiage setting. They've got to have a lot of life and spunk, and they must want a challenge." After talking with four or five applicants, they selected Joy Seaver. "Something about her just stood out," says Dianne. "She's crazy as a coot, for one thing—you have to be, to live out here."

The Isle au Haut school kids regularly go off the island on minitrips, such as when they took the train from Portland and had a "Duckboat" tour in Boston. In addition to grant money, the island benefits from its seasonal residents. "The summer people support this school wholeheartedly. Sales and donations at pie auctions on Labor Day weekend have totaled more than six thousand dollars," says Dianne. "They *are* good pies," she adds.

Thanks to the past generosity of credit-card giant MBNA, weeklong bus trips have also been part of their program—Washington, D.C., and Prince Edward Island one year, Gettysburg and Pennsylvania's Amish country another. Ahead of time, each child did a report on one aspect of what they were going to see. Parents usually outnumbered students on these trips, Dianne says. "We didn't like to leave the teacher with full charge of someone else's kid away from home for a week."

Specialists in art and music have sometimes come to the school from the mainland one day a week, and grants have helped pay for an island resident, Kathie Fiveash, to create inventive programs for the students in particular areas. Dianne's son Nicholas has been especially excited by some of these programs.

Dianne describes being on a field trip in Massachusetts. "I'm looking at buildings, and so on, and Nicholas is looking at trees. He wants to know what they are. He's always said he wanted to be a lobsterman, but the other day he said he'd like to work with invasive plants." Dianne would prefer that he not be a fisherman—it's too hard a life, and she thinks he could do better using his brain. "He's definitely a science kind of guy. I don't know one bird from another, or plants, or anything, and he gets disgusted with me when we're kayaking because I don't hear the same birds he does."

Dianne feels they're very lucky on Isle au Haut. "Each and every child, no matter where we go, we hear compliments about how well behaved they are, and how they know their stuff." She feels the island is unique. "We support our teacher, for one thing. We're paying Joy forty-two thousand." Isle au Haut kids have a good record for receiving scholarships to boarding schools, and not only because of their unusual background, which undoubtedly appeals to admissions directors. "They're smart kids, good students," says Dianne.

Like many of the other small islands, Isle au Haut has faced times of low student numbers. A century or more ago, the island had three grammar schools. Much more recently, they were down to a single student, who is now in his mid-twenties. But then, during 2002–03, they went from six to eleven, including two boys from Hong Kong

Kathie Fiveash with Isle au Haut students Victoria MacDonald and Hannah Lamson
(COURTESY OF LINDA ARCHAMBAULT OF THE LOBSTER CONSERVANCY)

whose school had closed down during the SARS epidemic. (Islands are not entirely iso-lated from the rest of the world!) Their mother had a house on the island. "We knew them, of course, but we got to know them better." The other three new children moved onto the island full-time, but at the end of the 2003–04 year, another boy came for a cou-ple of months. Far from being difficult for a new student to fit in, Dianne says, "It's great for all the kids when we do add one. They're like siblings, and they are pretty sick of one another by spring."

But they're not sick of school—and one major reason is the Enrichment Program developed by island transplant Kathie Fiveash. Always a naturalist, for many years Kathie had been in Cambridge, Massachusetts, teaching at a fine school that shared many of her ideals, but she had had enough of stores and restaurants and movies. She'd known Albert Gordon since she was in college, and in 2000, when he asked if she'd like to try life on Isle au Haut, she thought maybe she would. A graduate of Harvard Law School who had rejected a life in Corporate America, Albert had been on the island for twenty-five years, supporting himself there as a builder. Early on, he traded labor for a piece of land overlooking the Turnip Yard, the ledge-filled passage between the eastern shore of Isle au Haut and a mile-long island now inhabited only by sheep, and there he built a bright, open house with a 180-degree view from Mount Desert Island to the open ocean to the southward.

"I've just gotten twelve baby chickens," she enthusiastically tells anyone who comes her way. "I've always wanted chickens!" The pullets are in her garden shed, overlooking the Turnip Yard. Soon the chickens will get a yard adjacent to the garden, which is already fenced against deer, as all gardens on Isle au Haut must be. The hens will strip the ground bare, which Kathie hopes will discourage voles from invading the vegetables, and they'll do in some insects themselves, too. Multi-purpose birds. Kathie raises a good share of the food she and her friend Albert eat.

Gardening isn't as simple on Isle au Haut as it might be in some places. Brenda Hopkins says that whenever visitors from the mainland ask her what they can bring over when they come, she says, "Bring a bucket of good dirt!" As on many of the islands, there's not much good soil on Isle au Haut. And then there are the deer.

Kathie's first project on Isle au Haut was surveying the southern part of the island for duck habitat. The largest winter concentration of threatened harlequin ducks is off Isle au Haut, and her first summer, as the field practicum for her master's degree in environmental studies, Kathie was checking out seaweed in the particular areas the ducks concentrated, to provide data for drawing correlations.

When that was done, she learned that it's hard to find work on an island. "You have to make it for yourself," says Kathie, who did just that. With a grant from MBNA, she created a yearlong program at the school, focusing on Isle au Haut habitats. She took the kids out into fields and bogs and forestland, into the rocky intertidal areas, onto the clamflats, and to particular areas that had been disturbed by humans in the past. The children talked with older people who could remember what things were like on the island in earlier times, such as before the opening of the gravel pit. "It was a way of looking at how people change things," Kathie says. She met with the kids three afternoons a week, once outside; for the two classroom sessions, the students were divided into two groups by age. "They get a lot of individual attention," Kathie says. "There's a teacher and a full-time ed tech, too."

That year, she also volunteered to teach music. The next two years, the school hired her to teach music, and she taught all the students to play the recorder.

For the science enrichment program, in the second and third years she again got grants from MBNA, but the school contributed to the program too, as did the local Thorofare Foundation, supported by summer people. Year Two's focus was on invasive species, of which there are three major examples on the island—Japanese barberry, Oriental bittersweet, and Japanese knotweed. "It's interesting," says eleven-year-old Nicholas Barter, "because they're not supposed to be here." The students did a survey of the island for Japanese barberry—mapping where it can be found, learning the biology of the plant, and writing and drawing as they went along. They sent a mailing to the island's taxpayers to inform them about the locations and hazards of this threatening plant.

"Nice fields of hay-scented fern are being taken over by barberries," Kathie says, "and they are choking stream and road edges, displacing such beautiful native plants as blueberry, sweet fern, huckleberry, and steeplebush. Adults remember playing in streams that the kids can't play in today—the plants are thorny and unpleasant." A strategy used by invasive plants, Kathie explains, is to have brightly colored berries that attract birds, which in turn spread the seeds everywhere they wander and fly. Ten years ago, turkeys were introduced onto the island. They love barberry—and are probably seeding the whole island.

(Isle au Haut is not the only island being threatened by barberry. In 1990, Bill Livingston and others from the University of Maine at Orono published a study of the forests on Great Cranberry Island. In addition to the barberry matter, one of their findings—perhaps not surprising—was that the forest cover was quite different where the land had been disturbed by people. Members of the Monhegan preservationist group, Monhegan Associates, Inc., read about the study and said, "Hey, that's us!" and contacted Dr. Livingston, who ultimately did similar research on Monhegan.)

Another aspect of Kathie Fiveash's program during the second year was studying endangered Atlantic salmon. To do this, she used "Fish Friends," a curriculum developed by the Atlantic Salmon Federation. The students collected enough money to buy a thirty-gallon cold-water tank, and they raised salmon eggs until they hatched and grew into little fish about five weeks old and an inch long, ready for release. In Ellsworth, they met with a member of the Union River Watershed Association and learned about the Union River while they released the tiny salmon.

The third year's program was based on a workshop Kathie had attended called "The Silver Wake," a curriculum on plankton and ocean food-webs. Plankton—microscopic plants and creatures—live in the upper layers of the sea and are the foundation of ocean life. "They're what everything eats that everything else eats," says Kathie. The program demonstrated how life in the sea is an interconnected web. Kathie invites guests to come to the island and work with the kids—she kicked off the plankton project with a visit from a friend's brother, Robert F. Baldwin, author of the children's book *This Is the Sea That Feeds Us.* "In return, we put them up and gave them a chance to explore the island," says Kathie, ever-innovative about how to stretch the dollars she has available.

The children learned about water sampling, identifying the various constituents of the local plankton and looking for harmful algal blooms such as red tide. They set up a saltwater tank—using the same tank they'd used the previous year as a cold-water tank for the salmon—and filled it with creatures from the intertidal areas. There they found another invader, the Asian shore crab, which came to New Jersey on ships in the 1980s and has been spreading up and down the coast. It's a small, very aggressive crab is thought to eat lobster larvae, among other things. When the class identified the Asian shore crab, it was the most northerly one recorded to date. They wrote to local fishermen asking that they bring in small and interesting organisms that came up in their traps, and they received various fish, shrimp, hermit crabs, sea slugs, starfish, and urchins, which in larval form are all part of the plankton. Using a microscope, they were able to identify many of these creatures in their larval form in their water samples.

The second part of the year's program was raising larval lobsters, with the help of the Lobster Conservancy, a group based in Friendship, Maine, which describes its mission as "sustaining a thriving lobster fishery through science and community." In a specially designed tank, they were able to observe three distinct planktonic stages and finally the emergence of tiny but recognizable lobsters. They let them settle in an aquarium for a little while and finally released them on the shore near the school. That project was intense for Kathie, who says she had to be at the school three hours every day tending the minuscule creatures that seven or eight years hence might end up being edible lobsters in the traps of Isle au Haut fishermen. The final aspects of that project involved learning about the economy of lobstering and the biology of lobsters, learning about their courtship rituals, seeing their hearts beat and dissecting them—all with the help of a lobster biologist with connections to the island. By happenstance, lobstering wasn't the full-time livelihood of the majority of the children's families, but it certainly is a large part of the life of the community.

Kathie doesn't know how long she'll be on the island. She admits it's a cold and lonely place in winter. "All my life I've worked with people—in school in Cambridge, there were a lot of teachers and committees. It's hard doing everything on my own." And the people on Isle au Haut aren't demonstrative—she's had to get used to that. "It's a different social style." But the teachers with whom she has worked have been wonderful about accommodating her projects, and the fact that she's continuing to receive funding from the town shows that she's appreciated. In fact, all the money for her stipend now is coming from the school board.

In 2004, the Isle au Haut Ecology Project won the Maine State Board of Education's "Making the Grade" award for enrichment programs. Kathie sent in the application for the award: "Normally, your principal would nominate you, but we don't have one. I had to toot my own horn." Obviously, it was a horn worth tooting.

Kathie wishes it were not so difficult for her to get together with her family. To visit her children, who are grown and living in Massachusetts and New York City, requires a day of travel, and it takes a day and a half to see her mother in California. But, she says, "My life is a lot less high-pressure, more relaxed. The work situation and time in my life are not all stressed out." She's living in accordance with her own values: "From an ecologist's point of view, the way most people in America use resources is crazy. An economy that can only thrive on continuous growth is unsustainable and destructive. I like living where there aren't stores, movies, restaurants. I like not spending money. . . . Different people are on the island for different reasons. For me, it was a withdrawal from American materialism."

Kathie is so upset with the Bush administration that she has made the successful effort to live under the taxable income level, and has so announced to the IRS. She calls her situation one of voluntary simplicity. She likes the close contact with nature, and growing her own food. "On the other hand," she says, "it's important to make a difference—sometimes I wonder if I'm doing enough."

She thinks that if she were to have grandchildren, she might move off, but she doesn't know. "There are things you give up, things you get." In the meantime, the children of Isle au Haut are certainly benefiting from her presence.

Off-Island High Schools

For those islands without a high school, certainly ninth grade presents a special concern. Casco Bay's islands have less of a problem than those downeast: Long Island has a contract with Portland for most of their students in the sixth through twelfth grades, and the other Casco Bay islands are part of a mainland municipality anyway. Portland and Cumberland both opted to send their middle-schoolers ashore at least in part so they could make friendships in their mainland schools during this particularly critical time. By high school, island kids are used to the boat commute, and the ferries to Peaks and Chebeague run early and late and cause fewer limitations on kids' school activities than the islands down the bay or down east face. Students there presumably have little more pressure to change school systems than do suburban kids anywhere. Long Island and Cliff Island students are somewhat limited in their after-school activities because the last boat leaves Portland at quarter of six in the evening.

The more easterly islands without high schools have to make some kind of accommodation for their older students. There are financial issues, but the social issues can also be significant. It's said of each island that it is the idyllic place for young kids to grow up. Everyone agrees that in nearly all cases, the elementary education that island kids receive is excellent, preparing the children academically for whatever school follows. "There's a lot of one-on-one teaching, and more knowledge going through there than in a big classroom," says David Bunker of Great Cranberry (which, at this moment, has no students in its school). But certainly, the down side for kids is social, and the problems come with the transition to high school, never an easy time for *any* teenager.

An advantage to boarding schools—which many islanders attend—is that many other new students also arrive in ninth grade, making the entry easier for the island kids. "It was hard at first," says Jill Philbrook of Swans, who went to Maine Central Institute in Pittsfield, "but then I never wanted to come back—I even asked my mother if I could stay for Thanksgiving vacation. I lost a few friends when I went to boarding school and wasn't on the island to hang out, but the ones I was real close with, I still am. And one I met in high school comes out occasionally."

The adjustment to an off-island school is a matter of concern. "There aren't enough kids to learn social skills," says Isle au Haut's Bel MacDonald, whose granddaughter is approaching high-school age. "All the cliques are formed in eighth grade, and the island kids have to break in, in ninth." When it has eighth-graders, Isle au Haut sends them to visit the mainland high school on Deer Isle one day every couple of weeks, in hopes of easing the adjustment the following year when they go off-island. Whether they go to Deer Isle/Stonington High School or somewhere else, at least they've had some experience of being in classes with more than a few kids. And if they do end up there, they will have had some contact with their fellow students. But, said another parent, "They still don't get to know their classmates very well—the only time would be lunch, and that's very short."

Only a few years ago, as part of their effort to encourage families to stay year-round on the island, the people of Isle au Haut decided to adjust the mailboat schedule to allow students to commute to school at Deer Isle/Stonington. Previously, high-school students had to move ashore, one way or another. The problem is that it's not terribly safe for the boat to travel after dark, particularly during times of ice. Even with the revised boat schedule, it has not been possible for Isle au Haut commuters to make it to school in time for the first class, and during daylight saving time, they have had to miss the last class, too. "Teachers don't always get it, either," I was told. For instance, an Isle au Haut boy had to take algebra as independent study because he couldn't be there at the time the regular class was scheduled.

At this writing, there are only two high-school-age students from Isle au Haut, and they are both attending the Liberty School in Blue Hill and boarding with a family there, so the boat isn't presently an issue. There are five seventh-graders this year, though, and the school committee has to address financial arrangements and transportation issues before that group makes its plans. The town of Isle au Haut pays tuition (equivalent to the Deer Isle/Stonington tuition fee) for any school a family chooses; the town has also paid either transportation or board. (Transportation for daily commuters is not insignificant. In addition to the mailboat charge, three dollars each way, a special bus is needed to pick up the kids at the Stonington dock in the morning and, during daylight saving time, take them back in time to meet the boat again—an annual cost of some $4,800.) The hope is that the mailboat can push its departure time in the afternoon another fifteen minutes, which would allow the students to stay for their final class as well as to ride the regular school bus to the dock.

Swans Island's school is on a different scale, with around thirty students, K–8. The problems facing the other islands confront those with relatively larger populations, too. Most of the Swans kids go to Mount Desert Island (MDI) High School, commuting on the state ferry to Bass Harbor. I was told that they used to tend to stick with their Swans Island friends. There were enough of them that they could stay in a group and eat lunch together, and they didn't make the effort to form new friendships. "The kids there have an attitude about Swans Islanders," a Swans Island graduate from MDI a number of years ago told me. Others don't believe this is a problem any longer.

On the Cranberries, with early and short boat runs, commuting is relatively easy, although after-school participation in sports or extracurricular activities still requires staying overnight or finding private transportation.

As for the islands from which it is impossible to commute, whole families are more likely than they used to be to move ashore when their first child approaches or reaches high school. Some families move back to the island just as soon as their children graduate—and some never come back. Wyatt and Lorena Beal left Frenchboro when their son reached seventh grade—as they had expected they would from the time they moved onto the island—and they aren't sure whether or not they'll end up back on the island.

Even from an island like Isle au Haut, where commuting is possible, families sometimes leave when their kids reach their teens. One family with three kids moved off not long ago—their son was on the chess team and played basketball, and they felt they needed to stay off-island. Now they live ashore permanently.

Nicholas Barter is in the group of children nearing high-school age on Isle au Haut. "What are we going to do when Nicholas hits high school? Fortunately, we don't have to deal with that right yet!" says his mother, Dianne, but she knows she doesn't want her son to board, even though her husband went off to school himself. "In this day and age, a kid doesn't need to be exposed to all that. I don't want my boy learning personal hygiene from other thirteen-year-old boys! But if they're going to do sports or after-school stuff, they have to stay over there. If Nicholas is going to play sports, we'll have to figure out something."

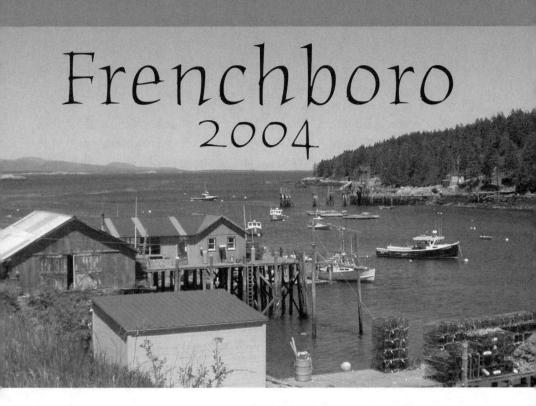

Frenchboro
2004

Graduation

he first graduation ceremony at Frenchboro's K–8 school since 1995 took place in 2004. Joe (or Joey) Charpentier, who had lived with his grandparents on the island for the previous seven years, was the oldest of five students during his last year in Frenchboro's one-room school: Cody, Dylan, and Joey's little sister Jesse were first-graders, and Lance was in third grade. Wyatt and Lorena Beal's son Mariner, Joey's age, had moved off the island two years earlier.

Graduation was a big deal. Lobstermen came in early from hauling in order to be cleaned up by three o'clock, a special boat ran over from Bass Harbor to bring celebrants, and one of the speakers came in his own boat, as did we. We rowed ashore an hour ahead of time and checked out the museum, across the street from the school. There's an interesting collection of items from earlier days on the island, as well as a gift shop that sells T-shirts, sweatshirts, and hats—both the baseball type and nice knitted ones—along with other crafts made by islanders or people with island connections. The revenues from the shop are used toward expansion and maintenance of the

Frenchboro Harbor, looking north toward Mount Desert

museum, volunteer Donna Hasal told us. Frenchboro is a common destination for yachting people, and the 2003 guestbook was signed by visitors from thirty-nine states and fourteen countries. Many want to have a souvenir of Frenchboro.

Now a seasonal returnee, Donna attended the Frenchboro School. Her father, Clarence Howard, grew up on Eagle Island; her mother, from Frenchboro, went out to Eagle Island to teach. As has happened so many times on the islands, the teacher met a local man and one thing led to another. After their marriage, they moved to French-boro, where he was a sardine fisherman. Donna's older sister went all the way through the Frenchboro School, but the family moved to Camden when Donna was in third grade. By then, Clarence owned Marshall Island, near Swans, and operated his fishing busi-ness with several boats from there. During the school year, the family lived in Camden, and summers were spent on Marshall Island. It wasn't until the late 1970s that Donna found her way back to Frenchboro, and, since retirement in 1990, she and her husband live there from April to November.

People started gathering at two-thirty, a half-hour before the graduation festivi-ties were to begin. David Lunt, longtime town father, wore a crisp new red Frenchboro hat for the occasion.

"People always come early. Never be late for anything on this island, or you'll miss it completely," said Donna. Not all islands are like that. "Island time" is a concept I heard more than once, referring to a somewhat casual approach to appointments on some islands.

We wandered across to the school, which has the required ramp leading to the door on one side and steps up the other. Immediately on opening the door, we knew this was a place where people do things. Up at least six feet, the wall was totally covered with children's written and computer projects, as well as examples of phonetic spelling and maps. A poster based on Ezra Jack Keats's counting book *Over in the Meadow* adorned a large part of one wall. Third-grader Lance Bishop had researched the scien-tific classifications of each of the creatures and posted the list. The original work only went as far as ten, but Joey had continued the series with verses for eleven through twenty. There were layered pictures of mealworms turning into darkling beetles—the students had studied metamorphosis. A timeline stretched around the top of three sec-tions of wall, with such milestones as William the Conqueror, Columbus, Leonardo da Vinci, and, more recently, Frenchboro School (1842), Martin Luther King, and Richard Harris (with credit for his role as Dumbledore—Harry Potter was apparently as impor-tant on Frenchboro as anywhere else). Bookcases were full to explosion, horizontal sur-faces were home to piles of books and papers. Enthusiasm shone everywhere. The teacher, Lorna Stuart, was pleased that we saw it that way—she said that some might see only end-of-school-year chaos—but this was obviously a happy home to a varied group of spirited young people and their equally eager teacher. On a centrally placed table was an array of graduation cards and gifts for Joey. The front of the room had a small raised stage with a podium. It was decorated with ceiling-high trees painted on kraft paper, left over from a recent operetta put on by the children with the help of a trio of professional musicians from off-island. The students had opted to leave them up for graduation.

Desks and tables had been pushed back against the wall, and chairs were lined up on every inch of open floor space. Even so, there weren't quite enough places to sit, and people ended up on makeshift seats. "Anyone who sits on the blue table takes his life in his hands," Lorna warned her husband as he parked himself carefully on it. Each chair held a blue program for the day, and within each was a copy of the *Visitor's Guide to Frenchboro, Outer Long Island,* which Joe had created during his eighth-grade year, "because I want to share the island with those that visit my home during the summer."

Although the island has only about forty year-round residents, fifty or sixty people of all ages—from babies to the oldest members of the community—attended graduation. Reverend Rob Benson from the Sea Coast Mission's *Sunbeam* boat was there, too. At three o'clock sharp, Lorna moved behind the podium and welcomed everyone. She asked that past graduates of the school stand, and about six people did. She also asked anyone from North Carolina to stand, too, and four people arose, summer people and friends.

"We have sixteen children on the island," Lorna said, as some of the smaller ones fussed a bit. "Isle au Haut would kill for this problem, I'm told." Frenchboro is unique among the islands in having a growth spurt. Their homesteading project—to recruit new families—has been very successful. Not so many years ago, the school was down to a single student. Now there's concern on the island about how the one-room school will handle the number of students they expect in another five years. It's a difficulty that everyone's happy to face.

Speaking at Joe's graduation were the principal, Dr. Craig Kesselheim, and the incoming superintendent, Dr. Rob Liebow, both of whom came from off-island and made appropriate remarks showing respect for both the school and its 2004 graduate. The main address was by Dr. Edward Brazee, a professor of middle-school education at the University of Maine at Orono. Dr. Brazee had been an e-mail correspondent and a mentor of Joey's for some time. "I'm a college professor," he said, "but I like to tell people I was a real person at one time." He taught at the middle-school level for eleven years, and he feels that eleven-to-fifteen-year-olds are often undersold. Not Joe. He gave credit to Joe for his columns in the *Bar Harbor Times,* and an article entitled "Alone and Just Fine, My Life as a School's Sole Seventh Grader," which appeared in the newsletter of the Maine Association for Middle Level Education. Joe helped Dr. Brazee—and thereby others—understand the possibilities of Maine's pioneering program to provide laptop computers to all of the state's seventh- and eighth-graders.

Dr. Brazee gave Joe three pieces of advice, noting that in the normal situation, a student could say that advice given at graduation was really for the person sitting next to him, or other members of the class—but not in this case. One: Don't be afraid to depend on others—but know how to depend on yourself. (This is a lesson that is perhaps particularly important, and also available, for anyone living on an island the size of Frenchboro.) Two: People matter, tests don't. And three: Don't buy lobsters in Iowa. He suggested that Joe adopt this phrase as a kind of trademark, as it will fit into nearly any discussion—whether of economics or literature or personal relations—and he, from Frenchboro, will be the only one who really knows what it means.

Perhaps the most entertaining part of the program was a multimedia presentation by Maegan Haney, who had spent the year on a grant as a technology specialist on Frenchboro, Swans Island, and Islesford, as well as in Tremont, on Mount Desert Island. It started with children saying with various degrees of articulateness what they liked about Joey and, after a montage of photographs of Joe at all ages, ended with advice from some of the elders in the community. Lorna spoke last, addressing the meaning of integrity. "Integrity is a person who is who he says he is." Joe, she said, is full of integrity. He has received a full scholarship to the Northfield–Mount Hermon School in Massachusetts.

After being presented with his diploma, Joe took the podium. He claimed not to be much of a public speaker, but that's not what anyone in the room would have said. He spoke of some cherished moments during his life on the island and remarked that the myriad assessment tests he'd spent most of the last year taking probably left him with permanent scars. He listed a number of books he'd read recently, including of course Harry Potter, but also *Lord of the Flies*, Ruth Moore's *The Weir*, Kenneth Roberts's Arundel series, and James Loewen's *Lies My Teacher Told Me*.

"The one thing I haven't learned is how to leave a place I love," he said. "A person doesn't have to be born in a place in order to call it home." Then he laughed. "One day I will build a mall out here for you," he said to his schoolmates.

Someone cried out, "Build us a bridge!"

"That was next!" he zapped back. "Or a bridge to the mainland," he read from his notes. He thanked everyone. "Now, let's eat!"

Everyone wanted be the one to congratulate him first, and he shook hands and grinned and looked even near-strangers like me in the eye as he thanked us. Gradually the crowd moved down to the church parish house for an extraordinary array of refreshments, after which, at six o'clock, the regular Friday passenger boat would take people back ashore.

Town Meeting: Elections, Budgets, and a Place for the Post Office

Ten days after graduation, it was time for Frenchboro's Town Meeting, attended by approximately the same number and cast of characters as the first event. In Frenchboro, as in most Maine towns, it is at Town Meeting that all decisions about town budgets and policies are made, and town officials are elected. There are thirty-seven registered voters in Frenchboro, and most of them were present on Monday night, June 21, along with Joey and Lance and some small children. At first I felt awkward, since I had no business with the meeting, but every woman whose eye caught mine immediately smiled a welcome. Not just the few I'd spoken with previously, but all of them, and no one seemed curious as to why I was there. Of course, it's entirely possible that since I had spoken with such a high percentage of the residents—though even one might have sufficed—they all knew who I was and what I was up to. But perhaps it was just accepted that a person might be interested in an important event in town. Many of the men were welcoming too—and Joey and Lance—but I didn't feel particular negativity even from those who didn't look me in the eye. It's my guess that's how many of the native islanders behave with any stranger or near-stranger.

On one end of the Community Building, supporters of the preschool had laid out an array of pies and cheesecakes and other sweets for a Dutch auction. A table on the far side offered cookies and coffee and punch at a quarter a pop, the proceeds also going to the preschool. People milled around checking out the goodies.

As town clerk, Lorna Stuart opened the meeting and read the first article: Elect a moderator. Three men were nominated for the job, and all declined it; finally, Rachel Bishop accepted the job and took over running the meeting for the remaining thirty-seven articles. The pattern of declined nominations continued through all the elections, starting with selectpersons—as they're called in official doings in Frenchboro if not on the street, where they're still known as selectmen, even the women who have served. In recent years, there had been five members of the board, by whatever name. All were elected each year. (Later in the evening, both these policies were changed. The meeting voted to go back to just three, to be elected to two-year terms—but staggered in 2005 so that, in theory, there never could be a completely green board.) It took a dozen nominations to finally get five people both present and willing to serve; three of these were continuing in the job, one was returning to the board after a year's hiatus, and one was new. They said it's a Maine law that an absent person cannot be elected to a position. As far as I can determine, it's not actually a state regulation, but it's certainly a sensible policy for a municipality to adopt, and I wouldn't be surprised if it's why sometimes Frenchboro people skip Town Meeting. There were forty positions up for grabs on this Monday night, including all the members of various committees.

At the very back of the room, a small clutch of young fishermen—plus Tim Wiggins, not so young (he's a grandfather)—were sitting and joking among themselves. Rachel asked them to keep it down at least once. Sometimes one of them would nominate one of the others for something, which the nominee would either accept or decline, but partway through the long list of positions, one of them hadn't agreed to take on anything. One of his friends attacked him: "What are you going to do?"

"I don't want to do nothin'," he said.

After three people declined, Tim Wiggins accepted the position of harbormaster, grumbling, "I can't speed anymore!"

Few of the positions had more nominations than there were jobs, and none of the unopposed candidates received a negative vote. For those few jobs where more than one person was nominated and didn't decline, ballot slips were handed out and counted. No one needed to feel uncomfortable either about voting for or against a neighbor or seeing who was voting for or against him or her—although probably the results were predictable.

As well as continuing on as selectman, and even though his term as fire warden wasn't up for a year, twenty-year-old Zachary Lunt accepted the position of truant officer. "He's got the most kids," someone said. (His girlfriend has three youngsters.)

"I can handle it," he said.

For the various boards and committees, one by one, Rachel asked if there were people currently on them who didn't choose to continue to serve. There were always one or two; sometimes they simply switched to another board or committee. The one committee that wasn't filled was Waste Management. "What's it do?" a couple of people asked. Although a couple of wags joked, "Manage waste!" no one seemed to have an answer. Finally someone quipped, "In other words, nothing." No one was nominated to replace any of the three who stepped down.

Waste management has been a touchy subject on Frenchboro, as on many of the islands. It has been said that a committee's job in those places is actually about raising awareness, not doing anything concrete yet. "You have to look at it in terms of lifetimes, not years." The issue seems to be whether or not the state or any other non-island entity can tell "us" how to act. Trash removal is difficult from any of the islands, and Frenchboro more so than some. The town does have a number of unique problems. In the summer, the island is a common stopping-off point for visiting yachtspeople, all of whom seem to want to bring their trash ashore. Some of the islanders don't understand the mechanics of what can and can't go into a dumpster. A metal headboard, for instance, fits into the dumpster, but it can't gracefully make the transfer from the dumpster into a compactor. And, most significantly, for waste removal, the island is dependent upon mainland truckers, who must ride an infrequent ferry that may not run in bad weather. "I can't tell you all the problems that can happen," says Dave McEachron, a member of the Waste Management Committee, "but we've experienced them all." Even a seemingly simple matter like a cable breaking on the truck becomes a disaster when it has had to make a reservation for the ferry, has come all the way across to pick up the full dumpsters' trash—and then he can't load and must start over.

The majority of Frenchboro voters have consistently taken the position that no one is going to tell them what to do, and recycling appears to be the lightning rod of the solid-waste discussion. The fiscally conservative town has been concerned about the decreasing market for recycled goods, and many individuals also fear the mechanics of recycling. Perhaps they haven't recognized the costs of not using some of the opportunities available. As an example, for some time the island has not had a way to dispose of old appliances, and derelict washing machines are piling up in barns and yards and under wharves. Eventually, these will have to be dealt with, and it won't be cheap when the time comes. In the meantime, however, anyone who might have had an interest in solving the problem has met a solid wall of resistance. Many issues on the island divide people into two camps, and often the two sides are predictable. On solid waste, Dave says, the split is foggy. Perhaps it comes down to people who have lived in a place where recycling was working well and those who haven't.

But in any case, it was not likely to be the subject of much action during the next year. "The most involved people have, at least temporarily, thrown up their hands and decided we'd better deal with other issues, like the post office," says Dave.

The budget items went more quickly, with little discussion. A dessert-bidding break split the evening in two, and people milled around the back table, raising their offers for the delicious-looking sweets.

When the article about raising money for the preschool came up, the recommended amount of $500 went through with no comment. This was not what had happened in 2003, the first year of the program, when the taxpayers weren't sure a preschool was necessary. But finally the $500 was passed then, too, and the preschool happened, with Becky Lenfestey in charge. "It's challenging out here," she says, "because any time you want to do anything, you have to do it yourself. You wear a lot of hats here." (Her acceptance of the position of town clerk earlier demonstrated that.)

The preschool has been described as one of the most positive changes to come to the island. That there suddenly are so many young children on the island is both a surprise and a pleasure, and everyone seems to be uplifted by the preschool.

Later on, I asked Becky two simple questions—"How do you fund the preschool?" and "Where do you meet?"—to which her responses were the same: "Well, now, that *is* an interesting question." The total budget the first year was about nine thousand dollars. There aren't a lot of toys, nor has there been a large play area for the children. Parents pay a tuition of a thousand dollars a semester, and the rest is raised by one fund-raiser after another, with a small amount of help from a couple of foundations and the Sea Coast Mission. The townspeople ran a bake sale, a crafts sale at Christmas time, and two dessert raffles (described by one resident: "We lug it up there, buy it back, and lug it home"). The raffle at Town Meeting raised $262, which isn't too bad for a gathering of so few people. "It's a lot of work," Becky says of the preschool itself, "not just the teaching part. But it's very important for the kids to meet together and get into a routine, preparing for school." Her salary is $6,500—but she often ends up paying for supplies. She and her husband paid one child's tuition in 2003–04, and two in 2004–05. "But I can't complain," she says.

In 2003, the preschool was first licensed for a room at the church. But there were heating problems and pipes burst and they had to move—requiring a change in the license—to another space, which they shared with the part-time technology specialist and the minister from the Sea Coast Mission. (Rob Benson and his family spend a weekend a month on Frenchboro.) Future prospects for the school are still unclear. Loans might be available for building, but the whole project is too uncertain to make a long-term financial commitment. And where would it be built? Not on the Lenfesteys' property, for a number of reasons: Grants would be iffy and their homeowner's insurance would be canceled. And what would happen in a few years when the children reach high-school age and Becky moves ashore? (The Lenfesteys have purchased a house in Lamoine for that time, although Mike will still fish from Frenchboro, and they'll be back summers. "But you can't depend on the fishing industry forever and ever, anyway," she says.)

Back to Town Meeting. Several people went home during the break, before the school budget issues and before the one seriously controversial topic came up—where to put the Post Office.

Historically, the Post Office was always in the home of the postmaster (or postmistress) or in a store. The island had no Post Office for many decades after it was settled; in the early 1890s, the Post Office opened and was named Frenchboro, after a lawyer from Bass Harbor who helped navigate the government morass to get it established. Since 1928, there had been only three postmistresses, one for twenty-four years, one for twenty-five, and finally Lorena Beal—from 1998 until she moved off-island in 2002. Then no one wanted to take on the job, so the town itself signed a contract with the Postal Service to sell stamps and sort the mail, with office hours six days a week, for three hours a day. The contract requires that the office be locked up when it isn't open. The Postal Service wants the office to be in a public building of some sort, rather than to move around according to who's running it. As a temporary measure, the post-boxes were set up inside the Community Building, and the kitchen, which is lockable, served as the office. But this meant that the kitchen was unusable once the Post Office was set up there.

Town Meeting, 2004, was the time to vote on the final Post Office plan—the decision had already been tabled at two previous meetings. There were four options, all of which required construction. The first and least expensive option was to build a facility within the Community Building. The second two possibilities required adding on to the Community Building—either for the town office (with the Post Office then moving into what was currently the town office) or for just the Post Office. The final option was the conversion of a building at the bottom of the hill at the ferry terminal.

There had been discussion around the island about the work itself. No one on the island does construction for a living, although many of the fishermen are competent carpenters. But being a public project, the state would require bonding and insurance and various hoop-jumps, and people from off-island hesitate before agreeing to work on an island, where transportation is always an issue. "But," said Selectperson Linda Lunt before the meeting, "there'll be more problem getting a majority to agree on where to do it than there is to build it." And the way the Town Meeting warrant (agenda) was written, one of the options would have to receive a majority vote. If none did, the least popular option would be thrown out and they'd vote again, until one got a majority.

Finally, a couple of hours into the meeting, the warrant article on the Post Office came up. The first question from the floor was whether there was a reason not to continue as they have been. Yes, a number of people said. It's in the kitchen. And it's now impossible to get to the electrical circuit board for the building, too, as it's in the kitchen, which can't be used as a kitchen.

David Lunt wanted the building at the ferry terminal to be used, and said so. "Me too," said one of the guys in the back, loudly. He wanted to take advantage of an existing building, and he thought it could double as a ferry waiting area, too. He felt it would be cheaper to utilize what was already there.

But does the town own that building?

Half of it. Or maybe all of it, but the ferry service keeps stuff in part of it, and they would continue to do so.

And does the town own the land under the building?

Well, no, Maine Coast Heritage Trust does. But they're supposed to be handing it over. Probably.

There's no bathroom in the building. There's no insulation. It's an open-stud building on cement blocks, basically just a fish house.

And access is difficult, down that hill, particularly in winter. The hill would have to be sanded every day instead of just when the ferry was coming.

"Actually, it don't matter if you put it in the building at the ferry landing," one of the young guys in the back joked. "It won't be there another winter anyway." The snowplow operator (whom he named) "would come down through and knock it right into the ocean."

The discussion continued—about how much space was required, how much would it cost to heat it if it were in this place or that, compared to how much additional heat was used in the Community Building this last year because it was there, and what kind of access was required for handicapped people.

Rob Stuart, just elected selectman after a year off the board, summarized the whole situation in a tactful and articulate manner. The least feasible option, he said, was number 1. The town needs the Community Building space for getting together—community is important. So is the kitchen.

(Later, he expanded on this thought. Because islanders see themselves as self-sufficient, they expect the rest of the world to take care of itself, too. It's very easy for island individuals to become isolated from one another, and then it's easy to become paranoid, assuming people are thinking things that in fact they're not. But when people work together and even do something as simple as eat together, they understand each other better.)

At the meeting, he continued. It doesn't seem wise to spend money on a building we perhaps don't own—in a difficult part of town to get to—on land we don't yet own. The next two options involve adding on to the community building. "The town office has not been used appropriately because it's not big enough. The records aren't kept there—you have to go all over town to find things. Business isn't being done there. It would be most helpful if we expand with a bigger addition for the town office, and ask the officials to do their business there, which will make them more accessible." Then the existing town office could be turned into the Post Office. It's important to consider what the town needs in the long run.

The vote was taken by secret ballot, and the results were perhaps surprisingly clear, with fourteen of twenty-five voting for the most expensive option—building on a new town office and using the old one as the post office. There were just four votes for using the building at the ferry landing.

Traditionally—just about from the first settling of the island—members of the Lunt family have run Frenchboro, and have done a fine job of it. Over the last forty or fifty years, David, in particular, has been the dynamic force on the island. He's been the progressive thinker, the one responsible for many improvements, the economic leader. It was he who first wired the island for telephones; he was among the men who convinced the state to bring a ferry to the island on a regular basis; and, to a large degree, the successful homesteading project can be attributed to David. He has been involved with various organizations off-island—Island Institute, an advisory board for Acadia National Park, the Maine State Ferry Service Advisory Board. "He's a smart guy," says his son Dean, author of the island history *Hauling by Hand*, certainly required reading for anyone with an interest in Frenchboro, "and he's devoted his life to the island."

The Lunt family is still deeply involved, and they will continue to be, as most of them still make their homes and livelihoods there, but, as the Post Office vote showed, times are changing. No longer does something happen simply because the Lunt family, and David in particular, says it should.

Island
Infrastructure

1ittle conveniences—such as electricity, water, telephone, Internet service, and trash disposal—often are far more complicated on the islands than they are ashore. They are also more expensive. Electricity users on Islesboro, where the power comes via a relatively short cable from the mainland, pay Central Maine Power Company the same rate as do all the rest of CMP's customers (presently 11.68 cents a kilowatt hour), whereas on Monhegan, where electricity is created on-island with diesel generators, the cost is currently fifty cents a kilowatt hour.

Water comes primarily from individual wells, some of which are better than others. Solid waste is one of the most problematic infrastructure issues today on several islands, and there are differing ways of approaching the subject. Not a one of them is inexpensive.

Getting property insurance on many of the islands has become a problem, particularly, I'm told, since September 11, 2001. Fire protection—or the lack thereof—is often a critical factor. On our hypothetical Smith Island, the status of the Fire Department is under discussion, but everyone turns out if there is a fire. There are trucks, but they're hardly modern. There's a fire warden who has no training; he has the job because he's willing to make sure the trucks are maintained and winterized—not that the trucks are terribly useful in winter anyway, unless there's a water source right near the fire. The trucks have to be kept drained, because there's no heated space to keep them in. One man has attended firefighting training, which makes some people think he's gotten too big for his britches.

On Smith, as on all the other islands, efforts are being made to improve fire protection as quickly as possible, but it's not easy. In the meantime, the cost of insurance has risen significantly, and those who are unfortunate enough not to have coverage—or who got angry and canceled their increasingly expensive policies—find themselves unable to get insurance at all.

The Murrays and the Matinicus Plantation Electrical Company

"I got a new hole in the floor," said Paul Murray of his truck. "If I drop something, it goes through." His truck came to Matinicus as a mainland truck, but it doesn't go to the mainland anymore. It's fifteen years old. That's typical of Matinicus vehicles, but Paul—who is, incidentally, the tax collector—says that 75 percent of them are excised and licensed, even though some consider it unlikely anyone would ever care. The excise tax stays on the island, so it makes sense to people to pay it. (Not all the islands feel this way. Isle au Haut and Monhegan, for instance, have few if any registered vehicles.) "At least out here, you know exactly where the money is going." Paul and his wife, Eva, have an array of vanity plates over the coat hooks in their entryway. If the state is going to charge them for a vanity plate every year, at least, the Murrays say, it'll have to come up with a new plate each time. They're not going to pay for nothing. That, too, is typical of Matinicus. Their collection includes GRD CNYN, NRTH RIM, N KAIBAB, LOAF, ANADAMA, and now DONUT, giving homage to two of their interests. The baking in the Murray household—along with various other jobs for which Eva gets paid—allows them to visit such places as the Grand Canyon, which they feel is important to their son's and daughter's education. And they just plain enjoy it, anyway. They are home-schooling the children, saying it fits their schedule better than the island school. "We make a major effort not to allow them to be limited by living here." They have music lessons and go to the library and skating, and they travel and go visiting and the kids spend time at summer camp—for them, not as an escape, but instead to spend time with other kids. The family likes to get to Portland for at least one Sea Dogs baseball game and a Pirates hockey game each year. Emily has now had her first tennis lesson. It's certainly less convenient from Matinicus, and expensive—it costs $300 for Eva and the two children to fly ashore and back—but there are plenty of opportunities to broaden the kids' lives.

A business card for Paul or Eva would have to unfold several times to include all their titles and areas of expertise. Paul's licenses include Master Electrician, Propane/Natural Gas Technician, and Apprentice Boilerman, and he holds a commercial driver's license. He's the local representative and service technician for the telephone company, he is the propane gas dealer on the island, and he operates the island's power system. He also sometimes grades the roads and plows snow for the town, and he opens, closes, and generally maintains, repairs, and caretakes a number of summer houses and cottages. He does electrical, electronic, and mechanical repairs on lobster-boats and visiting yachts. He fixes fax machines and other appliances that on the mainland would probably be replaced by a quick trip to Wal-Mart, and he helps dig graves for people and pets.

Paul Murray in the Matinicus Plantation
Electrical Company building

Eva holds paperwork that licenses her as an elementary and middle-school teacher and an Emergency Medical Technician with basic wilderness certification. She too holds a commercial driver's license. She is the town treasurer, administrative assistant to the assessors (the officials of a plantation, which Matinicus is). She says this position is like being a town manager, only without any authority. She's also town clerk, director of Matinicus Island Rescue, town health officer, school bookkeeper, and acting "garbage czar" (solid-waste and recycling coordinator). She's clerk of the church (ironic, never having been a member of any church) and runs a bakery in summer; she serves as a ballot clerk for elections; she has acted as substitute teacher when needed; and she is one of four substitute station operators for the electric company. They have both substituted as sternmen from time to time. Paul bought Eva's engagement ring with money from sterning. Some of these jobs have small salaries; some don't. She says she could make more money bagging at Shaw's supermarket.

Matinicus's telephone system is a small part of the Island Telephone Company—which, combined with the independent companies serving Matinicus, Swans Island, Frenchboro, and Isle au Haut—is itself a tiny subsidiary of Telephone and Data Systems, Inc. There are microwave links to Stonington and Owls Head, which then relay the signal to Swans Island, the hub of the island systems. The main computer and a full-time employee are there. Paul installs telephones on Matinicus, tends the equipment at the tower, and receives a monthly retainer to be available when something needs doing, such as picking up company representatives at the airport. This is not a terribly demanding job, but it needs doing. The best benefit, Paul and Eva agree, is the annual Christmas party at the Samoset Resort in Rockport. The company puts up the whole family there, and the Murrays find it a treat. "They're good people to work with," he says, "although some of the decisions from above or the PUC don't always make sense." Both the phone company and the electric company are subject to oversight by the state's Public Utilities Commission.

Paul's propane dealership serves ninety to a hundred customers. About eight times a year, a truck brings a load of hundred-pound propane bottles on the ferry, which

Paul delivers as needed. The Coast Guard requires that there be three empty spaces around the truck on the ferry. If he were to have a bulk-propane truck come out, he'd have to hire the whole boat—which would be prohibitively expensive, as well as impossible: the boat only stays at the ferry landing for an hour, and the truck wouldn't be able to get around to fill everyone's tanks in that short time.

The most significant of Paul's infrastructure jobs comes from the power company. He's responsible for the electric generation system that provides power for the entire island.

Island-wide power reached Matinicus in the 1960s—and, in fact, that's how Paul's family first came to the island. His father and his uncle had an electrical contracting company in Cape Elizabeth, Maine, and through a cousin who married a woman from Matinicus, they were hired to wire up houses for the new centralized electrical power. Paul's parents liked the island so well they retired there in 1974. After five years working for Central Maine Power Company, Paul came to the island in 1982.

The power company on Matinicus was originally privately owned; in the mid-1970s, it went bankrupt. The bank said, "Don't change anything, just keep it going." Toward the end of that decade, a federal grant made it possible for Matinicus Plantation to buy the system, which consisted of poles, wire, a small building, and a few not-very-good generators. Matinicus Plantation Electrical Company was born. A few years of experimentation with different equipment and some more federal money brought them to the very dependable system in place today. "We have far fewer and far shorter power failures than they do in South Thomaston," says Eva, who has relatives in that mainland town.

Twice a day, Paul goes down to the little building near the harbor—downtown, you could say—where the Post Office and the ferry landing are, and where there was a store not so long ago. The building is warmed by a Modine blowing heat salvaged from the engines, which are in a separate room in the back. Paul dons earmuff-style hearing protection before he goes in with them. "The greatest invention in the world," he says, "radios in ear protectors."

The system is automatic and has been in place since 1983. There are three engines. One is designated as lead engine, and the panel—which, with only a few additions, is similar to what one would find in a hospital or similar-size facility—automatically picks up another if the demand calls for more. The second one runs for ten minutes, checks to see if it's still needed, and drops off again if it's not. There are lights in place that run on batteries in case Paul has to work on the system when the power's off.

On the wall are two clocks, one run by battery that Paul keeps set to the National Institute of Standards and Technology radio signal, and the other, run by island power and dependent on the speed of the engines, is "Matinicus time." It represents what the clocks and time-dependent electronics in everyone's houses say. On our visit, they were ten seconds apart. "I'll catch that up soon," said Paul.

There are dials and knobs and settings, and a needle records the island's power demand through time onto a running tape. The section of tape that happened to show that particular February day ranged from 17.7 kilowatts to a high of 40, but the system reaches about 120 kilowatts several times during the summer and peaks somewhat higher than that immediately following an outage. Charlie Pratt, who ran the system for its first years, loved information. He was always looking for patterns, but Paul says that on such a small system, all it takes is for someone to flush his toilet at a different time to change the pattern. There is a clipboard holding pages of columns of figures recorded twice-daily, representing engine parameters—oil pressure, temperature, engine time, and the like. Another clipboard shows daily fuel use and the high and low loads for the day. In a cupboard are large, tidy piles of old records. Paul, who worked with Charlie for sixteen years and took over running the system when Charlie died, keeps the same sets of data. "I'll keep them until I see if they're useful or not. But I don't know what I'll do when the cupboard gets full."

An alarm system calls Paul's house and his telephone-company pager if anything goes wrong. "Alert Condition Two," it tells him in a computer voice. (There are other conditions for which the alarm system might notify him, but none that are in use at the power company.) "Two or three times a year it happens," Paul says. "The radiator might be down, or there might be a high water temperature on the running engine." Wherever he may be on the island, it won't take Paul long to get to the power plant and see what's ailing it; when he's planning to be off-island, he lines up someone else to receive the calls from the machinery. Presently the backups include one of the assessors, who works as a sternman on a lobsterboat; a retired engineer from Central Maine Power; and an artist with roots in Portland and time in New York City who happens to have the necessary knowledge, plus Eva.

A standby engine in a separate building outside can run the whole island if need be, with a disconnect switch. It works the same way that a home generator does when the power's down, but at 150 kilowatts, it's much larger than a home system. That building also is kept warm from the main system, and a battery charger keeps the batteries at full strength. Paul runs the backup from time to time in order to be certain it's operational and ready to go.

The system could run for three and a half or four days without refilling the day-tank, which is inside the building to keep the fuel warm, but each morning, Paul turns on a pump from the fuel-tank farm up the hill above the power building and fills it. He records on one of the clipboards how much fuel comes down. In winter, it uses seventy or eighty gallons a day, and in summer sometimes reaches 120, totaling 32,000 a year.

The tank farm holds 17,000 gallons and is topped off about three times a year, when the little oil tanker from Rockland, the *William McLoon*, comes in with a delivery for the island's fuel company.

On the mainland, most distribution lines carry 7,200 volts. On Matinicus, they're only 2,400 volts, but that's still hot; you don't want to go grabbing one. Transformers for the low voltage are harder to come by than those used on the mainland, but a company in South Dakota rejuvenates old ones, and Paul keeps a couple of them on hand.

Maine's Public Utilities Commission regulates the company, just as it does any other municipally owned electric company, of which there are a number in the state—Kennebunk, for instance. "We're the same, just smaller," says Paul. The total annual budget for the company is not quite $100,000. But they've been fortunate in that the income has covered the expenses; they've not raised their rates since the new company was set up. Electricity costs about twenty-seven cents a kilowatt hour plus a fuel adjustment (a total of thirty-eight cents and a bit as of March, 2005), which isn't insignificant, but the PUC insists that municipal power companies only break even. No money is being socked away here. Town Meeting on Matinicus votes $5,000 a year toward the power company— the idea is that because there's power available, property is more valuable. The only cost increases to users have been in the fuel allowance, even though Paul and the bookkeeper both get cost-of-living increases. Paul receives a salary, plus he's paid by the hour for line work—that time can't be predicted. The wires are pretty dependable in summer, he says, but there are usually two or three failures each winter from ice or wind. Paul tries to inspect a third of the wires each year, looking for problems and fixing them before they became critical, but it doesn't always work out. "The concept's good, but you can't stop trees falling down." Trees on Matinicus have shallow roots, hitting bedrock soon, and tend to topple easily. He reads the meters once a month—by bicycle in summer and by truck in winter. "It's a fun trip," he says. Collection is rarely a problem—in twenty years, they've only had to write off three or four accounts, and for one of those, the man has died. "It's hard to turn anyone off, because you know everybody."

The town office is in an old schoolhouse that was used until the mid-1960s. As tax collector, Paul has official office hours every Wednesday afternoon. "I was hoping that people wouldn't knock on my door at home at five in the afternoon, but they still do."

To date, water hasn't been much of an issue on the island, although quality varies from place to place. The most valuable land is on the shore—so appealing to summer people for its views and romantic aspect—but the well water there is apt to be rusty. Property there has no soil for gardens or septic systems, and people get battered by the wind. Year-round residents are more comfortable farther inland. Six or seven people get their drinking water from the Murrays, whose forty-three-foot-deep pounded well provides good water and plenty of it.

Little things become big things on Matinicus. The former funeral director in Rockland didn't like to go over to the island on the boat with a body; he flew. People didn't like that, and some wouldn't use his services. The new fellow "interfaces gently" with the island.

In the state of Maine, embalming isn't required unless by local ordinance; when a lifelong resident of Matinicus died not long ago, his sister was adamant that he not be taken off the island, and he wasn't. But even when funeral directors do get involved, the funeral itself is a local affair. "Funerals aren't handled by overpaid professional strangers," I was told. "The grave is dug by neighbors, and the get-together afterward is also a neighborhood thing. People bring out extra people, and nobody charges a nickel." The "boat minister" often presides (the minister from the *Sunbeam*, the Maine Sea Coast Mission boat).

The island cemetery has no deeded lots. "If you're from here, or can convince the island you deserve a plot, you can stake out your spot in advance, or your family can when the time comes," says Eva. "It's informal. There are jokes about 'I don't want to be next to *him*,' but it all works out." One guy decided that as long as he was to be buried on the opposite side of a tree from another person, it would be OK. The roots would be between them.

Charlie Pratt not only had his plot staked out, he had his stone prepared (all except the death date) and in place. More than one person came back from being away, saw that stone, and was surprised that Charlie had died without their knowing about it. Oh, no, they were reassured, he's just getting things ready. Instead of a polished marker, some people have chosen natural beach stones—some with a plaque and some not marked at all.

Two stones were repossessed. One day, Paul was surprised to see a truck on the ferry that he didn't recognize—usually everyone knows what's coming on the ferry. The truck went back on with something under a tarp in the back. A week or two later, Paul noticed that two stones were missing from the cemetery. He called the monument maker, who said the families hadn't paid for them. One was brought back in short order, but it was two years before the other came back.

The infrastructure on Matinicus is indicative of the nature of the island. "The essence of us as Community is questionable," says Eva. Other than emergencies, when everyone pitches in, things are taken care of by individuals, which can be stressful for the people involved. Paul has had times of burnout. Eva is aware of the possibility in the future. Probably every other person active in the community before and since has also reached that point, or will.

"What's going to save this place is the Stone Soup Committee," Eva says. "Whenever someone says 'It's never going to work,' someone steps up to the plate.

When there's nothing left to eat, then people show up with carrots or potatoes for the soup." Eva cites the parsonage as an example. The church owns it, and in July and August, various volunteer ministers come out and live in it. During the school year, the teacher often lives in it. But there is no individual owner to take care of it, and a year or two ago it had become really ratty-looking. "You can't keep paint on with nails out here," says Eva. Everyone knew it needed painting, but no one could muster up the interest in doing the job. Except Jasmine Tinker. She is relatively new to the island and has the right personality for community organizing. She took it on, enlisting artist Maury Colton, familiar with the mechanics of structure painting as well as the artistic kind. Between them, they got the job done. "Thirty people came out—lobstermen, summer people, lawyers, veterinarians, small children—truly in defiance of 'it isn't going to work.'" Says Eva, "She was the cruise director, and he was the painting director."

The Island Institute contacts Eva from time to time, volunteering to send some-one to do whatever the island would like done. "Why they call me, I don't know," she says, though it's clear she's had years in the cruise director's position herself. "Well, that's fine, I say, but where are they going to live?"

Matinicus, more than the other islands, takes care of itself—one person by one person.

The Cables of the Fox Islands Electric Cooperative

The Fox Islands Electric Cooperative (usually just called the Co-op) provides North Haven and Vinalhaven with electricity from the mainland, through cables that run from Glen Cove (part of Rockport) to North Haven. When the cables were laid in 1978, there were four of them, and any two would keep the regular power in business. (Three-phase power, on the other hand, needs three cables, so when two of the four were dysfunctional, the island's nineteen three-phase customers had to be bypassed.) Sometimes a cable would fail when one was already out and not yet repaired. When a cable went, all the customers on both islands lost power until they could switch the power to the spare cable—usually a matter of two or three hours.

There are two possible reasons why, over time, the cables started failing: chafing and snagging. Partway along the crossing, the bottom becomes shallow and the cable has to go over a rock outcropping—chafing there was probably inevitable. Draggers or other fishing vessels may have snagged the cable, as happened often between Swans Island and Frenchboro before that cable was buried. Also, tanker barges sometimes catch lobster gear on their hawsers. There have been reports of sometimes a hundred or two hundred traps being snared this way and pulled across the bottom, possibly grabbing or twisting an electrical cable in the process. It's probably not surprising that the cable became weakened over the course of twenty-five years.

During the first twenty-two years of service, there had only been seven "breaks" (the power was interrupted though the cable itself was not severed), but starting at Thanksgiving time in 1998, there was a series of failures, although, since only one cable went at a time, service continued. On Thursday, June 17, 1999, the Co-op finally was able to schedule a repair of a cable that had been nonfunctional since January. As a reporter, I went along to observe.

Coordinating the weather reports with fifteen men from five companies, two tugboats, a barge, and a lobsterboat was perhaps more of a job than the repair itself. The crew from Prock Marine Company left Rockland at four-thirty in the morning in order to take its barge and crane over to North Haven to grab that end of the cable. Greg Canders of Bangor, who was on hand that Thursday, had dived onto the cable back in January to attach a bridle and buoy so they could pick it up with the crane when they came back. A lobsterboat came from Vinalhaven to pick up the three Central Maine Power (CMP) cable-splicers in Rockland at six-thirty. I joined this group. When we reached the barge, it was within a mile of where they believed the break to be.

The problems appeared to be externally caused, according to engineer Wally MacDonald, who came from Prince Edward Island to oversee the project. ("I'm just kind of an ornament out here," he claimed, but admitted that if something went really wrong, he'd be the one making the decisions.) The team was underrunning the cable, running it up over rollers, across the barge deck, and back down into the water. There was a tug on either side of the barge; the smaller one, to port, was directing the barge as it followed the cable toward the mainland at about one knot. Prock's Terry Nichols explained to me in clear detail just how the operation would work. (If you ever need anything explained, ask Terry.) Everyone else knew; they'd been through it before.

They were all waiting for the big Snap.

To allow the men on shore to estimate where the failure was, a 10,000-volt charge—the "thumper"—was being sent through the cable every eight or ten seconds from Glen Cove. Everyone said we'd both hear and see the snap when the damaged section of cable cleared the water.

A couple of Prock guys kept a lookout forward, in case anything should get caught in the cable as it cleared the water. They carefully freed a couple of lobster traps that hadn't been moved from the cable corridor despite everyone's best efforts at notifying the fishermen about the project. Everyone else was just hanging out, waiting. People snacked on Twinkies and Nutribars. As soon as the CMP splicing crew had arranged their tools and equipment, they too headed for their lunch boxes, even though it wasn't much after seven in the morning. The big tug's color television showed the news to anyone who cared. Nobody did.

Greg, the diver, had a GPS that indicated exactly where we were and a chart marked with their best guess as to the location of the break. No one was surprised when the barge passed that spot; the previous time, the people operating the thumpers had underestimated the distance to the break by two thousand feet. Perhaps previous splices along the line confuse the distance readings.

As the cable came up from the water, most of the time it was remarkably clean, with only an anemone or starfish glommed on every so often. When the bottom is muddy, as it is most of the way across, Terry explained, the cable buries itself and stays clean. In one place, the cable was covered in both animal and vegetable growth; that was where it had been lying directly on rock.

Finally, *snap!* Every eight or ten seconds, a flash of light and a loud snap. The tug backed down to stop the barge. Mike Romer of Fox Islands Electric called the substation to turn off the thumper, and immediately all the men went into little clutches of activity. Some of Prock's men grabbed yellow ropes, come-alongs, and chains to affix to both ends of the cable and take tension off the break. Others set up steel sawhorses. The CMP guys climbed into their coveralls, gathered all their tools, and fired up their propane burner to heat buckets of tar.

Nothing was said; everything just happened. Ron Lord, then manager of Fox Islands Electric, observed, "It's hard to tell who the boss is on the Prock crew—they all just do what they're supposed to. I can stand here with my hands in my pockets—and pay the bill." The bill for this entire operation was expected to be between $25,000 and $50,000, depending on how things went.

When the length of cable crossing the barge was slack in the middle, CMP took over and everyone else eased up and started joking around.

The splicing process is intricate and time-consuming. The cable has several layers, going from inside to out: the actual transmission wire, rubber, PVC, copper, another PVC layer, sheathing wires wound around the outside, cloth, and finally, if it's on a reel, talc to lubricate it.

Once the cable is cut and carefully measured, collars are anchored in place on each end, and all the layers are stripped down and smoothed and made receptive to tape. They crimp a copper tube over the bare ends of the transmission wire, and then they tape. They tape and they tape and they tape, using five different kinds of tape. They connect the sheathing wires with copper and then apply more tape.

Everyone was glad the temperature wasn't zero, plus or minus, as it had been the last time they did a splice. You can't tape with gloves on. In January, they tried to hold plywood around the fellow doing the taping, but it was cold, no getting around it. This Thursday was perfect, everyone agreed. No wind, no sun. Sweatshirt weather.

Finally the splice was made, and they put it all into a tube, a splice box. As Terry described it, "When they draw it up, they create a little pucker in it so they're not pulling on the splice at all." Finally, they pour hot tar into the "can," as they call the splice box. The completed splice should be impermeable and strong and permanent.

Wally MacDonald said, "This is splice number ten for the CMP guys, and they've never had a failure yet." Bob Dube, Dan Conner, and Gil Guevin were the only splicers CMP had. "It's a dying art," said Bob.

As the CMP men picked up all their toys and headed for the lobsterboat and their sandwiches, the crane started up and the Prock guys went back to their yellow ropes and come-alongs. The divers never had to do anything, which was fine with everyone. Slowly, the cable dropped back into the water and all the boats headed for home.

The cable was tested later in the day. In January, after the last splice, it tested at 60 megohms (a rating in the 200s is considered good). This time it showed 310. "I hesitate to be too optimistic," Ron Lord said (justifiably, as it turned out), "but it's looking good."

Ron has since retired and has been replaced by Dave Folce, who had twenty years with electric co-ops across the country. He also worked for ten years at an investor-owned electric company and says he wouldn't do that again. "They seem to worry more about their investors than their customers," he says. Co-ops are locally owned and work for their members, who are the owners and have a voice in the decisions made by the company. Co-ops, he says, are part of the community they serve, and he's more comfortable in that situation.

After the 1999 repair, an increasing number of faults caused temporary outages, with thirteen in the first ten months of 2004; in September, for the first time, three cables were down at once. The islands were dark for more than a day. (Dave Folce heard that a whole load of generators came across on the ferry after the outage that day.)

The time had come to replace the whole shebang, and fortunately, the project was ready to go as soon as the materials could be created. For the winter of 2004–05, though, the Co-op had to spring for a $267,000 generator as backup. That was enough to cover both islands' needs, other than the three-phase customers, all but two of whom had their own generators anyway. Like any diesel generation, the Co-op's new plant was expensive to run as well as to purchase.

The engineering for the new cables was a chore, of course. Dave and a team of consultants, headed up by Wally MacDonald and electrical guru Chuck Swanson, had been on the plan for some time, and in the fall of 2004, the contract was signed to lay the cables in March 2005. Yes, March seems a tough time to be out on the ocean laying cables, but NOAA, the National Oceanic and Atmospheric Administration, wouldn't allow the crew in the water after April 9, due to the spawning season of the endangered Atlantic salmon. They did receive an extension, which allowed another couple of weeks for the work, not that April's a whole lot better.

It's a project of an unusual scale for an electric company of this size, or even for larger ones, which can normally work on a part of their system each year. The cost of everything—planning, permitting, and laying the new cables, plus removal of the old ones—was calculated at $6.8 million. Permitting alone was a big deal, and they hired a consultant just to guide them through the rigmarole. The Army Corps of Engineers was the lead agency; everything goes through them, but permits were needed from the U.S. Fish and Wildlife Service, the National Marine Fisheries Service, the National Register of Historic Places (for the land portion of the run), the Maine Coastal Zone Management Agency, the Department of Environmental Protection, the Department of Conservation, the Department of Transportation, the town of Rockport (starting point for the cables), and the town of North Haven (end point for the cables).

The biggest share of the cost, $3.6 million, was for the wire and materials, including its transportation from Sweden. The cable came on a specially designed freighter, coiled loose in a huge basket-type affair, and the trip took forty-five days. It is a single multicore cable this time, with three conductors inside it and a fiberoptic line too, in case someone's interested in leasing it. "It's foolish not to throw that in," says Dave. Cable of the specifications they needed doesn't just sit around in a warehouse waiting to be delivered, so time was an issue. They had only the short window to get the ten-day job completed, and you don't stop in the middle. Once they start, they have to keep going. They actually added another mile to the distance of the crossing, skipping south from Glen Cove to an old crossing site from Owls Head in order to avoid the rock outcropping. The new cable was buried six feet into the bottom, to protect it from the mechanical troubles the old ones faced.

The Co-op did receive a federal grant for $2.6 million, money set aside to assist rural areas with high energy costs—which, with costs nearly three times national averages, Vinalhaven certainly has. The rest was borrowed and must be paid back from the rates charged over the next thirty years.

The old cable must be removed, too. The new route would close off fishing grounds, so the old cable crossing route must be returned to the fishermen. The cost of this was estimated at $250,000. Some salvage might be possible—the cables in between the splices were still sound and useful for industrial use. But would there be a market?

Meanwhile, the Co-op has been looking into other ways of saving on electric power. They chased down and were granted $219,000 for solar projects for the islands' nonprofits—the eldercare home on Vinalhaven and the medical center and schools. The eldercare facility, for example, expects to meet all its needs for hot water from the solar installation—a huge saving, as they do all their own laundry. On a bright day, the arrays generate more electricity than can be used or stored, and it goes back into the Co-op system—their benefit is that they get that energy free. Normally, they are forced to purchase any such surplus from the owners of private solar systems that are equipped to send it into the overall grid. Their meters literally turn backward.

Hoping to further mitigate the expense of the new cables, Dave and the Co-op's board of directors are also looking into wind generation. An anemometer on the western side of Vinalhaven has demonstrated that a wind facility would be productive, and as many as ten turbines could be placed so they would be fairly difficult to see from the island. Dave would like to start with a single unit, to get acceptance. Landowners have been receptive to the idea, though of course there are issues to be addressed: aesthetics and the impact on birds being perhaps two of the more dramatic, along with paying for the project.

Four turbines the size of the one in Hull, Massachusetts, whose hub is 164 feet off the ground and has blades 77 feet long, could provide all the power the two islands need, but of course the production would be intermittent, so the cable system would still be needed. But any excess power could be sold back to the mainland at a profit. There are grants available to build such a system, but they're usually matching grants, and, with the cable project, there's no money available locally. Still, the idea is being studied, to be ready if the time came that it could happen.

Dave was hoping for a 2004 cable installation but knew that might be a dream, as indeed it was. But everyone wanted to get going as fast as they could, and September's problem just encouraged that. The spring of 2005 brought the new cable on line.

The Internet Comes to Swans Island

As recently as 1999, Swans Island had no Internet access. Telephone service came, and still comes, from TDS, for whom the Island Telephone Company is a tiny part of their total business—and one into which they're understandably not inclined to put much money. They wanted no part of adding what they felt would be an unprofitable service.

Belinda Doliber, who had recently retired from running the annual Fishermen's Forum in Rockland and had some time on her hands, decided it was time to get Internet access, so she contacted the Island Institute. "The whole country of Bangladesh had e-mail before we did," she says. "It was ridiculous." State Representative Marge Kilkelly took on the project. Marge found two wireless Internet companies interested in working with the island, and she was in the process of writing a grant application for the needed hardware, estimated at $300,000, when a short piece about her efforts appeared in the paper. "All of a sudden," Belinda says, "TDS notified us that they would provide dial-up service and bury cables across to the island." That was the end of the wireless companies.

Telephone service comes to Swans, as to some of the other islands, by microwave, and it works well. TDS gives better connections than did the previous company, Belinda says, but they're expensive—the only place they can call for free is Swans Island, and when the Dolibers first came to the island, calls to other towns cost forty-four cents a minute. TDS wouldn't offer unlimited Internet access, and they charged a dollar an hour. That doesn't sound like very much, but the first person with e-mail capability had a one-month bill for $500. Everyone on the island wanted to use it.

TDS never did bury the cables, and they refused to allow other providers to use their wires on the island, so no other provider could come in. The issue went to the Public Utilities Commission in Augusta, which put a stop to TDS's monopoly. "Now we have options," Belinda says.

Matinicus, with access by a wireless provider in Rockland, has service as good as on any island—or indeed, any other community in the state. The Internet age has certainly come to the islands, even though some are still limited to dial-up service. The opportunities will only be increased as good high-speed access reaches more islands.

Solid Waste, Then and Now

There's an old dump on a beach on Smith Island. Everywhere, there's evidence remaining of its earlier function: in the intertidal area, there is nearly as much glass as rock—sea-washed glass in uncountable colors. Many islands have similar beaches—I call this one Glass Beach.

Standing here, facing the sea, you're looking south and east across islands and islands of all sizes. The morning sun has warmed it, and afternoon sou'westers and nasty southeast storms alike have sent the waves onto it for more than seventy years since the islanders stopped leaving their refuse here.

The sea glass comes in recognizable shades—old Coke bottle aqua in the soft and inimitable curves, Canada Dry ginger-ale green, and Noxzema blue (but not much of that, as the beach has been too much picked, over the years).

There are pieces of very light lilac, a color that some very old clear glass takes on as it ages, greens in a hundred shades, clear chunks softened to a white surface and thinner clear sections, and beer-bottle browns, along with browns both lighter and darker.

Sometimes lettering stands out, identifying companies both extant and long gone: a single piece of a clear Gordon's gin bottle, and myriad shards of Cantrell something-or-other, in green.

Each glass shape has its own feel. Some are entirely rounded and smooth while others have kept a sharp edge or have broken to one; some have pebbled surfaces or logos. Some are recognizable by their shapes: bottoms and necks of bottles, sections of Mason jar lids; and some are amorphous, broken at random angles with bends and twists which hide the original form.

Some have settled with time; I saw one former bottle neck melted around a pebble, clearly visible today enfolded in glass. They say glass is a liquid.

Driftwood tree trunks lie along the top of the beach; visitors sit on them and admire the sea and the breaks of rock and tree that interrupt it. Invariably, glass pieces are lined up along a flat place on the wood, arranged perhaps by a child with bright examples of each color, or, as I have done myself, in a long line of one hue graduated subtly by shade, from clear to the darkest.

You could never find a sample of every green the beach offers, though. You think you've done it—your spectrum of just this one color is complete—and then your eye catches yet another shade.

Each of these remnants was part of an object once, made by someone, used for something, tossed aside by another person. Did this particular bit come from a bottle used to store pickles made year after year from island cucumbers? Or did it merely provide transport for a product from Away, simply consumed on the island? Was it purely decorative? A vase, maybe? Was it broken and thrown away, or thrown away intact and broken by the beach? Was it simply trash, or was it then treasured as it is now?

Beach glass is collected by nearly every beach wanderer and kept for itself or turned into *objets d'art*, corny or beautiful or both. I have always been a beach-glass collector—I even have Band-Aid boxes and wooden containers dating back to childhood, each containing a few glass treasures. But on the Glass Beach, I feel compelled to leave every piece behind.

I wish others had done the same, but the location of this beach treasure has been known to too many, for too long. The summer-resident owner has heard reports of people coming with five-gallon pails and hauling them off, full to the top with sea glass. There's plenty left, but the supply is not infinite. The ecology of islands is fragile in ways the Audubon Society and their ilk may never have considered.

DISPOSAL TODAY

Solid-waste disposal is one of the most difficult and expensive problems facing any American community today, a fact only more true on islands. Traditionally on the Maine islands, anything unwanted that would burn was burned, anything that would sink was sunk, and much that didn't sink was thrown overboard just the same; the rest was thrown in the dump, whether an official island dump as on Vinalhaven, or in the back woods. Perhaps islands had an easier time than did inland communities, in that they did have that huge ocean to take away garbage and trash—and, on the scale that materials were tossed in earlier times, no tremendous harm was done. With the coming of plastic, however, it was obvious to everyone that the ocean couldn't take care of what was asked of it, and burning the stuff is unpleasant, to say nothing of noxious.

While there's rarely an acceptable way in any Maine community to deal with trash locally, it's obvious that no island can safely handle it all at home. Yet, traditionally, the islands have taken pride in being self-reliant, which they have had to be, and they've been conservative with expenditures, too. It's difficult for some island residents, particularly the older folk, to understand the reasoning behind others' environmental concerns—not all the dangers of pollution are immediately observable, and they can be hard to imagine. The state is regulating solid-waste disposal to a greater and greater extent, though. (When the state first banned burn barrels, people asked Paul Murray what they were supposed to do with their trash. He suggested boxing it all up and sending it to DEP.) Nonetheless, more and more islanders are becoming concerned about their own surroundings. Every island has a committee of interested people, official or otherwise, struggling to find viable methods of improving the situation, although the ideas from some such groups are more welcomed than others.

MATINICUS ISLAND RECYCLES!

Since its settlement, Matinicus always took care of everything on-island, each individual for himself. Every household had a burn barrel. Since nearly everyone went fishing every day, it was a simple matter to toss overboard anything that didn't burn. Generally speaking, disposal was simple enough.

The first category of solid waste to attract public attention was old cars. It had been easy for someone to buy an uninspectable vehicle for fifty dollars on the mainland and take it to Matinicus, where few people worried about inspection stickers; the trouble was that fifty-dollar cars don't often run for long. Over the years, many went overboard, but the hulks of a large number remained lying around on the island—with grass and ultimately brush and even trees growing up through them.

A number of years ago, a group of people tired of the wrecks came up with a cleanup plan. The first step was successfully convincing Town Meeting to raise $10,000 to drag off unwanted vehicles. Some seventy-three or seventy-four were piled onto a big barge, many in more than one piece. "It was not a pretty sight!" says Sari Bunker.

The best part of the plan was the fee to discourage dead vehicles from collecting again. As a plantation, not a town, Matinicus creates its own budgets and sets its own tax rates, but the state is responsible for ordinances. It took an act of the State Legislature to pass the $250 vehicle disposal fee now charged for any vehicle that comes onto the island. The money is returned when the vehicle leaves again, making a big incentive to send unused cars off-island, while also providing a method of paying for those that don't go off on their own accord. If a car is abandoned, the town officials now have the right to get rid of it. Shorty's Towing Service of Rockland has agreed that if a car can get onto the ferry, whether it runs or is pushed, Shorty will meet the boat in Rockland and drag the car off and away at no cost.

A side benefit—one hoped-for and turning out to be so—is that the vehicles coming onto the island would be better to begin with and remain useful longer.

Sari Bunker has the duty of overseeing this program, an honor she says she received by having a big mouth, often the way island people get jobs. Does she have a title? It's rather like nicknames on the islands—they're given informally and you may not know every one of them. Someone called her the Witchy Waste Ordinance Woman, and she guesses that's as close to a title as she'll have. (Sari has a second title, Ferry Nazi, which was given to her because she watches the ferries come and go, clipboard in hand, making note of vehicles going each way.)

In the summer of 2004, using funding left over from the initial disposal, the town hired the *Island Transporter* to come out and take another nine cars ashore that had been missed before and for which a disposal fee had not been paid. The intent was to clean up the most visible ones, those by the waterfront at Harbor Point. There are still others around the island on private property.

Not everyone loves the ordinance, but the island has had no trouble enforcing it. "I'm totally against this," one fellow told Sari, "but I don't mind paying."

Although most people try to take care of their trash properly, not everything on Matinicus is disposed of legally. Planning for a better system is a horror show, says longtime (but finally retired) Assessor Vance Bunker. It would be easy to make the situation worse than it now is, by having unreasonable requirements. Even today, what can be burned, often is. There is no feasible alternative. Burying would certainly have detrimental effects—if it were even possible in the bony island soil—attracting rats if not seeping unfortunate substances into the aquifer. A transfer station would not only be very hard to site physically, as the town owns no land, but also astoundingly expensive because of the requirements for storage and the ultimate costs of shipping off-island. "Burning is the only thing we can do," says current Assessor John Griffin. "It's not something we should be bragging about, but if the DEP thinks we're not burning, then they have bigger problems than I think."

Even the most environmentally concerned individuals tend to look the other way, feeling that they're making so much ground in other areas that the relatively small amount of burning is the least of their concerns. The assessors are looking into other options that might be possible eventually, including, somehow, a transfer station, ultimately the best solution.

That the island is a sole-source aquifer is a far bigger issue than the pollutants from a bit of burning. Years ago, waste oil was spread on the airstrip to keep down the dust; now it's mixed in with the power company's diesel fuel and burned. The airstrip is sometimes dusty—can't be helped, as there is no safe alternative. State grants have paid to replace a number of oil tanks around the island, further protecting the aquifer.

For two summers now, a private hauler has been hired to come to the island. Paid by the junk owners and loaded by John Libby and his Bobcat loader, he has taken off a great many appliances and other scrap metal, all of which traditionally was simply dumped into the sea. Refrigerators are the worst—they float, due to the foam insulation used in recent decades. A few years back, someone wanted to dispose of his old refrigerator, so he took it out and threw it overboard, as he'd always done in the past, but it didn't sink. "Well, I'll get it!" he said, and shot holes all through it. It still floated. He rammed it with his boat—no success. (He had to repair the gelcoat on his boat that winter, though.) It came ashore on a point that is now called Refrigerator Point. No one likes to think about the Freon in the thing.

Some trash still goes overboard. "The worst thing that ever happened is plastic," says Vance, who remembers a day when it was rare to see plastic washed up on the shore. "Ninety percent of the rest is biodegradable." Vance and Sari speak of seeing wildlife entrapped in plastic shopping bags or six-pack rings. "People the whole length of the coast are getting more conscientious," they agree. But they also admit that where they live is the worst place left. There are still those—people who don't give a shit, they say—who still dump. The islanders are taking more care about such matters, though, and any new construction is built following all the rules and regulations. Vance speaks of the state officials. "We try not to have 'em come around any more than they have to. If they made up for lost time, they'd have to move in."

"If the DEP wants to come out here and give us a hard time," says John Griffin, "I'd be glad to sit down and talk with them." He knows that the island is making serious efforts toward the proper handling of its trash.

Eva Murray says it's hard knowing whether to get involved in a particular issue or not. She says that (like Sari) she has a big mouth and no fear of microphones, and she finds herself speaking out. That's how she ended up with her position as garbage czar.

Individuals had been recycling for several years—taking a boxful of their own recyclables and returnables with them when they went ashore if there was room in the plane, but until the summer of 2004, there was no community recycling program. That summer, due to Eva's efforts, the island took a major step. She had already gotten a matching grant for a few thousand dollars from the State Planning Office to buy an eight-by-sixteen-foot shed. The city of Rockland had agreed to accept, at no charge, any recyclables that Matinicus could bring to them. They would also take, for a fee, "universal waste"—those common household items that contain lead and mercury, such as cathode-ray tubes, thermostats, and fluorescent bulbs. The idea was that, when necessary, Eva would rent a truck on the mainland and take the recyclables to Rockland. The last and most difficult piece of the project was finding a place to put the shed—the town has no unused land of its own, and everyone was concerned about whether people would simply toss trash bags around and make a mess. Finally, the trustees of the church agreed to allow the small building for recyclables to be placed temporarily on parsonage property.

"Matinicus Island Recycles!" announced the T-shirts worn by Eva and her fellow recyclers to get the word out. They plastered the island with notices about just what could and couldn't be recycled, and who to call to open the shed when someone wanted to drop off something. There is nothing mandatory about the program—it's simply available for anyone who wants to take advantage of it. "We're not twisting arms," says Eva, "we're just offering options."

On September 2, 2004, Eva brought a fifteen-foot box truck out on the ferry. The ferry only stays on the island for a short time, but Eva and a group of volunteers scrambled. They crammed into the truck the entire shedful of glass and cans and milk jugs and detergent bottles and newspapers, and, even more than anything else, corrugated cardboard, because everything comes onto the island by mail order.

"The program is so far appreciated by those who use it and peacefully ignored by those who don't," says Eva, who had been concerned that people would make fun of it or maybe even vandalize the facility. But there has been no such activity, and no mess.

"Slowly, people who I didn't expect would take an interest are beginning to take advantage of it."

MONHEGAN AND SWANS ISLAND SOLUTIONS

Both Swans Island and Monhegan haul off all their solid waste, with differing approaches. It costs a lot, no matter how you look at it.

"We have a system we can call legal to a certain extent," says Kathie Iannicelli of Monhegan. The exception is that in the winter, they break bottles on the beach. There the shards tumble among the pebbles and become sea glass. Summer visitors like nothing better than to walk along the shore looking for sea glass, and Kathie herself gathers it to make wreaths with the stuff. One can certainly say this is recycling. During visitor season, some glass is crushed and used as fill in foundations, and some is set aside

Loading the Laura B. *with trash to go ashore* (COURTESY OF MONHEGAN BOAT LINE)

to be tossed on the beach after the year-rounders get their island back. "We don't break bottles on the beach in summer," Kathie says. "It upsets people." She remembers a woman telling her she'd seen someone throwing bottles onto the rocks. Kathie asked her if she picks up sea glass. "Oh, yes, I love sea glass." But still, it's generally agreed not to strew the shore with broken glass at a time of year when people are likely to be strolling along it.

Other than trees and construction debris—which the island has received permission to burn on-site—the rest of Monhegan's trash is taken off-island on the mailboat, dumpsterload by dumpsterload. "It is a law-abiding and responsible system," says Kathie. Most trash is compacted and sent ashore weekly during the summer, less often in the off-season. A grant they received some years ago covered several backyard composters, and one of the hotels has decided to compost. One of the fishermen takes returnable bottles and cans ashore for the deposit money. Someone looked into making it a town business, but if they had to hire someone to get them ashore, it wouldn't pay.

Establishing a recycling program has been a frustrating effort. First, despite some people's efforts to sort their junk into the right categories, the contractor dealing with it on the mainland was simply throwing it all together with the regular trash. Now there's a new contractor, and the numbers will be crunched, but it seems that recycling may cost more than simply throwing all trash together. (On the Cranberries, this is the case. Their present contract calls for paying a bit over $100 a ton for general solid waste to be trucked off the island, and $210 a ton for recyclables.)

On Swans, as on any island, solid waste is expensive to deal with, but it's pretty simple. "There's not much choice in what we do," says Dexter Lee, longtime selectman. Recycling has not been attempted—it was considered too expensive even to set up the buildings to hold everything. All household trash is thrown in together, it's compacted, and then it's trucked off-island. The island has had a compactor for ten years—they are charged by the truckload going off the island, though the charge at PERC, the trash-to-energy plant in Orrington, near Bangor, is by the ton. A load goes off at least weekly in summer, and a couple of times a month in the dead of winter. The transfer station and compactor for household waste are open three hours a day, four days a week; there's an open pile for demolition debris and wood waste to be burned, and there's a junk metal pile. "Eventually we'll find somebody to take it off. They come with a truck—it costs us so-much a trip, and we get credit for the scrap value."

No matter what system is followed, on any island, trash management is tremendously expensive. Says Great Cranberry's Barbara Stainton about buying products like cereal at the supermarket ashore, "I'd like to take just the inner bags and give them the boxes back."

VINALHAVEN'S LANDFILL CLOSURE

The major issue facing Town Manager Sue Lessard when she arrived on Vinalhaven in 1993 was the landfill, which was still being used for all the island's trash. The state had outlawed such dumps long ago, and the mainland's local dumps had been closed. But for an island, not only was the replacement for local dumping—trucking everything ashore—going to be costly, but capping the landfill in the traditional manner would be vastly expensive. Tons and tons of clay and soil would have to be ferried or barged onto the island, and the only place where a barge could be landed is where the lobster fishermen sell their catch every day. Such an operation would seriously disrupt the local economy. The voters had shown no interest in the problem. In fact, the previous year they had voted down a seemingly innocuous plan to require annual ten-dollar stickers for vehicles carrying trash into the dump. They weren't at all concerned by the state and its regulations. "What are they gonna do, come get us?" people asked. This is a community in which 80 percent of the people are self-employed. "It's a completely different dynamic when the population works for someone else," says Sue. More of them are used to taking direction and will follow rules simply because they are rules.

Sue was sure there had to be a better solution—and there was. People did recognize that if they filled it up with trash, there'd be no island left, and when a local committee came up with a reasonable alternative, they went for it. They would institute a serious recycling program to remove as much trash as possible from the solid-waste stream, establish a pay-to-throw system for the rest in order to encourage the recycling, and truck everything to "America," as some islanders still call the mainland. Composting would be encouraged and facilitated all over the island, too. But the most innovative part of the plan was to cap the old dump with granite, ubiquitous on Vinalhaven. All over the island are piles of tailings and scraps left over from old quarrying operations; it would be a relatively simple thing to crush those and use the rock to cover the site. Of course, the officials at the DEP didn't think so. It had never been done before, and no one could imagine it. One individual said it wouldn't look good.

"What do you mean?" asked Sue.

"It would look rocky," she was told.

"Have you ever been to Vinalhaven?" she asked. Vinalhaven is all rocks anyway.

It took three years, but finally, permission was granted. Since that time, DEP has been touting the program as a prime example of a state and local partnership, and the engineering company that came up with the final plan won an award for engineering excellence for their innovative approach. The town—the same town that not so long before wouldn't tolerate ten-dollar stickers—raised $200,000 as its share of the cost; the state paid for the remaining 75 percent. The town built a transfer station next to the old landfill, which is contrary to DEP regulations, too, but Sue was able to show the officials that there was no other option.

Individuals were charged a dollar a bag to get rid of their solid waste—which cost the town $1,300 a truckload to dispose of—but the town accepted recycled material at no charge, and it only cost $150 a load to haul it ashore. It was not hard to convince islanders to start paying attention. The official recycling rate calculated by the state went from 9 percent—more than half of which credit came from the state returnable-bottle law—to more than 50 percent. Solid waste still represents a hefty chunk of Vinalhaven's municipal budget, but not nearly what it might have been.

Vinalhaven
Sue Lessard

No one had ever stayed in the town manager's job on Vinalhaven longer than three and a half years when Susan Lessard came to take the job in 1993. She was from "America," and she had no illusions about being anything else, but she accepted the job precisely because of some of the difficulties it represented. "There's no way you could do anything in a cookie-cutter manner," she says. "It helped me get better at my job, not give automatic answers." She enjoyed meeting the challenges, and, arriving with realistic expectations, she had no surprises. Not to say it was all easy going—the living arrangements, in particular, offered some unusual difficulties—but four years after leaving, Sue had only good feelings about the job and her performance there. She spent seven years on Vinalhaven.

Sure, at first she heard many people complain that she was no John Spear, her predecessor (though his tires were slashed and his windshield was broken, and she experienced none of that kind of thing). "They got used to me," she says. Six feet tall, with bright red hair down to her waist when she was on the island, Sue is a direct-talking person who gives no sign of being afraid of anything. The people of Vinalhaven respected that, she says.

"The day I knew I had been accepted was two years in, one day in February. Two fishermen dropped a plastic bag with ten pounds of shrimp on my desk. 'You win,' they said, and left." Sue had no idea what they meant, but she knew how to find out. Once a week, she ate a five o'clock breakfast in the restaurant where all the fishermen hung out. "They didn't feel spied upon—they took the opportunity to tell me everything the town wasn't doing right," says Sue. At breakfast the next morning, she told them what the two guys had done and said. "Anyone know what that's about?" she asked.

All their eyes were down, looking at their plates, and no one said anything. She asked the fellow next to her.

"It might have been a bet," he mumbled.

"If it was a bet," she asked, "what would it have been?"

Hesitantly, the fisherman said, "It mighta been that you wouldn't last a winter."

"And who might have been in this bet?"

"All of us," he admitted.

There were plenty of issues to be handled from the start, including the huge one about closing the landfill, but the first that could have been truly troublesome on a personal level worked out well for Sue.

The owners of federally documented boats are required by law to pay excise tax, just as are those that are registered with the state, but even though the tax would be deductible and the money would stay in town, most Vinalhaven fishermen had never paid those taxes. In the past, no one had dared to go after the money. Sue's secretary simply said that the fishermen didn't want to pay the tax, and when Sue wrote a letter to them all, the secretary wouldn't initial the letter she typed. Sue's message was simple, though; it was a matter of fairness, and the town could use the money. Everyone would have to pay the tax.

Some of the fishermen came in screaming mad. "More than one of them, if they came in after ten-thirty in the morning, might have been a little tanked. They'd been up since three." The staff was terrified. Not Sue. "We just have to get by something," she'd say to them. "You're not scared of me, and I'm not scared of you. If you need to yell, go outside and yell, but you're not going to yell at me."

They'd quiet down. "You're gonna guarantee that everybody's gonna pay it?" they wanted to know.

"I'm going to guarantee that everyone will pay it or they'll have a mechanic's lien on their boat, and the taxes will be taken from the proceeds when you go to sell it," she said. The town could recover three years' back taxes, and she got all of it. Some eighty-eight boats—say, an average of a hundred dollars a boat, three years—that's real money. The fishermen respected her for being fair.

More than once during her tenure, Sue lobbied hard for the fishermen. During her time on the island, both the state and the feds were changing the rules governing lobster fishing, developing zones, and limiting licenses. Sue went to Department of Marine Resources meetings and spoke on behalf of the local fishermen. A

Browns Head Light

big issue arose in 1995, when the Coast Guard was adding more safety requirements for the fishing boats that worked more than three miles offshore—life raft, survival suits, and so on. And EPIRBs (emergency position-indicating radio beacons), which alone would have set a fisherman back $1,500. Seventy-five percent of the Vinalhaven fishermen never went more than three miles offshore, except in a single strip out to Matinicus, the width of a four-lane highway; an EPIRB would be of no use to them. If a boat went down in those waters, a local person spotting a flare would be the one to save them, not the Coast Guard in Rockland picking up an EPIRB signal. Sue took it upon herself to argue about the EPIRBs. The only way to get around the requirement was with an exemption from Boston, so she wrote the commandant there, asking for an exemption just for the EPIRBs for people who could demonstrate that they didn't go outside that strip. He agreed, and the fishermen were of course very happy. "It wasn't even so much the money," Sue explains, "as that they felt local government was listening to them."

Toward the end of her stay on Vinalhaven, she also advocated against the major dredging planned for Searsport's Mack Point cargo-port project, which would dump dredging spoils—including tremendous amounts of toxic materials—onto prime lobster-breeding grounds off Vinalhaven. She argued vociferously before then-Congressman John Baldacci, the Army Corps of Engineers, and others, and ultimately the scope of the project was scaled back. The toxic spoils were not taken to sea at all; instead, they were handled in a more appropriate manner on land.

The selectmen's vote to hire Sue was not unanimous; some felt that, as a woman, she might not be tough enough to stand the island. Knowing that, Sue was never going to admit there was something she couldn't do. Her living arrangements did challenge her, however. Housing was provided by the town, which had leased the old Brown's Head lighthouse keeper's house from the Coast Guard when it was no longer needed. It had been used for various things since the lease: temporary quarters for the Knox County sheriffs when they spent nights on the island and for an economic-development person who was there for a time, and a grade-B movie was shot there. Part of Sue's arrangement was that she would have the use of the keeper's house, and in return, she was to maintain the grounds, which were open to the public.

The lighthouse sits above the Fox Islands Thorofare, overlooking North Haven and West Penobscot Bay. It is photographed countless times every summer by yachtsmen and ferry-riders, and it is surely one of the most romantic places imaginable—or at least that's the perception of people in America. But it's not that simple. For one thing, lighthouses by their very nature tend to be in inaccessible places, and this one is no exception. "It's at the end of the last dirt road off the last dirt road on the island," says Sue. It was a half-mile to her nearest year-round neighbor, and another couple of miles to the next. And the last part of the trip was the worst—down thirty-two very steep steps, around a corner, and down five more. Water was stored in cisterns in the basement, which in turn were filled by a plastic pipe running overground from a big tank over the top of the hill. In the summer, the system worked fine; Sue would flip a switch, climb up over the top to a pump, which would push water back up the hill and down into the cisterns. But in winter, it was a different deal. She'd flip the switch and climb the hill to fill the cisterns, but then she'd have to separate and drain each of several twenty-five-foot pieces of pipe where it ran nearly horizontal so they wouldn't freeze up, and then put it all together again. Having to do this made her very conscious of every drop of water she used. She took sea showers, rinsing, turning off the water, soaping down, and turning the water back on just long enough to rinse again. "To this day, I'm careful," she says.

The pipeline had to be kept clear of snow, too, as did all the steps. That's a lot of shoveling, but the steps had more problems than that. One morning, as Sue went to open the door to go to work, the door moved only a few inches. The bottom five steps and the landing were a solid, frozen waterfall. She called the office to say she was going to be late and described why. "Oh, that's the glacier," she was told.

Using her Boy Scout hatchet, Sue chopped off all the ice. By the time she got home that night, it was all back again. "I did that morning and night for six or eight weeks—at ten o'clock at night or whenever I happened to get home. I'd be singing or swearing or crying my eyes out, feeling this is not reasonable, but I will not ask for help!" Finally, the water went off in another direction and she had a reprieve; in the spring, she had the public works department fix some things so it wouldn't get so bad.

Then there's the oil for the furnace, which also was stored over the top of the hill and had to be pumped up and over the hill and down to the house. And the gas stove that for a moment Sue thought was going to set the house afire. It was replaced with an electric stove the next day. And not being able to turn on the television sometimes because of the whistling of the wind. She had to keep the TV volume so high that if there was a lull in the wind, she'd be deafened. Or the foghorn, which no one had thought to mention to her and which startled her, to say the least, the first time the fog came in during the middle of the night. Or finding strangers wandering around the outside of her house at all hours, checking out the lighthouse and not always respecting the sign that said the keeper's house was a private residence. "The island is not necessarily the kind of place you need to lock your doors all the time," says Sue, but she had to. Sometimes it was hard to find a place to park her car at the lighthouse, and once she came home after a tiring day to find a woman stretched out in the sun on her deck. "Don't bother," the woman told her. "It's locked." Sue told her that was all right, she had a key. "Oh," said the woman. "This must happen to you all the time."

"No," said Susan. "Most people can read."

The single biggest issue for Sue—as for many islanders, for that matter—was getting off-island. Her younger son was a senior in high school in western Maine, and she would get on the boat and drive to see him play sports and the like. She had a car on the island and another off—"Otherwise you had to plan for a ferry trip like Sherman's march to the sea." There was at least one spell of several months when Sue didn't leave the island; at the end of that time, she says all she wanted was to get to the mainland and into a store where she couldn't see all four walls at the same time.

A lot of Sue's time as manager was spent on ferry issues, as they affected everyone on the island. Who should have priority for truck reservations? The grocery store, which is feeding three thousand people in the summertime? Or the people trucking lobsters—that's everyone's livelihood. "I don't know how many gyms we filled talking about the ferry," she says. The ferry service left the matter of lines to Vinalhaven. In summer, there are always more cars wanting to travel than space on the boat. "We used to threaten them [ferry service officials] to have to come over—we would have gotten them over here and let them figure out how to get back. But they lived in fear of coming to the island. Vinalhaven is seen as only slightly more civilized than Matinicus," she said.

It is perhaps not surprising that the community adopted Sue, despite her being from America. "The people were tremendously kind to me," she says. "It was like having an island full of relatives to look out for you. I never worried that there'd be somebody going to 'get' me." Sue became well known—nationally, even—after serving on the commission that developed the Maine Lights Program to make arrangements for decommissioned lighthouses. The tall, redheaded town manager who lived in the remote lighthouse keeper's house was such a romantic figure that she was featured in many newspaper stories. *Good Morning America* came and filmed her, too. People came to the island to seek her out, but islanders would call her to let her know someone was looking for her. "We're not going to tell him where you are unless you want us to," they'd say.

And after a late-night meeting, Sue would always call someone to let them know she'd gotten home safely. Otherwise, someone would have come out to check on her. The fishermen brought her their first lobster of the season and taught her how to gather and cook mussels for her dinner. "The selectmen treated me well," she says. "Some took great pleasure in saying they didn't vote to hire me, and then they'd laugh like hell. I guess I turned out pretty well."

But for all of that, she lived a solitary life on Vinalhaven. It was probably inevitable. She was always the town manager, never just Sue Lessard, and it really had to be that way in order to do the job—even aside from her intrinsic separation from the folks who had known each other forever. She had to remain impartial whenever there was a controversy. And although right from when she first arrived, everyone wanted to stop in and talk about whatever was on their mind—everyone from the salt-of-the-earth year-rounders to the wealthiest New York financiers who summered there—no one invited her anywhere. At first, a big contingent thought that as a single woman she must have come onto the island to find a man, so the women didn't feel safe with her near their husbands and boyfriends. But after a couple of years, when she had been working a hundred hours a week, they knew that she had really come for the job. Besides, she was taking good care of a property precious to them. The townspeople cared about the lighthouse.

Sue's relationship with the lighthouse was special. "It was mine. I put my soul into making sure it was well cared for." She flew the flag every day, even though it would be beaten to death and need replacing every few months. It took six hours with a weed-whacker to cut the grass—between the slope and the bedrock poking through, a lawn-mower was useless. She bought soil for flower gardens and painted and repapered the house, which hadn't had much attention in years. "It's like a child—the more of yourself you invest in the care and feeding, the more precious it becomes to you.

"I learned more about myself and my ability to survive and cope in those seven years than before or since. Solitude does good things—and you can't run away from yourself if you can't get on the boat and go." She misses the island—though she says her only trip back to the lighthouse will be her last, as it's just not the same under some-one else's care. She still feels she's let the house down by leaving it.

But it's the people she misses most. "For being an outsider, they let me into their lives." People gradually understood more and more about her. She remembers being in the store before her first Christmas on the island and buying ingredients to make candy. "Oh, you cook?" someone asked her with surprise. "Over time," Sue says, "that morphed into 'Well, the kids must be coming!'"

There was a time when Sue's cookies served the lighthouse well, too. The Coast Guard was at Brown's Head doing maintenance on the light—they had a ladder, and she needed a ladder for some project. She left a bowl of cookies inside the tower with a note: "I'll trade you for letting me use your ladder." When she came back, the bowl was on her porch, empty but for a note: "You make more of these cookies and we'll give you any-thing." She says the Coast Guard people were another group of wonderful people she got to know during her stay on Vinalhaven.

Even though there are few people with whom she was very close when she lived on the island, Sue says she could go out there now and stay in anyone's house. After the departure of her replacement—who had thought only of the romance of it all and was soon disillusioned—people from the island asked her if she would come back. But mem-bers of her family have had serious health troubles, and being based on the mainland has allowed her to help. There are plenty of big challenges in her new job as town man-ager of Hampden, a community of more than four thousand people near Bangor, and she's enjoying the work there, too. She figures that her next job should be somewhere in a third-world country.

Community Health Care

Island Emergencies

a few years ago—I still remember it clearly—when I was at Lincolnville Beach well after dark, the scheduled ferry trips long since over for the day, I saw Islesboro's ferry, the *Margaret Chase Smith*, powering across the bay. Aboard, the flashing red lights of an ambulance silently, paradoxically, and ominously announced that someone was in trouble. For islanders, trips to the hospital include the extra challenge of a water crossing. The ferry lives on the island side on Islesboro, Swans, and North Haven, and one of Vinalhaven's two boats stays on the island overnight, for just such occasions. The islands served by mailboat have to wait for emergency help to come, as is the case in Casco Bay, but the distances are generally shorter. The more remote islands—Monhegan, Matinicus, Frenchboro, and even Cliff Island in Casco Bay—do face more of a challenge.

In Penobscot Bay, the air service, based at Knox County Regional Airport in Owls Head, is also called upon for emergency transport from the islands. On Matinicus, the ferry couldn't be involved—not only would it take two hours for the boat to get out to the island and two hours to get back again, but the wharf is only accessible at some tides. An emergency trip from Matinicus has to be by lobsterboat or Coast Guard vessel or by air, but the other islands, too, call on planes from time to time. "It was a major, major part of the service," says pilot Michael Ball, who used to fly for the air service. The calls always seemed to come in the middle of the night, he says. All too often, they were alcohol-related, but more than once he hustled pregnant women ashore to have their babies.

Lighting the runway is an issue at night on Vinalhaven, where a fire truck would park at one end and a car would shine its lights down the runway from the other end.

"Three o'clock in the morning, the phone rings, and twenty minutes later, there I am, landing over a fire engine," says Michael. "I felt like a hero, but it was routine for the people who live there."

On Matinicus, they have a lot of flare pots to mark the runway. Years ago, they'd line up a bunch of cars. "Whatever it takes to get the plane in," says Vance Bunker.

LIFEFLIGHT

The helicopter transport system LifeFlight is part of the emergency system on the islands. Although islands are a relatively small part of LifeFlight's service area, in the first six years of their operation, they carried a hundred patients off the coastal islands from Cliff to the Cranberries. Not only can helicopters operate without airstrips—which not all the islands have—but LifeFlight's helicopters are better equipped even than a land-based ambulance.

Owned jointly by Eastern Maine Healthcare and Central Maine Healthcare (the nonprofit parents of Eastern Maine Medical Center and Central Maine Medical Center), LifeFlight bases one helicopter each at the Bangor and Lewiston hospitals. "We're more like a hospital intensive-care unit," says Executive Director Tom Judge. "We carry the gamut of critical-care equipment." Blood and fluids, ventilators, infusion pumps for intravenous medications, serious monitoring equipment are all aboard, along with highly skilled personnel. There's an intensive-care nurse with emergency training in the field and a paramedic with in-hospital critical-care experience—both trained in advanced protocols that are otherwise limited only to physicians. Occasionally a specialized physician might come along, too, and emergency-room and other specialists are always available on the radio for consultation, both before the LifeFlight team arrives and for the team itself.

The pilots, too, have been through a rigorous qualification system, including instrument flight and other specific training requirements. Weather is the biggest concern—it is the pilot's call as to whether a particular flight can be made safely. Each island has a designated landing zone, and sometimes additional possible landing sites have been noted. What's needed is a spot a hundred feet square—ball fields are good.

To make sure everyone knows what to expect from everyone else, LifeFlight periodically does training sessions with the local emergency people, medical and others, on each of the islands. Some, like Vinalhaven and North Haven, have physicians and a clinic on-island; others have EMTs or not even that. In addition to noting what hazards might exist for their own future use, the LifeFlight personnel train the island emergency people about the specific landing-area requirements for the aircraft, and they teach the specifics about patient "packaging" for the flight.

"We need people to be secured a little better than if they were going in an ambulance," Tom explains. "We teach how they should be secured in the litters, how splints must be applied to fit into the helicopter, where the IVs are to be placed—there will be two IV lines in."

Except in extreme weather, a helicopter is kept at the ready on each of the two hospitals' roofs; the standard is that at least 90 percent of the time they can be in the air twelve minutes from the time a call is received. "Generally, we're up in eight or nine minutes," says Tom, who was a flight medic himself in the beginning and now—unfortunately, he says—he's doing more administrative work.

It takes about twenty minutes to get from Bangor to Vinalhaven, although by fortunate happenstance, when a young full-term pregnant woman had a massive hemorrhage, LifeFlight was already on the island for a training exercise. When the LifeFlight crew got to her, she was in shock. The island physician was with her, but she and her baby were in trouble. They couldn't detect fetal heart tone and she had no blood pressure. The helicopter flew her to Penobscot Bay Medical Center in Rockport—a nine-minute flight. "We gave her fluids and blood—without those, she would have run out of time," says Tom. LifeFlight later took her to Portland. "She's now back on the island with a happy little girl, but it was very, very dramatic. There was zero chance for that baby's survival, and no time left for her, either."

The helicopters have the flexibility to go point-to-point, directly to the closest appropriate hospital, whether Rockport, Bangor, Lewiston, Portland, or even Boston. Not many emergencies need such an intensive level of care—patients with broken bones and most illnesses could come off the island in a traditional manner, but for complex problems, LifeFlight is the answer. "The greatest impact a helicopter can have is in rural or isolated areas—like islands." Between the time factor and the critical care available on the helicopter, lives can be saved.

Occasionally, adverse weather conditions prevent LifeFlight from responding. One example was a few years back, when a patient on one of the islands was having seizures. The fog was just too thick, and LifeFlight couldn't make it out there. The patient went ashore in the usual island backup, a fast lobsterboat.

MATINICUS ISLAND RESCUE

Emergency medical help is an issue on all of the islands. The more populated islands of Penobscot and Casco Bays have health centers, with either doctors or physician's assistants (PAs), often with twenty-four-hour coverage. On a number of the islands with fewer residents, including Matinicus, EMTs come when there's trouble.

Matinicus Island Rescue (MIR) happened accidentally—when five island residents wondered whether it would be a good idea to get some actual training for the kinds of first aid that everyone was doing anyway. In 1993, they convinced paramedic Luke Church to come from Monhegan and teach a class. A lobsterman, two fishermen's wives, a former teacher, and a woman with experience in law enforcement in California and with Outward Bound all started spending four or five days a week, all day long, trying to cram what is normally about a 180-hour program into the short-daylight winter and early spring months—before everyone was out straight again with their normal work. They took turns housing Luke and feeding him. "Neighbors helped with children, and spouses endured gory pictures at the breakfast table, as the textbook was with us constantly," wrote Eva Murray in a piece for the *Journal of Maine EMS*.

One thing led to another. At the time, an EMT in Maine could not be licensed unless sponsored by a licensed ambulance or other health-care service. "We found out we were joining the system, like it or not, but on Matinicus, we also had to create the system." The five newly licensed EMTs were responsible for paperwork and for raising funds—not just for the expected supplies but also for such bureaucratic requirements as the licenses, memberships, insurance, and dues for the regional oversight agency.

Historically, the island had been served by a registered nurse hired to spend the winter on the island. In an earlier era, when Matinicus had more people and less connection to the mainland, the nurse delivered babies, handled emergencies, and provided home health care. As a young woman, Rena Bunker came to the island in that role, and she, like other island nurses and teachers before her and since, married an islander. She and Harold raised their children on Matinicus; Vance Bunker, longtime first assessor and one of the acknowledged high-liners on Matinicus today, is their younger son. The last nurse to come to the island under this system was Nina Young, who also married an islander, Clayton Young (described by Eva as "postmaster, storekeeper, amateur historian, native lobsterman, Colby College math major, world traveler, and all-around interesting guy").

The Nurse's Association, which had raised funds for the winter nurse, had long since disappeared by the time MIR was started. In the intervening years, Matinicus people had fended for themselves. "Islanders, being the kind of independent-but-responsive types they are, assisted each other in times of crisis. You knew who was likely to be sober when you needed help. You knew who might take a person to the mainland in their boat. You knew who'd been in the merchant marine and perhaps had some experience. On the other hand, some knew who had painkillers on hand."

The situation on Matinicus is different from that faced by a typical mainland-based emergency medical team. There is no ambulance, let alone one that can take a patient directly to the hospital. There is no official backup—not medical or legal or from law enforcement. On the other hand, there still exists the age-old tradition of people

Eva Murray
(COURTESY OF EMILY MURRAY)

helping their neighbors when help is needed. The EMTs get assistance from whoever's at hand.

"Our purpose is first and foremost to respond to emergencies," Eva says. Fortunately, there are very few actual emergencies on Matinicus, but there's a lot of community health nursing. "A lot of it comes down to being the 'just glad to know someone's there' kind of person. It's more a matter of someone wanting to talk about a kid who's a little sick but not terribly and should she do something?"

You're not off-duty, ever. Eva does tell people that she doesn't know the answer when that's appropriate, and she has to be concerned about exceeding the level of her license. But her license doesn't begin to cover all the situations she faces—nor would any level of any license, for that matter. "There's a lot of travel-agent work for summer people, acting as the go-between for a person not from around here, who doesn't know who to call."

And local people sometimes need arrangements made, too. An elderly island resident who'd just had a mastectomy wanted to go straight home after the operation. She has arthritis badly enough that she walked with a stick even before the mastectomy; by choice, she has an outhouse and does her laundry on a washboard. When she asked if Eva could do whatever a nurse would do for her, Eva was willing enough, but she didn't think it would be the best solution for the patient. The woman would be both unhappy and unsafe, and what about pain management? With Eva's help, some of the patient's mainland relatives arranged for a week ashore, after which she was much more able to cope at home. "Of course, she was madder than a wet hen because they put her in a nursing home for that week."

In the case of a fisherman who has a serious injury, he'll often just take himself ashore, even when he shouldn't be running a boat. And sometimes he would be better off getting hospital attention but refuses to go—and he won't call Eva for fear she'll somehow make him do it. "They don't want to miss a day hauling, or they can't go to the mainland because there's a bench warrant out for their arrest, or they just think they can avoid going."

Other times, people come to her looking only for first aid. She finds herself following protocol with paperwork just to protect herself—she knows a guy with a nasty wound ought to have a tetanus shot, or antibiotics, but those are beyond her scope, and he's only interested in a Band-Aid or in having his bloody face cleaned up.

Eva faces different stresses than the typical American EMT's blood-and-death stress. "It's more worrying if they don't go to the doctor—do I have to check on them? And you're apt to know all the patients—you have no psychological protection as you might when they're strangers." Sometimes knowing the patient makes even the mechanics more difficult. "I've found that everybody knows the stuff that doesn't matter much, like who goes around stealing screwdrivers or who got suspended from high school, but there's actually a lot that somehow gets under the radar. This definitely includes medical histories!" And the efforts to collect history from acquaintances, not close friends, may cause annoyance, or—particularly from elder patients—more (and illegal) expectations of the EMT. Sometimes younger patients she doesn't know well worry that she's a "narc" and will turn them in.

Eva finds the narc issue to be significant. She has no wish to be subpoenaed to testify against anyone and tries hard not to know if there's illegal drug use—but she also has no desire to appear to condone it. There have been times when patients insisted on going to her house, rather than taking a chance that she might notice particular substances in use at a party. She's had people bleed all over her kitchen. "I used to react immediately to the blood with expressions of care and concern. At this point, I'm about ready to start shouting, 'Stop right there, buddy!'" It's a tricky balance.

That Eva runs a bakery puts yet another wrinkle in her position. She sees two sides of things. If a person she knows to be diabetic buys a batch of cookies, what's her responsibility? "I'm not their mother—I can't say, 'Hey, don't buy those! They aren't good for you.'" A fellow came in and bought a bunch of brownies, which she assumed he'd give to his kids, but he gave them to his dad, who has diabetes. A while later, the old man called her up as a health-knowledge source. "If I eat too much sugar, will I feel kinda weird?"

Now there are only two EMTs on the island year-round, just Eva and fisherman Clayton Philbrook. As director of the two-and-only-sometimes-three-person Matinicus Island Rescue, Eva is responsible for paperwork and must be present for the annual inspection. She has taken it upon herself to write a members' manual and newsletters ("to remind people we exist"), and she spends far more time on fund-raising than she could ever enjoy. Occasionally, it crosses her mind that it would be easier if the MIR disbanded. "We didn't start it to have a bureaucratic morass, but sometimes it seems that's what we've ended up with." Without the formal organization, there would be no licensing fees or paperwork, and they could still lend aid to their neighbors. But the idea passes quickly. Tax-deductible donations are wonderful, and more important, liability issues, training, and support from beyond all justify the organization. MIR isn't going to disappear soon.

Eldercare

VINALHAVEN'S IVAN CALDERWOOD HOMESTEAD

"I've never done anything so hard as to leave home," says ninety-one-year-old Margaret Webster of Vinalhaven. "If you have to leave, this is a lovely place."

Her house is still in the family, but Margaret says sadly that it will have to be sold. "I hope not soon," she says. "It's hard to be away. I'd lived in my house only ninety years. Both my children were born in the same room my sister and I were. But I'm thankful to be here. We're so lucky not to have to go off-island."

Isabell Calderwood spent her last months in a nursing home off-island. Her husband, Ivan, wished he could somehow help so that older people wouldn't have to leave the island at the end of their lives. With no family to whom to leave his property, he realized that his own home could become an eldercare facility after he died. The house was the seed of what became a private, nonprofit home for a half-dozen—and then eight—elderly residents of Vinalhaven. Three years' effort went into organizing and gathering grants and renovating and adding on a new wing, and in 2001, debt-free, the home opened its doors.

An easy walk from downtown, the house is bright and cheerful and the center of many different activities. There are exercise programs, they play bingo, church ladies come for tea, the island's four massage therapists volunteer time, people put on slide shows, musicians come to perform, and schoolchildren visit in Halloween costumes, to sing Christmas carols, or sometimes to talk with the older people for school projects. Some of the residents have had cats—a cat lives in the home today—but once a week people come in with other pets. Puppies go over very well. They have birthday parties and ice-cream socials and potluck suppers. A guest-cook program, which gives a break to the staff, is fun for both residents and the visiting cook. One couple brought their kids and the kids made the meal. "The residents got a kick out of that," says Maura Michael, the administrator.

Other elderly people come in during the day to enjoy the company and the activities. "It's a hard sell," Maura says, tongue in cheek. "'You gonna come for lunch?' we ask them, and hook 'em in." Maura told me when I visited. " There's one gentleman who comes now—we weren't sure he was going to take to it, but he came twice, and the third day he called and asked if he could come again."

Probably the most important aspect, though, is that family and friends can drop in whenever they like, at whatever hour—and when visitors come, of course all the residents know them and enjoy seeing them. If someone stops by to take an elderly relative to the Fourth of July Parade, he may take another along too. Everyone loves to see everyone else's grandchildren and great-grandchildren.

In summer, two horses have been living out back. "It saves us mowing," says Maura, "and the residents like it." The back porch has raised box gardens where some of the residents enjoy working. One was looking sad. "I know I'm going to catch it from her," Maura said of one woman who was particularly involved with them but who had been off-island for tests lately.

Since this is officially a nonskilled home, the residents must be basically healthy and only need assistance with such mechanical tasks as dressing and bathing. The aim is to keep people on the island as long as possible, though, and sometimes the caregivers provide more help than is usual in such a home.

Except Maura, whose in-laws retired onto the island, the caregivers are all from Vinalhaven and are Certified Residential Medication Aides (CRMAs). Although there are no registered nurses, there's an RN consultant who comes a couple of times a month, and when needed. For day-to-day medical needs, they call the nearby Islands Community Medical Center. "Most things, we've been taught to handle," she says.

A huge part of Maura's job is looking for money. The annual budget is about $200,000, and with a majority of the residents on MaineCare (the state's version of Medicaid), fund-raising is important. Out back, Ivan's old barn has been set up to house returnable bottles. Volunteers separate and sort them, and every three months a tractor-trailer comes to take them away. Each trip produces $2,700. A fund-raising letter goes out to all of Vinalhaven's twelve hundred taxpayers each year and brings back eight hundred responses, with donations from $25 to $5,000. Summer concerts and local groups make donations. The annual auction is a big deal; in 2004, it brought in $5,000 from donations of all sorts—from homemade pies (which sold for sixty to eighty dollars apiece) to picnics on a lobsterboat.

"It's hard when one of the home's residents passes away," Maura says. "People stay in their rooms until everything's taken care of. But they bounce back, and they start to wonder who's coming in next."

There was a waiting list of nine when I visited. (All the residents are from Vinalhaven, or sometimes might be the parents of islanders.) The island doctor, the nurse, three board members, and Maura decide who needs the space most. "It's objective," she says.

Margaret has only lived at the Ivan Calderwood Homestead for a short time, and she never gave it much thought when the old house was being set up to be an elder-care facility. "I guess I always thought I was going to be in my own home, doing what I wanted, but there comes a day. . . . I'm fine if I had some legs," she says. "It's so nice and clean, I don't know how they do it, with so many in wheelchairs or walkers. "It's lovely. I couldn't find any fault. It's the ideal place."

ISLESBORO'S BOARDMAN COTTAGE

Islesboro has a relatively high proportion of residents over sixty-five years old, and there had long been talk of creating some kind of facility to allow older people to stay on the island after they can no longer live on their own. "There is no one on the island who's not being taken care of," says Bonnie Hughes. "People are getting ad hoc support," but it can be difficult, complicated, and costly. On the island, simple things like having door hinges fixed or getting the lawn mowed become nearly impossible—or, at the least, very expensive. The hardest part is that when the older people no longer can cope, they have to leave not just their home but the community that they may have lived in for their entire lives.

"We see people staying in their homes long past the point of safety," says Sharon Daley, who, besides working on the Sea Coast Mission boat *Sunbeam,* is the Islesboro case manager for the mainland-based Kno-Wal-Lin home-care agency. "It's difficult for everybody."

In June 2003, the Beacon Project was initiated, with the mission "to make it possible for our elders to remain here on Islesboro with dignity and comfort as members of the island community." The board of directors consists mostly of year-round residents, including Sharon, plus a couple of representatives from the summer community. Bonnie Hughes is the president. "Maybe the only way I can get out of that is to go into the home myself," she jokes. After they investigated programs on Vinalhaven and Chebeague and on the mainland—hoping to benefit from the not-always-smooth experiences of others—they decided that the first part of the plan would be to build a six-bed group home, modeled after the Ivan Calderwood Homestead on Vinalhaven.

"I think it's great," says Lydia Rolerson. "A lot of people will enjoy it, I know they will. Me, for one, if I need to go there for care." She has checked it all out: "I picked my room out while they were buildin' it." She says it makes her feel safe to know she'll have a place to go if the time comes when she can't take care of herself at home. "It's right near the PA's place, handy, and they're going to build a pond out back—you can look and see if there's any ducks or anything there. It's a nice location, set back far enough, with a lovely driveway—it'll be really nice." She tells about Blenda Hammond, who had recently turned 101. "I've known her a hundred years," she says. Not quite, she admits, laughing, but nearly—Lydia is eighty-five. "I don't know who in the world would be available to take care of anybody like that—she's having trouble walking now and uses canes. She's a delightful lady, and I'll bet she'd love it there.

"I'm just livin' one day to the next, tryin' to enjoy life as best I can." She's a cheerful woman who certainly seems to enjoy her life. "The good Lord willin', I'll be here tomorrow, and if I'm not, I won't know it," she says.

Only a little over a year after organization, they broke ground on the Boardman

Cottage, as the group home is called. Named for Paul Boardman, who died a few years ago, the home is being built on land acquired from his family at a generous price. It is ideally situated, directly across the Main Road from the town office and the health center. They hope for occupancy in the summer of 2005. "Looking back," says board member Sharon, "I'm amazed we had the nerve to even start!"

Raising the $800,000 for the building was just the beginning for the board, however. As the construction continued during the winter, they were looking for people who might be interested in moving in, making certain that they met all the various state regulations, and, most difficult of all, finding staff. Particularly in the summer, when the pay scale is high on the island, it can be hard to find employees. The building includes an upstairs apartment providing housing for one or two staff members, which might be important, since affordable summer housing is scarce to nonexistent.

To fill the beds is important financially if in no other way—the board members learned this from their visits to Vinalhaven and Chebeague, where occasional empty beds have been hurtful to the bottom line. The first priority for residents is year-rounders, and after that, if there are still spaces, parents of islanders or people with a longtime island connection could be accepted. Although three of the residents can be private-pay and fully covering their own expenses, because the facility is state-licensed, the other three must be reserved for people funded through MaineCare—which, even in the best of cases, doesn't reimburse the whole cost. The board expects the Boardman Cottage to have higher costs than many adult family-care facilities, though, because it is everyone's hope that the residents will be able to live out their days at the cottage. They know that additional care will be require at times, but it's their intention, if at all feasible, to avoid having to move anyone to a mainland nursing facility. The same goal exists at both Vinalhaven's Calderwood Homestead and the Island Commons on Chebeague, and of course the expenses mount. Having three private-pay residents certainly helps, but even if someone starts out paying his or her own bills, it may not be possible to continue doing so; the day could come when every resident is funded by MaineCare.

Fund-raising will be a continuing necessity, as it has been at the other islands' facilities. The Beacon Project has a number of moneymaking endeavors now—calendars, pie sales, and coffee at the ferry when the takeout isn't open. Some donors have expressed an interest in contributing to an endowment—the goal toward which the board is working. Keeping all the financial records will be a big job, one that will probably fall to Bonnie. "Once upon a time I was a CPA, so I'm comfortable with pushing numbers around," she says.

Once the Boardman Cottage is well established, the board wants to add a Meals on Wheels program, transportation for the elderly on and off-island, and adult day care.

"I don't like that phrase," says Sharon. "It makes it sound like they're children. But there's a need—maybe your elderly mother is living with you and you have to go to work, or you have to go ashore for a doctor's appointment—she could come in for the day." The Beacon Project wants to help people stay in their own homes, too, and to encourage people still living at home to visit the Boardman Cottage and play bingo and other games. There's no hairdresser on the island; they'd like to bring in a hairdresser once a week. They'd like to find a piano. All over the island, plans are being developed to incorporate the Boardman Cottage residents into town events and programs. The librarian is considering how to provide regular service, and there are plans to involve younger students from the school. A van will be available to take residents to potluck suppers and other island events. "This has the potential to be a real central place for the island, integrating older people into activities."

The aim is to keep the Boardman Cottage comfortable and homelike. The pitched-roofed, clapboarded building looks as if it belongs on the island, and little interior details, such as offset hallways, make it homey rather than institutional. The kitchen is big enough so that, in traditional Maine fashion, people can visit when someone's cooking. The kitchen/dining room/living room area can be divided into cozy smaller rooms or opened up for a big event like a community supper. Residents will be permitted to have pets. The living area is close to the door, so residents can see people coming and going. Because everyone on the island knows everyone else, a visitor to one is a visitor to all.

Considering her age, Blenda Hammond is in good health. "Her mind is excellent," says Bonnie. "She still plays bridge every week, and she wins!" Her family is gone, but Blenda is still in her own home, getting help from neighbors. She is thrilled that, at last, the island has the Boardman Cottage. "I just hope she'll have the opportunity to enjoy it," says Bonnie.

Preservation of Land & Community

althought every island is facing the same squeeze as ever-rising land prices make it difficult for young people to find housing, the effects of this differ from island to island. The first island to identify and act on the problem was Frenchboro, which saw its community dying as its overall population steadily fell. Over on Isle au Haut, as lobstermen aged and retired, the fishing grounds were at risk. The pressure on Islesboro and Monhegan has been different—their populations have been increasing during the last fifty years, but every kind of property has been attracting very high prices as it is bought up by summer people and retirees. On those islands, the risk is that they could become summer and retirement resorts, no longer home to working people and with no open space available to the public.

In the 1980s, it had become clear on several of the islands that the numbers of young year-round families were dwindling, and housing was the issue. It has become both scarce and expensive in large part due to the pressure from people from Away—whether summer people or retirees—to whom prices that are high for local young people seem low compared to where they have lived. Often island property sells before it's even officially gone on the market. Says Bob Howard of Cliff Island, "Somebody mentions to somebody else that he'd like to buy his house and it just happens he's ready to sell. The last house, word got out and seven or eight people were knocking on the door giving him bids. It wasn't a prime house, either—it wasn't on the shore."

The school is often seen as the key to community, and some islands have faced pupil-less schools. A number of projects have arisen, and continue to be created or expanded, specifically in the attempt to attract new, particularly young, families or to make it possible for young families to stay on their native islands.

All have succeeded in the long run, but sometimes, in addition to being politically controversial for social or economic reasons, it has been difficult to find applicants for the housing that had to be created, or to keep the settlers once they had come. Equally controversial have been attempts to keep land undeveloped.

Islesboro Islands Trust/Islesboro Affordable Property

"People are buying up good property that we used to tramp on when we were younger," says Islesboro's Lydia Rolerson, now in her mid-eighties. She is herself an alien, she says (her word)—she moved to the island when she was six months old. Although she has traveled widely, she has always made her home on the island, and she says she doesn't want to live anywhere else. "I call it my little corner of heaven." But, she says, the island is changing. She speaks of No Trespassing signs: "It's not our island the way it used to be."

Back in 1984, the first public meeting about an effort to preserve Islesboro's aesthetic by land protection was a total bust. Very few people attended, and those who did were regaled by a former Massachusetts resident who was between cocktails and dinner and who had experienced all the bad things that could happen with such a program. Two of the three instigators of the meeting thought perhaps the time wasn't right for a preservation effort after all, but Steve Miller felt more passionately than ever that it was important to keep working. Propjet planes had brought Islesboro within an hour of Boston, New York, and Philadelphia. A big property on the island had just changed hands and was going to be subdivided—more than a hundred acres with three and a half miles of shorefront, the first such project in a hundred years.

That particular subdivision, Hermit's Point, was handled responsibly, but for the first time, the character of the island was under serious threat.

Steve had come to Islesboro a little more than a decade earlier. Disillusioned with the newspaper business, almost on a whim he took a job as janitor in the Islesboro School. "At the end of two weeks, I thought I had made the worst decision of my life." He was doing physical labor of a sort he'd never done before, and it was hardly exciting work. But, after a month in which he hadn't been off the island, he went to southern Maine to apply for another newspaper job; on that trip, he realized he didn't want to leave Islesboro. He wouldn't work as a janitor forever, but he would stay on the island.

Like many island people, he did a little of this and that, finally going to work as a caretaker for summer people. "I got involved with plants and the earth, and it opened up all kinds of work here." He married an island woman, had a couple of sons, and realized that Maine—and Islesboro in particular—had a special beauty that no one talked about very much.

Steve and his friends started a lower-key attempt to organize a preservation effort, meeting in people's living rooms. A core group of natives and transplants became interested, and they were wondering how to take the next step. Steve doesn't remember now how it happened that Dark Harbor summer people Liberty Redmond and Elizabeth Guest were invited to one of their meetings, but they came, and the next meeting was held at Mrs. Guest's in September or October of 1984. The summer ladies had invited more people. After a general discussion about how to proceed, the Dark Harbor crowd instructed Steve, Ed Lawrence, and Dev Hamlen to go and make it happen. With money from that group, a Boston law firm was hired to do the legal work, and by spring, the Islesboro Islands Trust (IIT) was officially created.

There is a perception that it all started with the summer people, but in fact it didn't. The summer people provided the money to pay the start-up bills, but it was a local initiative that began the process. The board of trustees was set up to include two year-round residents, two summer people, two at-large members, and a representative of the town government. For many years, Lydia Rolerson was on the board. Maintaining the balance between local and summer people has been difficult at times, as meetings would often be scheduled in summer when that group was in residence—but islanders have a tough time getting together in summer. "Just about everyone I know," says Steve, "works ten or twelve hours a day all summer."

The Trust started out with a bang, purchasing both Hutchins Island—which was being marketed by an international realty firm as a private kingdom—and the southern two-thirds of Spruce Island, buying it right out from under developers. The fund-raising team of Mrs. Redmond and Mrs. Guest went around to everybody on the island with their dog-and-pony show and brought in the $250,000 needed for these purchases. Says Steve, "For an organization that hadn't existed a month before, that's dramatic!" He describes the time as a watershed period, creating dramatic awareness among all segments of the island's population. People understood how vulnerable the island was, and they supported the Trust's efforts.

The Trust also became involved in education and in town affairs, working in the school and making a financial contribution to the Comprehensive Plan process, which allowed a more complete environmental assessment than otherwise would have been possible.

Since 1985, the Trust has made several more significant purchases, including properties that provide public access to the water.

The Islesboro Islands Trust served as a model for Vinalhaven, which soon started its own trust, the Vinalhaven Land Trust. Steve says that they've done a better job of keeping their finger on the pulse of the year-round community. Lately there has been some criticism of the IIT. Some of the issues raised against the Trust seem to be ones of detail—how much the executive director (Steve) is paid, or whether he has a conflict of interest in chairing both the Comprehensive Plan Committee and the Islesboro Affordable Property group. But there are more significant queries: the effect on the tax base when properties are put into "open space," with its lower tax assessment, and the criteria upon which land purchases are based. After all, one could argue, every inch of the island is of significance. There's a question about the stated goals of the Trust and whether, given the opportunity, the islanders would modify them. And the point has also been raised that the people who live on the island are also a part of its ecology. "Is environmental protection, which IIT was created to promote, really only a device to establish a sort of enormous (green) gated community for a select few?" asked a letter in the *Islesboro Island News*.

Sue Hatch, member of the IIT board, responds: "Development stresses the ferry, the water table, fire and medical services." She feels that the island is close to maxed out, and that restricting development will save money in the long run. While the taxes brought in by Trust properties will not equal what they would if those parcels were to be developed, the services required by those properties will now and forever be considerably less than if they were built upon.

Certainly, though, affordable housing is a big issue too—one seen by many as more important than preservation of particular parcels of land. The irony of this last dispute is that while it has been stirred up by people who are apparently against the Trust, the trustees themselves are tremendously concerned about it, as is evidenced by their own involvement in and their executive director's work with Islesboro Affordable Property (IAP).

Housing has become both expensive and scarce on all the islands. On Islesboro— perhaps more than on many of the other islands—traditional homes have been bought not only by newcomers but also by owners of the huge summer "cottages" who want more space for their expanding families as new generations come along. Or they simply want guesthouses. Occasionally a beneficent person will sell a house to a local person for a reasonable price, but property is very scarce for young families.

Islesboro Affordable Property was founded in 1993; within two years, it had built eight units of housing. IAP sold the houses—but not the land under them—to island residents. There are many puzzles in the affordable-housing game, one being how to determine who should be eligible for such a program. It was Islesboro's position that it should not be only for low-income people, as those of moderate income have an equally difficult time finding housing on the island, and they are essential to a community. "It took a lot of doing," says Steve, but they were able to convince the IRS that IAP should be granted nonprofit status. They have also had difficulties convincing state agencies that the function of the project is not so much about housing as about preventing community degradation. Without young people in the community, there soon will be no community. This is an issue faced by every island with a year-round population, and it has been demonstrated to be true on those islands that no longer have winter residents. Invariably, closing down the school is the last straw.

A sophisticated set of criteria was set up to select the applicants who would get to participate in the housing project, which was named the Ruthie James Subdivision, in honor of the longtime summer person (and year-round resident for the last few years of her life) who sold the twelve-plus acres to IAP. The criteria were reviewed and amended for a second phase, for which plans are now being made. Besides income level, commitment to the community must be measured in some way. Of the current residents of the original eight IAP houses, five grew up on the island and three were from Away, but all were living on the island when they were accepted into the program. Three of the original owners have moved out and off-island—"It had a lot to do with lovelorns," says Bill Boardman, who is on the IAP board. There was a divorce, and someone met someone from the mainland and moved off, and a local man's wife, from Away, didn't like living on the island. It's not easy to predict who truly is and will remain committed to a place. So far, IAP has not provided a steppingstone to another property on the island.

Some people feel there were disappointingly few applicants for the houses; there has even been grumbling about why so-and-so didn't get an interview. The board members handed out applications to a number of young people in the community who are either still living with their parents or in minimal cabins somewhere, but they never filled out the forms. "I get fed up with trying to hold people's hands," says Bill, who recognizes that many young people, particularly men, go through a stage when "they don't look to do much more," as long as they have some kind of roof over their head and a can of beer in their hand.

A second issue that must be dealt with is what happens financially when a family wants to sell one of the IAP houses. Naturally, a property owner wishes to receive some benefit from an increase in value—but the property must remain affordable. At a time when just about any house on Islesboro brings far more than the same house would bring anywhere else in Waldo County, the market value of a home is less and less affordable every year—hence the need for IAP. The committee created a formula by which to determine the selling price of one of the properties in the program: The rate of increase of median income in the county is applied to the original price of the house, and that gives the price. The owners will have built equity as they paid down their bank loan, also. In addition, the original owners, who, following island tradition, worked on the construction of their homes with their own time and hammers, are also allowed a fixed number of dollars' worth of sweat equity. No one gets rich from having participated in the program—on the other hand, they are able to live on the island, which otherwise would have been difficult if not impossible. It has been the resale issue that has stopped some people from applying, however.

The issues of land preservation and community retention—which in large part is about affordable housing—are faced by every island; the pressure from summer visitors is felt everywhere. Like some of the other islands, Islesboro at least has taken some steps to try to solve some of the problems. It is still too early to judge how successful they have been, but the efforts continue.

The Frenchboro Homestead Project

Perhaps the most successful community-building effort in the long run, the Frenchboro Homestead Project may have had the rockiest start. In 1985, the Frenchboro Future Development Corporation (FFDC) received a block grant of $366,830 from the state to help attract new settlers to the island, along with a low-interest loan. A thirty-acre parcel of land was contributed to the effort, a local fund-raising drive brought another $250,000 to the island, and the Frenchboro Homestead Project was underway. David Lunt, then a selectman and one of the originators of the project, says that it was the

Frenchboro Future Development Corporation housing

first time anyone had tried anything like this. "We made mistakes in the beginning, and we changed as we went on. We were flying by the seat of our pants." The idea was to provide housing for young people at reasonable cost, and to protect it with restrictions on resale in order to maintain prices at an affordable level and keep ownership in the hands of year-round residents.

Talking with some of the first homesteaders, more than once I heard someone speak of "the breeders." Islanders used that term to refer to the newcomers; it took the applicants aback when they first heard it, but it was an honest reference to just what was hoped for: children.

The island, officially named Long Island but known by everyone as Frenchboro, was never one of the more populated, peaking in 1910 with 197 residents. The 1940 census showed 119, the next twenty years showed a drop to 57, and by 1990, there were only 44 people living on the island—and that population was aging. To remain a viable community, there had to be some younger people. For young people to live there, how- ever, the school had to remain open. An attempt had been made in the mid-1960s to bring children to the island by taking in foster children, which, although not without problems, had indeed vitalized a dwindling school. But in the 1980s, once again the school was in need of children.

The town also wanted to diversify the local economy, which was based entirely on fishing. They hoped to find people whose nonfishing occupations would allow them to work and support themselves in some way from the remote island.

The plan was to build seven houses, set one aside for the teacher, and find home- steaders for the other six. The national media picked up the story—it's an appealingly romantic notion, to go live on a Maine island and help that island to remain a commu- nity. Before the new organization was prepared for any applications—when they were still many months or even years from being ready to start building—the town had received more than three thousand inquiries, many from people with less-than-realistic expectations. There was nothing to do but read them, David says. A dozen finalists were invited to come to the island for personal interviews.

Elaine Beote was working in an insurance office in Massachusetts when the word got out about Frenchboro. Her husband, Steve, was a fisherman. "I saw the piece in the Sunday paper and said, 'Hey, this'd be great!' You know how you do, but you don't really mean it?" But Steve thought it looked terrific. They felt they had nothing to lose in making the application, so they went ahead, thinking they'd never hear any more about it. When they were invited to the island for a weekend interview, they still thought nothing would come of it, but since they'd never been that far downeast before, they went. On the ferry with them were five other couples who also had been invited to Frenchboro that weekend.

"It's like a fishbowl—everyone's at the ferry, looking to see who these people are. Everyone was staring. But they were nice." The applicants stayed with island families, who threw a potluck supper for them on the lawn of the church.

All the year-round residents of the island lived around the harbor, but the land where the new houses would be built was up behind the village, past the fire station and the dump. There was nothing there except a path, but it was beautiful. The interviews took place in the firehouse, with the applicants at one end and everyone else in a circle asking them a million questions.

A couple of weeks later, the Beotes received a letter saying that the islanders would like them to move to Frenchboro after the houses were built. "It had never been a real thing to us," Elaine says, but as she and Steve talked it over, they realized that they were indeed interested. "We had only been married a year or two, we had no kids yet—it was a good time to try something like that. We could always come back if we didn't like it."

Several of the families who made that final cut did plan to make their living in other ways—in data processing and as glassblowers and weavers—but it was a while before Frenchboro was ready for the newcomers. Of the twelve families at the first interviews, only the two lobster fishermen actually moved out to the island, the Pietrowskis and the Beotes. They arrived on the island in 1988, and after that, the island abandoned its hopes for diversification. The rest of the newcomers, like the islanders, would be fishermen. Brendon and Jennifer O'Leary were among them.

At that time, state law required six months' residency before a lobsterman could get a license to fish, so Walt Pietrowski and Steve Beote went to the island to work on their new houses before their wives moved to Frenchboro. To establish her family's residency, Jennifer O'Leary went to the island before Brendon. During that time, she too worked on the development houses, staining and painting. Early on, though, she encountered the problems that ultimately would lead them to leave the island. "No one would talk to me," she says. "It was a beautiful place, but there wasn't a sense of warmth." The feeling she perceived was: It's us and it's you, and *you* have to fit in.

Several people have said that it's the women who had the hardest time. The men were fishing—yes, sometimes their traps were checked or even cut, and of course they couldn't say anything or it would just get worse. Says the wife of one former homesteader, "They wanted you to make it and stay, but they didn't want to share the wealth. We didn't have as much gear as some—if you did as well as someone already there, that didn't go over so well." It would have been easier, she says, if they'd been able to make a living in some other way. "But," says Mary Pietrowski, "it's the happiest Walt's ever been. He fell in love with the place, and he was doing something he loved."

Mary loved hiking the trails and hearing the snow fall, and she says it was a wonderful experience for her children. Her older daughter was in kindergarten there, and she remembers the teacher calling off school and taking the kids ice-skating. Another time everyone hiked to the other side of the island and saw a beached whale.

Elaine says both she and Steve enjoyed the life. Their son was born while they were on the island. "It was a nice place to bring up a baby—half the time we didn't close the door. Neighbors didn't knock, they just walked in. If anybody comes on the island, everybody knows they're there. We never locked a car door. There were no drugs. I never felt afraid of anything."

Elaine became town clerk and registrar of voters, but that didn't make her an islander. "Everyone was friendly, but I never felt close to anybody. I was comfortable enough that if anything ever happened, I could pick up the phone and get help, but I always felt the outsider." She loved the island itself. "It's a beautiful place, but you had to be comfortable with yourself to live there. If you couldn't be comfortable being alone, the winters were very long and isolated. I didn't feel I needed people around. There was always something to do—I never got bored—I was busy all the time. I loved my house."

There are inconveniences on Frenchboro, certainly, the most dramatic being the very real isolation—perhaps the most of any of the year-round Maine islands. The car ferry now makes three round trips a week from Bass Harbor (on Mount Desert Island), and on Fridays (except in winter), there are passenger-only runs, but at any season, if you go ashore on the ferry, you have to wait till the next day that the boat runs to get back again. There is no airstrip. Elaine and Steve went off-island for groceries on a Wednesday once a month. "We couldn't afford more often." They had to find a place to stay on the mainland and to buy their meals there, and they had to have a cooler to protect perishables from the heat or cold. Once in a while, they'd take their own boat, but she says that was even more of a hassle. You had to have a vehicle over there to get to the stores in Ellsworth anyway, and then when you got back to the island, you had to lug everything back up to the house.

Elaine feels that the separation of the newcomers on the hill from the islanders around the harbor made a big difference. Not only were they newcomers—they were physically segregated.

Wyatt and Lorena Beal, who stayed on the island full-time for sixteen years, initially applied for the Homestead Project, but they were able to buy a house on the harbor before the new homes were ready. They had other advantages: They were from Beals Island, not so far away and with a similar economy and fishing style; they knew people from Frenchboro, and people there knew their families. Of the original group of newcomers, they were the last to leave, and they still have their home on the island. Lorena's father and brother are on the island now, and Wyatt still fishes Frenchboro waters, but from Bass Harbor, except in summer, when they come back to the island. "I like being there," says Wyatt, "but I see it every day when I go to haul.

"They invited us there, treated us like the rest of them. There were just a few fishermen left, then, and elderly—they're all gone, now, except one. There's more fishermen there now than there was then, and more gear. They've used us good out there," Wyatt says. But he and his wife knew from the beginning that they'd be leaving the island again. "You kinda have to go ashore," he says. "You could board your kids out, but we decided before we moved on there, we weren't going to let someone else raise our kids. They can get into trouble even with us watching them."

Wyatt and Lorena moved to Tremont on Mount Desert Island when their son Mariner reached seventh grade—they wanted to give him a couple of years of socialization before he went to the big Mount Desert Island High School. One year, Mariner had been the only child in the Frenchboro School. Their daughter was six when they moved off. Both children have more friends than they would have had if they'd stayed on the island, and the Beals believe they'll have an easier time in high school. Wyatt doesn't know what will happen when the children are through school. "I don't know where we'll end up," he says. "I'm comfortable about anywhere I go."

From the first batch of homesteaders, except for Wyatt and Lorena, Steve and Elaine lasted the longest, eight years. Even the Crossmans, who had lived on the island as youngsters, didn't make it. They were very young when they married, and they split up and left the island. Elaine says that ultimately it was the women who were the deciding factor in leaving. For some, the physical isolation was too much. For others, it was that they weren't accepted.

Mary Pietrowski had no problem with any of the islanders. "I stuck to myself a lot." Her girls were little, and she had plenty to do at home. It was a conscious choice not to get to know any of the natives. "Tipping my foot in the water instead of jumping in was a good idea. I was pleasant, but I didn't get involved."

Most of the homesteading men were fine, say their wives; they were fishing all day, and men have different expectations of other people than do many women. But one woman remarks that fishing out there was not the end of the rainbow. "When my husband came, immediately they acted like he was one of the fold—but he wasn't; they ripped us off left and right." Bait cost two dollars more on Frenchboro, but if you bought it on Swans Island, she says, they wouldn't buy your lobsters, or they'd underweigh your catch, or your traps would be cut. Of course, what she doesn't acknowledge is that Frenchboro is a one-company town, and then largely a one-family town, too. The company is dependent upon Frenchboro fishermen. Naturally, the family and their friends would not be happy when someone they had invited to join them went against them.

The lobstermen from the westward had to get accustomed to a whole new way of fishing. Where they came from, they had set trawls of eight or ten traps on short warp (line), the bottom wasn't rocky the way it is downeast, and they weren't used to the tides of eastern Maine. But the fact is that the Frenchboro Homestead Project got started during a slump in lobster fishing. No one was doing well at that time. David Lunt attributes the lack of success of the early homesteaders to that "down" spell, the newcomers' lack of fishing experience in cold, rough waters like those around Frenchboro, and their unwillingness to take advice from the local people. "Two or three of them would have made it if we'd had good fishing times," he says, "but they was in trouble from the start."

Although even today there are people on the island who believe that many of the native islanders wish they'd never started the homesteading, David contradicts the notion that the newcomers weren't accepted into the fishing community. They wouldn't have set up the program, he says, if they weren't going to share the fishing resources. "We only have so much land and so much bottom," he said. "You've got to have so many people to protect that bottom. Our fishermen were getting older—we had to rejuvenate, bring down the average age." Otherwise, fishermen from surrounding towns would have taken over the Frenchboro fishing grounds. Elaine saw this, too. "We were amazed how much they needed people there. Population was dwindling, and it was getting older. Fishing was going to phase out. They had no choice but to take us."

Finances were tough for them all. To augment Steve's fishing, Elaine worked as a teacher's aide for awhile, and for a time she took care of the teacher's young children. Cleaning summer people's houses was a plum job, but unless the local women couldn't handle it, she was shut out of that. "I made decent money when I did it, but they weren't good about letting people in."

Jen O'Leary picked meat from crabs. "Do you know how many crabs it takes to make a pound of crabmeat?" She says she never worked as hard as she did on the island, "and we walked away with nothing. We went into such debt trying to keep afloat." They ate a lot of what Brendon caught because they couldn't afford hamburger. "I learned so many ways to fix lobster and scallops—I can't eat it to this day. What I wouldn't have given for a cheeseburger!"

One of the other homesteaders says that her family also ate a great deal of lobster. "For the most part, it was legal [within the harvestable size limit]," she says, but if some were not, it was hardly the first time that undersized lobster was consumed by a fisherman's family.

It was when their son neared school age that the Beotes finally decided to move. When they'd come to the island, there were thirteen kids in kindergarten through eighth grade; by the time their son would have gone to school, he would have been the youngest of only three students. The boy is very outgoing and involved with everything in Kittery, where they now live. "If we hadn't had him, we might have stayed longer. We really liked it there. Not the politics, but the place."

Much of the political difficulty centered on the houses—the rent or mortgage payments, and the expectations. It seems that the deal wasn't fully understood, or it changed as they went along—that's how it seemed to the participants, and David says as much. The former homesteaders don't blame the islanders, but rather the management of the program, part of which was through the Rockland-based Island Institute, which some feel was out of touch.

What's certainly clear is that several of the early homesteaders were deep in debt when they left the island, having lost all the savings they had before they moved there. But no one with whom I spoke had regrets about having been in Frenchboro.

"It didn't totally fail—nor totally work out," says Elaine. "It's a fun place to live—I really liked it, and we both had a hard time leaving, but we had to put our son first. I know we did the right thing. I'm glad we were there; we'll have good memories the rest of our lives."

"We followed a dream," Mary Pietrowski says. "We're teaching our kids that they should always try something. Even now—well, it didn't work out, but at least we tried it. It's a good life lesson. Money comes and money goes—but an experience like that comes only once in a lifetime. We ended up chucking everything we had, but we survived and are better for it."

And even Jen O'Leary, whose overall recollection is more negative than those of the others, says she wouldn't have traded the experience for the world. She wouldn't want to raise her children there, but she'd like to take them out there, just to show them what it's like.

Further development was made possible when, with the help of the Island Institute, the Maine Coast Heritage Trust, and the Sea Coast Mission, land that had been for sale on the open market was obtained for another five lots. These were sold with conditions similar to those on the houses—including a buyback clause and a "soft mortgage," whereby up to $20,000 of the mortgage is forgiven over the years. Buyers don't receive a big benefit from selling, but they won't go in the hole, either. The purchasers of these lots have built their own houses.

The FFDC has an agreement with the Maine Coast Heritage Trust to get more development land in the future, too.

Since that first bunch of settlers, others have attempted the move to the island. Some have stayed, some haven't. But now, all the properties have been bought, and their owners have become part of island life. Some of these have ties to the island, including one of David Lunt's grandsons and Wyatt Beal's brother-in-law and Danny Lunt's stepson. (Says Kyle Spratt, "I never would have been able to stay and fish without staying with my mom. That's great, but no one wants to hang out with their mom.") Others are from nearby mainland communities—Addison, Columbia, Bass Harbor, Dennysville. No one is from far away, except perhaps the one fellow from Portland, whose wife lived on the island when she was younger. Occasionally, the feelings between some natives and some homesteaders are uncomfortable—but then, any issue on such a small island will separate people, and the separations are as often on other distinctions as on that one.

Most important, the goal of the project has been fulfilled. By the summer of 2004, there were fifteen children on the island of elementary-school age or younger. While several other islands have shown a slight increase in population or school enrollment, Frenchboro alone seems to be really thriving.

While it has been difficult for young people to settle there, on Frenchboro the combination of land shortage and inaccessibility has left the island with a distinct character—with a working community, much protected land, and, compared to the other islands, relatively few retirees and summer residents. The FFDC is making it possible for some to live on the island who otherwise wouldn't be able to. Perhaps this does change the island's political makeup—but times change everywhere, no less so on the islands, and for the most part, the folks who live on the island choose to do so because they want it as it is.

Isle au Haut Community Development Corporation

As on other islands, Isle au Haut's lack of affordable housing became a topic of much discussion in the 1980s. Should they attempt some kind of project? It was during that time that summer resident Matthew Skolnikoff moved onto the island to write his master's thesis; somehow, he never left again. His education having been in project management for third-world countries, he had learned skills that were applicable to rural Maine too. After listening to the discussion for a couple of years, he jumped in. "Well, do it or don't," he said, and ultimately it was he who headed up the nonprofit Island Community Development Corporation (ICDC), which was created in January 1990.

The voters at Town Meeting opted not to be involved monetarily—they didn't want the town to assume the financial risk. Undoubtedly, some wondered how new people would fare in their small community, too. Dianne Barter, a member of the ICDC board, says that when she was a youngster, the island store didn't even sell film. "God forbid anyone would take a picture and show it to anybody else!" It might attract more people. But the town did recognize the value of the project and voted to donate six acres for three rental houses.

Matthew went to work. Using a combination of grants and loans, the ICDC got the houses built before looking for tenants. They were completed in 1993, and they had no trouble attracting tenants. Until lately, no house was ever vacant more than a month. There were always several applicants, and always at least one was found acceptable. Although the houses are intended to be affordable, the ICDC emphasizes applicants' ability to support themselves once on the island. "That's not only to be sure they can pay the rent," says Matthew, "but they also must be able to pay all their other bills." Applicants are also asked what useful skills they might bring to the community— auto mechanics, firefighting, prior community experience. "It's a plus to have children," says Dianne. But just as important is the sense of people's character. "It's not like everyone has to get along and be one big happy family," says Matthew, "but toleration is a good quality."

All of the tenants stayed at least a few years, and about half of them have subsequently bought land on the island and made their homes there, suggesting that the application process has worked pretty well. There is an unwritten rule, Matthew says, that no one should stay in the rental houses more than five years—and, in fact, it may take five years before a family knows whether or not island life is for them. "The first year, they love everybody," says Dianne. "The second year, they're starting to get involved in politics, and they realize they don't really like about 25 percent of the people here. By the fifth year, they're debating whether they're really gonna stay here or not."

Entirely separate from the ICDC, town land has been made available to people who have proven themselves valuable members of the community. The policy has been to require people interested in purchasing lots to have lived on the island for at least one entire year before asking, and then a townwide vote is taken on their application. Seven lots have been sold, and all but one of those people sailed easily through the secret ballots at Town Meeting. Perhaps interestingly, the only close vote was about a fellow who subsequently left Isle au Haut. Because there were no stipulations on the initial sale, that property is still in his hands. "That defeats the purpose," says Matthew, and the practice was subsequently changed.

The ICDC rental houses are all now occupied, though one was empty longer than desirable. Live and learn. The ICDC had voted to sell one of its three houses to its tenants, with the provision that, barring particular circumstances, they would have to stay on the island eleven months a year. Were the purchasers ever to leave the island, ICDC would have first refusal at a calculable price. The formula was specified and included only what the owner had put into the house with board approval. But, thinking the owners were staying indefinitely and with no idea they'd actually have to buy it back, the board had approved nicer flooring, a $50,000 addition, and a big barn. Then, in a matter of months after all the additions to the house were completed, the family left. The ICDC had to borrow money to buy the house back, and now, in order for it to pay its own way, they have to charge a higher rent for it than for the other houses.

Although this has not always been the case—and may not always be—presently it is stipulated that people should bring their work with them and not depend on either the fishery or such jobs as caretaking and handyman work, which would otherwise be done by current residents. Only one tenant was an island native to begin with. But the program has attracted new people who are content on the island, just as was hoped.

North Haven's Futures Committee

The Futures Committee has just come alive on North Haven, asking the tough questions about keeping the island alive and vibrant. Eighteen years ago, a similar committee made a series of proposals to the community, some of which led to distinct, concrete improvements such as the creation of the *North Haven News* and the establishment of the North Haven Foundation, whose purpose was to help startup businesses like the Y-Knot Boatyard. It also recommended making an effort to create affordable housing on the island, but that idea was voted down overwhelmingly at Town Meeting.

The new committee has identified various areas of concern, including jobs, island-wide high-speed Internet connection, transportation between the island and the mainland as well as across the Thorofare to Vinalhaven, societal issues such as alcohol use and bad home situations, and, once again, affordable housing. Tom Marx, superintendent of the North Haven Community School, has been among the score of people attending the meetings, and he expects that, once again, concrete recommendations will be offered to the townspeople. "We can't just sit by and watch the community disintegrate, and then eighty years from now look back and say, 'What a shame that happened,'" he says. It's unimaginable that this time the question of affordable housing will not be addressed in some manner.

Monhegan

lone among the Maine islands, Monhegan has built its economy around visitors as well as fishing and summer people. Visitors, as opposed to summer people, don't stay on the island. They may come for a day trip, or perhaps even a week's vacation, but visitors have no tradition of spending summers on the island, nor have they any commitment to it. It is possible to become a summer person without owning property, and many islands, including Monhegan, do have regularly returning renters who qualify, but Monhegan is set up to handle people whose stay is shorter and perhaps made only once. Monhegan encourages visitors to walk on the trail network (clear instructions are posted for proper use of them) and generally is very welcoming of people who've come from Away to enjoy the island. It is the only island that consistently has groups of strangers wandering around its roads and

From Monhegan looking across the harbor to Manana Island

trails, taking pictures of people's houses and the laundry hanging behind them and wondering where the bathroom is.

Three private boat companies serve the island. The mailboat runs year-round from Port Clyde, although but three times a week in winter, and occasionally the weather prevents that. From Memorial Day to Columbus Day, the mailboat runs three times a day and cruises come out of Boothbay Harbor and New Harbor. Altogether, there are six or seven round-trips to the island a day in season, with the ability to carry as many as 149 people on each trip.

(Isle au Haut, with its chunk of Acadia National Park, and the Cranberry Isles also have easy access for visitors, but the number of visitors to those islands doesn't approach that of Monhegan, and the impact on the local economy, particularly on Isle au Haut, is minimal.)

Listed on Monhegan websites are at least seven businesses offering accommodations—which, combined with weekly and monthly rentals, provide overnight bed space for at least three hundred people. For much of the high season, all are full. Food is available on all levels from deli takeout to fancy dinners. (Help is hard to find. As the season has stretched, college students can no longer provide all the service needed, as used to be the case—in recent years young Eastern Europeans have come to the island to fill the job niches in the lodgings and restaurants.)

The island is unique in that 480 acres—by far the greater share of the island—are preserved in their natural state. A private organization, Monhegan Associates, Inc., was established in 1954. Among other things, it seeks "to preserve for posterity the natural wild beauty, biotic communities, and desirable natural, artificial, and historic features of the so-called 'wild-lands' portions of Monhegan Island, Maine, and its environs, as well as the simple, friendly way of life that has existed on Monhegan as a whole." The seventeen miles of hiking trails traversing this protected land draw visitors from the mainland every day during the season.

The island has long been a mecca for artists, some very well known, who summer on the island or come for shorter periods and display their works in their own studios and in private and co-op galleries. (Naturally a cause for resentment among the traditional and serious Monhegan artists are individuals who take advantage of the island's arty mystique and rent cottages in which they set up "studios" and sell mediocre paintings and crafts.)

The spring and fall bring out hordes of birders, lured by the impressive number of birds that use the island as a jumping-off place on their way to their breeding grounds or winter homes. Around every corner during those seasons are another two or three khaki-wearing, middle-aged people with binoculars and huge-lensed cameras, peering at the sky and trees for the ultimate sighting of some rare migrant.

"Summer and winter are entirely different places out here," says Doug Boynton, who grew up as a Monhegan summer person but has lived on the island year-round since he graduated from college thirty-five years ago. "People think of this as a rural place, but in summer, it's one of the more densely populated places in the state." Doug gave a summer talk about winter life on Monhegan. "They're fascinated by it, but they have no idea. In summer, I don't know anybody. In winter, we're a very isolated small town."

In winter, Monhegan has far more in common with the other Maine islands than it does in summer. Only the two small stores and the laundromat are open through the year, and there are no new faces. "In March, there's a list in the store of people, dogs, and cats," says Doug, "and the dogs and cats outnumber the people. Sometimes the cats alone do."

The 2000 census showed seventy-five residents; at any given time during the winter months, sixty people are likely to be on the island. On Monhegan, this number includes the fishermen, whereas on many of the other islands, their counterparts have departed for warmer climes or at least the mainland during the coldest months. Monhegan is unique in its closed season on lobsters—no lobsters are taken between June 26 and the beginning of December. Lobstering is permitted for 180 days, starting on a date in December ("Trap Day"), chosen in advance by the fishermen. In 1909, the State Legislature formalized the closed season that the islanders had already imposed upon themselves.

The fishing schedule gives lobstermen the advantage of the higher prices common in winter—December is usually highest, with a strong European demand at Christmastime in addition to the American market—and leaves the summer free for other occupations. Traditionally, lobstermen used to fish for mackerel, herring, and groundfish in summer—lobsters were secondary to other fisheries on Monhegan in those days. Now, the other fisheries are dead or the next thing to it. According to Doug, historically there was a pyramid describing fisheries-related employment. At the bottom, with the greatest numbers, were the fish. The next tier up represented the fishermen. Next were scientists, studying the fisheries, and finally, on the top, with the smallest numbers, were the enforcers of fisheries laws. Now, he says, only slightly facetiously, the pyramid has flipped over. "If there are two codfish, there are three fishermen, a thousand scientists studying the situation, and ten thousand enforcement people. It's frightening!"

In 1996, the regulations were strengthened so that the local fishery is largely controlled by the island fishermen, of whom there can be no more than seventeen. At this writing, there are only fourteen. (Interestingly, the parents of only two of those lived on the island.) They have the say as to who can fish there, as no one may join them without a two-year apprenticeship with a current Monhegan lobsterman. In return for having their protected zone, no Monhegan fisherman may work in any state waters beyond their own, nor may they fish in federal waters except during their own season. In summer, nearly half the fishermen are still on the water in some capacity, though—operating charters, fishing for tuna, or helping researchers. The rest, including Doug, are on the island doing other work—carpentry, in his case. There's certainly plenty to do, and they're glad for work.

All the fishermen on the island start setting out their traps on the same day—Trap Day. "Between Thanksgiving, Trap Day, Christmas, and New Year's, we're going full tilt that time of year," says Doug. "Trap Day is the biggest community event." They all load their boats ahead of time and pile the rest of their traps on the pier. There's a wharf crew of twenty or thirty—some paid, some not—and school lets out or the day is made part of the curriculum. On a signal—sometimes there's even a gun—the boats speed from their moorings to set their first traps. Only three boats can get into the pier at a time, so as they come in to reload, it's first-come, first-served, and everyone pitches in to get the boats in and out again to make room for the next. It takes up to three days to set all the traps, but with this system, they feel everyone has an even shot at getting the best locations. "It's like the Oklahoma Land Rush, everyone trying to get to the better spots," Doug says. The first weeks of fishing are most productive. "The first six weeks, we go whenever it's possible. By midwinter, it's two or three days a week, but by the end of January, we've caught most of the lobsters still crawling out there. When the water's cold, they don't move."

The cooperation shown on Trap Day is perhaps unique among fishermen. Although each year the date is set well ahead of time, if perchance some fisherman isn't ready—illness, or boat troubles, for instance, or if there's really bad weather—they wait. Loading at the pier is always dangerous, even in good weather. A westerly gale is particularly treacherous at Monhegan's unprotected wharf, and it's a good reason to postpone setting. "Till everyone's ready, nobody goes," Doug says. It has even happened that a boat has broken down coming off the mooring, and everyone has gone back and waited until the disabled vessel could be repaired. The season still ends on the date set by the commissioner, regardless of what day it actually started. Trap Day gets postponed for one reason or another once every four or five years.

The Monhegan lobster fishery "is not the gold mine everyone thinks it is," Doug says. It's desperately hard work, cold and miserable, to say nothing of dangerous, and it uses a lot of fuel. Each fisherman has to go ashore to sell his catch and to buy bait and fuel. Monhegan has good-quality, hard-shell lobsters that ship well and bring a good price, but with the exposed wharf, it would be very difficult to run a lobster-buying, fuel, and bait business on-island. "Everything's just a little harder out here," says Doug.

Ironically, after the common efforts on Trap Day, it's every man for himself. The fishermen move from dealer to dealer, depending on who offers the most money—the price may vary as much as fifty cents a pound, depending on who's been most successful with his marketing efforts. There's no more discussion of price on the radio—everyone uses cell phones now, to keep news quiet and protect any edge they may have.

The most dangerous aspect of fishing on Monhegan is puttung the boat on the mooring and getting ashore, Doug says. Everyone has a story of a skiff flipping over on the beach while trying to get off or on. "Some days we can't get to our boats. You've got to be ready for a hurricane all the time."

Doug's own near-death story is unusual, however. During what came to be known as the Perfect Storm, he and a bunch of people were moving traps from a stack near the shore. The seas were beginning to build, and when the wind's just right, the harbor fills from both directions. That's what happened. The beach is at the lowest point, and Doug saw that it was going to overflow. He yelled at everyone to get to higher ground. The sea came in and took a float, 150 traps, and ten big logs on which he'd stacked the traps—and threw them all up the beach. He himself was trapped halfway into his truck, the water shoving the door onto his legs. "It all took about three seconds, but I had time to think, 'What a stupid way to die!'"

He says his is the only sea saga that takes place in a truck.

The trucks are an interesting element on Monhegan. Because the village is compact, there's certainly no need for vehicles just to travel from one house to another, but things have to be moved, and pickup trucks do the moving. The stony village roads are just barely wide enough for one truck, and a booklet available at the pier informs visitors that trucks have the right-of-way over pedestrians. (A good thing, too, as otherwise no truck would ever get anywhere in summer, what with all the people wandering around.) A truck from each of the inns meets every boat in the summer to pick up visitors' baggage; when they can, the drivers of those trucks help move freight to locations along the way. An island ordinance says that only businesses may have trucks—the idea being to try to limit their number—"but it's not all that successful." Doug says that people think there are only ten or twenty pickups, but there are at least thirty, maybe considerably more. No one knows. "Ordinances are only useful if there's a huge consensus behind them," he says. "The jail's not very full here."

Some of the trucks are of relatively recent vintage—conceivably, there's even one with a current license plate somewhere on the island; others seem to be held together by reputation more than actual steel and likely have not been licensed for years.

"Fairy houses" perhaps shouldn't be mentioned, but how can they not be? For generations, the little houses have shown up all along the island's trails. They are constructed of little pieces of dead leaves, of stone, of sticks and pinecones, and they sit quietly and inconspicuously behind trees. Of late, however, sometimes their builders have gone too far. For instance, there's the palatial one that islander Kathie Iannicelli describes as "a half-million-dollar house," with a long "driveway" marked with pincushion mosses the creator had pulled out of the ground. "As I understand it, they die if they're moved," Kathie says of the mosses. "It wasn't subtle, it wasn't charming, and it wasn't in keeping with the rest of the place. Who'd live in there, anyway? We know fairies like things simple. What would they need a driveway for? Fairies fly!"

Perhaps control over fairy houses exemplifies one of the problems on any of the islands with significant summer populations. The question comes up again and again: Why don't more year-round islanders get involved with this organization or that one (in this case, the Monhegan Associates)? The organization was founded by a group that included islanders—Sherman Stanley has been vice president since its inception in the mid-fifties—but it's most often summer people who serve as trustees. Says one year-rounder, "It has become an irritation to have people not here year-round making decisions about your home."

This person asked fellow islanders why winter folk don't get involved. "Well, you've been to the meetings," was the reply. "There are better things to do."

While it is an unusual island person who doesn't care about the issues that concern the Monhegan Associates, "everyone has a different way of expressing it," I was told. "The summer group creates a long way around and gets bogged down by stupid stuff. People get turned off, tired, and leave." The fairy houses are an example. At the annual Associates meetings, "there'll be a two-hour discussion of whether there should be fairy houses." Some people recognize how much fun they are, and an equal number ask, "Can't you just walk and enjoy and not leave your mark?" And there's always the question, Could they stop the creation of the little houses if they wanted to? "People are tied to their good memories—as kids, some in both communities made them."

The Monhegan Associates, without officially condemning the fairy houses, no longer mention them in their printed material. Instead, they post signs asking that people keep the trails pristine and, specifically, not disturb vegetation nor leave anything behind.

There are other issues that divide people on Monhegan, ones where the conversation is more intelligent than that about the fairy houses and sometimes less emotional. It still gets touchy because of personal experience, but, just as with the fairy houses, the split rarely is strictly along the summer/winter line. "There's ownership by the winter community that the summer community can't feel. One group lives it, and the other comes in and bustles around and talks about it. But sometimes, they're the only ones actually doing anything about an issue," Doug admits.

It's a paradox. Most islanders recognize that the summer people are devoted to the island, fascinated by its winter life that they don't themselves experience, and contribute tremendously to its welfare. "There are not enough people here in winter to do the essential things," says Doug. "We simply don't have time to take on extra." (This comes from a man who is on the boards of both the Monhegan Associates and the fledgling effort to create some sort of affordable housing, Monhegan Island Sustainable Community Association.)

That so much of the island was set aside to be wild is important to all, but what does "wild" mean? Should trees be cut when they fall across trails, so that people can get through? What about parasites and invasive species? The deer herd had caused trouble with both, by carrying ticks that spread Lyme disease—for a time, Monhegan had one of the highest infestations of Lyme-carrying deer ticks in the state—and, by overgrazing native vegetation, thus allowing invasives such as Japanese barberry to flourish. A few years ago, the decision was made to eradicate deer from the island.

In 2003, Dr. William Livingston of the University of Maine made a study of the forest on Monhegan. He observed that on former cleared sites, white spruce is dying off due to parasitic attack by dwarf mistletoe, which causes the cancer-like overgrowth known as witches' broom, leaving ugly patches of dead trees and creating a fire hazard. But he was even more concerned about the Japanese barberry, which chokes out regeneration of other species beneath it.

Common sight in summer

Japanese barberry was imported by man—directly or with the assistance of deer, birds, and breezes—and is spreading wildly around the island, not only precluding natural succession of native plants but obstructing passage through the forest. While this is contrary to the natural ecology of the place, to say nothing of ugly, it could also be disastrous economically because Monhegan is so dependent upon visitors. Should an attempt be made to curtail its advance? Is it feasible to make such an attempt? Dr. Livingston thinks it may be, and in 2004 an effort was launched to eliminate at least some of the barberry by cutting and burning and sometimes poisoning it. This weed shrub leafs out earlier than most plants, creating a window of time when it is susceptible to herbicidal treatment with less risk to other species.

Since the departure of the deer, there is already evidence of increased hardwood regeneration. The deer were removed in order to combat Lyme disease, but the return of hardwood saplings has been a side benefit. Deer eat nearly everything but barberry, which flourishes in the open space left when other vegetation is gone. The surviving young hardwoods should help to discourage the spread of barberry.

But not everyone on the island is concerned about the barberry. "Some of the winter people," says Kathie, "have the sense that nature heals itself. If you stand back far enough, you'll see this planet has tremendous self-healing possibilities." And vegetation changes over time. "Are we trying to keep this the same as it was? And isn't that futile?"

"Barberry's not a big issue for me," says Doug. "I'm more worried about the community and whether it can survive than whether Mother Nature can maintain the balance in the wild lands." His personal concern is with affordable housing, knowing that every year people come to the island and fall in love with it and would like to try living there year-round—but it's impossible with no reasonably priced real estate or even winter rentals.

On Monhegan, any house, whether winterized or not, brings at least half a million dollars on the open market. Clearly, this is not conducive to young people establishing homes on the island. "It's no different from coastal towns on the mainland," says fisherman Robert Bracey, "but there you can move inland. Here, they drive you off and you're living on your boat."

The Monhegan Island Sustainable Community Association (MISCA) was established in 2003 with the goal of purchasing existing residential property and making it available for sale to people of low and moderate incomes. To some degree, there was a historical tradition of winter people selling their homes at reasonable prices to other winter people, but that's not always possible. The founders of MISCA wanted to institutionalize the practice, while ensuring that the property would remain affordable by including covenants limiting the profit an owner can make on resale.

The choice was made to buy existing buildings rather than to find land on which to construct new ones, in order to maintain the island's policy of land conservation. MISCA sells only dwellings, not the land beneath them. Only full-time residents of low to middle income are eligible to buy. If purchasers were to make their primary home elsewhere, they would have to sell back the MISCA home. The criteria for choosing among applicants for a particular house include the length of time they've been on the island, their commitment to the community, their ability to make a living on Monhegan, and the suitability of the available house for the family. "We want to help people who are going to be successful," says Doug Boynton, MISCA's president. The hope is to get six or perhaps even ten houses in the pool in the next ten to fifteen years.

The IRS initially denied tax-exempt status to MISCA. Several trustees drafted a letter describing the island situation and the specifics of the first project—the purchase of the old island store in the village—and when the eligibility requirements had been honed down to the satisfaction of Washington, MISCA finally received 501(c)(3) status. The first year saw individual donations of more than $43,000, corporate and foundation donations of $25,500, and public grants of more than $14,000, all of which provided enough money to purchase and renovate the old store, which now houses the Post Office, the town office, a store, and the laundromat. There are also two residential units, which have been sold.

Monhegan is a dichotomy, being one of the islands most distant from the mainland yet the most visited. Despite its many differences from the other islands, it shares some of the very same concerns. At least, it is not dependent upon crustaceans to maintain its financial viability, and it's not likely to become strictly a retirement community. It's already largely service-oriented, but it seems to continue to attract newcomers, which is as well, since for whatever reason, it has less depth of multigenerational native population than perhaps any of the islands. It may have a good shot at remaining a viable year-round community long after others might have lost that capability.

Casco Bay Islands

he islands of Casco Bay, in southern Maine, are very different in many ways from those farther east, but they share many of the same concerns. Their ferry connections to the city of Portland and the town of Yarmouth certainly leave them less removed from the rest of the state. Only Islesboro comes close to the same frequency of scheduled service as is provided by the Casco Bay Island Transit District and the Chebeague Transportation Company, quasi-municipal nonprofit operations. Still, even Islesboro depends on private enterprise for early morning and evening ferries like those scheduled regularly in Casco Bay—and when you've landed in "America" from Islesboro, you're still miles from employment or shopping or entertainment, not in downtown Portland.

Of the year-round islands, Portland claims Peaks, Great Diamond, and Cliff; Chebeague is a piece of the town of Cumberland. Only Long Island is a town in its own right, and it only became independent when it seceded from Portland in 1994. That door has been closed on the other islands, all of which at one time or another might have chosen to follow Long Island's lead. Because of the ease of connection to Portland, there has never been as clear a delineation between natives and those from Away as there is on the eastern islands, nor is it always quite clear who lives on the island and who only vacations there. Many people from the Portland area have houses both ashore and on the island and go back and forth with regularity or irregularity. It is possible to commute ashore to work, and many do just that. The island schools in Casco Bay run only through fifth grade; students take the ferry for middle school as well as high school. There have always been closer connections between summer and winter residents on the Casco Bay islands, with intermarriage common. (This is not to suggest that when some particular local issue arises, no one is going to accuse someone else of being from Away and therefore of lesser stature. But the attack may be taken less seriously by others in earshot than on some of the other islands.)

Each of the winter communities in Casco Bay has seen an increase in population in the decade between the last two censuses, though not necessarily in school attendance. Only Little Diamond has lost population, and no one now lives there all year.

Before its secession vote, Long Island invited town officials from the downeast islands for a weekend. "People came from the Cranberry Isles, North Haven, Swans, even Matinicus—I can't remember where all they came from," says Mark Greene. They stayed in people's houses and there was a potluck dinner in the VFW Hall ("Yes," says Mark, "Long Island has a VFW hall—it's one of the smallest in the world, but we have one!"), and there were a lot of good and interesting discussions about life on independent islands.

"Every one of them, to a man and woman, was absolutely surprised by Casco Bay," says Mark. "They were shocked. They had all thought it was like Old Orchard Beach, or Peaks—not that there's anything wrong with Peaks," he adds quickly. Casco Bay islands—except perhaps Peaks—really *are* islands, the visitors realized.

Long Island, the Rebel

Long Island is one of the outer islands in Casco Bay—"down the bay," they call it—and it has yet to become as gentrified as Peaks or even Chebeague. It still has a significant fishing community, and the forebears of about half the winter community have lived on the island for several generations. Many islanders are related to one another. The island is seen by some from Peaks, at least, as still having the sense of community that has been lost on that inner island. "They do things together out there," says a Peaks Island fisherman, sadly wishing his own community was like that. (To be fair, many on Peaks believe it is.) Residents of Long Island say that its location is ideal—close enough to Portland to be able to take advantage of the good things it offers, but far enough out that they're not affected by the bad.

Dawn Johnson is seventy-six. She looks back on the changes on Long island with acceptance and good cheer. "My mother always said, 'Things change,' and they do." Many islanders left after World War II. "The older people died off," she says, "and a lot of the young ones wanted to get off the rock and moved away—but when they started having children, they wanted a place on the island to come summers so their children could have the joy of the island." Other Long Island summer people have come in July and August for generations and generations. "We're one big family," she says. "We get along well with the summer people. My father played with them when he was young, and I played with the next generation, and my kids played with the next. There's such a closeness." In fact, Paula Johnson, the wife of one of Dawn's sons, is from a many-generation summer family. Paula has been teaching on the island for many years—she now has the sons and daughters of former students in her class. Even though half the people now on the island have come from Away, many of those, like Paula, are former summer people with a long history on the island.

"When you live on an island," Dawn says, "you see the girls pregnant, you hold the newborn babies, you watch them grow up—they're the island's children, and they're all beautiful." She laughs, but she means it, too. "It's a wonderful place, and everybody loves it," she says. How often does she go ashore herself? "As little as I have to," she answers quickly. "To your doctors' appointments and to get your pills, and grocery shopping for what you can't get on the island. Buy big and stock up," she says.

Another daughter-in-law, Lynn, has only been on Long Island for fourteen years, but she and her husband, Steve, have no plans to leave. "Peaks Island is too big and Great Diamond is too small. Cliff is just that much farther down the bay. Long Island is just right," she says. In the winter, she knows just about everyone she sees. Summer is a different case, though. "It's odd to get on a ferry and know nobody." Lynn used to commute to Portland to work.

There are about twenty-five boats fishing from Long Island these days, and many sternmen commute out on the early boat from Portland, which gets in at five-thirty. There are more people commuting off the island than on—including all the students from sixth grade up (twenty-two, in 2004–5)—but not Lynn anymore. Since her husband stopped fishing and started building boats, she works in the boatyard with him, bookkeeping and sanding and painting. "There's a lot of sanding and painting in finishing a boat," she says. She's glad to have him home in winter and not shrimping or dragging. "You worry about them out there—we've lost a few to fishing. You just never know."

Steve's twenty-seven-year-old son works with him and lives in a house on family land. "Not everyone's that fortunate," says Lynn. Long Island has faced the same problems of high land costs as have the islands beyond Casco Bay—primarily, the difficulty for young folks to get started on the island. But being part of Portland gave it and the other city islands another problem: skyrocketing property taxes.

By Maine's Constitution, taxes on real property are to be assessed on the property's "just value." The courts have interpreted that phrase to mean fair market value—what a willing buyer will pay a willing seller. There have always been objections to this system, but in 1990, when the city of Portland revalued all the property within its boundaries, it was required to assess all land in this manner. It should have come as no surprise to anyone that compared to inland properties, shore frontage had increased in value manyfold. Smaller communities all along the coast have experienced the same phenomenon, and it caused a shift in tax burden there, too. But the impact was particularly dramatic in Portland. Mainland property owners saw far less increase in land values, and commercial property had already lost value due to the economic slump Maine was experiencing. Portland's islanders suddenly received a far greater share of the total bill.

For ages, Long Island had felt itself at odds with the city, of which it was but a small part. "We were always being shat upon by the city," says Mark Greene, whose great-grandparents moved to Long Island in the 1890s. The city constantly threatened to pull back on what few services they provided to the island—whether school, police coverage, trash service, or road maintenance. Taxes raised on the island were nearly double the funds spent there by the city, and the islanders didn't like it. For twenty years, whenever one of these issues arose, Mark, always active, spoke up at local meetings. Secession was the answer, he kept saying.

Although of island stock, Mark had the misfortune to be born and raised in Massachusetts. His mother was among the many who moved away from Maine before World War II, but the family always spent Christmas and summers on the island, and he himself always kept as much of a connection as possible to the island. In his teenage years, he worked every summer on Long Island, and although he and his wife weren't able to find teaching positions in Maine, they lived within a two-hour drive of Portland so they could always come back on the last boat every Friday. He bought a house on the island, along with some rental property, and ran a lawn business there. "I worked my tail off so we could afford to be here," he says. The one good thing about his experience in small towns in central Massachusetts was that he saw how powerful the local town-meeting form of government could be.

When suddenly islanders found their taxes tripled—and at a time when even fewer services were being received from the city—Mark's cry for secession suddenly seemed sensible. It wasn't long before a core group of islanders were meeting in Mark's living room every weekend. Everyone pitched in on the research, looking at facts and figures and estimates and guesses about expenses and requirements and responsibilities. The mood changed. Says Paula Johnson, "The movement was started by the revaluation, but it quickly turned into 'Let's make decisions for ourselves.'"

A vote in October 1991 went ninety-eight to two in favor of a referendum on forming an independent town, and shortly thereafter, legislation was introduced in the state House of Representatives to allow a secession vote in November 1992. Portland wanted all its citizens to participate in that vote, not just residents of Long Island. "With that kind of thinking, we'd all still be part of England," says Mark. "They said it with a straight face, too!" (But, in fact, this is precisely the change that the State Legislature passed soon after Long Island seceded. It's not at all likely that a coastal town will ever again lose its tax-revenue–producing cash cow. And with a new revaluation, not yet finalized at this writing, it is clear that the shore property has once more risen in value far more than has inland property. Again, the islands will take

Representative Herb Adams swears in Mark Greene as moderator of Long Island's first Town Meeting, December, 1993.

a huge hit unless there is a constitutional change.)

At a legislative hearing, Mark articulated the central issue as "preserving an endangered way of life." The island still was a small fishing community, even if it had been part of a larger city politically. In the spring, with little objection, both houses of the State Legislature passed the bill permitting the November island vote. A few of the state's elected representatives were happy to stick it to the big city, and others simply believed in the principle of self-rule.

Then followed a summer and fall of heated discussion. Mark, admitting that he has a bias, describes the most vociferous of the naysayers as having something to lose personally by splitting off from the city. They worked for the city, or thought they could benefit more behind the backs of a distant City Hall than they could with local officials. Some islanders—many of whom had always lived as part of the city of Portland—had no understanding of how a small town works. Mark found himself fielding such questions as "Who will plow the snow?" He remarks that it's a lot like the breakup of the old Soviet Union. Things weren't too good for people under the Soviet system, but everyone knew what to expect from it. Being part of the city gave everyone something to bitch about, with a clear target for their displeasure. Many people are still unhappy that the USSR broke up, he says. "Democracy is not always smooth, and sometimes it's not pretty."

But the island's final vote was very clear: 129–44 in favor of secession. The taxes saved in the first five years after the rebellion were enough to pay the sixth year's, and in 2004, the island tax bills were 33 percent less than what they would be under the city's rule. The island did vote to add a dollar to the mill rate to create a kitty to fight a liquefied natural gas (LNG) facility, if one were to be proposed again for Casco Bay. (In addition to the many and very real environmental and safety concerns shared by people in all areas where an LNG facility has been proposed, the islands are worried by the impact on both ferry traffic in the bay and the fishery, as a very wide berth must be given to ships in the approaches.)

"That we could do that showed how nice it is to have our own control," says Nancy Jordan, who was very active in the secession. She believes that Portland never

The new addition to the Long Island school

would have made such a commitment, that the city would have seen LNG only as an economic benefit to the area.

"It has been a lot of work," says Mark about independence. There is tremendous responsibility, but people have stepped up to it. "It's done wonderful things for the community."

Perhaps the most visible and dramatic accomplishment of the new municipality is the construction of a school addition. "Everyone who sees it is overwhelmed," says Paula Johnson. The town raised $867,000 to build a multipurpose room and library—and all of that money, save one small state grant for a refrigerator, came from private grants and donations. "Before that, the most we ever raised was $11,000 to buy the beach, years ago. The community is incredibly proud of that building."

Mark admits he has been surprised that the island has not been as environmentally conscious as he expected. In the past, it had been easy for everyone to agree that the city was wrecking the place with whatever ordinances it suggested. "I thought we could protect things better, acting locally." But start tinkering with land-use ordinances—things like lot sizes—and the community splits. He speaks of the same divisions found everywhere—one he calls the Montana camp (the "it's my land and I'll do what I want with it" people) and the other the tree-huggers. "But no one has ever figured out how to balance protecting land with private property rights," he concludes.

His biggest fear had been that they wouldn't have enough people to do all the jobs that needed to be done, but that has been less of a problem than he expected. "We're running out of people to be selectmen," he says, though. "We've always gotten someone, and we've had good people, but we've kinda cycled through them. It's tough being selectmen in a small place where 'most everything's volunteer. They end up having to do a lot themselves, fixing planks on the dock, or whatever needs to be done. That gets old." And Long Island is in an unusual situation in that it is the only small town around. In other parts of the state, they might be able to share services with other small towns, but there are none around Casco Bay.

For the schoolchildren, secession has made little difference, but as teacher, Paula had no idea what was coming when Long Island struck out on its own. "I always wondered what in the world the school department needed with all those people in the central office—and now I know. That was the biggest eye-opener, what a lot of paperwork is involved in the administration of a school." The first year, it was easy to think, well, nobody ever reads this stuff, there's no need for all these reports. "But there are people who read it, even more than there used to be, due to No Child Left Behind." Paula makes a lot of grant applications, too, as well as filling out all the various reports, and while she says the paperwork has intensive times, including during the summer, she estimates a minimum of five extra hours every week on administrative paperwork. "I just wasn't aware of how much there was."

Still, she's clearly happy about the town's independence. "We know exactly where every penny goes," she says. "We all vote. Town Meeting is very heavily attended—'most everyone is there. We were often neglected by Portland—once we seceded, the other islands got a whole lot more attention. Portland no longer ignores them."

The main issue facing the school, as on all the other Maine islands, is population numbers. After years of a steady sixteen-to-twenty-four students, the numbers of on-island elementary students have dropped recently, with fourteen in 2003–04 and only eleven in 2004–05. As is the case on all the islands, the problem is the lack of affordable housing. One of the selectmen, Steve Train, has taken on this issue and is looking into options. It's difficult, as has been well demonstrated elsewhere, yet even a single affordable dwelling can make a big difference. One family moved to the island not long ago with three children and another on the way. Another such family would bring a significant and welcomed increase in the school. Perhaps a little help might come from off-island: Great Diamond Island has no school, and one mother there, whose son is only three now, is hoping to send him to Long Island as a tuition student. Even a single student helps.

The town has a contract to send most of its older students to Portland schools.

"I personally think it's very good we seceded," says Lynn Johnson. "I think a few other islands are jealous. We're able to make our own decisions as a democracy. You might not get your own way all the time—you never do—but it's your neighbors and friends deciding things. We have a little more control of our destiny. The people out here are very family-oriented, with families going way back—no one wants to see older people be taxed out."

Chebeague Island

Although Chebeague is in Casco Bay, with the easier connections to the mainland that the ferry systems there allow, it still shares many characteristics with the other islands, including the tendency for young people to leave. Like nearly everyone her age, Kim Martin left the island when she finished school. Her friends couldn't wait to get out, she says, and while she didn't feel the way they did, she knew she had to leave. "It's stagnant, if you don't get away." She's back now.

"I didn't assume I'd come back, but the island always was home." Of the cities in which she and her husband lived during the first ten years of their marriage she says, "I had a constant feeling I didn't belong there." She says she's been much more at ease since she returned to Chebeague. An RN, she's been exploring her creative side more than she could when she was in Massachusetts, and she likes the space, freedom, and lack of structure for her younger children. "I have family all over the island to look out for them," she says. But it's hard with children in high school, playing sports and wanting to be involved in other extracurricular activities—"football, for example," she said a couple of weeks before school started for the year. "My son has to be at school in Cumberland at seven, and the first boat leaves at six-forty. He wouldn't get there till seven-twenty or so, and the coach is very punctual. He wouldn't be able to play." The Martins' outboard was on the fritz, so they bummed rides at six in the morning, or sometimes the boy stayed at Kim's mother's in Yarmouth. "They wouldn't be able to do sports without my mother." Basketball season in particular, with its late practices, often saw Martin children at their grandmother's. This is hard for Kim, though. "I was always right there, involved. It's hard to delegate."

Just as on the outer islands, some parents rent an apartment ashore during their children's years in school ashore, which start in sixth grade for Chebeague Islanders, just as for the island children going to Portland schools. A friend of Kim's has swapped houses for a year with a woman who wanted to try out life on the island. But it's hard for young people to find a place to live on the island, where it's rare that a livable house is offered for under $250,000. It's not necessarily easy for older people, either. Kim's mother, Pam Johnson, grew up on Chebeague and now lives in Yarmouth, where she's a real-estate broker. "I always thought I'd move back and open my own agency, but now I don't think I could afford to," says Pam.

There is talk of creating some kind of affordable housing, an issue that is controversial. Some people don't like the idea, but Kim thinks it's important. "We're either going to be a summer resort," says Kim, "or people will have to accept that kind of development to help people live here."

Chebeague Island is part of the town of Cumberland, a fact that has both positive and negative sides. Among the pluses are a town police department and access to a town planner. The minuses are mostly about property value, which—in addition to creating a lack of affordable housing—imposes a tax burden similar to the one the Portland islands have. High assessments bring high taxes to an island that ends up paying a disproportionate share of the town bills. To educate its forty-odd students the way Long Island does—locally for the first years and tuitioning its middle- and high-school students to mainland schools—might cost about half a million dollars. But because the island is part of the Cumberland school district, they're paying about four times that amount toward the town's education bill. "That doesn't even pass the straight-face test," I was told.

"Someone buys a house on the island for a million dollars, and we're all millionaires." That's fine if they want to sell their houses too, but not so fine if they don't. "It's according to the state constitution, so we're in big trouble."

Town Councilor Donna Damon was among the people urging a land-bank taxation system during the statewide push for property-tax relief a year or two back. The idea was to allow people to enter their property into a program like the state Tree Growth Plan, which allows taxation on the basis of its actual use, rather than its fair-market value, thus reducing property taxes. Then, if the property were sold, the back taxes would be paid up. Interestingly, Donna came upon this concept from the point of view of the town, rather than just from that of a taxpayer. Many years back, a distant family member of Donna's was able to stay in his own home until his death because the town had kept his assessment low. While contrary to the state Constitution, this was certainly a humanitarian gesture—one possible in a day when townspeople knew each other and looked after one another. After the old man died, his niece sold the property for what was then a huge price. "If someone's making a profit, some of that should go back to the town," says Donna. But she couldn't even get her own council to accept the scheme. "It's hard for people on the mainland to understand. We live in a mobile society and don't have a sense of place anymore. Most people are transient." Many people in mainland Cumberland are on the "twelve-year plan"—they come into town for the excellent school system and move on when their children have finished school.

But the people of Chebeague most definitely do have a sense of place. Evidence of this is the difficulty experienced by the town of Cumberland in privately raising the last half-million dollars for a new auditorium, while Chebeague, just in a dozen years, received donations totaling $350,000 for their library, $750,000 for a new recreation center, and another $500,000 for the historical society. During this same period, they also opened an assisted-living center for the elderly. Cumberland simply sees that as evidence that Chebeague Islanders have plenty of money and needn't be worried about taxes, but what it really shows is the investment that members of the community—even summer people—have and continue to make in their own community.

"The island is the one constant in their lives," says Donna. "When we built the rec center, we thought the town was going to kick in a hundred thousand dollars, but they didn't. We went back to our major donors, and one guy, who's been coming here since he was a little kid, said he would pay off the mortgage if we'd have a mortgage-burning party. That was $162,000 right there!" Mainland Cumberland has the same kind of money, but they seem to be less willing to invest it in their community. And the fact that there are such donors in no way says that less-wealthy residents are able to pay property taxes at the level required of even a modest house.

Chebeague, unlike the islands of Portland, which are simply part of a mainland district, at least has representation on the Cumberland Town Council. By charter, each of the four neighborhoods in Cumberland, of which Chebeague is one, has a councilor, even though all are elected by townwide vote. Donna has been in the position twice, once in the early 1980s before she raised her family, and again now. She is in her second term of her second go-round.

Taxes and property values aside, it certainly costs more to live on the island than ashore. Freight charges have to be added to every commodity on the island: a jar of mayonnaise that sells for $1.99 at the mainland supermarket will bring more than four dollars on the island. People-transportation is expensive too. Even if a young couple were able to find a place to live on Chebeague, the costs of commuting to work or school would make it prohibitive. When Donna and her husband were both traveling ashore to work each day, and their daughter and son were at school on the mainland, they had to budget four thousand dollars a year for commuting costs.

The economy of Chebeague is more diverse than that of most of the Maine islands. "I think of it as a three-legged stool," says Donna, leaving the increasing numbers of retirees out of her formula. Fishing is the major industry still, with forty-five or fifty people employed—almost all in the lobster fishery. Not all the sternmen live on the island, although some are islanders by upbringing. Due to the same old issue of affordable housing, young island-born men either live with their mothers or get apartments in town.

The second leg of the stool is made up of on-island businesses such as might be found anywhere: people run stores and inns and consulting businesses as accountants or engineers, and there are builders, a plumber, and an electrician. In fact, a few years ago, the electrician, Kim Boehm, was living in Yarmouth and working for someone else. He and the crew started working on the island when a mainland customer who had a summer cottage on the island begged them to come out and do some work. "We were skeptical, worried about how to get around, what if we forget something, what about the boat, all that, but he arranged it all. You'd have thought we were movie stars, 'Oh, my God, there's an electrician in town! Can you come back tomorrow and do thus-and-such?'" They'd be working on a new house, and people would pull over and ask the contractor, 'Hey, can I borrow your electrician when you're done with him?' They'd practically kidnap us."

Kim started on his own about then, doing more and more work on the island. His divorce and coinciding tax increases led to his selling his house on Cousins Island, and by then, 95 percent of his work was on Chebeague. It was logical for him to move out there, and because he came from a small town in the first place, he liked the remoteness. He found a reasonably priced property in the center of the island. "The boat? It beats commuting forty minutes on the Interstate, at least if you like boats." (He knows there are people who don't like boats, but he says he wouldn't involve them in his life.)

"You don't want to move out here and make it how it was where you came from," he says, speaking of people who rent an island cottage for a week and first thing they do is call the landlord because they can't get the History Channel. "For God's sake, walk the beach or count the stars. Like anything else, it's what you expect of a place that matters. You have to have your head up—there's only one store, and it has limited hours, and there's no drive-through McDonald's. On the other hand, people who live here tend to take care of each other. If I'm out of potatoes, I'll go next door and ask for some—and if they're not home, I'll go in and get some. And if they're out of town and it snows, I'll shovel their doorstep. We take care of each other because we're all we have." Kim quotes a saying he heard: "Do the best with what you have to do it with." That's island life.

But he likes the idea that in twenty minutes he can be on the mainland headed to Portland. "Okay, you want some culture—there's arts, theater—within an hour you can be at the mall. Now that's a whole 'nother world!"

There was a downside for him, he says. He had been romantically involved with a woman who feared she'd never get him off the island, and she didn't see any future for herself out there. "Employment is limited," he admits. There were other issues too, of course, but she's gone.

"But Chebeague overcompensates for its limited social opportunities," Kim says. "There are a disproportionate number of programs. A big rec center with a pool, and they keep that open at night as a teen center, and they show two classic films at the library every Friday night—Hitchcock or something. It's an excellent library, and it has a huge video collection."

Kim has done a lot of electrical work on boats, too. "It's a skill not that many have." He completely rewired five fishing boats last spring. "The fishermen were thankful. People do botched jobs, and they depend on that boat for their livelihood. And the barter system is alive and well out here." (Oh, yes, he assures anyone who cares, every scallop he trades for is reported to the government. Right.)

And back to Donna's third leg—the group of people like her and her husband, who commute to work. These people include teachers, engineers, accountants, and lawyers who lend their expertise to the island with in-kind donations to projects like the rec center.

The island is served by two ferry systems, Casco Bay Lines and the Chebeague Transportation Company (CTC), which is a for-profit stock-based corporation "from which no investor will ever get a penny," I was told. But its users support the company; it has no subsidy. There has been talk about restructuring it as a nonprofit. The local company makes a fifteen-minute run between Chebeague and Cousins Island, a bridge-linked part of Yarmouth. There are nine or ten round-trips a day, Monday through Saturday, between six-forty in the morning and ten forty-five in the evening; on Sunday, the eighth and last trip back to the island leaves at seven-thirty.

The Casco Bay Lines ferry brings most of the freight onto the island, and it connects the islands to each other as well as providing a link to Portland. They provide five or six trips to and from Chebeague each day in summer and four the rest of the year, allowing an easy commute to Portland for regular business hours.

When Donna and her engineer husband, Doug, first moved into their island home, he was commuting to Stratham, New Hampshire. He took an early boat, did his design work in his head on the Maine Turnpike, left work at five, and caught the six-thirty boat home. Now he is commuting to Auburn. "It's easier than when we were first married and he was commuting on the Southeast Expressway out of Boston," she says. "Now I always know when he'll be home. I had no idea, then."

The CTC boats have been running since the early 1970s, when the company bought out the island water-taxi owner, and this has separated Chebeague from the other Casco Bay islands. "It used to be that all the people knew each other, because they met on the Casco Bay Lines boat," says Donna. "Now we're set off. A couple of generations have grown up here never having known the people from the other islands."

But there are still connections. When she heard that the state had suddenly sprung the idea of a liquefied natural gas terminal on Hope Island, between Chebeague and Cliff Islands, Donna went to work. As soon as it was light, she called fishermen on Cliff and Long Islands, and by seven-fifteen in the morning, everyone on the boats all over Casco Bay knew what was going on.

Donna has no idea whether her own children will end up on Chebeague. "When I was first married, I never would have thought I would be back. When I was in high school, I hated it. I wanted to be with everyone else—my senior year, I spent ninety-two nights away. I might as well have been at boarding school." When she was at college, she still said she hated the island, but the girls in her dorm, who had heard her many stories about Chebeague, corrected her. They loved hearing the tales—they said they felt as though they knew everyone out there—and when they pointed out to her that she enjoyed telling them, it made her stop and think. It wasn't long after she was married that she and Doug wanted to return to Maine, and just as soon as one of them got a job—it happened to be Donna—back they came. A piece of land on Chebeague came down to her from her family, and they started work on a house. Five years later, before her daughter was born, they were on the island. Even though she doesn't dare guess whether either of her children, now nearly grown, will come back, she knows she's home.

(Donna has also made a name for herself as the savior of Crown Pilot crackers. In 1996, Nabisco did away with a number of products, including Crown Pilots, of which they only sold about 241,000 pounds each year, compared to 150 million pounds of Ritz crackers. They hadn't realized how important those crackers are to New Englanders for their chowders. Donna went on a campaign, starting with the *Inter-Island News* and ending up on *CBS News Sunday Morning*. In response, 3,500 people called the company, and the crackers were put back in production. Traditional chowder suppers were again possible.)

Peaks Island

Residents of most other island communities in Maine look down their noses at Peaks, with its fifteen-minute ferry rides scheduled nearly every hour from about six in the morning until nearly midnight. But its residents say it's still very much an island, even if their access to the mainland is only limited for a short time each day. Due to its proximity, it has always been a bedroom community for Portland, and now close to a thousand people—of diverse backgrounds—make their homes there year-round. Many decades ago, Peaks was a haven for low-income families, but this phenomenon is rapidly changing as the island further gentrifies. The real-estate values on Peaks have just risen and risen—the latest city assessments suggest that island values have increased 200 percent since the 1990 valuations were made.

It wasn't until the economic boom of the 1980s that Peaks started to become the fashionable address it now is. Professional people and artists and others of a relatively liberal bent moved onto the island, attracted to it in the form it then had. As the numbers of residents increased, various improvements were made. There's a question of chickens and eggs here.

Dean Camp was born in New Jersey, but he had Peaks Island roots and grew up there. "The island has changed a huge amount in the forty years I've been here," he says. It's less blue-collar than it used to be. Even though professionals have been moving onto Peaks and commuting to Portland to work since the 1980s, they didn't change the island much, he says, compared to what's happened in the last ten years. "Baby boomers who've done very well for themselves have come and remodeled rundown cottages into million-dollar monstrosities. That's when things really changed."

Summer patterns have changed, too. "When I was growing up, the families would be here with their kids all summer—now it's all weekly rentals. They come from wherever, and if there are four people, they bring three cars and are racing around in front of the stores. It's hectic."

In winter, Dean still knows most of the people on the street on Peaks, and they greet each other, but they're acquaintances or people for whom he's worked, "not people you walk in and watch a ballgame with."

It's still beautiful on the island after Labor Day, Dean says, but he and his wife are considering moving off. "Most of the guys I grew up with are gone—there's only two or three left. They loved the island but felt the burden of the boats—we're at the point where we're getting tired of it too." Even with the liberal schedule, he speaks of the same difficulties that people face on more distant islands because of the ferry: grocery shopping, going to the movies, medical appointments. "Whatever you do, you have to think about the boat."

Peaks never was a big fishing village, but now there are only one or two full-time fishermen. Corey Johnson still fishes, and he also does excavation work in spring and fall. "Most everyone commutes ashore," he says. "There's not many old families left. The price of real estate is just outa sight. Peaks isn't really a community the way Long Island is—I don't think there's any community spirit. It's not like we have any form of government here."

The degree of discomfort or inconvenience that comes with living on an island, says John Carroll, who moved to Peaks in 1984, "provides a self-selection mechanism," determining who will move there. "The barriers change—the threshold lowers—opening up to different people." Before the current car ferry, there was a smaller one, the *Rebel*. Its seating was not very good, and people often ended up outside. It was difficult to get vehicles to the island, particularly heavy trucks. There was a wooden pier with a single light on the end of it. (Dean says that, at least when he was a kid, there was usually no light at all. "We always broke it out.") A cobbled street led up the hill past a junkyard to the main street. Some who came to Peaks wondering if they'd like to live there decided that while it was a nice place, it was just too difficult, and they looked elsewhere.

The new ferry, the *Machigonne II*, came on in the late 1980s, allowing easy access for all kinds of vehicles. On-island construction expenses declined as materials were more easily brought over. Major changes were made to the pier, too. The cobbles made it hard to walk or drive, yes, and they could be slippery, but they kept vehicle traffic down and they looked good. The islanders tried to save them, but the stones were all ripped up in favor of a wide, concrete expanse with as many as fifty-four lights of various descriptions. "Coming in by ferry at night, it looks like you're approaching an airport," says John. "And now you can't see the stars." He's not sure whom the lights protect. "Nobody ever fell off the dock because it was dark," he says.

People who come to check out the island now have a different greeting and a different response. "It affects people's choices," says John. "It would affect mine. I'm not sure I'd move out here now. It's easy to accuse me of being a Luddite or trying to close the door after myself, but I moved here for what it was. I would have been happy to leave it that way." The second wave of newcomers who started arriving ten or twelve years ago came with different expectations.

Another change is that summer renters, of whom there are more and more, find it easier and for that matter less expensive to bring their cars to the island than to find a place to park them ashore while they're vacationing. There are no two points on the island more than a fifteen-minute bike ride or a half-hour walk apart, but once the cars are there, it's easy for their owners to drive "down front" (the islanders' term for the ferry-landing area) or to the back side, rather than walking or bicycling.

There's actual traffic congestion on the island now, and residents say that visitors don't know how to drive appropriately on the narrow roads. The vacationers' vehicles are too big, and they drive too fast. The island's twenty-mile-an-hour speed limit exists for good reason.

Planning for growth is always tricky, because improvements made to accommodate past growth always attract more. No one was trying to change the island by building the new, comfortable, and convenient ferry—but the effect was just that. Another aspect of the new boat, points out John, is that the seemingly inexhaustible demand for bringing cars onto the island provided a cash cow to Casco Bay Lines, which operates from the proceeds of its fare boxes. The increased traffic on the *Machigonne*, and the concurrent decline in the character and quality of life on Peaks, has supported the islands down the bay (or "downbay," as they say). "It's a trade-off, and it's not necessarily Peaks that benefited," adds John.

The island is still home to a relatively liberal-thinking group, but, says John, "I suspect the percentage of truly eccentric people is down. Of course, you always hear that: 'You should have been here ten years ago, when it was really crazy.'"

When the new boat was put to work, the rest of the ferry schedule was adjusted, too. The *Rebel* had run infrequently, and other trips were made by smaller Casco Bay Lines boats, which often stopped at Peaks and then continued on to the other islands. The *Machigonne* was purpose-built to serve only Peaks Island, and although smaller boats sometimes run to Peaks, that's as far as they go, now. "The five-thirty—the main home-bound commuter boat—used to stop at Peaks and then go down the bay," explains John. "We'd ride home every night with the people from the other islands." Now, much day-to-day interaction between Peaks Islanders and those from the islands down the bay has been eliminated. "It's just another of those little things that slip away."

"Everybody knew everybody," says Brenda Buchanan, who first spent time on Peaks when she was in law school in Portland and moved onto the island in 1995.

Peaks Island Land Preserve

Perhaps ironically, it is the devout wish of many newcomers to Peaks Island—who are often regarded as the cause of the island's changes—that it remain as it has been, that it be preserved where possible. The Peaks Island Land Preserve (PILP) was organized in 1994 in order to buy twenty-six acres, the Battery Steele property, which was being offered for sale for development. Battery Steele was the largest installation remaining from World War II, boasting two sixteen-inch guns when Peaks was heavily fortified by the U.S. Army to protect the Portland area, where Liberty ships were being built and large fuel tanks were in place on Long Island and elsewhere. The battery itself is a popular hiking and picnic destination for islanders and visitors alike—there's a magnificent view out to sea from the top.

PILP now has ownership of (or conservation easements on) 150 of the island's 720 acres. The largest project was securing the easement on about a hundred acres, also formerly military property. It had been donated as a park to the city of Portland in

The southern embrasure of Battery Steele, once the site of huge guns. Myth has it that they were only fired once, and they broke every window in the village. (COURTESY OF STEVE SCHUIT)

the mid-sixties as part of an effort to spur people to move to the island. Over the years, part of the property had been used as a source of gravel, and another piece became the island dump and subsequently the transfer station. About ninety-eight acres remained in its wild state, and PILP convinced the city that it would be a better steward than the city could be. An active group of volunteers has taken on its management, working to protect habitat by clearing brush to lower fire risk, maintaining trails, and lessening the impact of invasive species that threaten the forest health. Japanese bittersweet was brought onto the island during World War II to provide camouflage, and now it, along with various other imported species, is choking out other vegetation.

A current project that is more unusual is the protection of the walking path through the village. A path runs from the school all the way across the island, but the most-used section traverses the village and ends at the Peaks Island Health Center. It cuts between houses—sometimes fenced on either side in a five-foot-wide corridor—and no one remembers when it wasn't there. It has no formal easement, however, and PILP is hoping to establish one before someone suddenly starts worrying about liability and shuts it down. "It is a feature that makes Peaks Peaks," says Brenda Buchanan, a member of the PILP board who has been involved with the organization since 1998. She has also joined the board of Oceanside Conservation Trust, which is involved with preservation on all the islands of Casco Bay.

Brenda is pleased to have become a part of the two land preservation organizations. "It's a wonderful opportunity to know people on all the islands," she says. "They all feel it's a privilege to live in such a beautiful place, tuned into nature, and are concerned about the same kinds of issues—the impact of taxation, keeping schools going, the ongoing impact of tourism." Peaks Island Land Preserve and Oceanside Conservation Trust work closely together, establishing a double layer of protection where they can, with one organization having fee rights to the underlying land of protected parcels and the other holding a conservation easement. "It may be belt-and-suspenders," says Brenda, "but if something were to happen and Peaks had to forfeit ownership, say, then the property would still be protected."

Brenda specializes in real-estate law, and sometimes finds herself advising clients when they're having a difficult time making a purchase work. She believes strongly that if something is right, the opportunity will present itself, as it did for her—she fell into her own house by serendipity. "There's a karma to the places we find ourselves," she says. It's not a particularly lawyerly-sounding belief, but, she says, it seems normal on Peaks. She says the people there (including lawyers) are a singularly creative bunch—practical, resourceful, and resilient. These are characteristics she feels are necessary for an island-dweller. "You have to know how to carry the right gear with you when you're coming to town, and how to get a bulky new purchase home in a windstorm."

Management consultant Don Stein and his artist wife also came to Peaks a few years ago. It was the sense of community that drew them to the island, along with what he sees as a rural feel. "You're twenty minutes from a wonderful city, yet it's a pretty, pretty place, with the coastline, and still the inland parts are like the woods of northern Maine or Vermont. And there are a lot of very interesting, creative, talented people," says Don, who, like Brenda, is involved with PILP. "A lot of folks know each other. If you're in a pinch, usually there are people who can help. A large number of Peaks Islanders volunteer for cleanups and brush clearing." While the ferry does require planning, it has its advantages. "The boat provides a source of social engagement—you see and even meet people there. It's not like the mainland, where you don't necessarily even know your neighbors."

It seems that Peaks has remade its community, one that provides a powerful and emotional connection for its new residents, even as it loses its old ones.

Great Diamond Island

As the American deepwater port closest to Europe that doesn't freeze over, Portland is significant historically, and a number of former forts and batteries surround the harbor. On Great Diamond Island, Fort McKinley was built to defend the harbor during the Spanish-American War. More than a thousand soldiers were housed there until the facilities were retired after 1945. The island definitely has a sense of "sides"—inevitably, in fact, if only because the Army had built a fence across the island, physically separating the two halves. The fence was incorporated into development plans, and the island has ended up cut in half physically and in every other way.

The largest percentage population increase on the islands between the 1990 and 2000 censuses came on Great Diamond, which has no school, no Post Office, and a store only in summer. In 1975, only one family was living there year-round. Twenty people were there on census day in 1990, and, because of the development of Fort McKinley, seventy-seven in 2000. (It's more like 140 at this writing.) But some who moved to the island intending to stay year-round have gone ashore after a single winter. It may be only twenty minutes to Portland by boat, but it's still an island.

In summer, there are about five hundred people on the island, all told.

In the late 1980s, a developer had great intentions for the old fort, with plans to create Diamond Cove, a gated, resort-like community with five hundred upscale residences. Understandably, the forty or so year-rounders and summer people on the "public" southern end of the island were alarmed by the scale of development being proposed for their quiet little island. But the project was to be separated from the rest of the island by the fence and a closed gate, and covenants prohibited vehicles within the development.

Although the first grandiose endeavor went belly-up, the Diamond Cove project came to life on a more modest scale. With 121 units possible, it is still very significant—especially when compared to what previously had been on the island. The lovely old brick military buildings have been restored, and other homes have been built, creating a whole new community with a seasonal store and restaurant.

Architect Scott Teas and his wife, Mary Beth, first visited Casco Bay's Great Diamond Island when he was asked to work on the development project. It was a beautiful Saturday, and it happened to be their anniversary. While he was measuring the old Army quartermaster's supply store, Mary Beth wandered around the elegant buildings that had been abandoned after World War II. The developer suggested that Scott might like to take a building as payment for his work. "That was all it took!" says Mary Beth. Working weekends and summers and whenever else they could, they did most of the restoration of their house, which had always been the military doctor's residence. Four years later, in 1998, they moved onto the island. "Portland seems very far away," says Mary Beth. "It took me forever to remember that it wasn't a long-distance call to phone over there."

The island has been in the news a great deal, with the subject under scrutiny nearly always the same: golf carts. "I was hoping you wouldn't ask me about golf carts," said Mary Beth. But golf carts have caused tremendous friction both between the two sides of the island and perhaps within each community. Everyone wants to protect the island, but the various factions have differing ideas of what needs protecting and how to make it happen.

By the late 1990s, many people on both sides of the island were using golf carts to get around. Between the two communities, there were perhaps a hundred golf carts. The gate restriction had never been enforced. "No one thought anyone cared," says Mary Beth. People on both sides had taken pains to include each other in community events, such as the Fourth of July celebration and potluck dinners, and the island was beginning to feel like a single community.

A handful of people on the public side thought there should be no golf carts; everyone should walk. Sometimes teenagers loaded up carts with friends and rode around and around, which anyone would find annoying. And the Maine courts had decided golf carts were "vehicles," so, said the complainers, Diamond Cove residents shouldn't have them at all. Although there were attempts at negotiation, eighteen people from the public side filed a lawsuit against the city for not enforcing the development's covenants. Only two of the plaintiffs were year-round islanders. "Ninety-five percent of the island was heartbroken," says Mary Beth. "We had come so far toward being one island." Friendships disappeared.

Betsy Weber and her husband, Ted, grew up on Cousins Island and bought property on Great Diamond in 1972. In the early 1990s, they were involved in an attempt at secession after Long Island made its escape from Portland. "It didn't come to pass, but it went on for four years, and some very positive things came out of it," she says. The city gave Great Diamond some real attention: decent equipment for their fire department, good training for the firefighters and emergency responders, and finally, the establishment of the full-time city/island liaison position now held by Tom Fortier (about whom, more below). She's pleased that the old fort has been developed. "It was derelict for many, many years. This is a good example of recycling." But the latest revaluation—with island property values increasing two or three times and even more—has upset people once again. And still the golf-cart business hangs on.

"This never was a walking island," says Betsy. There was a truck on the island when she arrived in 1972; back in 1920, there was even a trolley. The golf carts serve well to help people get from house to pier or from one part of the island to another.

"Should we control traffic and the number of vehicles? Yes. But neighbor to neighbor," she says, not by lawsuits and interventions. "It's not right for me or anyone to say, 'You can't use the roads.'" She gives as an example that there's very little space at either pier. "You should drop your stuff and go home, don't block the pier. But to legislate who can have what, when, is not right." People must accept change. "I still want dirt roads," Betsy says, but she understands that people who've bought houses lately—at high prices—expect smooth roadways. Still, she says, she has an issue with people who, now that they're here, want to change the way things are. And she'd like to be able to drive up to Diamond Cove to the store or the restaurant if she wanted to, but the gate is now closed.

Diamond Cove is an odd community, because everyone arrived as a newcomer at about the same time. There were no traditions. It has been described as dysfunctional, with an ineffective board overseeing the planned unit development's infrastructure needs of water treatment, open space, common buildings, grounds and road maintenance, and so forth, and many people object to any decisions they make. The work itself, of course, is done by people who commute onto the island and have no stake in it. Some in the development are starting to complain to the city about lack of services—but, says Tom Fortier, that was the deal in the first place.

The public side of Great Diamond hasn't changed much over the years—nor does anyone want it to—but it seems to get tangled up in the mess on the Diamond Cove side more often than many of its residents would like. But with fights about trees being in someone's view, and then the trees being felled illegally, and various suits and disagreements with the developers, some say Diamond Cove has always been a contentious place. It is still beautiful, though.

Little Diamond Island

Little Diamond, attached to Great Diamond by a sandbar except at high tide, until not too long ago had one family year-round and many summer people. It is changing now from strictly a summer island to one with a three-season population. A trio of couples— including Mark Tierney and his wife—is on the eighty-acre island nine months a year. Mark is a relative newcomer to the island, having summered there only since 1979. He and his wife built their primary residence on the island in 1997–98, and they have spent nine months of each year on the island since then.

Seventy percent of the property owners on Little Diamond are from Maine, and the majority of those own houses in Portland or Cape Elizabeth. The Tierneys' other abode is in Bethel, in western Maine.

Total year-round living isn't feasible in most of the residences. There are no roads, so there can be no snow removal. The majority of the fifty-two houses have water only half the year. When the island is inhabited, the city of Portland does provide weekly trash pickup using a small dump truck that crosses the sandbar from Great Diamond. There's a golf-cart–based fire engine for the volunteer firemen. Emergency response time from the city fireboat that serves as off-island transport in medical emergencies is good.

Most of the houses on Little Diamond are old, unwinterized, and of normal scale, not huge and ostentatious. A new one is built every couple of years, but zoning has pro-hibited the construction of mega-mansions on most of the island. Most lots are only a quarter of an acre, so the setback requirements preclude a large footprint. In addition, the height of any new structure is limited to twenty-seven feet. Five contiguous lots were recently bought in order to protect them from any building. The group that raised the money for that project is hoping to buy up as much as possible of the remaining land.

The major problem facing the island is one shared by all the Portland islands, but perhaps not to quite the same degree as on Little Diamond: taxation. Actually, Little Diamond's issue is assessment, more than taxation. According to Mark, the tripled taxes of 1991 were acceptable to the landowners of Little Diamond because they were based on actual fair-market-value valuations, and they accept their responsibility to pay on that basis. But the proposed new assessments, with Little Diamond having the great-est increase of any of the islands, he says are not reasonable. Sales on the island and on next-door Great Diamond don't support the values that have been assigned to Little Diamond properties. At this writing, the city has not been willing to reconsider them. "It's as if they're saying, 'You people are wealthy, you can afford to pay,'" says Mark.

By a forty-seven-to-three vote, the island's property owners have agreed to fund a class-action suit against Portland if it's necessary. "We just want a fair valuation based on current market sales," he says. "We assume we're going to pay increased taxes."

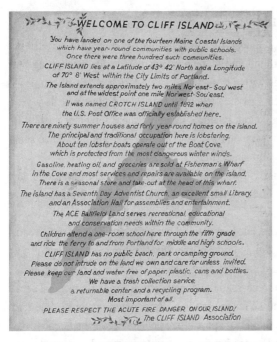

Sign at ferry dock on Cliff Island

Down the Bay on Cliff Island

Of all the Casco Bay islands, Cliff is the farthest from Portland and, with eighty-seven residents as of the 2000 census, has the smallest winter population. It remains largely a fishing community, and even its summer community seems more like the winter one than is the case on many islands. "They're high-end people, but they're real down-to-earth," says Bob Howard. "The houses aren't big enough, for one thing. It wouldn't attract someone who wants the real high-end lifestyle. The guy next door could be the head of some big corporation and you wouldn't know it." Bob, like others with summer roots, moved to the island full-time in the 1970s. "A lot would like to have done that but never figured out a way, and a few who tried have moved off since." The Howards and a number of other families have been coming to Cliff since before 1900, but nowadays people can't stay as long as they used to, and there are more and more weekly rentals. Some of the renters come year after year, though, and have developed strong attachments to Cliff Island.

Bob, a builder, finds plenty of work for himself and one or two helpers. Another carpenter works alone, and the third contractor on the island has five or six employees in winter and a dozen in summer, mostly summer kids. "All the summer kids here seem to want to work. It's not like the Hamptons," Bob says.

While fewer than a dozen people work full-time in carpentry and construction, there are ten or twelve lobsterboats and sixteen or seventeen islanders involved in lobstering. A boat comes out six days a week to buy lobster and sell bait.

It's not an easy place for a woman to find a job. Three or four are now lobstering, including one with her own boat. Some who were really hooked on the island worked as carpenters, and there are the teacher and teacher's aide positions—islander Judy MacVane, the current teacher, is the wife of longtime teacher Earl MacVane, who is now fishing. In summer, there's house painting. "Most women seem to go off and not come back," says Bob. But that's true of many youngsters of both sexes. It's often hard on teenagers on any of the Casco Bay islands, between the boat ride and having friends off-island. The grass is always greener somewhere else, no matter where teenagers call home. The majority of Cliff Island young people go off to college and a lot don't come back. Occasionally one moves off and comes back again, like Gordon Griffin's son James, who went to Maine Maritime Academy and shipped out with the merchant marine for a time, but when he married and settled down to have a family, he moved back and has gone lobstering. A few commute to shore; they cross paths on the bay with a few stern-men who come from town to work—along with plumbers and electricians and the like, when they're needed.

A few problems faced on all the islands may be slower getting to Cliff than to some of the others, but they've come. "It's slowly becoming a summer resort just like everywhere else, and kids can't afford to buy," says Gordon, who says he's been on the island "a while." He was born and raised there, as was his father. His grandfather came as a youngster from Vinalhaven. Gordon himself served twenty-three years in the U.S. Navy and then returned to Cliff to fish. He had one of the first fiberglass boats around—when he first got her, she had a 455 hp Olds engine converted for marine use. "She'd go like a scairt rat." She's on her third engine now. "I'm getting too old to be going, anyway," he says. He used to help his father, who was one of three boatbuilders then on the island. "If I was younger, I'd like to build a boat now. Building 'em now is a dying art." (He's speaking of wooden boats, of course.)

On Cliff Island, the effort to attract newcomers to live on the island year-round was not conscious so much as fortunate happenstance. One year, it looked as if there would be just one child in the school. "We tend to be in the news on and off," says Bob Howard. *Yankee* magazine did an article about the island, and then Harry Reasoner ran a piece on television. Several families came as a result of that coverage.

One woman moved to Cliff with her husband and children after the *Yankee* article appeared. Her husband moved off again, but, says her friend Stephanie Howard-O'Reilly, "for a long time it was perfect for her. She did lots of odd jobs—cleaned, shoveled, mowed, painted, took care of old people—you name it, she did it. You have to be willing to push and push and yet not disrupt things too much—it's hard to become an islander. It let her be there for her kids."

It has been said that Cliff is the snobby island. "We just don't associate with those other islands," says Bob. "I don't know why, we just don't know them that well. The kids know each other, but they get over it! We see people on the boat every week or two, probably only one way—and we usually have our nose in a book and don't pay much attention to anybody."

Cliff always felt removed from the city it was part of, but the situation has improved lately. "Being part of Portland used to be a pain in the ass," says Bob. "When the [Long Island] secession came around, they started to kiss our feet. They pull a lot of money out of here. They put more money in roads and to keep the school going now than they used to, and they listen to us more. There's roadside trash pickup every week now, and recycling—of course, part of that would have happened with the times. No one was thrilled with throwing trash off the wharf." The school is run by the city, but the islanders have some input hiring the teacher. "It's been a lot easier than doing it ourselves. Things can get real nasty with such a small population. There are so few adults to do everything. This way, you can bitch at the city, someone far away."

Stephanie Howard-O'Reilly grew up on Cliff Island and went to school there through fifth grade. Her teacher, like most people on the island at the time, was a cousin of hers. He used to lobster part-time, and now he's fishing full-time. But she admires Earl MacVane's teaching: "To him, everyone's smart. Earl was able to find something that each kid was good at." She goes on: "I had the best oceanography as a kid—everything was hands-on. We made our own undersea water-viewers, and we had the opportunity to touch everything. We'd find tracks and do plaster-of-paris castings—all things I remember to this day. On the mainland, people laugh at me because I know odd information about oceans, trees, or animals that they don't know."

When she was twenty-eight, Stephanie returned to Cliff. She says that after a bad marriage, she went back to the island to teach because it was safe. She believed she knew where the dangers were, anyway—but in fact she didn't know. "I have a vision of the island when I was young, of this perfect little world," she says now, "but the last time I lived there, it became horrid." It wasn't the fault of the school. She had eight students, and later six. She didn't need a grade book, as she knew just exactly where each child stood, what they could do and what not. "A kid might be doing second-grade English and eighth-grade math." She had a second-grader doing fourth-grade work with his older sister. "He's going to have trouble when he gets to town—nobody will keep up with him." Fifty percent of the students were special-needs–qualified. Stephanie doesn't know if this is happenstance or not. She says the situation was the same when she was a student there. "Perhaps parents with kids who have troubles are attracted to the small school, where you go at your own speed."

But as a teacher, it was hard for her to keep perspective—and she says it was hard for the community, too. Decisions she made at school affected the island, but she couldn't make them with the objectivity that someone with fewer connections might be able to do. And she was still young, relatively. "Your mother, grandfather, aunt all have opinions, you see the kids 24/7, their parents talk to your parents, and suddenly you're a child again." She couldn't handle it, so she moved off again—before the love she still had for the island turned to hatred. Other teachers have returned to the island of their youth to teach with greater success. They were older when they came back—maybe that's the difference.

Portland's Island Administrator

Tom Fortier is the island/neighborhood administrator for the city of Portland, in the city manager's office. He acts as the liaison between the Portland islands and the city government and has been in the position for five years now. The existence of his position in Portland City Hall is a direct outgrowth of the secession movement of a few years earlier. He says people always offer him condolences, assuming his job is tough, with all its meetings and negotiations and mediations between the islands and the city. Island residents are seen as a volatile group, and indeed, he was surprised to find that public meetings on the islands are easier than those on the mainland. "I've found the islanders to be very communicative and respectful, just passionate about their issues," he says. "It's a cool job, and I enjoy it immensely. People just want to be heard and respected." He's glad that he came to the job well after the secession movement, for he brought no emotional baggage with him, and he feels he can see matters objectively. When he first took his position, there still was a bit of rancor between some people on Long Island and the city, but it has settled down now. More recently, the city worked out a firefighting mutual-assistance plan with Long Island. "I'm not sure that would have happened a few years ago." The mood has changed.

Island
Churches

every island has at least one church. People may never go to it except for weddings and funerals, but it's important to them. In summer, ministers come to serve some churches that have no regular services the rest of the year. There are churches that were established specifically for the summer people, like the Episcopal church on Islesboro, and at least one originally primarily for their servants, the Catholic church, again on Islesboro, which also only holds services in July and August. North Haven's winter church, nominally Baptist but served presently by a Congregational minister, cedes its building to the Episcopalians in summer and moves over to Pulpit Harbor. This sharing arrangement was agreed upon when the church was built. On other islands, church has been held twice each Sunday—once in the morning for the summer people and again in the evening for the islanders, using different hymnals. "You have one that's got the good hymns in it," says the Reverend Ted Hoskins, whose personal and pastoral ties to the islands are deep and of long duration, "and another that has the straight ones the summer people like. 'This new hymnal is very nice,' they'll say very politely, 'but we like our hymns out of the other one.'"

On the islands, says Ted, "faith isn't something you parade around and shout about, but I have no question about the islanders' faith. It's behind the realities. You don't stay on the water without some connection. It's always awesome, whether it's dead quiet or roaring over top of you."

Ted followed in his father's tracks as summer minister on Isle au Haut. For many years, his job from September through June was as the pastor of a fifteen-hundred-member church in Connecticut, and for two months each summer he lived on Isle au Haut. "Ministers have long vacations and short salaries. For a change of pace, you look for a place with a parsonage where you can store your kids for the summer. You go on with the ministry—most of us are addicted to it anyway, or we wouldn't be doing it, so we keep right on."

In 1995, he joined the full-time staff of the Sea Coast Mission as pastor to the outer islands (more usually referred to as "the boat minister"), working from the *Sunbeam*. "God's Tugboat," as some islanders call the vessel, makes regular trips around to Frenchboro, Swans, Isle au Haut, and Matinicus. The boat minister regularly visits Monhegan, too, with or without the *Sunbeam*. "The preaching is not nearly as important as the presence," says Ted. "That's the significant gift we give.

"I would knock on any door. If there was smoke coming out the chimney, I put a knuckle on the door. It's nothing to do with going to any service, nothing at all. They have the same problems as anywhere else—alcohol, drugs, truancy, divorce—we're born, we die, and we do a lot of stuff in between. I know pretty much everyone on any of the islands we visited. It's a privilege of being a pastor, to know people. You come in and sit down and have a cup of coffee or a shot of Scotch or whatever's going. Most people are delighted that I didn't talk about religion—I'd do that if they wanted, but they had to initiate it."

Paul Joy, Swans Island High-Liner and Pastor

Paul Joy's boat is named *Sparrow*. She already had that name when he bought her in Brooklin (Maine). It wasn't until he drove by the church there after buying the boat that he remembered about the friendly little sparrow that landed on his shoulder when he first came to Brooklin twenty years earlier, or about the scripture that was handed to him as he started Bible School at that church. "Fear not therefore: ye are of more value than many sparrows." He thought then of the hymn with the refrain:

> *I sing because I'm happy,*
> *I sing because I'm free,*
> *For His eye is on the sparrow,*
> *And I know He watches me.*

"Here I was bringing a sparrow from Brooklin. I had no idea way back then that the sparrow would be such a part of my life. It was the kind of thing that brings goosebumps to your arms, like the good Lord saying, 'I saw you then, and I see you now.'"

Paul was born in Bangor, spent most of his growing-up years in Brewer, and went with his mother to Portsmouth during his sophomore year in high school. "It was my mother's worst time of her life, but it was good for me, for I met my wife-to-be there, at Sunday School. It was love at first sight. We went to Bible School together and then got married."

He had always wanted to be pastor of a little church where he could wear a flannel shirt and boots, and he used to drive around looking for one, maybe an abandoned

church where he could start his
own congregation. It was difficult
to get hired—no independent
church wanted a pastor with five
children. He would have been willing to work, too—they couldn't
starve to death—but he couldn't
find a church. He had to learn a
trade. He went to Washington
County to learn diesel mechanics
and commercial fishing, and he
worked on fish draggers out of
Portland. "You made a pile of

Paul Joy (COURTESY OF DONNA WIEGLE)

money in a hurry," he says, but it was very dangerous work. "Most of the people I fished
with are no longer alive—they went overboard or had some other accident."

Through all this time, he never said no when anyone asked him to preach. In
1982, a fellow from the Church of God approached him and asked if Paul would come
help him, splitting his own salary of $300 a week. "You don't do these things for money,
anyway," says Paul, so he agreed, and he ended up on Swans Island. "I saw the place
and fell in love with it, and here I am," he says. "I'm a hermit at heart. I don't get up in
front of people because I want to, it's because I have something to share.

"The Church of God on the island at the time was almost like a mission church.
They couldn't afford a full-time minister and benefits and all that—most times in a mission church, you work alongside the people anyway."

Paul and his family did leave the island for two years, when his oldest children
reached high-school age. He and his wife didn't like the idea of boarding the youngsters
off the island, nor of breaking up the family just so the older ones could play sports or
be involved in other school activities. While they were away, there were two pastors in
his place on Swans, a year each. The second one built a brand-new church and then
immediately announced he was leaving. The overseer asked Paul if he would consider
going back. They didn't want to lose momentum with the new building, and nobody else
would want to move out to the island in the middle of winter. "All my family wanted to
go except my oldest daughter, who was about eighteen then. She said, 'I'll go back for
the rest of you,' and just about six months later she was married to a fisherman on
Swans and has been happy here ever since. She's been blessed with two little boys."

Paul doesn't admit it, but others say he's a very successful fisherman. His whole
family fishes, too, although one boy works primarily as a carpenter and only fishes on
the side. All ten of his children live on the island—four of them are married and three

have children of their own. The three girls married fishermen, islanders all. "That makes me related to almost everyone on the island." The youngest at this writing is five, and she goes out with her mother. The next few have student licenses and fish fifty or more traps apiece or stern for their elder brothers. The older ones are also fishermen, including the oldest girl, who has a little boat of her own, *Madam Blueberry*, and her husband lobsters too.

While they were ashore, they got to know a grandmotherly Baptist woman with whom the high-school-age children can stay overnight when they have basketball or other reasons to stay late at school. "It hasn't been easy, but it's been good," says Paul. "They learn a little bit of independence, too."

For the past fifteen years, Paul has also delivered the mail from Swans to Frenchboro four days a week. He picks up the mail and packages from the carrier on the wharf, and his sternman runs home. "I give him an hour lunch break and then when I get back, we're ready to go at it again.

"It's a service to Frenchboro, and not everyone wants that job. It's not always fun, though if it's real bad out, you don't go." In the fall, as the days get shorter and the lobstermen are doing well, taking an hour or so off in the middle of the day might be an inconvenience, "but we work around it. It's one of those things you do to help people out, and it helps me, too. Unless you have other skills, and I don't—I'm a punisher of lumber, when it comes to carpentry—there's not much to do in the winter."

The church has grown, but Paul doesn't like to say how many members it has. "I think sometimes other churches get discouraged," he says, "because they don't have a lot of children. But if you have ten of your own children, you attract children, and they come to Sunday School. All the children, now they're having children of their own—anybody with children wants to put them in a place with other children. It takes almost a lifetime to build a church on a small island," Paul says. He's been at it for more than twenty years. Just looking at the names of lobsterboats around Swans Island, it's obvious that there's an active church of a certain flavor: *Atonement*, *Born Again*, *Daily Bread*, *Genesis*, *Never Alone*, *Praise the Lord II*, and *The Fifth Day*, just to name a few. (On the fifth day, God created the sea creatures.)

Swans is unusual among the Maine islands in that it has four active churches. Even the much larger island of Vinalhaven only has two. "It was said for years that if you're going to live out here, you've got to realize it's a faith community," says Paul. "The pastors on Swans are great. We had a baptism with all four churches—Baptist, Methodist, Advent, and Church of God." Some of the baptism candidates were from other churches and some were from the Church of God. It didn't matter. "We're all family. They might call themselves something else, but we're all family, not just the family of God, but literally, too."

Matinicus church

Matinicus Summer Ministers

Usually two or more ministers volunteer to spend time during July and August on Matinicus, which otherwise depends on the boat minister, with or without the *Sunbeam*. Says Eva Murray, "It is not just about Sunday church services, either—these ministers don't have much to do except socialize, but sometimes they become a really neat part of the summer scene." Some hit it off well on the island and come back again, while others "become the subject of re-telling of their mishaps for years."

Denomination isn't important. "Any mainstream Protestant, moderate-to-liberal will do. No fire and brimstone," says Eva, who finds it ironic that somehow it has fallen to her to make arrangements for and talk with prospective summer ministers. "I never thought I'd be a 'church lady'!"

The church on the island is more like a community hall, Eva says. "A nice thing in the summer, and a place for a Christmas party, occasional weddings, and funerals. An average summer congregation contains an assortment of people from various Protestant churches on the mainland, and also might include a Catholic priest (Father Tom, whose family has a summer place on the island), a Quaker [Eva's husband, Paul], people who say they just like the singing, carpenters from a messianic community called the Twelve Tribes, kids who are just curious about what's going on, and those whose religion cannot be explained in twenty-five words or less (such as myself). It is usually a very small group and seldom includes the lobstermen unless there is something special going on."

Vinalhaven's Union Church

For six years now, Vinalhaven's Union Church has had a female pastor, Reverend Michelle Wiley. If her gender weren't enough, she was divorced when she came to the island, and subsequently she dated and ultimately married an islander. The church is independent and nondenominational, and its members are adamant that it remain that way, but historically it has been a relatively conservative organization, theologically and in other ways too. People in a free-spirited independent fishing community went to church to hear about good and evil, right and wrong, no questions asked, Reverend Michelle says, but her own approach is more open. "Atonement and salvation are God's realm," she believes. "We're here to nurture, take care of one another, provide opportunities for discussion, enlightenment, and prayer so the spirit can grow. My job as pastor is not writing a rule book about who gets saved, or how many hoops to jump through." Her conviction that all of God's creation is good sometimes rubs up against the more rigid black-and-white beliefs of some in the congregation.

That she was hired at all was a huge risk for the church. "It was in part driven by people who've moved onto the island," she says. She was first hired for eight months, and then for two years more, and only after that time was she voted "called and settled," which means that as long as everyone is content, she stays, with no more regularly scheduled votes.

It's ironic that there'd be any question about having a female pastor in a community where in the past not only church but business was often left to the women while the men were at sea. "We give authority to men," Michelle remarks, "but it's the women who did the work to get things done because the men were gone. It's still that way on Vinalhaven—the vast majority of businesses are owned or managed by women, and the men are at work on the water.

"It's comical," she says, "that educated people from Indiana or somewhere lament that the fishermen aren't in church—but they never have been. To see the men, you've got to be willing to go to the waterfront, go to a party, and not be afraid to open a beer."

Michelle's last congregation was in Camden, where people would consider a suggestion and say, "Oh, that's a neat idea, let's try it for six months." That's rarely how it goes on Vinalhaven. If the bean suppers haven't been drawing as many people as they'd like, perhaps they could try serving something different? Gasp! No, we couldn't! They've always been bean suppers!

Some of the older church members remember when the *Sunbeam* used to come in, bringing a doctor, but now they feel they've been forgotten by the Sea Coast Mission. Times have changed—there's a full medical center on the island now, doctor and all. But the Sea Coast Mission pays thirty percent of Michelle's salary. She feels her work includes the community at large, not just Union Church and its members, in part because of the support of the Mission. Part of what she is enjoying in her ministry is helping the church to redefine its relationship with the Mission, and to see her—and the members, if they could just believe in themselves—as the outreach that the boat used to be. "I'm hoping that if I say it to them enough, they'll believe it," she says.

The congregation has stayed about the same size during the past forty years, averaging fifty or so each Sunday in the off-season, nearly twice that in summer. It is, as it has always been, mostly women, and few of the churchgoers are young. Sunday School always seems to have participants, but not nearly as many as in earlier years—before soccer, television, and rowing, before both parents worked six days a week, before stores were allowed to be open on Sunday. Michelle wonders whether they could try something other than Sunday School to offer support to the young, to nurture and help them see that the church cares about people, but again, tradition is strong. At least for the time being, Sunday School will remain as it has always been.

"Being a pastor on an island is similar to the island itself, surrounded by the wind and waves," she says. There's a constant ebb and flow, and sometimes the storms are fierce and create isolation. "Yet, with every sense of loss, there's community, too." One such storm was her hiring in the first place; another arose over the war in Iraq, a huge issue on Vinalhaven. Before the invasion, the island was seriously split, with some believing that to attack Iraq was unconscionable, while others felt it was necessary and right. Michelle and Bob Candage, the elder of the Community of Christ Church, tried to play referee—"We have to live with one another," they tried to say to both sides. "Pray for the soldiers, pray for wisdom." As in the rest of the country, emotions were high and communication between the well-defined sides was lacking.

Vinalhaven may be populous enough that distinctions between categories of people can remain stronger than on the smaller islands, where everyone has to associate with everyone else on a regular basis. There are people on the island who keep their social beliefs to themselves, who might come up to Michelle in the coffee shop and commend her for speaking out on a particular issue but who wouldn't go to church. Maybe a bean supper, that's it. Some who write checks for a particular cause don't want fanfare. "We're from the island—we need to be of the island—please don't let people know we think this way," they say.

Friendships are seen as alignments. Someone in Michelle's position has to be careful with whom she is seen in public. "I'm always pastor, even if I'm out at a restaurant. On the mainland, you're anonymous. It was very hard at first," she says. Over the last hundred years, Vinalhaven has had a huge run of pastors, their tenures averaging just two years. The short pastorates have been due, partly, to those community dynamics, as well as to all the factors that may make it difficult for any newcomer on an island. It's simply more intense for a minister, who is supposed to look and act the part at all times. It's hard for church members to trust a pastor who in all likelihood will be gone soon—Michelle still senses some of that reluctance, even after six years. "They're not sure I'm going to ride this out with them."

But she is. "I have a sense of hopefulness, of commitment. I'm reexamining my sense of call, of what kind of minister I'm being called to be, what gift I might have to share. I meditate on it, and I sense that my work here is not completed. Sunday-morning attendance may not be growing as the church would like, but I've been able to help people in the community to grow and thrive, not necessarily just church members. It's good for me here."

Helping Hands from Off-Island

traditionally, the islands have been populated with "I'll take care of it myself" types, and by and large, they've done just that. But there have long been off-island organizations whose goal was to help them, and there still are today.

A Trip on the *Sunbeam*

Since 1905, the Maine Sea Coast Mission has been active—starting with a single missionary sailing a small sloop along the coast with the goal of providing Christian leadership to fishing villages and lighthouses. In the first half of the twentieth century, even the most remote lighthouses were manned, and, says former boat minister Ted Hoskins, "some of those rocks are pretty small." The Mission—headquartered in Bar Harbor—has grown to a large organization with twenty-eight employees, countless volunteers in several programs along the coast, and an annual budget of nearly $2.5 million. "The Mission is nonsectarian, absolutely," says Ted. "If God cared about that crap, I wouldn't have anything to do with Her."

The present boat, the *Sunbeam V*, was launched in 1995. While the official blurbs emphasize the formal Christian goals of the Mission, many of the projects of the Mission are not specifically religious in nature, including much of the boat's endeavor. "I feel we're doing God's work," says Executive Director Gary DeLong, even though they collaborate with many people and organizations that are secular in their approach.

The *Sunbeam*'s work is built on respect for humankind in general and the island communities she visits in particular. The Mission's major projects are on the islands and way downeast in coastal Washington County. Of the communities they serve, Gary says, "We've been with them long enough that the needs emerge from them."

It can be noted that there is presently not one member of their constituency on the Mission's board of directors—some feel that this is anachronistic if not downright condescending. The board members serve, of course, because they believe in the program, and their role is more about making sure the resources are available and that the organization is being managed responsibly than in establishing program policy. Program oversight is left to staff, with an increasing role played by active subcommittees that include people from the programs' communities.

The Mission has recently obtained a grant from the Maine Health Access Foundation to consider how best they can help to improve health care on the islands. Eight islands are involved—Frenchboro, Isle au Haut, Islesboro, Matinicus, Monhegan, North Haven, Swans, and Vinalhaven—along with the providers ashore who have worked with the Mission on the telemedicine project. "It's exciting to think 'outside the box' about how to improve the health of islanders," says Gary. One of the ideas that has come up, in addition to increased mental-health services, is dental care, or at least a traveling hygienist. Gary laughs. "Every time I think I have a really good idea, I go back and see that one of my predecessors has already done it!" In years gone by, the *Sunbeam* used to take a dentist out to the islands. Gary doesn't actually know why the practice stopped, but maybe the time has come to do it again.

Going along for the ride on the *Sunbeam* trip just before Easter 2004, I saw nothing but good.

"Most people are glad to see the boat come, even if they have no relationship with the minister," says Vance Bunker from Matinicus, the *Sunbeam*'s last stop on my trip. "We all know Dave and Betty." Dave Allen has been the captain for more than thirty years. His wife, Betty, has worked as steward for nearly all of that time. (She's of island stock herself; her grandparents grew up on Frenchboro and her father on Vinalhaven.) Pastor Rob Benson and his wife Cristy are the newcomers on the boat; Rob became the pastor to the outer islands in 2002. The engineer, Mike Johnson, and the nurse, Sharon Daley, have both been aboard a couple of years longer.

It's only in the last decade and a half that Betty has become an art teacher, too, and children and adults alike look forward to seeing what she has found for them to work on. It started accidentally—Matinicus school kids watched her decorating a cake and wanted to give it a try, so on her next trip, Betty brought cupcakes for them to decorate. Then she worked with knitting, crocheting, weaving, and when she started taking painting lessons herself—also happenstance—she began teaching that, too. "I never set out to do anything, it all just evolved." Two of Betty's own paintings are posted on the boat's galley wall, over the jars of doughnuts and muffins. One is an oil

Dave Allen

portrait of herself at age four or five and the other is a lighthouse painted in water-color on a plastic sheet, a technique she shared with some of the women of Isle au Haut. Her work may not be headed to the Museum of Contemporary Art in Manhattan, but she enjoys it, and so do the visitors to the *Sunbeam*.

At Frenchboro, our first stop, teacher Lorna Stuart and her five students—the entire school population of Frenchboro that year—came aboard and sat around a table in the salon of the *Sunbeam*. Betty brought out plastic palettes, tempera paints, and a big jar of paintbrushes and offered each painter a choice between little wooden skiffs and flowers in flowerpots made of pine and a dowel. Lorna, eighth-grader Joey and his sec-ond-grade sister Jessie, Lance, and the twins Dylan and Cody all painted industriously while chattering with each other and the crew of the *Sunbeam*. I was duly introduced, and the older children, with enthusiasm and more politeness than I expect of children today, told me of their special projects in school:

Betty Allen

Joey had videotaped a documentary about life on Frenchboro, and Lance had written an island myth, "Why the Tide Goes In and Out." Both children offered to send me copies of their work, which I felt honored to accept.

Rob Benson had made some posters announcing the upcoming Easter service and he left the boat to walk around and put up his notices.

This was Lorna's third year teaching in Frenchboro, which had had eleven teachers in the fifteen years before she took the job. They were looking for someone who would stay. Lorna and her husband, Rob, both ordained ministers with extensive experience in education and other fields, had recently come to the island in quasi-retirement, and the match was made. They also run an Internet business—disposing of unneeded books donated to university libraries—and they are building a magnificent house.

Lorna's husband drove me around, providing a guided tour of the island's paved roads—the whole mile-and-a-half. We saw the harbor and the former store and the Lunt lobster company; then we went past the affordable-housing project and up to the old cemetery, past another Internet business and a B&B, up by the school, the library/museum/gift shop, past the town building and ball field, and back down by them again.

Along the way, he pointed out the riprap project alongside the road across the end of the harbor—the road had been eroding, and though the town got a grant to do the work, no bids were received from the mainland. No contractor was willing to take the chance of tying up equipment should the three-times-a-week ferry be canceled (as it sometimes is). Earlier, a fellow had come in to do some blasting and ended up having to leave his equipment on the island for a week before he could get it back to shore. The town had to do the riprap itself, using materials available on the island. Rock is one thing there is plenty of on Frenchboro. The island has steeper terrain than many, and its harbor is spectacular from above, but the trees have such shallow root systems that if one blows down, its neighbors are likely to fall too.

After the students walked back up the hill to their normal classroom, Cristy painted one of the tulips, taking good suggestions from Betty about how to liven it up.

Wearing a wrist support, Linda Lunt came by to talk with Sharon, the nurse who runs the telemedicine program on the *Sunbeam*. Sharon's office is in a small room ahead of the galley. It's too small, really—although the layout of the boat was designed by Dave and Betty, no one had thought of telemedicine in 1995. This little space was originally designed to allow the pastor to meet quietly with one or two people. Many other features of the *Sunbeam* are laid out ideally, like the snack center, which is at the outer end of the galley counter and across the passageway; people can grab sodas, nuts, fruit, or any of the desserts and muffins that Betty always has available.

With her telemedicine offerings, the *Sunbeam* provides a tremendously useful service, one that saves islanders vast amounts of money and time because Telemedicine

Cristy Benson and Eric Murray's chemistry lesson

allows conferences by two-way television between the boat and a doctor's office ashore. There are five medical facilities associated with the program—four on the mainland and one on Vinalhaven—offering a wide variety of services, from simple blood draws for testing to wound care to pediatric assessment and geriatrics. Sharon faxes histories and vital-signs data to the appropriate provider. She also has instruments that allow her to show the practitioner extraordinarily detailed, close-up pictures of a patient's inner ear, for instance, or their eyeball, or a wound. The sounds from her stethoscope can be amplified and shot across the airwaves to be interpreted. Doctor and patient can look one another in the face on the interactive TV screen as they talk; even mental-health counseling with providers ashore is possible on the *Sunbeam*. (I wondered if the physical distance between counselor and counselee would make the process more difficult, but Sharon says that in some cases the separation actually makes it easier.)

For residents of the outer islands, even the simplest of procedures ashore ends up being extremely expensive, time-consuming, and possibly anxiety-producing, as well as ferociously inconvenient, for they might have to stay overnight, or even several nights, just for a simple test or checkup. The Mission charges nothing for its contribution to the visits that islanders can make with their doctors, and it has negotiated low fees for lab work and other routine matters.

Sharon and the *Sunbeam* are also an official WIC site, providing nutritious foods, nutrition education and screening, and referrals to other services for low-income women, infants, and children. Just as regular medical attention can be difficult to get from an island, the federal WIC benefits are simplified by the participation of Sharon and God's Tugboat. "The numbers are small," Sharon says, "but important." At that time, there were twenty WIC clients on the islands.

Linda received some kind of good news through the television hookup from ashore and bounced out of the telemedicine office. "I don't have to be still anymore!" she announced gleefully. "I'm going home to not be still!" It's obvious that stillness doesn't come easily to Linda, a very enthusiastic person who acts as sternman for her husband.

The next stop was at Minturn, on Swans Island, which we reached just at lunchtime—always a good time on the *Sunbeam*. The bell rings, and people pile into the salon and fill their plates from the counter.

Because there are active, year-round churches on Swans Island, Rob has less of a pastoral role there than on the other islands where we stopped, though he's happy to talk with anyone. Sometimes, talking about the Red Sox is as important as religious subjects, anyway. On Swans, the *Sunbeam* provides medical services, but everywhere she goes, her people help to build formal or informal networks among the various islands. Earlier in the year, people from the Cranberries came over to Swans on the *Sunbeam* for a turkey-pie dinner and to talk about car ferries. Some on the Cranberries wish they had one—but some on Swans wish they instead had a mailboat like the one that serves the Cranberries. Fire protection, affordable housing, waterfront access, fishing regulations—these issues face all the islands, and sometimes the *Sunbeam* can facilitate islanders' sharing their experiences with each other.

"My job is a learning experience for me," Rob says. "Not because it's complex, but because it wouldn't have been right to come in and implement a lot of things. Change is gradual. It's not up to me—I'm an occasional part of these communities, and I don't have a dog in any fight. Families and communities change over time, and I can be patient with that. I see opportunities to gather resources, channel, create experiences where opportunities can arise." He cites the example of a Vinalhaven folk-music group going for Easter to the Cranberries, where people had expressed an interest in music but hadn't known how to implement it. "They're not the Kingston Trio, but they're pretty close," says Rob of the folk group. "You have to see a horizon to start aiming at it. A performance is fine, but a performance and jam session—the fallout is that people say, 'Hey, we can do that too!'"

Rob admits frustration with some of the situations he faces. As an example, he described (in entirely anonymous terms) a report he'd received of a woman who was being abused by her husband. Because she hadn't spoken with Rob herself, he couldn't act—but he did learn all he could about the resources available, and he knows that a couple of women from her island have spoken with her, to let her know she needn't tolerate this. When she's ready to act, he's ready to help her. And in the meantime, her husband has been warned by fellow islanders, so Rob feels that he may not dare manhandle his wife again. Or so he hopes.

(I was told by a Vinalhaven woman how it is that sometimes domestic violence seems to be more common on an island than on the mainland—as with so many island issues, it's simply because everyone knows everyone. If passersby see a well-bruised woman going into the medical center, they can surmise what happened. "Whenever anything happens, good or bad, you know the people," she told me, "so it feels bigger.")

Rob accepted his job in part because his wife and young son could accompany

The Sunbeam *grounded out at Matinicus*

him on the boat. At the time of my trip, Peter was two and would soon be joined by a baby brother. Having his family aboard lets Rob be part of their daily life, and Cristy is herself part of the *Sunbeam* presence. Her own background as a high-school math and science teacher was useful on this particular trip when we got to Matinicus, where Eva and Paul Murray are home-schooling their two children. Eva and Eric had come to a point in their chemistry studies—Eva was keeping ahead of Eric, but not by that much—where help from someone better-versed in the subject matter would be welcomed. So Cristy and Eric spent two hours deep in atomic configurations. Cristy also enjoys spending time with other young mothers on the islands. Each personal connection made, each friendship, is yet another piece of the web of support that the *Sunbeam* weaves.

Early on, Rob was surprised by the level of trust that he received, but the boat has been such an integral part of island life for so long that her credibility extended to him. I felt it myself. There have been some powerful and effective ministers in the past—most recently, Ted Hoskins—but undoubtedly the gentle continuity provided by Dave and Betty is key.

This was Cristy's last trip before the baby's arrival, but Rob says there are times when it's good not to have his family with him. It's easier for islanders to invite one person into their home than three or four. When he's alone, Rob can hang out in the evenings with a bunch of pot-smoking sternmen if that's how things happen. Much of his ministry on the islands is simply hanging out with people, just as much of the boat's service is simply giving people a place to visit and different folks with whom to visit.

Sharon had no appointments lined up ahead of time at Swans, but three women came aboard. One wanted her cholesterol checked, a second just came to keep the first one company and chatted with the *Sunbeam* group while she was waiting. The third was wearing ripped jeans covered with paint. "I didn't expect the boat to be here today, as you can tell. I was up on the roof and saw her coming in." When she emerged from Sharon's office, she scooted right back to work. The schedule showed two hours blocked off for patients—an hour with one provider and an hour with another—but there was no more business.

I went up to the pilothouse to talk with Dave, who takes his role as captain easily. "When Sharon says, 'Let's go,' we go," he said. "I always say I've been retired for thirty-some years. It's a wonderful job, calling all the islands your hometown. It's been a good job." He speaks of building the current *Sunbeam*. "Betty and I worked with John Gilbert of Boston, the architect, and with Washburn & Doughty, the builders. Curtis Blake, a member of the Mission board, called his neighbors, and the boat didn't cost the Mission a cent." The seventy-four-foot-long steel *Sunbeam* is built essentially the same as a western-rigged purse-seining fishing boat. Dave feels comfortable with that form, he says, because he used to fish. She's high in the bow and her pilothouse is forward, which gives good visibility, keeps her dry, and provides a lot of room below. He does wish, however, that they had put more power in her. A single-screw boat with only a 359-hp propulsion engine, she cruises at ten knots, but with her bow thruster, she's maneuverable going into the island piers and her home berth, in an inside corner of the marina at Northeast Harbor. She has two generators, putting out 50 and 30 kilowatts respectively. "The Coast Guard adds up everything on the boat that might use electric power and adds ten percent more, and that's how much you have to have," he explains. "She could run half a town."

She was reinforced to be able to break ice—during the previous winter, she had plenty of opportunity. Dave broke out Northeast Harbor a couple of times, as well as the channel at Isle au Haut, but once even the *Sunbeam* couldn't make it through York Narrows, on the approach to Swans Island. And she must tolerate sitting on her own bottom, because on every trip to Matinicus, she grounds out. She has a cage over her propeller to keep it from snagging lobster-trap lines. "You can't go around doing good while you cut off people's livelihood," says Dave. In the pilothouse is a photo of the propeller cage.

The *Sunbeam* has all the modern electronic equipment, including "The Cap'n," a computer navigation program that integrates with GPS and the autopilot and makes the trips from island to island far easier for the helmsman. An old stopwatch is mounted overhead—Dave says it's from the previous *Sunbeam* and was used for dead-reckoning navigation. "It's not used much anymore. Mike used it for blowing the horn in the fog, but now that's all automatic. Life's some simple compared to twenty years ago," he says. The *Sunbeam* has a satellite dish for television, too.

While keeping his eye on the sea and the instruments before him as the *Sunbeam* made her way to the next stop, he downloaded photographs from his digital camera onto his own laptop computer. He had a question about burning them onto a CD and asked Mike. "Me and computers," said Dave. "Every five minutes, I gotta call Mike to straighten out the computer."

The boat has two telemedicine trips scheduled each month, and she occasionally makes other trips in the winter—such as the one not long before my ride when they took a band out to Isle au Haut for a contra dance. (Mike mentioned that he hadn't really felt like going to a dance that night, but he felt it was part of his job. And he had a good time.) Another recent trip, an annual event now, took ashore the two home-schooled children and the three public-school students on Matinicus for a sports trip. They went swimming, rock climbing, and ice-skating, and played basketball. "I was pleased to be invited," said Rob. "It's good to interact with the kids as a person, not always as a minister."

The following weekend, the *Sunbeam* was going to several islands for Easter services. Later in the month, a farewell party on Matinicus was planned for Dr. Rick Donahue of Vinalhaven. He was leaving after serving as family physician to both islands for eight years, both by telemedicine and directly. Vinalhaven's Islands Community Medical Center is the closest medical facility to Matinicus. The *Sunbeam* would pick him up on Vinalhaven and transport him to Matinicus so people there could have final appointments with him. Afterward, a gathering in his honor was planned at the school.

In late May, an interisland program for the schoolchildren was scheduled. In the summer, the boat makes a number of what Dave calls "VIP trips"—fund-raising events, as well as participation in such activities as the Bar Harbor Blessing of the Fleet boat parade and the Frenchboro Lobster Festival. A special event is the annual Eastern Star picnic on Matinicus, with which they are involved because it's important to Paul Murray's mother and aunt. "It's a favor to them, and we're glad to do it. We couldn't get along without Paul," says Dave. "If anything's broken, he comes aboard and fixes it. Electric work, or moving skiffs—you name it, he does it. I don't think Matinicus could function without Paul being out there."

Isle au Haut was the final destination of the day, and we tied onto the town float there in time for supper, five o'clock. The mailboat had just come and gone, leaving a big Dell computer box on the wharf, sent by UPS to the island. No doubt someone would be down to pick it up. For the first time since morning, the generator was turned off and the *Sunbeam* was silent. She's not nearly as loud as many vessels I've been aboard, but Mike's right when he says that it's a huge morale booster when the generator isn't running.

Isle au Haut and Matinicus both provide shore power for the boat. When the boat grounds out at Matinicus, she can't use her generators—they are keel-cooled and need water. But the islanders say she's welcome to the power. On Isle au Haut, too, it's simple generosity. "What happens to the light bill here?" Betty asked one of the islanders in the morning. "It's on the town?"

"Yes, the town pays the dock electricity."

"So we should be careful with what we use," Betty said, deciding to postpone running the dishwasher.

"No, don't worry about it. It's worth it to the townspeople that you come."

"Every little bit helps," said Betty. When we were underway again in the morning, she turned on the dishwasher.

After supper, Mike and Sharon asked me if I'd like to go for a walk ashore with them. Absolutely. When Mike was through setting up the *Sunbeam* for the mailboat to come alongside in the morning—putting out fenders and opening the gate on the outboard side—we took off. With the time change, there was more daylight than there had been for their recent walks, so they chose to turn right coming off the pier instead of left, as they had been doing lately. We didn't go by any of the town's official buildings, but we saw a number of houses, their dooryards filled with lobster traps and with bedrock showing—lawns are a struggle on that stony island. We passed through a part of Acadia National Park—mostly scraggly evergreen trees, some uprooted, but we saw our first skunk cabbage of the season peeking up from the muddy roadside—and came to a house with a lovely southern view of the open ocean, where we sat, protected from the breeze, and enjoyed the almost summery air. As the sun approached the treetops, we headed back to the boat, glad then that we'd worn hats and gloves. A golden retriever joined us for the trip back to the pier but trotted off toward home when we went down the ramp onto the boat.

On the *Sunbeam*, a group had come aboard to try the various desserts Betty had spent the day creating. She had made four and offered three to us with our dinner, but she had saved one until the Isle au Haut people were there. She and Dave are on low-carb diets, and she always sweetens some of her desserts artificially for them and for the diabetics; those plates she leaves on the counter over the dishwasher, while she puts the real-sugar ones out on the end. Everyone knows that. Everyone knows 'most everything about the boat. People come aboard and head right for the glasses, ice, and soda, or for the coffee or the muffins, or for the games. It was dominoes that night on Isle au Haut, with three women and two children from the island playing with Betty, Sharon, and Cristy from the boat. Rob came along in a bit and sat in for Cristy when Peter started fussing; when someone came to talk with Sharon, I sat in for her. While everyone tried to win, this was no cutthroat competition. Still, eleven-year-old Nicholas was pleased when he won handily.

Everyone visited easily with everyone else. I had spent an hour or more on the phone with Dianne Barter earlier in the year and enjoyed meeting her face-to-face, along with young Nicholas. And I'd been meaning to call Bel MacDonald to learn about the Isle au Haut mailboat. There she was, with her granddaughter Geneva, a sixth-grader, whose dad, Danny, I'd also spoken with. He's in charge of the fishermen's co-op.

Bel answered my questions about the island-owned boat services and spoke of life on the island. She'd come from Deer Isle in 1959 and admits it was a difficult move. There was no power then, nor telephone. There were thirty people year-round—she's seen the population as high as seventy-two and as low as seventeen. She confirms the several-year transition time I've heard from others: the first year on an island is romantic, reality hits in the second, and it's the third year that determines whether you stay or go. "It does take that long," Bel says. (Dianne, on the other hand, says that they can tell in a month or so if people will make it, by what they do with their time, but it was also Dianne who said it took five years for someone to really know if they belonged.)

The game broke up around eight-thirty or nine, and everyone headed home or to bed. I had a cabin with upper and lower bunks, and I opted for the top one, as it had a porthole. The view out the window on that moonlit night was wonderfully peaceful, the nearby lobsterboat *Geneva Sue* gently turning on her mooring in the breeze. (Yes, *Geneva Sue* belongs to the father of dominoes-player Geneva.) In the morning, the white boats in the harbor nearly glowed in the sunrise.

Breakfast was not as well attended as on the previous trip to Isle au Haut, Betty said. There were twenty, then. Only Billy Barter and Bel joined us this time—he brought a bucket of huge clams for Betty, who made a delicious chowder at lunchtime. Billy's boat, the *Islander*, has the big numbers that indicate he has a federal lobster license. He used to fish offshore, but doesn't anymore: "The cold air don't like me."

The mailboat from Stonington came in at seven-forty-five and tied alongside *Sunbeam*, bringing a half-dozen carpenters and other workmen who were renovating houses on the island. After unloading, the crew from the mailboat grabbed a quick cup of coffee and some doughnuts and muffins. "It's nice to have a restaurant that comes to you twice a month," one of them said. A number of people boarded the mailboat for her trip back to Stonington, including Dianne and Nicholas, who was going ashore for an orthodontist appointment. Sharon sent along the blood samples she'd taken the day before, as they would get to the lab a day sooner than if she took them back to Northeast Harbor.

Dave, who makes an effort to walk a mile every day, said he'd like to go for a walk but he guessed he'd save it for Matinicus. "I like to go up to the airport and see all the stewardesses," he said.

"Yup," said Bel. "They're probably all sunbathing, this time of year." (Though everyone was excited about the warm sunny weather, it was still far from suitable for sunbathing, even if there were stewardesses—which there most certainly are not.)

There was some talk about the steepness of the ramp from the float up to the pier, and about a new float, which was on a mooring out in the anchorage. It was supposed to be taller in the water than the present one, which would change the angle of the ramp at low tide. "Us older people just set back and watch," said Bel. "And complain when it's hard to get up the ramp." Everyone looking at the new float agreed with Bel—it wasn't going to significantly change the angle of the ramp. "Far be it from me, for I'm just a woman and I don't know this stuff. I'm pretty dumb," she said. "Oh, well, wait a little." As Rob had said the day before, things change slowly.

Sharon came in, pointing at her watch. "Aw, these guys can have a little down-time," said Mike.

"They can have it on the boat! I have an appointment," she said. Off to Matinicus.

There was a bit of chop on the ocean, but the *Sunbeam* didn't care in the slightest. She was listing noticeably to starboard, and I asked Dave about it. She has two water tanks, he explained, port and starboard, five hundred gallons apiece. They work off the port one so that she'll lean the right way at the pier on Matinicus when she grounds out. "We have enough list today, no question. We used a lot of water yesterday." Without the lean, if she fell away from the pier, she would give a sudden, startling lurch. It has happened three times—twice when she caught on bolts on the newly rebuilt pier, and once when she went down onto lobster traps that, unbeknownst to Dave, had fallen off the pier.

I had a chance to sit down with Mike, who was at the helm. I was interested in his remark about the contra dance being part of his job. "Betty's here cooking," he said, "but she's always here to chat with people. Dave's captain, but it's the same. Fifty percent of the job is socializing, hanging out with island folks. We all enjoy their company, or we wouldn't be here." Mike said he didn't always go to church, but soon after he signed on to the *Sunbeam,* he saw that being a friendly, social person was just as important as changing the oil, and that's why he'd joined in at the dance.

Sharon finally got Rob to sit down with her and work out the scheduling for the following couple of months. From Sharon's perspective, a lot is involved in making the schedule. Each telemedicine trip requires the coordination of the boat and the five providers; if you schedule too far ahead, someone will go on vacation and mess it all up. You get four offices all lined up—they'll handle this hour on this day and that one on the next—and then on the fifth call, they can't do the hour that's left. So Sharon has to go back to one of the others and arrange a switch. She dreads the phone calls. The tides have to be taken into account too, both at Matinicus and at Frenchboro—where the boat has to keep backing up as the tide drops—so the days chosen and the order of the islands visited are worked around the tide tables. On top of all that, they have to know the state ferry schedules; they don't go to Frenchboro on days the ferry's coming in, as they'd be in its way.

Mike asked Dave to take over while he took care of a couple of things. "There's a couple of boats"—he checked the radar for their distance—"within half a mile." Fishermen were setting traps off Saddleback Ledge.

"Call 'em and tell 'em to get out of our way," Dave joked as he took over. On we went, chugging easily along at ten knots.

No one was talking. Dave was reading the ads in *Uncle Henry's* (a popular swap/sell publication), looking up regularly to be sure that there was nothing between the boat and Matinicus. Mike was stretched out on the settee in the pilothouse. Betty popped up, wondering how long it would be to Matinicus. Dave checked the computer. "Twenty-two minutes," he said.

"OK, lunch when we get there," said Betty.

Paul Murray was on the wharf, waiting to catch the lines, when we pulled in. "What time's the ferry coming tomorrow?" Rob asked him.

"Ten, I think."

"Think we can get out before they come in?" Rob asked Dave.

"I'll tell you tomorrow afternoon," Dave answered. "If we're afloat, we can. If we're not, we'll wait till he goes."

Sharon asked Paul if a particular couple was on the island. "Yes, they are," he said. "In fact, they went up to the church this morning and took down the Christmas tree. Spring's here."

Someone invited Paul and his family to supper. "At five? Can we bring anything?" Paul asked.

After lunch, Rob and Cristy took Peter in his stroller for a walk, and I joined them. We stopped to visit with Kenny and Maud Ames, an elderly couple whose house looks out across the harbor; Rob left off a few jigsaw puzzles for Maud. She and I talked about her cat, a very important part of her life, and Rob talked with Kenny about his truck and one thing and another. The next stop was with Natalie, a young pregnant woman who had grown up on the island and was then living at her parents' house, across the road from Kenny and Maud. Cristy and Peter stayed with her and her two children while Rob and I moved on to Kathleen Ames's house, which has no driveway— she's never driven. She greeted Rob with the news that she was thinking about moving into the Methodist Conference Home in Rockland. They talked about that for a while—there were pros and cons, and in any case, she wouldn't move until fall. She said she might be able to go look at it when she goes ashore in another month for an appointment. Rob said he'd be happy to go with her if she wanted, but she said that wasn't necessary. Then the talk turned to Betty's desserts—Rob promised to bring her some in the morning—and to other goodies that Kathleen enjoyed. She used to pickle beets but hasn't had much of a garden lately.

The visiting filled most of the afternoon, and not once was God's name mentioned. There was some discussion of hymns at the last stop, the Rankin house—Rob was still planning his Easter service, to be held that night, as the *Sunbeam* would not make it back to Matinicus over the weekend. We stopped by the church to be sure the heat was on.

After supper, Rob had to be satisfied with his service, for the time had come. He went up to the church ahead of time. Sharon and I walked up, and Eva asked her son, Eric, if he'd like to drive. He said no, thanks. (Where does a thirteen-year-old boy turn down a driving opportunity? Only in a place where driving is commonplace for him.) With Cristy and Peter and her children all loaded in, Eva drove the old Subaru up to the church.

With some fifteen people in attendance, Rob's service was simple and pleasant. I saw only three people there that I hadn't met, and I spoke with one of them, the schoolteacher, afterward. Everyone was dressed in jeans or the equivalent, sneakers, and casual shirts, including Rob. The kids volunteered help and cheerful commentary a couple of times—Rob asked for the one and accepted the other happily.

When we returned to the boat, she was high and dry. Dave and Betty were watching a movie in the pilothouse. Mike hadn't gone to the service either, and he was stretched out on a sofa in the galley, reading. He takes good care of his body, both as a runner and a relaxer.

The next morning, my porthole was right up against the pier, and again there was no water to speak of beneath us. As I brushed my teeth, the tap water came out of the faucet at an angle reminding me that we were atilt.

Dave asked me if I'd seen the lobsterboat across the pier from us at two o'clock in the morning. (I hadn't.) "All lit up, loading traps." They were catching the tide to get the traps ready to set the next day.

Sharon and I made rounds, delivering cucumber pickles and pickled beets to Kathleen—Sharon happened to have some aboard—and sugar-free desserts to Kenny and Maud, diabetics both. The teacher passed us, going to see if Natalie's daughter would like a ride to school. When we got back to the boat, Sari Bunker was there getting ready for her job as Ferry Nazi, keeping track of vehicles coming onto and leaving the island. She reported to me that her husband, Vance, had approved a piece I had sent to him, and when I scribbled down a rough draft of another paragraph and asked if she'd pass it on to him, she suggested I take it to him myself. He was at work on his pier just down the harbor. I walked the long way around, by road, not knowing yet about the passage along the shore—on and off piers and through everyone's traps, up wooden stairs and down rocky paths and across boardwalks to where the *Sunbeam* was tied up. It was a lot longer by land, but everything came in by boat, after all, until just recently when the planes got the mail contract. Vance OK'd my paragraph.

Of the *Sunbeam*, he said, "It's very important. Funerals and prayer services for those who want them, even if they're not religious, and weddings—those would be very expensive if we didn't have the *Sunbeam*. It may not look important, but sometimes it is. Ninety percent of the ministers, in the time I've been here (sixty-five years?) will come to the house and talk with you. If you have a problem, you can talk about it, and if not, fine. After they've visited with the old people, they might have a drink with you."

Back at the pier, people were gathering. The ferry was coming. The one monthly ferry trip during the wintertime is a big event on Matinicus. I had decided to leave the *Sunbeam* at this point and go back on the ferry, realizing it gave me an opportunity to talk with the ferry people. It also would save me five hours of steaming and one in a car. I went back aboard the *Sunbeam* to visit a bit more with Betty while she prepared lunch. "We've had some memorable guests on the boat over the years," she said. "A few who thought I was their servant, who would tell me what they wanted to eat and when." She laughed, thinking of it. "One couple was getting off the boat and I told them supper was at five. 'We don't eat at five,' they said. 'All right,' I said. When they came back at six-thirty, there was nothing left and everything was all cleaned up. I didn't say a word. They didn't miss another meal."

"There've been good things, too," she said. "Going up Somes Sound one time in April, there was a sailboat upside down, people we knew. We were the only boats in the sound. They never would have survived if we hadn't seen them. We had a diesel-fired cookstove on that boat—they some enjoyed that, cuddled up to it.

"'Course some of the stories I could tell, you couldn't print," she said. "I can honestly say, though, that in twenty-seven years the only thing I've ever hated is the schedule. David has always put the *Sunbeam* first—our entire life together has been absolutely controlled by the boat."

"We're very fortunate to have the *Sunbeam*," Bel MacDonald of Isle au Haut had said. "In wintertime especially, for the socializing."

Paul Murray concurs: "Betty and Dave and Mike are just as important as Rob and Sharon. The 'ministry' of a warm place to have some of Betty's sweets while you talk to Dave and Mike in the wheelhouse is just as welcome after a long spell of looking at the same twenty or twenty-five people for a month as the service Rob would do up to the church or the trip to town Sharon might save someone for the medical exam that can be done over the video link."

The Island Institute

Founded in 1983 and based in Rockland, Maine, the Island Institute has always had as its ambition the support of islands and island communities. Its outlook and approach have changed over the years—most recently, it has oriented itself toward partnerships with islands, creating island-initiated projects through the Island Fellows Program and funding for island projects and scholarships.

Controversial since its inception, the Island Institute is still met with suspicion from time to time. People know the Institute has an agenda—and whose is it? It's not that it's bad, necessarily—it's that it's not ours, some islanders have said. "It seems they come down from on top and kind of stumble around trying to make it good."

Others look at the financial side. "I haven't much use for them," says one. "They like to put their name on a lot of things they don't really do themselves. If they make an appearance on something and it goes through, it comes out in their newspaper that they're the big hero." He admits this is just his own opinion, but it bugs him. "I just had someone donate nine thousand dollars for the fire department, and it came through the Island Institute even though he lives a quarter-mile from me."

There certainly is an irony in the Institute's work. They want to help islands sustain their way of life—certainly a fine objective—but there's the correlative and paradoxical "We admire your being self-sufficient and we're here to make it possible for you to be that way."

Just the same, it's clear that more residents of more islands have good feelings about the Island Institute than don't. In the twenty-plus years of its existence, it has taken on a wide variety of projects—from technical assistance in a number of fields to providing seed money for community programs to facilitating communication among islands as well as between islands and the world at large. Recently, and with great success, the Island Fellows Program has sent recent college graduates to applicant islands to work in schools, libraries, town offices, fisheries co-ops, arts-enrichment, and adult-education programs. The goal is that the Fellows bring with them skills that they can leave behind when they go.

Dana Leath was a Fellow on Long Island in 2001, mostly working with the school and the recreation committee. She assisted the teachers technologically, updating their computer, adding a scanner and a digital camera, and helping everyone understand how to use these tools. "I'd show the kids so they could show their teachers."

(Everyone knows that eight-year-olds are more fluent with technology than most adults.) She coached a small, multiage track team and arranged a track meet against a Chebeague Island team.

"It was magical to be part of a two-room school—to be the gym teacher and the librarian and the kindergarten math teacher. And it was neat to be someplace where all you had to do was have an interest in something and they'd say, 'Go for it!'" She says it's an extraordinary experience for someone just out of college "to be involved in so many things, making decisions and designing programs while getting a window into a different way of life." She loved the island and the islanders' sense of independence—of course, this is the town that seceded from Portland, a David-and-Goliath story if there ever was one—and she admired the way they were solving their own problems, using the local control they'd won.

Dana, whose background was in agriculture, had planned to become an Extension agent when she finished her education, but after her experience on Long Island, she took a full-time job with the Island Institute in Portland as the Community Development Officer. She is charged with "supporting the convening function of the Island Institute"—organizing and networking islanders so they can consider specific interests—firefighting, historical societies, land-use planning, and the like. Dana also administers the Island Community Fund, which provides seed money, and she is helping to leverage additional funds for projects. She provides support for other island organizations such as the Casco Bay Forum and the new Islands Coalition.

She would have loved to stay on Long Island, but the commute to Portland is much easier from Peaks, where she lucked into a year-round rental house that is actually more reasonable than what she had been able to find ashore. She's still keeping in touch with the friends she made on Long Island.

Mike Felton, who was a Fellow a few years back, also subsequently went to work for the Institute. "I was interested in the relationship between education and community," he says. "You can see it at work on Vinalhaven. It was awesome to get fully immersed in another community. It was intense and powerful to really get to know people well and for them to get to know you well. People took me in and were supportive of me—and they fed me!" Of course, there were occasional tough days, but they asked him to stay on another year, and he wanted to return. "It was such a different community than any I'd ever experienced." He had been at Bowdoin College in Brunswick, fifty miles to the west as the crow flies, "but even Bowdoin's a long way from Vinalhaven."

Having spent two years experiencing a small school from the inside, Mike spent the next two years working for the Island Institute as the Education Outreach Officer.

During that time, he traveled to almost all the islands with schools and had a chance to observe small schools from the outside. "The teachers are invested not only in the school but also the community, in its survival and vitality. That's why island schools can be really strong." He learned that some really successful urban schools are patterning themselves the same way. He talked to people in Boston schools where parents have to volunteer at the school in order for their children to attend, and he learned about housing projects designed with the school in the middle. The schools are the center of community life. "That's the Vinalhaven model," he says.

Now, at twenty-seven, Mike is back on Vinalhaven as School Leader. He has taken all that he has learned in four years with the Island Institute and is applying it back on Vinalhaven. He is amused to go to educational conferences where well-known speakers are talking of new and wonderful techniques of school management, and he finds himself saying, "Wow! We're doing that!" His own aspirations? He hopes to stay at least five years on Vinalhaven. He's married (to a longtime summer resident whose grandmother and uncles and sister are now also living on the island full-time) and has bought a house. "I can't think of a better school to be at. I enjoy going to work. This is one of the things I wanted to do, to see a school blend with its community and transform itself. But one thing I've learned in my short years is that the older you get, the less you know what's going to come next. I tend to think things fall into place. This keeps all my focus now. When I first came out here, I thought I'd be here a year. Now I don't have a fricking clue."

Other Institute Fellows have worked with libraries, marine research, after-school recreation programs, helping with comprehensive planning, teaching music and art and any number of other projects. Mike speaks with enthusiasm about Geographic Information System mapping projects with which Fellows have been involved. "With the Fellows, students were doing real work, with value to their town or the fisheries." One project had students on lobsterboats dropping buoys overboard and using a GPS to mark how they drifted. Mapped, this information showed local currents around the islands, which allows them to extrapolate where lobster larvae might drift to. "They're doing real oceanography, using the same technology that scientists use when they study the larger currents of the world."

The possibilities are limited only by the imaginations of the island people, who have to apply to the Institute for Fellows. The island is responsible for finding housing—not always easy, and often Fellows have to move several times, as Dana had to do while she was on Long Island. The Institute provides a small stipend and health insurance, but everyone wins.

Maine Island Youth on the *Harvey Gamage*

Since 1994, as one piece of a much larger mission that includes forty-four programs aboard three schooners, the Ocean Classroom Foundation has offered young islanders an opportunity to sail on the schooner *Harvey Gamage*. The first year, it was just a three-day trip, but since that time, more than two hundred young islanders have sailed on nine- and ten-day voyages along the New England coast. "It's an opportunity for them to put island life in the context of a bigger world, of other maritime communities," says program founder Alix Thorne, who summers on Islesboro.

For a ten-day trip in 2004, there were twenty-two students from Long Island, Vinalhaven, North Haven, Islesboro, and Deer Isle—all just entering or just out of eighth grade. A very enthusiastic Keith Drury of Vinalhaven was one of them. "It was the best time ever!" he says.

They boarded the *Gamage* in Mystic, Connecticut, after checking out Mystic Seaport; then they went into New York City. "We went right past the Statue of Liberty, and I got to steer into New York!" burbles Keith. "We were under sail, and then we had to motor because it was getting too crazy. The captain was standing next to me and there were boats flying right past us. He was like, 'Do this,' 'Do that,' and I was really worried—Am I doing it right? Will I screw it up?—but it was OK."

They stayed in New York a couple of nights. "We walked all around the city and saw places built with Vinalhaven granite, like the pillars in the back at St. John the Divine Cathedral. They let us go off on our own in New York for three hours! We just had to stay in groups, but I had no idea they'd do that! They're responsible for twenty-two of us, and they'd be in terrible trouble if one of us got lost. It was really fun. We went on the subway. I'd been on subways before, but not in New York—about half of our group had never been on one before, and when it started up, half of us fell right over. One kid had lived in New York—he was laughing his butt off."

The kids were divided into three watches, and it happened that Keith's watch drew the midnight-to-0400 watch three of the four times they sailed through the night. "It was quite annoying—but it was really awesome. That's definitely the hardest watch—you can't decide whether to go to bed or stay up till twelve, and then you go to bed at four and in two hours you're up again—you only get three-and-a-half hours' sleep. But then you sleep when you're tired—stay up all night and sleep in the day. We never got that tired.

"On watch, we got to be on the helm and stand bow watch and do boat checks—see if there's water in the bilge and stuff—and it was our responsibility to clean the boat. And we did charting. We had galley duty, too. The cook was funny—she was always singing. She made me make up a Sun Dance—it was foggy and nasty and she said if I danced, it would clear up, and I started dancing and it did clear! 'What'd I tell you?' she asked me. Then when we were in port, we'd have one-hour watches with two of us up all the time to make sure nobody tried to board or anything."

The best part for Keith was meeting other island kids. He knew a couple of them a little, such as the ones from North Haven—he'd been on the cross-country team with them, and he'd run into them sometimes when he was over there. "One guy from Islesboro I didn't know, but I'd played basketball against him and he'd guarded me. I know them much better, now," he says. "There were tons of really awesome people. Nobody was mean or a jerk or just not fun to be around—some got annoying sometimes, but you have to expect that. I get annoying sometimes.

"Living on an island, you can't get away from the people there," he says. "You can't get a fresh start. If you mess up once, everybody knows, but you get on the boat and you have a completely fresh start. In the city, you get it every day."

Keith wants to go to college, but he's not sure what he'd like to study. At thirteen, he has plenty of time to think about it. Maybe politics, but he likes math, too. Maybe architecture. But he'd like to coach something, too. He does not want to be a fisherman. "Too many people are fishermen—if you were to ask kids, more than half probably want to go fishing, but definitely not me. Yeah, you make a lot of money, and I like boats, but I don't like nasty fish guts on my hands, and diesel engine fuel all over you. Me and my dad have sixteen traps out in the summer just for ourselves and our friends, and if we fill up the crate, we might take it over town and sell them. I like doing that, and I might go with a friend sometime just to make some money." But there's no question in his mind—lobstering is not for him.

Some youngsters who started sailing in the Maine Island Youth program went on in the maritime world, sailing in full-semester educational programs and even ultimately getting their Coast Guard licenses. Keith may not have those ambitions, but he certainly hopes he can go on the *Gamage* again next year.

The Genesis Fund

To date, six islands have benefited from the expertise and the loan dollars from the Genesis Community Loan Fund, which works with Maine communities to develop a variety of projects—from transitional housing for people with special needs to a therapeutic horseback-riding facility. After what Associate Director Garrett Martin describes as "tangential involvement" with Frenchboro's and Islesboro's affordable-housing projects, Genesis became more deeply involved with the creation of the Ivan Calderwood Homestead—Vinalhaven's eldercare facility—and it has continued with other island community efforts.

The name would suggest that Genesis was primarily in the loan business, and it does indeed provide loans. When the owners of one of the units in the Ruthie James Subdivision on Islesboro divorced, they had to sell the house. Islesboro Affordable Property had first refusal, but even in the short term, IAP didn't feel comfortable using its own capital to purchase the property. Genesis came to the rescue with a bridge loan to carry them until they resold the property, which happened in short order.

But loans, while very useful, are only a single part of the services Genesis provides to communities. Perhaps of more importance is their expertise navigating the legal and regulatory processes required for such projects as the Calderwood Homestead and now Islesboro's Boardman Cottage. They also make it a point to be familiar with public and private sources of funding, grant money, for municipal efforts.

The islands are unusual, and various islands have found that their situations don't fit the guidelines of government programs. In the minds of federal bureaucrats, affordable housing is aimed at people of low income. The fact is that it's very hard for a low-income family to establish itself on a Maine island—job opportunities are few and expenses are high. Yet there's a demonstrated need for housing. Sometimes traditional grant providers can be shown why an island project should qualify, and at other times it's wiser to look elsewhere. Garrett and the Genesis people can act as connections to other funding sources.

On Monhegan, for instance, when the island wanted to buy the old store and create a couple of affordable-housing condominium units, Garrett was able to help in several ways. It started with helping them gain their nonprofit certification, then going through the development process, and finally acting as a go-between between the islanders and Camden National Bank, which financed both the overall project and the individual mortgages for the units. "It's a matter of obtaining a level of comfort on both sides," Garrett says. "If you just plugged the numbers into the formula, it wouldn't work. This is a part of doing business in small communities. There's an accountability that exists but doesn't necessarily translate when you run the numbers. Still, everyone on the island has an interest in their not defaulting," he explains. "But Camden National gets it." Camden National, with a branch on Vinalhaven, is the only bank with a presence on one of the islands.

In the past, the Genesis Fund has been a quiet player, behind the scenes, Garrett says. "But timing is so critical, making sure resources are in place when they're needed, that we will now turn the tables and be a little more proactive." There are two aspects to this new approach—being aware of what projects are under discussion and trying to create a pool of money to be distributed via matching funds. In the past, islanders have been very good at finding money within their own communities, but they have not been as aware of the open-market funders that Genesis can tie into. Nor, as individual tiny communities, have they been as successful with them when they did find them. "We've seen that it could be of benefit to coalesce the island voices in order to make the larger funding community aware of them." The hope is to put money into the till now in order to fund projects when they come up; this will act as an incentive for local fund-raising as well as provide a real financial boost to specific projects.

The Maine Islands Coalition

"The Maine Islands Coalition is a collaboration of island communities to discuss and, when possible, reach consensus on issues brought forth by our communities, and to advocate for the economic and environmental sustainability of year-round island communities." So says the new organization's mission statement, approved in early 2004. Eva Murray of Matinicus dropped in on its November 2004 meeting in Rockland during the lunch break for an EMT training course she was taking. John Griffin, Matinicus assessor, had mentioned the coalition to her the night before—first she'd heard of it, but she agreed to stop by, at least. "We've been leery of getting involved in any more organizations," she told Cliff Islander Roger Berle, chairman of the coalition. "We worry about the exposure to regulatory agencies—we're doing the best we can, but not everything is entirely according to the book yet. The other thing is the increased bureaucratic load—there's no one to do it.

"Five years ago," Eva said, "no one on the island was willing to even discuss doing anything at all, but now islanders are starting to think of joining civilization in

Hockamock Light, Swans Island

some ways. Now various agencies are asking, 'Why aren't you doing this?' 'Why aren't you applying for that grant?' and 'Why aren't you doing that other thing?' But there's no one to deal with the organizing, work, or even paperwork. So, about whether we want to be involved with the Maine Islands Coalition, those are our issues."

Roger mentioned that the coalition wanted Matinicus to be represented, because they were anxious to find the commonalities affecting all the islands. Eva spoke of going to a gathering of island teachers some years back. There was a discussion of field trips, and Eva was taken aback at the differences between her students and their families and those on other islands. She couldn't imagine taking her students on any of the suggested trips, and she mentioned behavioral issues and lack of parental interest. "Oh," she was told, "just have the mothers bake cookies."

"That was when I realized that not all the islands have the same problems," Eva says.

That, too, is part of the value of the coalition—to share problems and solutions and find not just commonalities but also differences. "That's why we're here," said Roger, "to listen to each other."

Even though Little Diamond is not home to anyone year-round, the island was voted in as a member of the coalition. The coalition members decided to consider on a case-by-case basis any other island that might like to join, knowing that the summer-only islands share some of the same concerns as the year-round ones.

Speaking as a group, the islands will have more clout than if each tiny community were to represent itself alone. Working with them are Genesis's Garrett Martin and various state legislators—Representative Hannah Pingree of North Haven joined the discussion by conference call from San Francisco, and Senator Dennis Damon of Trenton was present at this particular meeting. The Island Institute provided the meeting room and staff assistance, but the coalition is an independent organization.

Many of the issues faced on one island are faced on others. Affordable housing is one that the Maine Islands Coalition has recognized right off the bat, and they've set up a subcommittee to consider just that issue. Tax reform is another. The entire state is upset about high property taxes, and the islanders want to have a voice in how the system will be reworked.

High-speed Internet access is another mutual concern, and—despite the remark by one representative that part of the charm of living on an island is living without some of the conveniences—the rest of the group agreed that good Internet service for those islands that don't have it—most of them—could certainly provide opportunities for sustaining communities. It was felt to be more effective to devise a comprehensive plan for all the islands' Internet coverage than for each to push for its own.

Solid-waste disposal is another issue that faces all, and perhaps solutions can be shared—both large conceptual ideas and specifics like particular compactor models that have worked well on a small island scale.

When Pat McEachron raised concern about conservation land on Frenchboro, though, the islanders' views clearly differed. Frenchboro feels the pinch of having so much of its land taken off the tax rolls: Maine Coast Heritage Trust has 900 acres, and David Rockefeller has 250 acres under an easement to Acadia National Park. On the other hand, the representatives of Cliff, Little Diamond, and the Cranberry Isles all spoke of the benefits of preserved land: "Your problem is one that a lot of towns would like to have!" Land in the reduced-taxation rates of Tree Growth designation is also an issue on Frenchboro, and that issue is shared by other islands. To register land in Tree Growth requires a forestry plan, but there's no mechanism to see that the plan is ever followed, and the program sometimes is used solely as a method of evading property taxes. Vinalhaven recently assessed a $130,000 penalty on Maine Coast Heritage Trust for taking land out of Tree Growth. "We were just trying to follow the law as it stands," said Town Manager Marjorie Stratton, though one could sense that perhaps making an example of them wasn't altogether bad.

Pat McEachron also pointed out Frenchboro's reliance on salmon pens, which have been controversial along the coast but represent about 10 percent of their tax base: "If they go, it might be good for the bay, but the impact on us would be heavy."

The coalition may represent a strong part of the islands' future as they try to maintain their viability as true communities and not simply summer colonies, especially if there comes a time of less prosperity from fishing than exists on many islands today. The coalition members are establishing priorities and defining areas of agreement and disagreement so they can best speak in Augusta, lobbying for the mutual benefit of the islands.

Afterword

I t has occurred to me that I may be documenting the swan song of traditional island life in Maine. As Ted Hoskins says, the period since World War II has been one of great change, and we haven't finished it yet. During the war, men moved their families off-island and went into the service or to work in the shipyards or in other war-related efforts, and many never came back. Not that the population drops started then—for the eighty years preceding, Maine islands had been losing residents—but this was the critical time for many, and the beginning of the present crunch for some. Island schools closed during that time—Criehaven in 1941, Eagle Island in 1942—and in recent years, schools on Matinicus and Great Cranberry at times have had no pupils. They were not closed, though. Once a school is officially closed, it's gone, and that pretty much shuts down the vitality of a community.

With a few creative exceptions, employment opportunities on the islands involve lobsters or summer people. People from Away are waiting to buy any property that comes up for sale. Who could blame a former fisherman for selling his house for far more than the price he or his parents or grandparents paid for it, even taking into account the decades (or centuries) of inflation? For that matter, who can blame him for taking an offer higher than any local person could afford to pay today? Islesboro—where fishing is marginal at best, and which has a relatively good ferry connection to the mainland (not that the people of Islesboro would agree)—has in the last several years approached becoming a retirement town. The fishing base on both Great Cranberry and Peaks Islands has nearly disappeared. Peaks's proximity to downtown Portland makes it enticing to commuting professionals as well as retirees, though allowing its school to remain vital.

Criehaven lost its winter residents not long after the war; Frenchboro, Isle au Haut, the Cranberries, Cliff Island, Monhegan and even Islesboro have formally or informally solicited homesteaders from off-island or created programs to help their own young people to remain. Other islands are considering such programs.

Lobstering has been so rewarding of late that it hasn't mattered that the rest of the fisheries are moribund or nearly so. Big, fast, new lobsterboats are moored in

Carver's, Matinicus, and Burnt Coat Harbors, as well as all along the mainland coast, and the pickup-truck dealers have been more than gratified by the successful lobster harvest. But a precipitous condition such as hit Long Island Sound a few years back could come along, or the lobsters' breeding cycle could be disrupted—there are scientists who fear that it already has been. In the instant that the lobster catch drops significantly, many of the islands will be left to the retirees and summer people and to those few who cater to them who can still afford to live there.

Older fishermen warn their younger compatriots not to count on the lobsters always being there—they remember days when lobstering barely paid the bills—but it's easy for the newer entrants into the field to assume things will continue as they are. If a bad patch comes, I just hope that the islands will somehow be able to weather it.

Islesboro's Red Top *has been fishing for lobster since she was bulit on Beals Island by Harold Gower in 1968. What comes next for her?*

YOU KNOW YOU'RE REALLY FROM MATINICUS WHEN . . .

Compiled by Eva Murray, with the disclaimer: "I wasn't born here, I don't fish, and I have no right to speak for this place."

- You ask one of the guys if he's heard the weather report, and he replies simply: "Sou'west." From this, you are able to extrapolate the next four days' expected temperature, wind speed, precipitation, and humidity.

- You save used gift wrap, old panes of glass, cardboard boxes, and scrap metal, but you might toss gift lobsters back overboard if you already had other plans for supper.

- You rush to the aid of people you can't stand. Every time.

- If you see a resident child or adult male walking, you immediately ask, "Where did you break down?" (There are a few exceptions to this rule, but everybody knows Tom and Paul are eccentric.)

- You pay $2.90 a gallon for gasoline, 35 cents a kilowatt hour for electricity, and $102.50 a tank for propane, but you really hate to pay more than three bucks apiece for lobster [prices as of November 2004].

- Instinctively, the first thing you do when your child says he doesn't feel well is look up at the sky conditions.

- One of the most fun things to do is think up creative street addresses for United Parcel Service.

- You know the weather is going to change because you're getting the Yarmouth, Nova Scotia, Coast Guard on the VHF.

- You laugh out loud when the appliance dealers try to sell you the extended service contract.

- "You can't get they-ah from hee-ah" isn't Maine humor—it's a weather report.

- You ask the dentist to do all six fillings the same day.

- The only reason you own a fax machine is to order groceries.

- No matter what it is you're trying to accomplish on the island, it all boils down to the problem of freight handling.

- You can be an ax murderer and be on the school board, you can be a Russian spy and be on the board of assessors, but if your laundry isn't done and on the line by five in the morning, you are likely to be subject to criticism.

- You might not bother to go in to the emergency room if you had a chainsaw through your leg, but you'd be ready at a moment's notice if somebody offered you a ride to Vinalhaven for an ice cream cone.

- You love it, absolutely love it here, 51 percent of the time. That is enough to make you stay.

Index